SIMPLY

T H E   B E S T

Freelance journalist and writer DAVID ROSS is an acknowledged football expert - the only person ever to appear on BBC TV's *Mastermind* to take British football as a specialist subject. Born in Dundonald, Ayrshire, he was educated at Marr College in Troon, Kilmarnock Academy and Teesside Polytechnic. A contributor to various publications both at home and abroad, he is also the author of the critically acclaimed *"Killie - The Official History."*

He has a son, Neil, from his first marriage. He now lives in London with his wife, Josephine, who is also a journalist. A member of the *Association of Football Statisticians* , David is a supporter of Kilmarnock, Middlesbrough and Dulwich Hamlet, while Josephine follows the fortunes of Ross County.

Cover illustrations:
Front:
(Top) George Best and Matt Busby celebrate Manchester United's capture of the European Cup in 1968 (page 57)
(Middle) Action from Norwich City's surprise victory over Bayern Munich in 1993 (page 63)
(Bottom) The Raith Rovers squad proudly display the Scottish League Cup after their shock victory (page 134)

Rear:
(Top) A relaxed Rangers team group - European Cup Winners Cup in 1972 (page 135)
(Left) Programme cover from Stockport's double figure victory over Halifax in 1934 (page 84)
(Right) After an absence of fifty years, Dumbarton head back to the First Division (page 115)

Published by:
Yore Publications
12 The Furrows, Harefield,
Middx. UB9 6AT.

© David Ross 1995

....

British Library Cataloguing-in-Publication Data.
A catalogue record for this book
is available from the British Library.

ISBN 1 874427 41 0

(Every effort has been made to acknowledge the source of illustrations
and to ensure that copyright has not been infringed)

YORE PUBLICATIONS specialise in football books, generally of an historical
nature, including Club Histories, Who's Who Books, and general interest - both
League and non-League. Three free newsletters per year are issued. For your
first newsletter please send a S.A.E. to the above address (see also page 144).

Printed by The Book Factory

ACKNOWLEDGEMENTS

Researching and writing the greatest moments in the histories of 132 football teams can be a time-consuming affair. And just when I thought I had completed my researches, sure enough, some team would go out and do something which forced me to change everything. For instance I had just written my account of Raith Rovers defeat in the Scottish League Cup Final of 1949 when they went and won the thing in 1994-95. But the staff at Starks Park responded favourably to my request for a new illustration from them. I would like to thank them and all other clubs and individuals who responded, namely: Martin Simpson (Aberdeen), Andrew Warrington (Arbroath), Iain Cook (Arsenal), Pam Bridgewaite (Aston Villa), Gordon Dickson (Berwick Rangers), Conrad Pilkington (Blackpool), Eric White (Brentford), Tony Millard Associates (Brighton & Hove Albion), Peter Cullen (Bury), Andrew Pincher (Cambridge United), David Steele (Carlisle United), Andrew Mullen (Cowdenbeath), James Coome (Crystal Palace), K.J.Avis and Paul Gilligan (Doncaster Rovers), Graeme Robertson (Dumbarton), Peter Rundo (Dundee United), Andrew Wilkie (East Fife), Derek Johnston (Everton), David Fisher and Norman Shiel (Exeter City), Jim Hendry (Falkirk), Forfar Athletic, Mark Agate (Gillingham), Greenock Morton F.C., Heart of Midlothian F.C., Sharon McAndrews (Ipswich Town), Mark Ingle and Dave Smith (Leicester City), P.C.G. Critchley (Manchester City), Jack Retter and Mansfield Chronicle Advertiser (Mansfield Town), R.Lindsay (Millwall), Motherwell F.C., Norwich City F.C., Robert Reid (Partick Thistle), Kim Slaney (Peterborough United), Hector Cook (Queen's Park), Keri Gooding (Raith Rovers), Donna McLellan (Rangers), David Downs (Reading), Brian Campbell (Ross County), Alastair MacLachlan (St. Mirren), A.T.Bullock (Stenhousemuir), Richard Harnwell (Stockport County), Reg Pike (Swansea City), Andy Porter (Tottenham Hotspur), John Lovis (Torquay United), Peter Bishop (Tranmere Rovers), Gabriela Lyons (Watford), Kate Evans (West Bromwich Albion), John Northcutt (West Ham United), Geraint Parry (Wrexham), D.Small (York City).

I would also like to thank the staff of the National Newspaper Library in Colindale, North London for their assistance, and also the staff of the Mitchell Library in Glasgow. Thanks are due to my publisher, Dave Twydell, for his expert assistance. Fay Twydell and Kara Matthews deserve a mention too for their hard work putting the book together.

My wife Josephine had boundless faith in this book from the time the idea first emerged right up to completion of the manuscript. At her request, the piece on her favourite team, Ross County, was the last to be written. Finally, I would like to express my gratitude to all those people who bought my previous book - 'Killie - The Official History.' It was the enthusiastic response that book received which made writing this one all the more pleasurable.

INTRODUCTION

Every football club - no matter how big or how small - experience a moment like no other. A time when all that has gone before is transcended in a single match. A time that will remain in their supporters collective memory forever. A time that defines what that club is all about. The purpose of this book is to tell the story of every club's greatest day. There are 132 clubs in the English and Scottish Leagues, each of them with a tale to tell. And while researching and writing 132 different stories has been a pleasurable task, it has also been, at times, difficult to pick out one outstanding game.

For while relatively few Manchester United or Celtic supporters would dispute that winning the European Cup represented the pinnacle of success for their clubs, for others it is much more difficult to define that special occasion. Spurs fans, for instance, may think especially fondly of the side which became the first to win the 'Double' this century. Yet the captain of that team - the late, great Danny Blanchflower - said at the time that success in Europe would be much more difficult to achieve. Two years later they became the first British side to win a European trophy. I have used Blanchflower's benchmark in this book.

Too often, it seems, we revel in a peculiarly British sense of insularity - the splendid isolation so descriptive of the late Victorian era. But these are the 1990s, not the 1890s, and, no matter which way we look at things, success in Europe is harder to obtain and a more prized achievement than anything on the domestic front. If a team has won a European trophy then that is what I have written about here. If successful more than once, then I have described their initial victory - with the exception of the European Cup, the most glorious trophy in club football. Who would argue that Liverpool's UEFA Cup win in 1973 should be ranked higher than that magnificent evening in Rome four years later?

That takes care of one category for inclusion in this book. There are others. There is no-one still alive who can remember Blackburn Rovers three FA Cup wins in successive years and Rovers have emerged as one of the best teams of recent years. But in a hundred years time, the records will still show that they won the FA Cup between 1884-1886, and those citizens on the threshold of the 22nd Century will have as little contact with our time as we have with the 1880s. So, until or unless the present-day Blackburn emulate or surpass their ancestors, it is the deeds of old that remain their greatest triumph.

Sometimes, where there have been conflicting claims for inclusion, I have selected the most dramatic. Both Motherwell and Kilmarnock have won one Scottish League title and two Scottish Cups. But Motherwell's title was secured well before the end of the season and their first Cup win was a walkover. Their second triumph produced one of the classic modern Cup Finals, so that game has been included. Kilmarnock won two exciting Cup Finals but their League triumph was on the final day of the season, away to their only rivals and achieved by four-hundredths of a goal. So that game was selected.

What of those clubs who have won little or nothing? Hartlepool have won promotion before, but it has usually been followed by an all too rapid relegation. So in their case I have picked their highest-scoring victory. For a Hartlepool side to hit double figures is a special event indeed. For others a sensational Cup triumph has seemed the most important. Berwick Rangers have won promotion and reached a League Cup Semi-Final, but the supporters of that club are virtually unanimous in thinking that the day they knocked their Glasgow namesakes out of the Scottish Cup was the greatest in their history. Walsall have a similar record but I have omitted their 1933 FA Cup win over Arsenal in favour of their League Cup tie with Liverpool on the grounds that Walsall, having drawn the first leg, genuinely believed that they were 90 minutes away from a major Cup Final - the best they have done in a knockout tournament. I have also omitted triumphs in the welter of Wembley finals in competitions where the top clubs do not compete. Reaching Wembley used to be the high spot of the season. In the era of ZDS, Freight Rover et al, that is no longer the case.

To justify every inclusion would require a chapter in itself and to argue the case for omissions would need another book. I hope that I have explained why I have let the spotlight fall on particular matches. I don't expect the reader to agree with all my choices, indeed I would be disappointed if anyone did, for football is a game when quite often the arguments start after the action is over. Healthy debate is the engine of enthusiasm and long may it continue that way.

Another intention in writing this book was to allow every club their moment in the sun. The big teams of London, Liverpool, Manchester and Glasgow have millions of words dedicated to them every year. Other scarcely appear in print at all, save for the results and League tables. I have tried to correct that imbalance by giving every team roughly equal treatment. If the reader closes this book having learned more about the history and traditions of some of the more unsung sides in the land, then the time and effort which went into the writing of it will have been well spent.

To give a flavour of the times, I have also included a section after each match entitled *'On The Same Day'*, outlining events which made the headlines in news, sport, and entertainment. But enough from me of what lies within, it is time to turn the page, select your team and read about the time when they were **'Simply The Best'**.

David Ross

October 1995

- CONTENTS -

F.A. Premiership and Football League Clubs

Scottish League Clubs

ABERDEEN Vs Real Madrid	May 11th 1983
AIRDRIEONIANS Vs Hibernian	April 19th 1924
ALBION ROVERS Vs Kilmarnock	April 17th 1920
ALLOA ATHLETIC Vs Celtic	August 19th 1922
ARBROATH Vs Bon Accord	September 12th 1885
AYR UNITED Vs Rangers	April 4th 1973
BERWICK RANGERS Vs Rangers	January 28th 1967
BRECHIN CITY Vs Meadowbank Thistle	May 7th 1983
CALEDONIAN THISTLE Vs Arbroath	August 13th 1994
CELTIC Vs Inter Milan	May 25th 1967
CLYDE Vs Motherwell	April 22nd 1939
CLYDEBANK Vs Celtic	April 14th 1990
COWDENBEATH Vs Rangers	September 21st 1949
DUMBARTON Vs Berwick Rangers	May 3rd 1972
St. Johnstone Vs DUNDEE	April 28th 1962
DUNDEE UNITED Vs AS Roma	April 11th 1984
West Bromwich Albion Vs DUNFERMLINE ATHLETIC	February 19th 1969
EAST FIFE Vs Kilmarnock	April 27th 1938
EAST STIRLINGSHIRE Vs Alloa Athletic	August 18th 1965
FALKIRK Vs Raith Rovers	April 12th 1913
FORFAR ATHLETIC Vs Rangers	April 3rd 1982
HAMILTON ACADEMICAL Vs Celtic	April 8th 1911
HEART OF MIDLOTHIAN Vs Celtic	April 21st 1956
HIBERNIAN Vs Motherwell	April 19th 1948
Heart of Midlothian Vs KILMARNOCK	April 24th 1965
Rangers Vs MEADOWBANK THISTLE (LIVINGSTON)	September 26th 1984
MONTROSE Vs Rangers	October 8th 1975
(GREENOCK) MORTON Vs Rangers	April 15th 1922
MOTHERWELL Vs Dundee United	May 18th 1991
PARTICK THISTLE Vs Celtic	October 23rd 1971
QUEEN OF THE SOUTH Vs East Fife	December 26th 1953
QUEEN'S PARK Vs Vale of Leven	February 22nd 1890
RAITH ROVERS Vs Celtic	November 27th 1994
RANGERS Vs Moscow Dynamo	May 24th 1972
Forfar Athletic Vs ROSS COUNTY	January 8th 1994
ST. JOHNSTONE Vs Celtic	October 25th 1969
ST. MIRREN Vs Dundee United	May 16th 1987
STENHOUSEMUIR Vs Partick Thistle	February 21st 1903
Raith Rovers Vs STIRLING ALBION	April 2nd 1949
East Stirlingshire Vs STRANRAER	April 23rd 1994

ARSENAL 3
Vs Anderlecht 0

April 28th 1970 - Inter Cities Fairs Cup Final 2nd Leg

Arsenal: Wilson, Storey, McNab, Kelly, McLintock, Simpson, Armstrong, Sammels, Radford, George, Graham.

Arsenal - England's premier pre-war club side - had endured their longest spell without any concrete success. Not since 1950 had they won the F.A. Cup and their 1953 triumph was their last League Championship success. In the League Cup they had lost two successive finals, the second being a humiliation at the hands of Third Division Swindon in 1969.

Managers had come and gone with alarming frequency and, as the 1960s wore on, the famous North London side had slumped into a regular mid-table slot. Yet a revival of sorts had taken place under Physiotherapist turned Manager Bertie Mee in 1968-69. Aside from the Wembley disaster against Swindon, the Gunners had finished 4th in the table, allowing them entry into the Fairs Cup.

Unlike capital rivals Spurs and West Ham, Arsenal had never enjoyed any success on the European scene so little was expected of them as they embarked on their 1969-70 campaign. They beat Northern Ireland's part-timers Glentoran but not before suffering an ignominious defeat in Belfast. A draw in Lisbon against Sporting followed by a comprehensive Highbury victory redeemed their reputation and a 1-0 overall triumph in a desperately close contest against French side Rouen sent them into the last eight where they turned over the Romanian outfit Dinamo Bacau, winning 7-1 at home and 2-0 away.

But it was their semi-final win over the emerging Ajax team, Cruyff, Krol, Keizer et al which made Europe take notice of the Gunners. A 3-0 Highbury lead was comfortably held on to as Ajax managed to win only 1-0 in Amsterdam. Their Final opponents were the skilled Belgian team, Anderlecht, the first team from that country to reach a European Final. They were a formidable side, from International 'keeper Trappeniers through veteran Swede Nordahl to the front three of Devrindt, Mulder and the superb Van Himst. They swept Arsenal aside imperiously in the first leg, easily building a 3-0 lead. Only an 85th minute goal from substitute Ray Kennedy offered any kind of hope for the Highbury return.

It was a monumental task which faced Arsenal as 51,612 supporters roared them on. Arsenal applied early pressure, using their aerial supremacy to unnerve the Belgians, but it was a cracking volley from teenager Eddie Kelly in the 25th minute which reduced the leeway to just one goal. The Gunners defence, led by McLintock, was seldom under threat but coped well when called on until early in the second half when, twice, Anderlecht almost scored. First, Wilson smartly nicked the ball off the feet of Devrindt's toes after a rare Simpson miskick. Then the 'keeper saw Nordahl strike the post before he beat out Mulder's rebound attempt on goal.

Trappeniers was in superb form too and it was 20 minutes from the end before the Gunners levelled the tie. Graham's through pass found McNab on a surprising jaunt upfield. He crossed to Radford who headed home. Arguments had raged before the match as to whether away goals would count as double if Arsenal won 2-0 or whether a third game would have to be played. One minute later such debate became redundant. Charlie George split the Belgian defence with a long pass to Jon Sammels. The striker hit a text-book shot, low inside the far post from 10 yards. The crowd sang and chanted their heroes through the final minutes until the final whistle blew. Then, after 17 long years, Highbury exploded into a riot of celebration. The Cup was won. *"The name of Arsenal will resound through the world again"* said the *Daily Telegraph*. Bertie Mee was ambitious: *"Now we would like to win the League and the European Cup"* said the Arsenal boss.

The latter proved beyond them but twelve months later, the reborn Gunners achieved the League and Cup double. Since then, many more trophies have gone Highbury way. The last-kick League title win at Anfield in 1989 and the double domestic Cup success in 1993 plus the Cup-Winners Cup in 1994. Magnificent triumphs to be sure but they were achieved by a team which had a proven track record. Such was not the case in 1970, when, on a night of high emotion, Arsenal rose from the slumber of almost two decades to proudly hoist what many believe to be the hardest trophy of them all to win.

For the first time in seventeen years, an Arsenal skipper holds a trophy aloft. Frank McLintock and the Mayor of Islington with the Fairs Cup.

10

ASTON VILLA 1
Vs Bayern Munich 0

May 26th 1982 - European Cup Final (Rotterdam)

Aston Villa: Rimmer (Spink), Swain, Williams, Evans, McNaught, Mortimer, Bremner, Shaw, Withe, Cowans, Morley.

Only the most romantic of midlands dreamers could have envisaged Aston Villa vying for the continent's greatest club prize as this famous old side slid into the Third Division in 1970. But the long-awaited revival of a team which had been predominant in England before the First World War was both surprising and swift when it finally arrived. Villa returned to the top flight in 1975 and, thanks to two League Cup successes, played twice in Europe in the 70s but without making any serious impact. Their 1981 League Championship victory saw the League flag flutter over Villa Park for the first time since 1910 but even then there were few prepared to suggest that the Birmingham club could emulate Liverpool and Nottingham Forest by keeping the European Cup in English hands for the sixth successive year.

Villa was given the softest of starts in the tournament, easily disposing of Valur from Iceland, but after that it was tough all the way. They won a hard away tie against the stolid East Germans of Dynamo Berlin before losing the home leg, only the away goals rule allowed them to enter the last eight. Another splendid away performance, a 0-0 draw with Dynamo Kiev, was followed by a 2-0 home victory in the return leg. But it was under peculiar circumstances that they played that night. For the man who had led them to the title, Ron Saunders, had resigned as manager a month beforehand in a dispute over his salary. The new boss was Saunders' assistant Tony Barton who guided his charges through this tie on a caretaker basis. Barton didn't receive a contract until that most inauspicious of dates, April 1st.

The newly confirmed manager steered his team through a difficult semi-final against Anderlecht, Morley's first-leg score at Villa Park being the only strike of the 180 minutes, to face the might of Bayern Munich in the Final. The Germans, three times European Champions in the 1970s, were still a formidable squad. In Paul Breitner and Karl-Heinz Rummennigge they possessed two of the best players in the world. And Hoeness, Dremmler and Augenthaler would have walked into many an ideal XI as well. The team from Bavaria were strongly fancied to end the English stranglehold on the Cup.

The 46,000 assembled in the Feyenoord stadium in Rotterdam didn't have long to wait to witness the first drama of the night. Eight minutes into the game, Villa's 'keeper Jimmy Rimmer, who had injured his neck in training, was forced to retire from the fray. In his place came Nigel Spink whose entire first-team career ran to just a solitary appearance, in a 2-1 defeat at Nottingham Forest on Boxing Day 1979!

Immediately he was called into action and in the manner of all the best comic strip heroes, distinguished himself with fine saves from Durnberger and recently crowned European Footballer of the Year (for the 2nd year in succession) Rummennigge. Spink's heroics began to inspire his team-mates and when the first half ended goalless it was Bayern who were the more disappointed side.

Bayern kept up the pressure at the start of the second half but Spink stood firm. Although having the most of the match the Germans couldn't really impose themselves on Villa as Cowans and Mortimer, heartened by what their young colleague was doing to Europe's No.1 player, effectively closed down the man who had come second in the poll, the usually lethal Breitner. With Evans and McNaught striving manfully to keep the heat off the tyro goalkeeper, the match gradually began to turn Villa's way.

In the 67th minute Gary Shaw passed to Tony Morley who accelerated past an astonished Augenthaler before squaring the ball to Peter Withe. The big striker drove his shot into the net off the post. Maybe not the most spectacular goal of a long and varied career but without doubt the most important. Bayern were stunned. They could not respond. It was almost a mirror image of the 1975 Final when Bayern had soaked up everything Leeds could throw at them before breaking away to win the game. Now it was England's revenge. The European Cup was on its way to Birmingham and if the hitherto unknown Spink was the hero of the hour then the luckless Rimmer could claim a consolation place in the record books. He had been the substitute 'keeper when Man Utd had won in 1968, so now he was the owner of two European Cup winner's medals having played for just eight minutes!

Ten years after playing in the Third Division.......

.... Aston Villa are Champions of Europe.

Withe scores the winner.

BARNET 4
Vs Crewe Alexandra 7

August 17th 1991 - League Division 4

Barnet: Phillips, Blackford, Cooper, Horton, Bodley, Johnson, Showler, Carter, Bull, Lowe, Evans. Subs. Stein, Murphy.

This small North London outfit had achieved little in the way of success in their 103 years of existence prior to 1991. They had won the Amateur Cup in 1946 and had squeezed 11,026 fans into their compact Underhill stadium for an Amateur Cup tie against Wycombe Wanderers in 1952. But they were chiefly known as the nearly-men of non-League soccer. Three times in five years they had finished runners-up in the Alliance Premier/Vauxhall Conference League; just missing out on the automatic elevation to League status reserved for that division's champions.

In 1990-91 that all changed as Barnet withstood early challenges by Kettering and Altrincham and held off the late bid by ex-Leaguers Colchester to win the title, scoring over 100 goals in the process. Now they looked forward to their first-ever game in the Football League.

Under the dubious - if imposing - figure of Stan Flashman, Barnet had prepared for life in the League with a close-season investment of close to £1 million being spent on ground improvements. A crowd of 5,090, almost double their non-League average, welcomed the League new boys onto the field. Within seven minutes those fans were cheering as Gary Bull, brother of England player Steve, slid the ball under Crewe 'keeper Greygoose to give Barnet the best possible start. But the newcomers' defensive frailties were exposed ten minutes later as Naylor equalised for Crewe and Futcher put the Cheshire club in front sixty seconds after that. Crewe's third goal, from Edwards in 27 minutes, seemed to have wrapped the match up but battling Barnet had other ideas. Five minutes from the interval, Carter scored to make it 3-2 at the break.

The goals continued to flow in the second half. Hignett netted from the penalty spot on the hour mark to make it 4-2 to Crewe. Then, in a repeat of the first period, the Barnet defence collapsed, losing two more goals inside a minute, Edwards and Hignett making it 6-2 with 20 minutes remaining. Barnet refused to buckle, Bull pulled a goal back with 15 minutes left on the clock. Still, the goal rush refused to dry up. Edwards got his hat-trick and Crewe's seventh three minutes later, only for Carter to grab Barnet's fourth with a minute to play. This incredible 11 goal League introduction ended with Barnet's ever-ebullient manager, Barry Fry, emerging from the dressing-room to claim *"This could be the quickest sacking on record, only 90 minutes into the League."* It wasn't, but Fry would be sacked, or resign, and be re-instated several times over the next two stormy seasons. Fortunately for the manager, his other post-match prediction was also slightly askew when he said that "I'll still back us to score 100 goals this season, but we might lose 300".

Neither target was remotely in sight by the season's end but Barnet did enough to prove themselves an asset to the League and did even better in their second season by winning promotion. Sadly, the club's perilous financial predicament forced the break-up of the side and the departure, for good this time, of Barry Fry. But the memory of that amazing debut game when Barnet scored four times, only to be well beaten will be vividly recalled for a long time by those who were there.

ON THE SAME DAY...

News: Freed Beirut hostage, John McCarthy, leaves RAF Lyneham, where he has been recovering from his ordeal.

Sport: The biggest crowd of the opening day of the season is the 46,728 watch Manchester United beat Notts County 2-0.

Entertainment: Surprise hit of the 1990 World Cup, Luciano Pavarrotti, appears in concert on BBC 2, marking 30 years since his operatic debut.

BARNSLEY 1

Vs West Bromwich A. 0

April 24th 1912 - FA Cup Final Replay
(Bramall Lane)

Barnsley: Cooper, Downs, Taylor, Glendenning,
Bratley, Utley, Bartrop, Tufnell,
Lillycrop, Travers, Moore.

No more than a modest 2nd Division side, Barnsley had astonished the football world in 1910 by reaching the FA Cup Final where they held Newcastle United to a draw before succumbing 2-0 in the replay. Yet in 1910-11 they sank to second bottom of the League. They were a better side this term and, with six survivors from their previous Final appearance, they went on an enterprising Cup run; the highlight of which was a Quarter-Final elimination of the holders, Bradford City, 3-2 after three 0-0 draws. There was another goalless game against Swindon Town in the Semi-Final before a 1-0 replay win took Barnsley to the Crystal Palace for a second Final.

Not surprisingly the Final also ended in a 0-0 draw. One paper's match report was written thus: *"3.30, West Brom kicked off. 4.15, half time, nothing scored. 4.24, game re-started. 5.09, final whistle, no score."* As succinct a summing-up of a non-event as the 54,556 who endured it would have wanted to read. On the Monday after the Final, Barnsley lost 2-0 to Derby in the League, hardly a morale-booster for the Wednesday replay against their First Division foes. But Barnsley had one thing in their favour, the venue. The replay was at Sheffield United's Bramall Lane ground. For the first time in it's history the F.A. Cup would be won and lost on Yorkshire soil.

A crowd of 38,555 assembled, paying receipts of £2,615.9s.0d, and although there were again no goals to cheer in the first 45 minutes, the play was of an infinitely higher standard. In a keen and entertaining match, Barnsley were well on top with outside-right Bartrop driving his side forward. It was a more even second half but both teams finishing was woeful, even the partisan *Barnsley Chronicle* said, *"The South Yorkshire men were very erratic in the vicinity of goal."* It almost cost them dearly, twice near the end of 90 minutes West Brom's Jephcott went close to scoring. But, again, the game finished goalless. For the first time, there would be extra time in the Cup Final.

West Brom hit the bar then their left-winger, Shearman, appeared to have been brought down in the penalty area but referee Schumacher waved play on. Barnsley retaliated. In the second extra time period, Moore's shot was only partially cleared, Bartrop's follow-up was blocked, then Bratley tried to force the ball over the line but somehow West Brom survived. Two minutes from the end, Barnsley's Tufnell broke away. He raced past the defenders, steadied himself as 'keeper Pearson advanced, and slipped the ball past him into the net. There was no time for West Brom to counter-attack. As the final whistle sounded the enthusiastic Yorkshire crowd invaded the pitch while West Brom captain, Pennington, warmly shook hands with his Barnsley counterpart, Archie Taylor. Taylor repeated the sporting gesture when the Cup was presented to him amid the cheering throng.

As soon as the news reached Barnsley, a huge crowd filled the streets. At 8.45 that evening the team arrived back in a motor procession to a tumultuous roar from the crowds in Sheffield Road. At the Clarence Hotel, Taylor hoisted the Cup high for all to see. The delighted masses yelled for Tufnell and the reluctant hero appeared, carried shoulder-high by his colleagues. The party had just begun. The press reported that, *"up to a late hour bands of enthusiasts paraded the town merrymaking."* Just 24 hours later, Barnsley had to play Chelsea in a home League game which they lost 2-0, a result which the euphoric Yorkshire crowd scarcely noticed. The Cup success galvanised Barnsley into a side which came close to promotion over the next few seasons. But the First World War intervened, League football was suspended for the duration, and seldom since have Barnsley looked like achieving top-flight status. What they do have though, is the comforting thought that the first FA Cup to be won in Yorkshire was lifted by a Yorkshire side.

ON THE SAME DAY...

News: Survivors of the Titanic disaster told their harrowing tale upon arrival in New York as an inquiry into the tragedy got underway.

Sport: Derby's win at Oakwell had guaranteed them promotion and the great Steve Bloomer led them to an ecstatic welcome from over 20,000 fans.

Entertainment: The Empire Theatre, Barnsley, is the setting for 'A Royal Divorce', not a prediction of life in the 1990s, but the story of Napoleon and Josephine. The following evening's performance was graced with the presence of the Barnsley and Chelsea teams as the FA Cup took centre stage beside the Bonapartes.

BIRMINGHAM CITY 0
Vs Barcelona 0

March 29th 1960 - Inter-Cities Fairs Cup Final 1st Leg

Birmingham City: Schofield, Farmer, Allen, Watts,
Smith, Neal, Astall, Gordon, Weston, Orritt, Hooper.

Despite a history dating back to 1875, Birmingham City has never been a name to unduly trouble trophy-engravers. Their highest League finish was 6th place in 1956, a year when they also played in one of their two losing FA Cup Finals. While they did win the League Cup in 1963, that trophy had still to be accepted as a serious competition by many of the leading sides of the day. Yet the Blues were among the early British pioneers of European football. By dint of its status as a major city, Birmingham was entitled to enter a team in the Fairs Cup. With Villa in serious decline it was their St. Andrews rivals who led the way. They were actually the first English club side to take part in a European tournament when they played in the inaugural Fairs Cup, a competition which sprawled over three years from 1955-58; the other English entrants being a London select XI.

Blues eliminated Inter-Milan and Zagreb in that first foray abroad before losing to Barcelona in a Semi-Final play-off. The second Fairs Cup was less unwieldy than the first but still lasted from 1958-60. Cologne, Zagreb and St. Gilloise all surrendered to the Midlands team as they forced their way into the Final to face Barcelona again. The Spanish outfit had won that first tournament beating London's all-star XI 8-2 on aggregate. So it was Blues who now became the first English club to play in a European Final, against a team described in the *Birmingham Mail* as *"Brilliant Barcelona, the best club team in the world."* An appellation which may well have been disputed by Real Madrid but not by many others.

Blues manager Pat Beasley didn't share the *Mail's* view. *"Over-awed? Why should we be"* was his response. Team captain Trevor Smith was more circumspect. *"A collection of geniuses,"* was his summation of Barcelona. The Spaniards had already visited the West Midlands during this season, when they thrashed Wolves 9-2 on aggregate in the European Cup, no bar in those days to playing in more than one Euro-tourney. The same Wolves ended the season by winning the FA Cup, and were just one point away from a history-making third successive English title.

Blues, by contrast, lay second bottom of the First Division when Kocsis, Martinez, Ramallets and Co. stepped out on to a rain and mud-soaked St. Andrews. But that night they were matched by the Midlanders. Maybe it was a roar of 40,500 fervent Blues fans which unnerved Barca. Or perhaps it was their arrogant refusal to even train before the game which told against them. One thing was for certain, it was impossible to tell which team was claiming to be the best in the world and which was struggling for survival in their domestic League. True, as a spectacle it was less than memorable. But Blues achieved what they set out to do. The creative edge of the Spanish was blunted by the hard tackling of Blues defenders. There were plenty of those. Eight players stayed resolutely behind the ball, forcing Barcelona into some desperate and ineffective long-range shooting. Birmingham 'keeper Johnny Schofield didn't have one direct save to make during the 90 minutes. But Blues couldn't force a way through either. The game ended scoreless. The supporters viewed that as a triumph. The final whistle was the signal for a rare St. Andrews pitch invasion by thousands of jubilant fans, proud of their team's performance in matching the maestros of world football. Pride was restored to English, and Midlands, football by this battling performance from Birmingham. Where the mighty Wolves had been torn apart, humble Blues had weathered the storm.

Alas, there was to be no repeat in Barcelona. Blues lost 4-1 in the return leg. But they had whetted their fans appetite for continental opposition. The following year Birmingham again marched all the way to the Fairs Cup Final, only to lose to AS Roma. Defeat by Barcelona's other team, Espanol, in the 1962-63 competition marked the end of Birimingham's European days. As they attempt to re-establish themselves at the forefront of the English game, Blues fans may take some consolation in the knowledge that they once led the way into Europe, the first English club to appear in a Euro-Final and a team which performed so well.

ON THE SAME DAY...

News: Deputy Labour leader, Nye Bevan, the architect of the NHS, is allowed home from hospital. Hopes that he has recovered from major illness are premature though; three months later he is dead.

Sport: More European success as Britain's Dave Charnley wins the European lightweight boxing title.

Entertainment: Top TV programme is the Western series 'Rawhide', starring Eric Fleming and his little-known sidekick, Clint Eastwood.

BLACKBURN ROVERS 2
Vs West Bromwich Albion 0

April 10th 1886 - FA Cup Final Replay (Derby)

Blackburn Rovers: Arthur, Turner, Suter, Douglas, Forrest, McIntyre, Walton, Strachan, Brown, Fecitt, Sowerbutts.

Blackburn was the mecca of football in the North of England in the 1880s. Rovers became the first Northern side to reach the F.A. Cup Final when they lost 1-0 to Old Etonians in 1882. Their local rivals, Blackburn Olympic, avenged this defeat and went one better by lifting the trophy at the expense of the same Old Etonians a year later. It was the first Northern triumph and also the last time that an 'old boys' team played in the Final. Rovers kept the trophy in Blackburn by beating leading Scottish side Queen's Park in both the next two Finals. They powered their way to a third successive Final where they faced dangerous opposition in West Bromwich Albion, a new rising force from the West Midlands. The first game, at Kennington Oval, ended in a disappointing 0-0 draw. A week later, the sides met again, this time at Derby County's Racecourse Ground. For the first time the F.A. Cup's fate would be decided out of London.

15,000 watched as the match got underway at 3.32 precisely. Right from the kick-off, Albion demonstrated that they would be no push-overs for a Blackburn team aiming to emulate the achievement of the famous Wanderers by winning the F.A. Cup for a third successive year. During the early part of the first half, it was Rovers who were under pressure. But Albion lacked the penetration necessary to capitalise on their territorial advantage. After weathering the initial storm, Blackburn took control. They penned Albion back inside their own half. In 26 minutes, Sowerbutts put the Lancashire side in front. But it was inside-left Fecitt who was Blackburn's outstanding player. His pass to Brown should have resulted in a goal but the centre-forward, and Rovers captain, slipped as he was about to shoot. Sowerbutts did get the ball in the net again but he was ruled offside.

The first period ended with Rovers still leading by a solitary goal. The start of the second half mirrored the first as West Brom laid siege to the Blackburn goal. Suter was outstanding in defence as was 'keeper Arthur. At length, Blackburn broke out of defence. From an Albion corner Brown won the ball and he ran the length of the pitch, but his shot was a weak one. Undaunted, the skipper repeated his lung-bursting run. This time he scored. A magnificent goal. Albion were a spent force now. The match ended in the now-familiar sight of Blackburn Rovers hoisting high the F.A. Cup. They had been described as a *"Northern horde of uncouth garb and strange oaths"* on the occasion of their first triumph, but there was no denying the superlative quality of their victory. *"Once more the Rovers have astonished the football world,"* said the admiring *Blackburn Standard*.

What an achievement it was. More than 100 years later no other club has ever captured the F.A. Cup in three successive years. Rovers themselves went on to win the trophy two years running in 1890 and 1891. Their bid for a second hat-trick ended in the last 16 in 1892 when they were beaten by the eventual winners that year, West Bromwich Albion. Two League titles shortly before the First World War and another F.A. Cup victory in 1928 were all that Rovers could add to their name before a long decline set in. Recent years have seen them again become one of the most powerful sides in the land, lifting the Premiership title in 1995. But for all their money and big names, few would wager on them ever matching those heroes of the long-forgotten 1880s.

BLACKPOOL 4

Vs Bolton Wanderers 3

May 2nd 1953 - F.A. Cup Final (Wembley)

Blackpool: Farm, Shimwell, Garrett, Fenton, Johnston, Robinson, Matthews, Taylor, Mortensen, Mudie, Perry.

Blackpool were the F.A. Cup's 'nearly men' in the immediate post-war period. Twice, in 1948 and in 1951, they reached the Final only to trail away as runners-up. For the legendary Stanley Matthews, a wonderful career seemed destined to end without a single medal to his name. Matthews was three months past his 38th birthday when Blackpool lined up against a strong Bolton Wanderers side in this match. No-one needed to be told that this was his last chance of glory.

With just 90 seconds on the clock, 'keeper George Farm fumbled a Nat Lofthouse shot and Bolton were ahead. Blackpool played poorly for the first half-hour and were lucky not to be further in arrears. But Mortensen took a hand in proceedings after 34 minutes. His shot appeared to take a deflection off Bolton's Hassall before entering the net but the goal was credited to Mortensen. Bolton came storming back though. Farm failed to come out to meet a cross from Langton, allowing Moir to put Wanderers in front again. In 55 minutes it appeared to be all over when Bolton's Bell (who had been a virtual passenger since his 20th minute injury) rose to head his side's third.

Matthews had been outstanding in a poor Blackpool performance and it was he who now inspired his team-mates into the greatest Cup Final fightback of them all. With 20 minutes remaining, Mortensen pulled a goal back. Even that didn't look to be good enough. Despite Matthews running all over the pitch as if he had *"the legs of an athlete of 18,"* as one paper said, his side were still behind with only three minutes to play.

But then Mortensen scored from a free-kick to level the scores and, in the final minute, Bill Perry broke away to score a fourth for Blackpool. Thus ended what Frank Butler in the *News of the World* described as the *"finest exhibition since the first Wembley Final in 1923."* Joe Smith, Blackpool's manager (and, ironically, a former double cup-winner with Bolton) sprinted onto the pitch, hugging Matthews and declaring *"lad, you won the Cup."* Smith was right. From that day to this the 1953 Final has always been referred to as *"The Matthews Final."*

Yet the ever-modest Stan would have been the first to acknowledge the role of those others who made this Final such a great one: Stan Mortensen, overshadowed by the other Stan maybe, but still the only man to score a hat-trick in a Wembley F.A. Cup Final.

Bill Parry, who thanks to Matthews and Mortensen, has become the most anonymous scorer of a winning Cup Final goal. Harry Johnston, Blackpool's skipper, who, like Matthews, Mortensen and right-back Shimwell, was playing in his third Cup Final for Blackpool in five years. Johnston became the first captain to receive the Cup from Queen Elizabeth II.

On the losing side was the never-say-die figure of Nat Lofthouse. His only immediate consolation lay in the winning of the Football Writers Association award as 'Player of the Year'. Five years later Lofthouse would finally get his hands on his own winner's medal, but in such circumstances (facing Manchester United shortly after the Munich tragedy) that - just like this Final - almost everyone outside Bolton wanted Nat's team to lose.

As for the amazing Matthews, he was asked if this Cup triumph was the climax to his career. Instead of a simple 'yes', he replied *"I hope to play for several more seasons,"* and he did. Matthews, who had made his England debut as far back as 1934-35, was recalled to the England side and played a further 21 internationals over the next four seasons; his last appearance being in a World Cup qualifier in Copenhagen, well after his 42nd birthday. In the domestic game, he played on until 1965, retiring at the age of 50 as the only footballer ever to be knighted while still playing the game.

But if he had answered that reporter's question in the affirmative, then it would have been no lie. For, of all his many feats, the day Stanley Matthews helped bring the Cup to Blackpool must rank as his finest 90 minutes.

ON THE SAME DAY...

News: The trial continues of John Christie. The notorious occupant of 10 Rillington Place faces four murder charges.

Sport: Roger Bannister knocks three seconds off the British record for the mile, raising hopes that the four-minute barrier would soon be broken.

Entertainment: Although TV is growing, radio is still popular. Millions tune into the Light Programme's music show with Henry Hall and Donald Peers.

THE FOOTBALL ASSOCIATION CHALLENGE CUP COMPETITION

FINAL TIE

BLACKPOOL v BOLTON WANDERERS

SATURDAY, MAY 2nd, 1953   KICK-OFF 3 pm

EMPIRE STADIUM

WEMBLEY

Chairman and Managing Director : SIR ARTHUR J. ELVIN, M.B.E.

OFFICIAL PROGRAMME   ONE SHILLING

BOLTON WANDERERS 2
West Ham United 0

April 28th 1923 - F.A. Cup Final (Wembley)

Bolton Wanderers: Pym, Haworth, Finney, Nuttall, Seddon, Jennings, Butler, Jack, J.R. Smith, J. Smith, Vizard.

Although one of the founder members of the Football League, Bolton had endured something of a chequered history. Four times they had been relegated to the Second Division, yet they had always quickly bounced back. Twice, in 1894 and 1904, they had reached the F.A. Cup Final, only to return to Lancashire with losers medals. Their opponents in the 1923 Final, West Ham, had only joined the League in 1919 and were playing in their first Final. So a new name had to be engraved on the trophy.

But this match was also notable as the First Cup Final to be played at the new Empire Stadium in Wembley. A vast crowd assembled to watch the match. The Metropolitan Railway alone ferried 60,000 passengers to the ground, disgorging them at the rate of 1,000 per minute. Officially, there were 126,047 people inside the stadium at the appointed kick-off hour, but the real size of the gathering was anywhere between 150,000-200,000 as barriers and gates were broken by the eager throng. It was a mass of people *"so unmanageable it seemed probable play would have to be abandoned,"* according to one report.

Eventually the spectators were herded off the pitch and into the terraces and stands. At 3.44pm the game got underway. It was Bolton who held the early upper hand. Twice, West Ham's right-back, Henderson, saved his side. Then, Bolton's David Jack got the ball and as a contemporary report stated *"took the ball in his stride, and showing perfect ball control, beat the West Ham defence completely, finishing a great run with a lofty drive, at which Hufton (the Hammers 'keeper) threw himself in vain. It was a magnificent goal."* And historic - the first-ever goal scored at Wembley. West Ham attacked, their centre-forward, Vic Watson, headed over the bar when faced with an open goal. There had been just five minutes played.

West Ham came more into a game which was full of *"rousing football, never a dull moment."* Once more the crowd surged onto the pitch. When play re-started, Bolton again seized the initiative but half-time arrived with no further scoring. Mindful of the crowd intrusions, both sets of players remained on the pitch during the break.

The second half was a scrappier affair until Vizard made a good run on the left for Bolton, beating Henderson and Bishop, before passing to J.R. Smith who hit a *"tremendous cross-drive"* for the second goal. It was a shot so hard that the ball bounced back yards into play. West Ham tried to come back into the match but Bolton's defence was rarely troubled. Bolton had won the first Wembley Final. If Jack had written himself into the history books, so too had J.R. Smith. For he had scored for Kilmarnock in the 1920 Scottish Cup Final, making him the first man not only to obtain winner's medals at both Wembley and Hampden but also the first to score in Cup Finals on those historic grounds. But the Wanderers star man was left-winger Vizard.

As Boltonians celebrated all the way back to Lancashire, the F.A. sought to avoid any blame for the fiasco of the match arrangements. They *"regretted the inconvenience,"* but said they could not *"accept responsibility"* as *"the arrangements were not in their hands."* An oblique swipe at the Wembley authorities and the first public row in a series that has continued on-and-off for over 70 years. One press report summed it up thus: *"The battle of Wembley is over. If future generations ask who won, they will be told a policeman on an old grey mare."* Not quite correct.

Legend has transformed the 'old grey mare' into a shining white horse in the commonly accepted version of events. As for Bolton, they were now on the brink of their greatest era. Twice more within the next six years, they returned to the scene of their greatest triumph and travelled North with the F.A. Cup proudly in their possession.

ON THE SAME DAY...

News: A crowd even bigger than at the Cup Final, an estimated one million, lines the streets for the wedding of the Duke of York and Lady Elizabeth Bowes-Lyon. She is already referred to jokingly, and prophetically, as Queen Elizabeth by the Prince of Wales.

Sport: Long-forgotten Nelson F.C. celebrate winning the Third Division (North) title with a win over Walsall.

Entertainment: The hymn which would later become the Wembley anthem, 'Abide With Me', could be heard by those in the London area with radios, sung by Miss Edith Russell Miller.

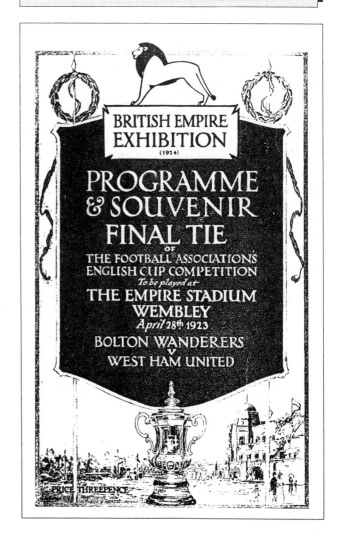

(A.F.C.) BOURNEMOUTH 1
Vs Manchester United 2

March 2nd 1957 - F.A. Cup Quarter-Final

Bournemouth: Goodwin, Lyons, Woolard, Clayton,
Hughes, Brown, Stiffle, Norris,
Bedford, Newsham, Cutler.

What a year this was for Bournemouth (or Bournemouth and Boscombe Athletic to give them the full title they used at the time). The modest Third Division (South) team had reached the last 32 of the FA Cup by virtue of triumphs over Burton Albion, Swindon Town and Accrington Stanley. It was then that the heroics started. Drawn away to Wolves, they shocked the nation by pulling off a remarkable 1-0 win in front of 42,011 at Molineux. That was followed by a 3-1 home win over Spurs, then second top of the League, before 25,892 supporters at the Dean Court ground. Now there was an even bigger scalp on offer, that of Manchester United, reigning League Champions, set to successfully defend their crown, and Cup favourites as well.

A record gate of 28,799 crammed into the compact ground to see their local heroes, assembled at a total cost of £4,000, take on the team which many reckoned to be the best in Europe. It was a blood-and-thunder affair, and after just ten minutes play, Bournemouth's Ollie Norris collided with United's centre-half Mark Jones. Jones was forced to retire from the fray, and in these pre-substitution days, 10-man United were compelled to re-jig their formation, with Duncan Edwards taking over at centre-half. The Cherries hustled their illustrious opponents for the next 25 minutes. Then, in 35 minutes, controversy. From a Bournemouth corner, centre-forward Brian Bedford headed goalwards, with 'keeper Ray Wood making no effort to save. The bemused Wood later explained, *"the corner kick had already gone behind. I was amazed when the referee gave the goal."* But give it he did. Boscombe (as the local press called them), reached the dressing-room nursing that precious lead. Bournemouth held on at the start of the second half. Their fans were beginning to sense that a third famous victory was on the cards and that the Semi-Finals beckoned their heroes, when disaster struck twice within five minutes.

On the hour mark, United's right-winger Johnny Berry cracked home the equaliser. Then, a fierce Denis Viollet shot was punched clear. Alas for Bournemouth, the fist in question belonged not to 'keeper Godwin but right-back Lyons. Berry scored from the resultant penalty.

Bournemouth tried to come back into it, but once the First Division side got their noses in front, that was the end of the South Coast side's dream. There was to be no more scoring. But it was a relieved Matt Busby who paid tribute to his team's foes. Without referring to the early loss of Jones, Busby said simply, *"I think it was one of the boys greatest fights."* His opposite number, Freddie Cox, replied, *"United were a fine team to lose to."* United lost the Final to Aston Villa that year and their team was wrecked in the carnage of the Munich air disaster less than a year later. For Bournemouth there has been little in the way of concrete achievement since that heady campaign in the fifties. A victory in the Associate Members Cup in 1984 was followed by the Third Division title in 1987 and a brief three-year tenure as members of the old Second Division which followed. In the F.A. Cup, Ted McDougall scored nine times in a single match against Margate, but their sweetest moment undoubtedly came in 1984 when they avenged their 1957 loss by beating Manchester United 2-0 in the third round.

Great as that success was however, it couldn't really compare to the time when the top clubs were being eliminated by Bournemouth one after the other, only the greatest team of the day preventing one of the most unlikeliest F.A. Cup wins ever.

ON THE SAME DAY...

News: Rocky Marciano, former undefeated heavyweight boxing champion of the world, is starting to carve out a new career for himself. He teams up with Jimmy Durante for a night-club song-and-dance act.

Sport: England's Test Cricketers are on the verge of defeat in South Africa.

Entertainment: TV weekend highlight was the Eurovision Song Contest.

The first F.A. Cup had been stolen from a Birmingham shop in 1895. The second was presented to F.A. President Lord Kinnaird in February 1911. The third trophy cost £52.10s (£52.50) and was made by Fattorini & Sons of Bradford. Since no team from that city had reached as far as the Semi-Finals of the tournament, few expected the new F.A. Cup to remain in the place of its 'birth'.

BRADFORD CITY 1
Vs Newcastle United 0

April 26th 1911 - F.A. Cup Final Replay (Old Trafford)

Bradford City: Mellors, Campbell, Taylor, Robinson, Torrance, McDonald, Logan, Spiers, O'Rourke, Devine, Thompson.

The match itself saw Newcastle pile on the early pressure. Bradford City were forced into some pretty desperate defending, breaking out only occasionally with some *"fierce, ugly rushes."* Whereas Newcastle were playing the *"prettier, more polished, cleverer football."* But perhaps elements of the much-vaunted Yorkshire grit were in evidence as City withstood all that Newcastle could throw at them.

Bradford City had other ideas. They were a potent First Division team at the time and they swept aside New Brompton, Norwich City, Grimsby Town and Burnley to reach the last four. A fine 3-0 win over Blackburn Rovers in the Semi-Finals set them up for an historic occasion. Their opponents were Newcastle United, the finest cup-fighting side of the times. In 1905, 1906 and 1908 they had reached the Final, only to lose on all three occasions. But in 1910 they had finally triumphed and few were prepared to bet against them winning for the second successive year.

But Cup fever had gripped Bradford. As early as 4 a.m. on the day of the Final, special trains started arriving in London. 36 rolled into Euston, a further 23 at St. Pancras and even more alighted at King's Cross, bearing the Geordie contingent. But the 69,098 at the Crystal Palace saw a dreadful game. It was, *"the poorest final on record"* said the *Bradford Daily Telegraph*. The replay, four days later, at Old Trafford, brought chaos to the streets of Manchester. 66,645 entered the ground, with a further 30,000 locked outside, such was the interest in this match. The scenes prompted one reporter to bewail the lack of facilities, pleading *"when will the F.A. ever build a Hampden Park?"*

As half-time approached, Bradford began to take the game to their rivals. A huge kick from Robinson towards goal was blown out by the fierce wind to Thompson who headed into the penalty area. As Spiers headed on towards goal, O'Rourke challenged 'keeper Lawrence. Thus distracted, Lawrence couldn't keep the ball out of the net. Spiers was the scorer though some present thought that O'Rourke had gained the last touch. At any rate, this goal seemed to sap the spirits of the Geordies. Because, for all their possession in the second half, they rarely threatened to equalise. The Cup belonged to Bradford City.

The aforementioned *Bradford City Telegraph*, under the headline *"A BRADFORD CUP FOR A BRADFORD TEAM"* described the goal like this: *"At 3.43 or thereabouts, the head of a certain person came into contact with an inflated leather sphere, which, in accordance with the laws of impact, rebounded, falling within a certain netted space near Manchester."* The paper also reported that it was the moment for great celebrations to start. Over 100,000 turned out to watch the Cup return 'home' and those celebrations were justified. For, neither before, nor since 1911, has a team from Bradford ever made the last four of the F.A. Cup and of the 100,000 celebrants, just one-tenth of that number turned up the following evening to see City beat Middlesbrough in a League game.

ON THE SAME DAY...

News: It was announced that Lord Kitchener would be in charge of the security arrangements at the forthcoming Coronation of King George V.

Sport: Yorkshire County Cricket Club moved, unsuccessfully, that County Championship matches be limited to two days play only.

Entertainment: Top turn at the Bradford Theatre Royal Is the Compton Comedy Company. Their Friday evening performance was marked by the presence of the victorious eleven and the F.A. Cup.

BRENTFORD 9
Vs Wrexham 0

October 15th 1963 - League Division 3

Brentford: Cakebread, Coote, Jones, Slater, Scott, Higginson, Summers, Brooks, McAdams, Ward, Hales.

For a brief period either side of the Second World War, Brentford had been a Division One club. But by 1962 they had slid into the Fourth Division. They had escaped from the basement quickly, securing the Division 4 title in the process. However, life in the Third was anything but easy and they had lost all three home games they had played by the time this fixture came round. With four first team regulars out through injury, their hopes of ending their dismal run looked remote. Their more optimistic supporters in the 10,500 crowd hoped that new signing Dai Ward, an £8,000 capture from Watford, might inject some welcome punch in attack. But no-one expected the goal blitz which took place this night.

With just three minutes on the clock, a Summers corner reached McAdams who promptly despatched the first goal of the evening. Five minutes later, a Hales corner was headed on by McAdams to Ward. The inside-forward hooked a spectacular overhead kick into the net to mark his Brentford career with the most auspicious of starts. After eighteen minutes play, another Hales corner caught the Wrexham defence flapping. Brooks' shot ricocheted into the net off McAdams who claimed the goal as his own. Three up in less than 10 minutes and Brentford settled down a bit, but still controlling play, allowing the hapless Welshmen little sight of goal.

Seven minutes from the interval, and with Wrexham beginning to think they had weathered the worst of the Brentford storm, centre-half Alan Fox contrived to knock the ball past his own 'keeper. Thus re-invigorated, Brentford returned to the attack. A Billy Hales header from a Brooks corner made it 5-0 at the interval.

There was no let-up after the break. Brentford kept pouring men forward. Wrexham had the worst defensive record in the League and it showed. Even their 'keeper, Steve Fleet, once understudy to the great Bert Trautmann at Manchester City, was having a torrid time. Brooks piled in a fantastic shot to make it 6-0. George Summers, at this stage the only Bees forward not on the scoresheet, rectified that particular error by grabbing the seventh. Even when Brentford made mistakes, they paid off. Brooks miskicked a high shot but it still landed behind Fleet and in the net for number eight. Near the end, Ward notched up the ninth to complete the scoring and give Brentford a win which stands as their record victory to this day.

For Wrexham, it was one more miserable result on their way to conceding over 100 League goals and relegation. For the home fans, it was wing play at its best, four of the Bees goals coming from moves down the flanks. Dai Ward had made a spectacular debut, scoring twice and having a hand in four more. The biggest problem lay with the Editor of the *Brentford and Chiswick Times*, whose match report began *"Where to start on this night of fantasy?"* Where indeed. Brentford have made only modest triumphs since and their support can only hope that one day a Bees team will emerge which can match, or surpass, the achievements of the record-breakers of 1963.

BRENTFORD FOOTBALL CLUB

OFFICIAL PROGRAMME
Season 1963-64

Football League Division III

BRENTFORD Nº 3162
v.
WREXHAM
Tuesday, 15th October, 1963
Kick-off at 7.30 p.m.

Photo by courtesy of " Middlesex County Times "
NEAR THING
Coventry City keeper Wesson turns aside John Dick's header with John Hales in close attendance.

Next Home Matches

MON. 21st OCT. London Challenge Cup
BRENTFORD v BARNET K.O. 7.30 p.m.
SAT. 26th OCT. Football League Division III
BRENTFORD v MILLWALL K.O. 3.15 p.m.

GROUND: GRIFFIN PARK, EALING ROAD, BRENTFORD

ON THE SAME DAY...

News: There is no hiding place for Premier Harold McMillan. He has decided to resign but, as yet, there is no mention of who his successor will be. (Eventually, McMillan was replaced by Sir Alec Douglas-Home).

Sport: The Cricket Writers Association give their prestigious *'Young Cricketer of the Year'* award to a raw youth from Yorkshire, Geoffrey Boycott.

Entertainment: The top TV show of the evening has a title which could explain the Wrexham defence's torment. It was the detective drama 'No Hiding Place'.

BRIGHTON & HOVE ALBION 2

Vs Manchester United 2

May 21st 1983 - F.A. Cup Final (Wembley)

Brighton: Moseley, Ramsey, Pearce, Grealish, Gatting, Stevens, Case, Howlett, Robinson, Smith, Smillie. Sub. Ryan.

Brighton have never been one of football's more fashionable names yet in the early 1980s the Sussex club played in the First Division. 1983 marked the end of their brief flirtation with top class soccer and they had already been relegated by the time they arrived at a rain-sodden Wembley as rank outsiders in their first F.A. Cup Final. But even though they were without their suspended skipper, Steve Foster, Brighton reckoned they could give Ron Atkinson's United a hard time. After all, littered among the bodies of their victims on the way to the Final lay Liverpool. England's premier, and well-nigh invincible, team had been humiliated by the men from the South Coast at their own Anfield fortress in a 5th round upset.

But the underdogs looked precisely that as a capacity 100,000 crowd saw Alan Davies and Norman Whiteside both go close for United in the early stages. But, after 15 minutes, it all changed. In their first real attack, Brighton caused panic in the Manchester defence. Neil Smillie's dashing run forcing McQueen to concede a corner. Jimmy Case's kick was cleared, but only as far as Gary Howlett. His centre darted accurately to the far post where the lurking Gordon Smith headed down past Gary Bailey in the United goal to put Brighton ahead. United's neat build-ups fell apart after the goal and the game turned distinctly ugly for a while. Case committed a bad foul on Ray Wilkins, then Whiteside did likewise to Ramsey, both offences going unpunished. Stapleton, McQueen, Whiteside and Robson all failed with attempts on goal. Brighton's confidence rose and Smillie went close before the break. Brighton retired at the interval, clutching their precious lead. Ten minutes into the second half and Duxbury surged forward for United.

He and Whiteside set up Stapleton for a close range equaliser. Shortly afterwards, Ramsey limped off, the victim of a severe Whiteside tackle. The game appeared to be flowing United's way. With just under 20 minutes remaining, Arnold Muhren found Wilkins free on the right. He saw Moseley off his line and sent a 25 yard chip curling into the far corner of the net.

With time running out, Brighton won a corner. Case's kick found Tony Grealish on the edge of the box. He stabbed the ball into the area where Stevens pounced to equalise. There were only three minutes left to play. So, into extra time it went. Both sides looked tired and ready to settle for a draw until the 114th minute. Michael Robinson, who had battled for every ball all day, broke through the middle. He cut the ball back to Smith. With the ball at his feet just six yards from goal and with only Bailey blocking his way, Smith shot straight into the keeper's body as the match commentators roared in unison *"and Smith must score..."* It was a miss destined to become legendary.

Brighton manager Jimmy Melia remained defiant, vowing *"We'll give them another hell of a game on Thursday."* Sadly for Melia and Brighton, it didn't work out that way. Even with Foster back, Brighton were no match for an inspired United. The Red Devils celebrated Sir Matt Busby's 74th birthday in style; 3-0 up at the break, they cantered to a 4-0 triumph.

Brighton's day of glory had come and gone. The dramatic first match had been their opportunity and they had spurned it. For their supporters there was only the memory of what might have been. As for Gordon Smith, there was a nightmare which would haunt him for the rest of his career.

(Back): Gatting, Stevens, Digweed, Moseley, Nelson, Robinson, Ritchie.
(Middle): Wilson, Ramsey, Ryan, Smith, Pearce, Stille, Yaxley.
(Front): Melia, Grealish, Case, Foster, Smillie, Ward, Aitken.
The pride of the South Coast - The squad get together years later for a benefit match.

BRISTOL CITY 0
Vs Manchester United 1

April 24th 1909 - F.A. Cup Final
(Crystal Palace)

Bristol City: Clay, Annan, Cottle, Hanlin, Wedlock, Spear, Staniforth, Hardy, Gilligan, Burton, Hilton

The Edwardian era was Bristol City's heyday. Promoted in 1906, they narrowly failed to lift the League title in their first season upstairs. Now they had won the right to appear in the season's showpiece match, and they had done it the hard way. Southampton and Bury had both been overcome on their own grounds after replays. Norwich became the only side City eliminated in 90 minutes. Then Glossop were overcome in a home replay. In the semi-final, there had been a rare old tussle with Derby County. A 1-1 draw at Stamford Bridge being followed by a 2-1 replay success at Birmingham before Bristol City earned the right to play in their first (and to date, last) F.A. Cup Final.

United were no great shakes and as the Final approached, most Bristolians were confident of success, despite having to take the field minus two of their most influential players, Rippon and Marr. The enthusiasm in the city was great. 150 special trains left Bristol for London and over 1,000 fans carried hammers, nails and wood with them. Not for fighting but for putting together wooden benches to sit on at Crystal Palace. The police made no complaints.

Overnight rain had left the pitch slippery, but Bristol City seemed able to cope with the conditions. Hardy and Staniforth combined to give Gilligan an early chance but his shot curled just past the post. In eight minutes, United's Roberts set up winger Wall whose fierce drive was blocked by Clay before Wedlock cleared. Surprisingly, the Manchester club were content to feed Wall rather than Billy Meredith. But the Welsh Wizard imposed himself on the game anyway. Clay fumbled a shot from Meredith but Annan was on hand to clear off the line. Man. United won four corners in quick succession but City weathered the storm. At length, they began to press forward themselves. Hardy and Staniforth again linked well together, setting Hilton off on a run. He returned to Hardy whose shot was well saved by 'keeper Moger. Immediately, United returned to the attack. Halse hit the bar but his fellow inside-forward, A.Turnbull, netted the rebound. The Bristolians among the 71,401 looking on were despondent. It was little compensation to later learn that Turnbull's goal was described as being achieved, *"flukily,"* by the somewhat less than impartial *Bristol Evening News*. City's woes increased when Meredith, who had been off the field injured, returned to taunt them, setting up further chances which his team-mates spurned. Despite the incredible United pressure, City reached half-time trailing by just the solitary goal.

The second half opened with a long-range Meredith effort just missing, but after that it was City who went on the offensive. With the wind now behind them, they charged downfield. Gilligan's shot was tipped away by a full-stretch Moger. United full-back Hayes was forced to leave the pitch injured, but the Old Trafford team were still on top. A few niggly fouls marred the atmosphere. Hayes returned but Gilligan forced his way through again. His mazy dribble ending when a frantic Moger raced off his line to clear the danger. At the other end, United's James Turnbull was through with only Clay to beat but he fired over the top. In similar circumstances, City's Hilton shot harmlessly right across the goalmouth. It was the Bristol club's last chance. Wedlock remained outstanding in their defence, refusing to allow United to add to their lead. It ended at 1-0, the closest Bristol City have ever come to winning a major honour. But back in Bristol, a rumour was circulating that the match had ended 1-1. Elation turned to depression inside the *Bristol Evening News* office at 5.10pm when the 1-0 defeat was confirmed. Meredith had been the difference between the teams and some Bristol wags suggested that had City got hold of the 'lucky toothpick' that the Welsh winger always played with, then the result might have been different. Clutching at straws is a recognisable trait in football, clutching at toothpicks more desperate still.

ON THE SAME DAY...

News: The Turkish Empire is in chaos with rumours of an attempted coup in Constantinople, amid the continuing massacres of thousands of Armenians.

Sport: Repercussions of the Glasgow riot caused by Celtic and Rangers fans at the Scottish Cup Final dominates the sporting press, with calls for stiffer penalties for offenders.

Entertainment: Any Bristol City supporters, unable to endure 'animated pictures' of the Final, showing in several theatres, can make their way to the Theatre Royal where *"after 1,000 nights in London"* they can see *"the great comedy drama,"* A Message from Mars. The unkind suggest that contact would indeed be made with the inhabitants of the Red Planet before the F.A. Cup is ever paraded through the streets of Bristol.

BRISTOL ROVERS 3

Vs Newport County 1

April 25th 1953 - League Division Three (South)

Bristol Rovers: Anderson, Bamford, Fox, Pitt,
Warren, Sampson, Petherbridge, Roost, Lambden,
Bradford, Watling.

In their 70 years of existence prior to this match, Bristol Rovers had featured largely as one of football's also-rans. But over 20,000 were already in their Eastville ground half an hour before the kick-off, knowing that history was in the making. Victory for Rovers in this game would secure the Third Division (South) title and earn the club not only their first major trophy, but also a first-ever promotion. An enthralling season had seen both Bristol clubs among the pack chasing the solitary promotion slot and crowds at Eastville had reached record numbers. Over half a million had watched the League programme and the average gate of 23,411 was the highest figure ever recorded in the city. The team assembled by manager Bert Tann was the most talented in their history.

The crowds kept rolling in. Seven minutes before the start, the Muller Road entrance was closed. 29,451 watched Rovers attack straight from the off, and they almost witnessed a sensational start. Newport defender Newall high-kicked in a desperate attempt to clear the danger. The ball teetered along his own side's crossbar before eventually dropping behind the goal. The corner was cleared but Rovers kept pressing. Watling found space before crossing to Roost. He laid the ball back to Bradford, and the inside-left - cleared to play just before the start - netted to send the home fans into a frenzy. Just two minutes had been played, Rovers were so in control that ten minutes had elapsed before their goalkeeper, Anderson, touched the ball. At the other end, Newport centre-half Wilcox was in superb form, whipping the ball off Roost's toes when the inside-right looked certain to score, then clearing a dangerous Petherbridge header.

In 31 minutes, disaster struck Rovers when Newport's Beattie put a close range effort past Anderson for a shock equaliser. There was a nervous nine minutes before Bradford struck again. His superb header restoring Rovers' lead. Problems piled up for Newport. Fearnley, their goalkeeper, fractured his collar-bone and right winger Birch took over in goal.

In the second half, Rovers were well in command but at 2-1 couldn't really relax. In the 65th minute, Bradford secured the match with another header, giving him a hat-trick. It was also his 34th goal of the season, a new record, pipping Lambden's 33 recorded the previous term. 3-1 it stayed. At the end of the match, thousands invaded the pitch, refusing to leave until team captain Ray Warren addressed them.

The club chairman who revelled in the magnificent name of H.J. Hampden-Alpass, was called to the Council House by the Lord Mayor of Bristol as a civic reception was arranged for the team. Almost 100 telegrams arrived congratulating Rovers. The £275 'talent money' awarded by the League was shared by the players. Bristol Rovers supporters had waited a long time for this success. Their jubilation was justifiable.

Rovers stayed in the higher sphere for nearly a decade, although they rarely looked like progressing any further. They have enjoyed the odd success since 1953, notably the 3rd Division title in 1990, but they have never been able to really sustain themselves at a higher level for long. Of the few moments of genuine success they have enjoyed, that initial promotion in 1953 must surely be the sweetest.

ON THE SAME DAY...

News: In the aftermath of the death of Stalin, NATO announces a massive arms build-up.

Sport: Top sprinter McDonald Bailey is suspended sine die by the Amateur Athletics Association, having been found guilty of infringing amateur status. His 'crime' came to light because of an advert in the Oxford Vs Cambridge sports programme for starting blocks, *"made to the requirements of E.McDonald Bailey Ltd."* He was the managing director of the company.

Entertainment:
   A real treat for radio listeners is a full hour of top 'soap', The Archers.

BURNLEY 3

3 Vs SV Hamburg 1
January 18th 1961
European Cup Quarter-Final 1st Leg

Burnley: Blacklaw, Angus, Elder, Joyce,
Adamson, Miller, Connelly, McIlroy, Pointer,
Robson, Pilkington.

In the 1990s it seems little short of absurd to think of Burnley as a team capable of living with Europe's elite. But in the 1960s they were a force to be reckoned with. A stream of talent flowed through Turf Moor and just a look at the team-sheet for this match indicates how strong a side they were. Most were internationals who had aided Burnley to a surprise last-day title success the previous year which had gained them entry to Europe's most prestigious club competition, but after eliminating twice-previous finalists, Stade De Rheims, Burnley had developed a run of poor form. Few, even amongst their own support, gave them much of a chance against a Hamburg side led by the great Uwe Seeler.

Despite that pessimism, 46,237 turned out on a cold January night to see if manager Harry Potts and his team could confound their critics once again. And they did. The match opened ominously when Pointer missed an open goal but Burnley were undaunted. They harried the Germans with the long-ball approach. Seeler didn't get a sniff of the action. Blacklaw set Pointer away and he in turn carved out an opportunity for John Connelly which just failed to come off. From a throw-in, McIlroy received the ball. Again, the pass was to Ray Pointer. The selfless centre-forward despatched his pass to the unmarked Pilkington and Burnley were ahead.

But even European novices like Burnley knew that a goal wouldn't be enough to take to Hamburg in the return. On the hour mark, Pilkington let fly with a screamer of a shot off his right foot and Burnley led 2-0. Then Pointer headed goalwards, only to be denied by 'keeper Schmoor. But the waiting Bobby Robson pounced on the loose ball to make it 3-0. Only now did Hamburg come into the game. Several shots were blocked or scrambled away. Blacklaw made two brilliant saves. Pilkington and Pointer were in top form as they tried to take the game back to the Germans. Miller was hit by body charges and hacking but shrugged it all aside. Just once was the Turf Moor rear-guard breached, when Doppel scored what most felt could be only a consolation goal. At the end of Burnley's 3-1 victory, the Hamburg players sportingly bowed to the Burnley fans whose wall of noise had inspired their side so much.

The appreciative Burnley fans rushed off to book for the second leg in Hamburg. The *Burnley Express* was full of praise for the team they had previously labelled a *"side of unpredictables."* In particular, they said of Ray Pointer: *"If ever he decided to stand still for 15 seconds, the grass would take encouragement and the sub-soil population come to the surface to see why there had been a stoppage in vibration."*

But it was eight weeks later before the second leg was played and Burnley were involved in maintaining a high League placing as well as progressing to the last four of the F.A. Cup. By the time they arrived in Hamburg, the momentum had gone. The 'consolation' Hamburg goal in Lancashire turned out to be a killer. Burnley were 2-0 down at the break before Harris brought them back into the tie. But 75,000 German voices roared their heroes on to a 4-1 triumph on the night and a 5-4 aggregate victory. This time there was no stopping Uwe Seeler as he notched two of the goals. For Burnley it was defeat but not dishonour. They would return to Europe in the sixties, but never with quite the same enthusiasm.

They had come so close to challenging Barcelona and Benfica for the title of Kings of Europe that it might seem unthinkable that in the 1980s Burnley came within 90 minutes of losing their place in the Football League, such was the decline of a once-great club. Perhaps the day will come again when Turf Moor again resounds to the thrill of European battle.

ON THE SAME DAY...

News: A famous confrontation takes place at the United Nations in New York when Soviet Union Premier Khruschev bangs his shoe on the table. British Prime Minister Harold McMillan responded by asking for *"a translation please."*

Sport: At the height of the battle over the maximum wage, the threat of a players strike hangs over English football.

Entertainment:
Top film at the Burnley Odeon is 'South Pacific'. Admission ranges from 3/- (15p) to 6/- (30p).

BURY 6
Vs Derby County 0

April 18th 1903 - F.A. Cup Final
(Crystal Palace)

Bury: Monteith, Lindsay, McEwen, Johnston, Thorp, Ross, Richards, Wood, Sagar, Leeming, Plant.

It's not a name whose very mention strikes fear into the hearts of opponents nowadays, but at the turn of the century, Bury were a formidable side. From 1895-1912 they were a First Division side to be reckoned with. Nor was Cup success an unknown quantity. In 1900, Bury brought the famous trophy back to Lancashire. Six of that side were regulars in their 1903 campaign.

It was not an easy route to the Final for Bury. They beat Wolves 1-0 at home before travelling to face the holders, Sheffield United. Another solitary goal success set them up for a time tie with Notts County and yet another 1-0 win. They met the competition favourites, Aston Villa, at Goodison in the Semi-Final and emerged triumphant thanks to a comprehensive 3-0 success. That victory marked Bury out as favourites in turn to lift the trophy. Their foes in the Final were Derby County, on a par with the Shakers as a League side, but lacking in Cup pedigree. Their top player, the legendary Steve Bloomer, would miss the Final through injury.

Thousands travelled South for the Final. With teams like Manchester United, Manchester City and Preston North End all in Division Two, Lancashire's support was there for Bury's taking. Indeed, Manchester United drew a crowd of only 4,000 for a League match the same day as the Final. A far cry from the 63,102 in attendance at the Crystal Palace who saw Plant and Leeming run the early part of the game for Bury. Yet it was Derby who almost took the lead. But their outside-right, Warrington, missed the chance. Twice, Leeming went close for Bury. Then Richards tried a shot which the 'keeper could only parry away. Bury skipper, George Ross, dashed in, slipping the ball past the Derby custodian, Fryer, to open the scoring. The captain was the hero again near the break, Derby's G.H. Richards looked certain to score until Ross, magnificently, cleared off the line. At half-time it was still just 1-0.

Bury's No.9, Sagar, hit the post in the first minute of the second half. Three minutes later, the same player powered through on his own. Fryer came out to meet him, the two collided and fell, but Sagar had already despatched the ball into the net for Bury's second goal.

Fryer was forced to leave the field. Morris took over in goal, Derby playing with just one full-back and relying upon the offside trap. It was a tactic doomed to failure. Plant's centre gave Wood a chance but he headed over the bar. Then Wood dribbled through on his own. Morris came out of goal but fell, dropping the ball. Leeming took advantage of the open goal to make it 3-0. 55 minutes had gone, and so had Derby's resistance. Even Fryer's return to goal did little to raise the Rams hopes. Thorp eluded his opponents and shot, again Fryer managed to parry it away. This time, it was Wood who was waiting nearby to take his chance, Bury's fourth. As the Derby fans started to stream out of the ground, Bury were relentless. Neat combination work from Sagar set up Plant again. His shot was unstoppable - 5-0. Fryer limped off again, this time for good. Leeming broke through, evaded Morris' lunge and scored number six. There was another fifteen minutes to play but that was the end of the scoring. The nearest attempt on goal came from Derby when Richards brought out the best in Monteith with a brilliant shot which resulted in another spectacular save.

"Never in the history of the Final has the result been so one-sided," said the *Daily Telegraph.* Yet it was a fully-deserved win. Bury had not conceded a single goal in Cup-ties, a record to equal that of Preston in 1889 and one which no other club has attained to this day. Bury's triumphant return to Lancashire was the pinnacle of their success. Although they again played in the First Division in the 1920s, the day of the small team was passing. The giants slumbering in Manchester would soon awaken. Now, Bury are usually to be found in the lower divisions but they can proudly point to the record books where this achievement still ranks as the highest score in an F.A. Cup Final.

It's 1903 - and this Bury team won the F.A.Cup without conceding a goal.

CAMBRIDGE UNITED 0

Vs Crystal Palace 1
March 16th 1990 - F.A. Cup Quarter-Final

Cambridge United: Vaughan, Fensome, Chapple, Daish, Kimble, Cheetham, Leadbitter, Bailie, Philpott, Taylor, Dublin. Subs. O'Shea, Robinson.

Since their election to the Football League in 1970, Cambridge United's progress had been steady rather than spectacular. In the F.A. Cup they had rarely figured as a threat at all. 1990 saw that change. A 4th round replay victory over 1st Division Millwall was the launchpad. Their 5th round tie with Bristol City went to three games before Cambridge eventually emerged triumphant thanks to a 5-1 win, Cambridge's record F.A. Cup success. Now they had the opportunity to become the first 4th Division side to reach the Semi-Finals of the tournament. Standing in their way was another 1st Division side, Crystal Palace.

But Cambridge's fans were confident that manager John Beck's side could create another upset. 10,084 crammed into the compact Abbey Stadium to see the home side start well. With only two minutes played, Alan Kimble's assured tackle set up a move which saw John Taylor speed down the left flank. He beat Palace centre-half O'Reilly and turned into the box to face 'keeper Nigel Martyn. With time on his side, Taylor fluffed the chance, his hurried shot was poorly struck and trailed a foot past the post. But the South London side had been warned. If they weren't aware before, then they knew now that this was going to be a real battle.

Cambridge were more than a match for their big-name opponents. In 23 minutes, Lee Philpott sliced a shot over the bar when a pass to Dion Dublin would have been more productive. Then Dublin himself had a split-second chance in the crowded penalty area but was forced wide. Six minutes from half-time, Michael Cheetham had Palace backtracking. His pass sent Colin Bailie into the box. But Bailie lobbed harmlessly to Martyn with both Dublin and Philpott waiting for a pass. The interval arrived with Cambridge receiving a standing ovation from their fans.

After the break, Palace began to move ominously forward. Their big stars such as Ian Wright, John Salako and Andy Gray were all far better in this half. Vaughan saved brilliantly from Wright at point blank range. Even though Palace were now in the ascendancy, Cambridge still had their moments. A good move down the left set up Taylor but he headed tamely at Martyn. With just eleven minutes remaining, Palace won a corner on the left.

Gray's kick was headed down by Cambridge's Daish. Barber, for Palace, tried to put the ball back into the middle, but Leadbitter intercepted, sending it out to the edge of the box. Palace's Geoff Thomas just beat Dublin to it and sent in a right foot shot which skidded between Chapple's feet and past the unsighted John Vaughan for a goal. Shortly after, Palace appealed for another goal but Gray was penalised for handball.

Cambridge put on a stirring finale. Fensome's fierce centre found Dublin but the striker's header was weak. Then, in injury time, Cheetham beat two defenders and crossed. Dublin blasted his volley over the bar and Cambridge's last chance was gone. The magnificent run was over. Palace manager, Steve Coppell, admitted, *"It was a soft goal. Any goal Geoff Thomas scores with his right must be soft."* Cambridge boss, John Beck, had expressed his view before the game: *"It's a case of Que Sera Sera."* Which is what the Londoners were singing as they left the ground.

Palace went on to reach the Final that year. For Cambridge, it was the start of an excellent few seasons. They won promotion to the 3rd at the end of this season, then lifted that division's title the following year before going on to end up 5th in the old First Division and reach the last eight of the Cup again. They haven't been as successful since but the memories of their glorious run of 1990 will stay in the minds of those who saw it for a long time to come.

CAMBRIDGE UNITED FC

CARDIFF CITY 2
Vs SV Hamburg 3

May 1st 1968 European Cup-Winners Cup Semi-Final, 2nd leg

Cardiff City: Wilson, Carver, Ferguson, Clarke, Murray, Harris, Jones, Dean, King, Toshack, Lea. Sub. Davies.

Famous all over the World for taking the F.A. Cup out of England in 1927, Cardiff City are little known outside South Wales for much else. This match was described as the most important since that historic F.A. Cup victory. For Cardiff were European regulars in the sixties. Although only a 2nd Division side, they were of a much higher standard than any other Welsh side in the Football League. It was a rare year when they didn't win the Welsh Cup, their passport to European competition.

The draw was kind to Cardiff in the early rounds. Neither Ireland's Shamrock Rovers nor Dutch entrants NAC Breda were even up to 2nd Division standards and both were despatched with ease. But the Quarter-Final brought Moscow Torpedo to Wales. Cardiff won 1-0 and lost the second leg by the same score, having been forced by the vagaries of Moscow's March weather to play a European tie in Central Asia, in Tashkent, capital of Uzbekistan. Undaunted, Cardiff emerged triumphant in a play-off staged in Augsburg. Hamburg were overwhelming favourites to win the semi-final but Cardiff excelled away from home, gaining a 1-1 draw which enticed 43,100 to Ninian Park to see a Welsh club just 90 minutes away from a European Final.

It was clear from the start that Hamburg were going to closely mark the one Cardiff player with something of an international reputation, John Toshack. But close attention to one player always leaves gaps for others to exploit. Such was the case after 10 minutes when, with Toshack lying injured, Dean pounced on a cross from King to open the scoring. Welsh jubilation didn't last long, however. Seven minutes later, the Cardiff defence left Uwe Seeler too much room and the German centre-forward laid the ball off to Hoenig who hit an unstoppable shot past Wilson. There was no let-up in the furious pace. Toshack, now recovered, led the Cardiff charge. Barrie Jones saw a fine effort saved well by 'keeper Oezcan. Then came a shot from Dean which looked a certain goal but which was charged down by Horst. The Germans played their part too, Kramer almost putting them in front. Back came Cardiff, Clarke beat Oezcan but his shot trailed wide. Cardiff's five-forward approach was clearly troubling Hamburg. From an excellent Jones cross, Lea's first-time shot flew just past the post. Then, from only four yards, King saw Oezcan smother his shot. On the stroke of half-time, a Toshack header was dramatically cleared off the line.

The second period was just under fifteen minutes old when Hamburg broke out of defence. Seeler sent over a harmless-looking lob, but it deceived Wilson and suddenly the Germans were ahead.

For the next five minutes they bombarded the Cardiff goal in an attempt to kill off the tie. But Cardiff were resilient. King and Clarke both made desperate attempts to score. Then, King, 12 yards from goal, blasted well over the top. Passes were now beginning to go astray as the pace took its toll. Suddenly, Schulz found himself in position, his shot beat Wilson, rebounded off the post and the gleeful Seeler netted, only to be given offside. Welsh hearts started beating again.

With a quarter of an hour remaining, a Barrie Jones free kick found Harris who prodded the ball home for the equaliser. That was the signal for a joyful pitch invasion. Then, Cardiff came close to victory as another Jones free kick ended with the Germans scrambling the ball off the line. It looked like a draw, and a play-off in Jutland. There were only fifteen seconds on the clock when Hoenig fired in a speculative 30 yard shot. Wilson looked to have it covered, but the ball struck his jersey and slithered from his grasp. Cardiff players and fans looked on in disbelief as the ball trundled painfully over the line. Cardiff were out, beaten in the cruellest fashion.

Cardiff's Scottish manager, Jimmy Scoular, remained stoic. He was *"proud of the boys."* For Hamburg, Uwe Seeler spoke with Teutonic efficiency: *"Soccer is a 90 minutes game and we won it in the last second. What more can I say?"* There was to be no glory that year however, as Hamburg lost 2-0 to AC Milan in the Final, but they have gone on to European success since, remaining one of continental football's biggest names. Sadly, the same cannot be said for Cardiff City. They had one or two more notable European nights but nothing like this. In domestic football, they are now on the long haul back from obscurity. Cardiff Vs Hamburg reads like a mismatch in the 1990s. In 1968 it was a game between giants.

ON THE SAME DAY...

News: New British Rail timetables reveal that, for the first time ever, there are no steam trains running anywhere in Britain.

Sport: A promising young English golfer, Tony Jacklin, lies 8th in the money-list in the USA.

Entertainment: Top-rated TV shows are the quiz-games, 'Double Your Money' and 'Take Your Pick'.

Carlisle United were the most unlikely of First Division clubs. Until the advent of Wimbledon in the 1980s, they were the 'smallest' club to take their place in the top flight. But their promotion in 1973-74 had been well merited. How they would cope with the big time was a question they seemed to have answered emphatically upon their arrival. They travelled to face Chelsea and Middlesbrough, winning both games 2-0. So, this, their first home fixture in Division One was eagerly awaited by the Cumbrian support, with 18,426 in attendance at the kick-off.

From the outset, Carlisle grabbed the game by the scruff of the neck. The midfield trio of Train, O'Neill and Balderstone ran the show. Up front, Joe Laidlaw played the game of his life. In 10 minutes, he nearly scored, ending a good run with a ferocious drive which brought out the best in Pat Jennings in the Spurs goal. After 21 minutes, Laidlaw again careered down the left, leaving defenders trailing behind him. He looked certain to score until brought down by Spurs' Mike England. The roars in Cumbrian throats were stilled when a diving Jennings parried away Balderstone's penalty kick. But only briefly, for the referee had spotted Jennings moving well off his line before the kick had been taken. Balderstone made no mistake with his second kick and, if more exuberant Carlisle fans are to be believed, the roar which greeted the goal could have been heard across the Scottish border.

There was no let-up by Carlisle. Just sixty seconds later, Train beat Jennings with a dipping volley from 25 yards, but watched, agonised, as the ball hit the underside of the bar before bouncing clear. Spurs, having endured a tortuous 45 minutes were happy to hear the half-time whistle blow, even if it was accompanied by the thunderous cheering and clapping of the Carlisle fans.

Spurs did come more into things in the second half but seldom threatened Carlisle's resolute defence. In 61 minutes, controversy stalked the game. Joe Laidlaw was brought down a yard inside the penalty area but the Referee waved away all appeals for a penalty. Until he noticed the linesman flagging. To the consternation of the home side and support, he awarded an indirect free kick **outside** the box! Carlisle continued to press but found that Jennings was in the kind of mood which made him one of the world's truly great goalkeepers, and, on this occasion, he had to be.

CARLISLE UNITED 1
Vs Tottenham Hotspur 0

August 24th 1974 - League Division One

Carlisle United: Ross, Carr, Winstanley, O'Neill, Green, Parker, Martin, Train, McIlmoyle, Balderstone, Laidlaw. Sub. F.Clark.

The match finished 1-0 amid scenes of great delight. Manager, Alan Ashman, was quick to praise his players, especially the midfield and the man of the match, Joe Laidlaw.

Just how significant the game was, only became apparent after the announcement of the rest of the day's results. But television and the press confirmed the historic moment when the tables appeared. There it was, for all to see.

Division One	P	W	D	L	F	A	Pts
1. Carlisle United	3	3	0	0	5	0	6

Carlisle, after their first home match, were top of the entire English League. What an achievement for the Cumbrian outfit. Even their crowd on this day, good by their own standards, was the smallest in the First Division. An indication of just how much they had achieved.

Of course, it couldn't last. In their next game, at home to Middlesbrough, Carlisle were beaten and knocked off the top. The rest of the season became a long, hard, and ultimately futile battle to survive. But for one glorious weekend in 1974, Carlisle could look down on Liverpool, Arsenal, Man Utd, Leeds and the rest of the soccer aristocracy. Even today, there are still many Cumbrians who can recall with pride the day Carlisle were top of the League.

ON THE SAME DAY...

News: The Blood Transfusion Service stops taking blood from prisoners at Wormwood Stubs and Pentonville jails. Overcrowding and poor sanitation was causing a high incidence of blood disease carriers among prisoners.

Sport: The ugly side of football shows its face. Kevin Olsson, an 18 year old Blackpool supporter is stabbed and killed at the game between Blackpool and Preston.

Entertainment:
As a tribute to the late Jacob Bronowski, BBC2 repeat the final part of his classic series, *'The Ascent of Man'*.

TED SWAINSON
...versatile

GEORGE SHEFFIELD
... true leader

JEAN HEWER
... " It's fantastic "

ALAN ASHMAN
... he returned

DICK YOUNG
... does everything

DAVID DENT
... pressures

WHAT Carlisle United had done was to climb out of the lowest ditch of League obscurity and, to the beat of a sound and steady drummer, march through 16 highly competitive years to the pinnacle of English football.
Yes, there they were at the top of the First Division. Of course, it might not last. Yes, the rest of the season might bring comparative failure. But no, it was

The Carlisle miracle, just like a Soccer story in the Wizard magazine when I was a boy...

by DANNY BLANCHFLOWER

That kind of ballyhoo was out of keeping for Carlisle. They needed something more sincere—a deep respect and a

the fantasy changed. I had never been there before.
The soft, green grassy pitch of "Brunton Parks" were full of

been built by the groundsman. In the boys' magazines the

caution or sadness haunted his eyes but his humour burled it. Along the corridor I bumped into a couple of players—full-backs John Gorman and Peter Carr. They had radiant smiles and bright eyes as we bantered about the game. I could sense their personal pleasure in

Beattie, Bill Shankly, and Bob Stokoe were managers here. Willie Carlin, Bob Hatton and Stan Bowles were players who restored faith and gained reputation here, and were sold for profit to help the club on its way.

CHARLTON ATHLETIC 1
Vs Burnley 0
April 26th 1947 - F.A. Cup Final (Wembley)

Charlton Athletic: Bartram, Croker, Shreeve, Johnson,
Phipps, Whittaker, Hurst, Dawson, W.Robinson,
Welsh, Duff.

Charlton Athletic had burst into prominence in the 1930s, moving from Third to First Divisions rapidly and establishing themselves as a serious force. They were one of those teams who may well have gone on to greater things, had War not intervened. Now, they were struggling to hold on to their top League place. Their opponents, Burnley, were near the top of the 2nd Division so a close match was in prospect. Charlton also had a score to settle, for they had made the previous year's Final, only to lose to Derby County. Their largely-ageing side knew they would never have a better chance of lifting the F.A. Cup.

Interest in the match was keen, with 3/- (15p) tickets changing hands for £4. Wembley was almost full to capacity, 99,000 were inside the ground, when the game kicked off. Both sides attempted to play to their wingers but the defenders were well on top. Attacks were soon cancelled out. Close marking and tenacious tackling was the order of the day. The most excitement in the first half came when the ball burst after 30 minutes play. Even this was nothing new for Charlton, exactly the same thing had happened in the 1946 Final. Of the wing pairings, Hurst and Duffy of Charlton seemed the slightly more effective. Manager Jimmy Seed endured the boredom along with everyone else as he wondered if his Cup dream was to be denied again. At half-time, the game was still scoreless.

In the second half, Charlton's Duffy appeared to be the most confident man on the park. He was certainly the only player capable of holding the ball for any length of time. But a precious goal rarely looked like coming. Indeed, the best chance of the match fell to Burnley. After 75 minutes, inside-left, Harry Potts, crashed the ball against the bar when placing it would have been better. For Burnley, Morris just missed the right hand of the corner with a ferocious shot from the edge of the area. Harrison put in a good effort from an awkward angle but Sam Bartram, in the Charlton goal, was equal to the task. Hurst, momentarily relaxing saw his attempted shot blocked. Robinson also went close for Charlton but full-time arrived with no sign of a goal.

In extra time, Burnley almost snatched it again. But Morris shot over the bar when stood almost underneath it. With 114 minutes played, the first replay since 1912 looked inevitable. Then, Robinson cut out to the right wing and fooled the Burnley defence by crossing back in to centre to Duffy, who stood, unmarked, on the edge of the box. He let fly with what one newspaper called "a shot of volcanic pace," and suddenly, Charlton were ahead. Duffy stood for a moment with his hands above his head, immobile, then he danced. Duffy was the only Scot on the field and he did a

Highland Fling, running 40 yards and jumping into the arms of full-back Shreeve. There was no way back for Burnley. The F.A. Cup was on its way to the Valley. Charlton Athletic, for the only time in their history, had got their hands on the biggest prize of them all.

That it was not the greatest of Finals was evident at the time. Often, the tenseness of such affairs affect the players performances. But according to one who should know, the great Alex James, it was, "one of the dullest games ever" at the ground. For Charlton Athletic that was of little account. They did something which they had never done before and have rarely looked like emulating since. The South London club declined after this victory, even to the extent of losing their ground. But the 1980s saw a revival with the team playing in the top flight once more and now that they have returned to their home at the Valley, who knows? Maybe one day a Charlton player will again dance a Highland fling on Wembley's turf.

ON THE SAME DAY...

News: Princess Alice, mother of Lieutenant Philip Mountbatten, refuses to confirm, or deny, rumours that her son is to wed Princess Elizabeth, the heir to the throne.

Sport: John Pulman records a snooker break of 139, one higher than the World record held by Joe Davis. But as it is in a private match, Davis's record still stood.

Entertainment:
Top new film in the West End is Michael Powell and Emeric Pressburger's 'Black Narcissus'.

CHELSEA 2
Vs Real Madrid 1

May 21st 1971 - European Cup-Winners Cup
Final Replay (Athens)

Chelsea: Bonetti, Boyle, Harris, Cooke, Dempsey, Webb,
Weller, Baldwin, Osgood (Smethurst), Hudson, Houseman.

For so long the butt of music-hall jokes, Chelsea were transformed in the 1960s, to become a symbol of the times; carefree, successful, and, above all, trendy. This change in the perception of the club was the work of their colourful manager, Tommy Docherty. Upon his departure, the less flamboyant, but no less competent, Dave Sexton continued to build Chelsea into one of the leading teams of the day. Their F.A. Cup Final replay victory over Leeds United in 1970 was a truly epic performance. And it provided the Londoners with entry into the Cup-Winners Cup.

Although often regarded as the weakest of the three European club competitions, this was not the case in 1970-71. Chelsea defeated teams of the calibre of Aris Salonika, CSKA Sofia, and Bruges to reach the Semi-Finals, equalling their previous European best. In the semis, they won both legs against compatriots and Cup-holders, Manchester City, to earn a place in the Final against Real Madrid. Real were still the most famous name in football, with players of renown like Pirri, Amancio, Grosso and Zoco in their ranks. They still possessed the incomparable Francisco Gento, fifteen years after he had played in the first Real team to win the European Cup.

So, outside West London, Chelsea were the underdogs for their Athens showdown. It didn't turn out that way though, Chelsea took the lead through Peter Osgood but relaxed too soon, allowing Zoco to equalise. In those days, there was no provision for a penalty shoot-out in the Final, so two days later the teams met again. Obviously, this arrangement took its effect on the travelling supporters, most of whom were booked on package deals. The 42,000 who watched the first match fell to 24,000 for the replay. One spectator Chelsea didn't want watching them was John Hollins, but he had been injured in the first game. Sexton was forced to tactically re-jig his side as well as bringing in Tommy Baldwin as Hollins' replacement.

Charlie Cooke, a world-beater on his day, was in great form for Chelsea and the talented Alan Hudson performed much better than in the first game. Pirri and Velasquez were denied the midfield control they had enjoyed in that affair. Up front, Chelsea were much more potent. Baldwin justified his inclusion and Osgood found greater freedom. After 31 minutes of largely Chelsea control, David Webb surged powerfully forward, forcing a corner. Houseman's kick was cleared by Real 'keeper, Borja, but Dempsey unleashed a thundering volley to give Chelsea the lead. Real were still trying to compose themselves when Chelsea scored again.

Harris set up Baldwin who quickly passed to Osgood. The centre-forward sent three defenders the wrong way before hammering the ball home to make it 2-0. Cooke, who had been persistently fouled by Grosso, retaliated, sparking off ugly scenes as an angry melee formed. It took some time for the referee to regain control.

Chelsea kept their lead until the break and dominated most of the second half too. But, after 74 minutes, Fleitas caught the defence off-guard, cut into the middle and scored. The weary Osgood was replaced by Smethurst and Real brought on the legendary Gento, but it was Zoco and Amancio who came closest to equalising. Zoco's header brought off a great save from Bonetti. Webb made a goal-line clearance from Amancio. But Chelsea kept their nerve. Eventually, the final whistle sounded amid scenes of jubilation on the pitch. Back home, it was the signal for the King's Road and the West End to come to a halt as thousands of Chelsea fans took to the streets. There would be no more stale jokes about a side who had earned European glory by beating the most famous team in world football.

Chelsea have had their ups and downs since then, but the 1990s has seen a revival, with the return of European football to Stamford Bridge. There is a belief that, one day, Chelsea will triumph on the continent again.

ON THE SAME DAY...

News: Prime Minister, Edward Heath, is *"optimistic"* about Britain's entry to the EEC after talks with French President, Georges Pompidou.

Sport: Mark Cox, the holder, loses in the Semi-Finals of the British Open Hard Court Tennis championships to Yugoslavia's Zelkjo Franulovic in straight sets. National honour was later restored by Gerald Battrick who won the Final. (British tennis players winning tournaments! Strange, but true).

Entertainment: Those not watching the match had the alternatives of American import 'Hawaii 5 0' or the home-grown, 'Budgie' on their TV sets.

CHESTER CITY 2
Vs Aston Villa 2

January 15th 1975 League Cup Semi-Final 1st Leg

Chester: Millington, Edwards, Loska,
Storton, Matthewson, Owen, Whitehead, Seddon,
Draper, James, Lennard. Sub. Moore.

Chester's name could be found in the record books at the start of the 1974-75 season. But only as the League's dullest club. They were the only team never to have been promoted, but things were stirring in Chester this season. Not only did they put together a promotion push but they worked miracles in the League Cup. They had never been past the last 32 in either Cup competition. They beat Walsall and Blackpool to reach the same stage. When they knocked out Preston 1-0, to reach the last 16, it was uncharted territory for Chester. But when it was announced that their next opponents would be the reigning League champions, Leeds United, that looked like the end of the matter.

For Chester though, this was just the start of their remarkable odyssey. They knew that Leeds had a reputation for losing cup-ties they were expected to win easily, as Sunderland and Colchester could testify. At Chester's Sealand Road ground, Leeds were humiliated as the 4th Division side ran amok, winning 3-0. Their next opponents were another top side with a reputation for losing to the 'rabbits', Newcastle United. Chester earned a creditable away draw 0-0 then knocked out the Geordies 1-0 at home. They had beaten two of the biggest names in football and reached the Semi-Finals of the League Cup. What next?

In an amazing season of upsets, not one 1st Division side had reached the last four but the other three sides left in the tourney would all go on to be promoted to the top flight at the end of the season. Norwich City, Manchester United and Aston Villa were Chester's potential semi-final opponents and it was the Birmingham side's name that came out of the hat alongside Chester's. Manager Ken Roberts prepared his men for an attempt at something which would have been considered laughable just a few weeks beforehand, a place in a Wembley Cup Final.

But Villa were a fair side and at the top of their form. They took the game to Chester. Grenville Millington, in goal, had his work cut out to deny McDonald and Hamilton. The first fifteen minutes were torrid for the Chester defence and, eventually, the inevitable happened. Ray Graydon's free kick fooled the defence and McDonald's well-place header beat Millington.

Chester battled hard to come back into the game. In 31 minutes, Ian Seddon burst through to fire in a fierce shot which brought off a great one-handed save from Jim Cumbes, the Villa 'keeper. At the other end, Graydon almost increased Villa's lead, but Millington saved well. Just on half-time, Trevor Storton sent the ball forward to John James, who helped it on to Derek Draper. Both Cumbes and Chris Nicholl failed to block Draper's shot and Terry Owen nipped in to prod home the equaliser. The majority of the 18,620 crowd rose in acclaim.

Yet this boost was short-lived. Five minutes into the second half, Villa were back in front. Brian Little's well-timed pass sent Graydon on a run and he hit a shot into the corner of the net despite the attentions of the on-rushing Millington. Ten minutes later it was nearly three. Keith Leonard was allowed a free shot which was scrambled off the line by Edwards before being booted clear by Storton. With 20 minutes to play, Gary Moore came on for James. Moore showed quickly that he had the beating of Nicholl in the air. With ten minutes left, Draper broke clear down the right and took advantage of a slip by Villa's Ian Ross to dash forward and slip a short pass to Moore who gratefully converted - 2-2.

In the closing stages it was all Chester. Edwards got through in the dying seconds but Cumbes pulled off a fine save. Draper and Seddon were missing from the team a week later in the 2nd leg. Moore and Mason replaced them with Redfearn as substitute. 47,632 saw Chester go two down in 28 minutes but rally back to 2-2 before Villa squeezed into the Final with a goal in the 80th minute.

Villa went on to win the League Cup. For Chester (now Chester City), it was a magnificent year. They gained that elusive promotion at the end of the season, but it is the memory of their cup-fighting achievements at their now-obsolete Sealand Road ground which still stir fond memories among Chester fans today, as well as haunting the nightmares of those who follow Leeds, Newcastle, and yes, Aston Villa too.

CHESTERFIELD 3
Vs Glasgow Rangers 0

October 28th 1980 - Anglo-Scottish Cup
Quarter-Final 2nd Leg

Chesterfield: Turner, Tartt, Pollard, Wilson,
Green, Ridley, Birch, Moss, Bonnyman,
Salmons, Walker. Subs. Crawford, Hunter.

The Anglo-Scottish Cup had originally been conceived as a competition for those clubs which fell just short of a place in Europe. The reluctance of leading English clubs to enter allowed a side like Chesterfield who had just missed out on promotion to the 2nd Division to take part in the tournament. They qualified from a group containing Grimsby, Hull and Sheffield United to face Scottish giants Rangers. Although the *Derbyshire Times* dismissed the current Rangers line-up as having *"inherited the club's reputation in name only,"* they still could boast nine Scottish internationals among the thirteen players listed for this match. Though Chesterfield had surprised even themselves by drawing 1-1 at Ibrox in the first leg, few were confident that they would progress any further.

Although top of the 3rd Division, Chesterfield were in financial difficulties, having lost £¼M over the year. They welcomed the boost to their income provided by 5,000 travelling Glaswegians, even though the police and local shopkeepers thought differently. Scared of potential trouble, there was a heavy police presence on the streets before the game. Only four pubs opened in the town centre and the only people to be seen in the town were Police and Rangers fans. Yet there were only seven arrests, just one of these at the match itself.

Rangers started confidently but persisted with playing the high ball to Colin McAdam, a fruitless enterprise. In 15 minutes, Chesterfield's Phil Walker, whose in-swinging corners had been such a threat in the 1st leg, adopted the same approach. 'Keeper McCloy committed himself hopelessly and the ball rebounded off the far post for Phil Bonnyman, himself a Rangers reject, to score. The home contingent in the crowd of 13,914 were ecstatic.

Five minutes later, Walker crossed again. McCloy stood transfixed as Ridley headed down for Bonnyman to score again. Rangers had a chance to get back into it when Jim Bett's free kick was firmly headed on by Derek Johnstone but Turner made a good save. McCloy, having a nightmare match, again missed a Walker corner but Sandy Jardine cleared off the line. Colin Jackson blatantly punched away a cross but the referee's whistle remained silent. Wilson's follow-up crashed off the bar. Salmons, faced with an open goal, hesitated, allowing McCloy time to recover and beat his shot down. McCloy missed another cross, this time from Birch, but Ernie Moss' header went narrowly over the bar. Chesterfield fans could hardly believe what was happening. At half-time they led 2-0 but it could have been six.

Rangers were a bit more positive in the second half. Johnstone looked likely to score but was fouled by Bill Green, which resulted in a booking for the Chesterfield skipper. The contest was finished in the 63rd minute when a four-man move in tight space ended with Ernie Moss sweeping the ball home to make it 3-0. Rangers were awarded a penalty but McAdam's kick was beaten out by Turner and Robert Russell sent the rebound wide. There were no more goals and Rangers left the pitch dejected. They had been humiliated by an exuberant Chesterfield side.

Chesterfield went on to beat Bury in the Semi-Finals and Notts County in the Final to become the unlikeliest-ever winners of the Anglo-Scottish Cup, but it was a success they deserved. They narrowly missed out on promotion once more, and now, as they read about the latest multi-million buys at Ibrox, they can recall the night when the Glasgow giants were humiliated at the Recreation Ground in what was undoubtedly Chesterfield's finest hour.

ON THE SAME DAY...

News: 87 year old film star, Mae West, is said to have almost fully recovered from a double stroke, suffered nearly three months earlier.

Sport: An 18-month police probe into Derby County's finances ends with the club getting the all-clear.

Entertainment:
Just as one set of Blues beats another at the Recreation Ground, a new film opens at the Chesterfield ABC, 'The Blues Brothers'.

COLCHESTER UNITED 3
Vs Leeds United 2

February 13th 1971 - F.A. Cup Round 5

Colchester United: Smith, Hall, Cram, Gilchrist, Garvey, Kurila, Lewis, Simmons, Mahon, Crawford, Gibbs.

For only the second time in their history, Colchester United had reached the 5th round of the F.A. Cup. On the previous occasion, in 1949, they had been a non-League side and their exploits had earned them respect. But, after 20 years as a fairly nondescript League side, their re-emergence in the last 16 of the tournament was greeted with less than a fanfare of welcome. For, on this occasion, there had been no giant-killing. The luck of the draw had aided Colchester's passage while more illustrious names lay strewn by the wayside. Indeed, the sports editor of *The Sun* went so far as to call them *"jokers,"* and suggested that the likes of Colchester had no right to be in the tournament at this stage. So much for the romance of the Cup!

The opponents at Layer Road were Leeds United, beaten Finalists in 1970 and strongly fancied to pull off the 'Double'. They were a side brimming over with international stars. Colchester, by comparison, had only one name who might easily have been recognised outside his own household, Ray Crawford, a veteran from the Ipswich team which won the League in 1962. But manager, Dick Graham, convinced his team that they had a chance of an upset. And the fans sensed so too. 16,000 of them rolled up to see their local heroes take on the mighty Leeds.

They were soon given something to cheer. Lewis and Mahon took the game to Leeds, slicing the much-vaunted defence apart. Mahon's shot hit off 'keeper Sprake's ankle for a corner. An early indication that Colchester meant business. After 18 minutes, Jack Charlton, Leeds' beanpole centre-half, fouled Simmons. Lewis took the free kick which left Sprake groping at thin air as Crawford headed into the roof of the net. The ground erupted. Six minutes later, Bobby Cram sent Gibbs away on the right. He crossed into the box. Up went Sprake. Up went full-back Reaney. And up went Crawford. Down went all three. Out swung Crawford's leg as he connected with the ball and it rolled over the line, off the inside of the far post. There was bedlam in the crowd, and also in the Leeds defence. Colchester continued to press forward. Simmons and Mahon both had chances to make it three. Panic-stricken Leeds were reduced to the sight of Charlton conceding a corner from near the half-way line. Their feared front three of Lorimer, Clarke and Jones made no headway at all against the resolute Colchester defence. At half-time it was still 2-0.

There was to be no let-up in the second half. In 54 minutes, Crawford robbed possession from Terry Cooper near the half-way mark and sent Lewis away. Simmons beat Reaney to the cross and as Sprake dithered, Simmons nodded home the third goal. Now, with disaster staring them in the face, Leeds fought. In 60 minutes, Lorimer's corner was met by a leaping Norman Hunter to make it 3-1. Crawford almost got a fourth but the exhausted veteran miskicked at the last. With 17 minutes to play, Johnny Giles came into the game at last, with a mesmerising run to make it 3-2. Leeds piled on the pressure. Charlton headed just over. Hunter went close, so did Jones. But Colchester still made chances. Crawford brought out a full-length save from Sprake. Three Colchester corners in succession ate up precious time. As the seconds ebbed away, Lorimer beat Hall, twice. He crossed for Jones to send in a goal-bound shot. Jones turned away in joy, so certain was he that he had scored, that he didn't even see Graham Smith hurl himself onto the ball right on the line. It was over. Colchester had brought off one of the biggest F.A. Cup shocks of all time.

The celebrations for Dick Graham and his men continued for days. A 45 minute record of the match was made, selling thousands. Who knows what the sports editor of *The Sun* thought about this result. Leeds finally got their hands on the Cup the next season. Colchester advanced to face Everton, and defeat, in the Quarter-Finals. But, in many ways, that didn't matter. For a place in the history books forevermore had been ascertained by that marvellous win over Leeds United.

ON THE SAME DAY...

News: There is a rush to spend old coins as Britain braces itself for the decimalisation of the currency two days later.

Sport: Everton, Colchester's next opponents, advance to the last eight with a 1-0 win over Derby County in front of more than 50,000 at Goodison.

Entertainment
George Harrison is at No.1 in the charts with *'My Sweet Lord'* and nine of the current Top 30 have sold more than 250,000 copies each.

Ray Crawford scores his second goal, while Jack Charlton and Leeds goalkeeper Gary Sprake can only look on helplessly.

COVENTRY CITY 3
Vs Tottenham Hotspur 2

May 16th 1987 - F.A. Cup Final
(Wembley)

Coventry City: Ogrizovic, Phillips, Downs,
McGrath, Kilcline (Rodger, 88), Peake, Bennett,
Gynn, Houchen, Regis, Pickering.

For most of their history Coventry City had toiled in the lower divisions. Promoted to the top echelon in 1967, their main claim to fame had been to stay in Division One while bigger names were relegated. They had done little of note in the cups and had only the most fleeting of acquaintances with Europe. So their arrival in the F.A. Cup Final took most people outside the West Midlands by surprise. But they had earned their place there. After beating Bolton at home, they were drawn away in every subsequent round. Their victory over Manchester United at Old Trafford should have alerted the rest of the country to the capabilities of the team shrewdly led by Managing Director George Curtis and Chief Coach John Sillett. Further successes at Stoke and Sheffield Wednesday set them up for an epic extra time win over Leeds United at Hillsborough in the Semi-Finals. Now they had to do battle with the hot favourites, Tottenham Hotspur, a team who had won the trophy a joint record seven times and who had never lost in the Final. Twice before in the 1980s, Spurs had carried off the trophy. Surely Coventry were there just for the day out?

After only two minutes, that seemed to be the case. Chris Waddle's accurate cross to the near post was met by Clive Allen who headed his 49th goal of the season. But Coventry were undeterred. Seven minutes later they equalised. Downs centred from the left, Houchen flicked on and Bennett neatly side-stepped 'keeper Ray Clemence before slotting the ball home. Both Clemence and his former Liverpool understudy, Steve Ogrizovic, were showing signs of nerves with Houchen a constant threat to the former while the latter put Coventry fans hearts into their mouths when he ran well out of goal to clear, but succeeded only in giving the ball to Glenn Hoddle. The danger was averted on that occasion. After half an hour of almost invisibility, Cyrille Regis at last got into things, putting Micky Gynn through but Clemence saved well. Four minutes from half-time, Kilcline failed to clear a Hoddle free kick, allowing Gary Mabbutt to give Spurs the interval lead.

In the second half, Bennett was more influential, his centre in 62 minutes gave Houchen a diving header to equalise. Houchen and Bennett both continued to threaten the Spurs goal but the 90 minutes elapsed with the score still 2-2. Coventry skipper, Brian Kilcline had been forced to leave the field just before the end of normal time but his replacement, Graham Rodger, served his side superbly. It was Rodger who sent McGrath away clear on the right. Mabbutt desperately raced back to cover but as McGrath shot at goal, Mabbutt's touch sent the ball over the lunging Clemence

into the net to create an unwanted piece of history; becoming only the second player to score for both sides in an F.A. Cup Final.

There were still 23 minutes of extra time to play but Spurs seemed shell-shocked by the own goal and Coventry grew in authority. The final whistle saw scenes of unrestrained joy from players, supporters and management. John Sillett's run across the pitch evoking memories of Sunderland's Bob Stokoe in 1973. It had been a superb match and both sides emerged with credit. They both had over 20 shots on goal and in 120 minutes of all-out football, not a single player had been booked. It was the best Cup Final for many years. Coventry City, the side who usually made up the numbers, were - deservedly - F.A. Cup winners of 1987. Even the Spurs fans in the 100,000 present couldn't really argue with that.

ON THE SAME DAY...

News: Tory MP, Harvey Proctor, facing charges of gross indecency with young men, resigns as parliamentary candidate at the outset of the general election campaign.

Sport: 'Don't Forget Me', wins the Irish 2,000 Guineas, the first horse to win both the Irish and English titles since 1969.

Entertainment:
BBC 1 features 'The Domesday Project'. Over one million people contribute data to mark the 900th anniversary of the Domesday Book.

CREWE ALEXANDRA 0

Vs Preston North End 5

February 18th 1888 - F.A. Cup Semi-Final (Everton)

Crewe Alexandra: Hickton, Conde, Bayman, Cope, Halfpenny,
Bell, Payne, Pearson, Price, Ellis, Tinsley.

Crewe Alexandra have had little in the way of concrete triumphs since their foundation in 1877. Somewhat incongruously the only trophy of any significance lifted by the Cheshire club has been the Welsh Cup, in 1936 and 1937. In the League, while they were founder-members of the Second Division, they lasted just four years before failing to be re-elected. Re-admitted to the League after the First World War, the only high spots have been promotion from the League's lowest division in 1963, 1968, 1989 and 1994. Even then they have failed to justify their elevation, returning downstairs after no more than a couple of seasons on three occasions.

So, to find a time when the best clubs in the land worried themselves about facing Crewe, it is necessary to return to the days before the founding of the Football League. In 1887-88 Crewe had a useful side. In the 1st round of the F.A. Cup they beat the then-powerful Welsh side Druids 5-0, a result which stands to this day as Crewe's record F.A. Cup victory. Crewe progressed to the 5th round where they made the football world sit up and take notice of them by beating the highly-fancied Derby County 1-0. They travelled to Middlesbrough in the Quarter-Finals and returned with an equally unlikely 2-0 success. Now people began to talk of Crewe Alexandra as potential F.A. Cup winners.

So it was that they prepared to face Preston North End in the Semi-Finals at Everton. Preston were the strongest side in the land. If Crewe could triumph over them then that unlikely Cup victory would be tantalisingly close. At first it looked that the match might not go ahead. Crewe protested that the Friday night thaw had rendered the pitch unplayable. But their opponents did not agree. The F.A. had to be called in to settle the dispute. They ruled that the match should to ahead and at 3.05 p.m., Crewe having lost the toss, had to kick off against a powerful sun. Full-back Conde was soon in action, twice breaking up Preston attacks. The Lancashire side's short passing game was proving surprisingly effective despite the slushy conditions. In 15 minutes a goal from J.Ross put Preston ahead. They relished taking the lead and piled on the pressure, winning a series of corners, but it was a soft shot from John Goodall, the most feared forward of his day, which made it 2-0. At this stage Crewe attempted a rally. Payne and Price forced their team-mates forward but the Preston defence was resolute. Some of their tactics were of a desperate variety, *The Sportsman* recorded that Payne almost broke free with the ball but *"his endeavours to stave off Ross senior by seizing him round the neck gave Preston a free-kick."*

Dewhurst and Goodall restored Preston to the offensive and it was no great surprise when Goodall's low shot secured

Preston's third goal. Just thirty seconds later, Goodall notched up a fourth. A long shot from Russell eluded Hickton and Crewe retired at the break 5-0 down. Crewe had the best of the attacking in the second period and helped by the quagmire of their own defensive area, they kept out Preston's sporadic raids. There was no more scoring but this had been far from a humiliation for Crewe. They had been facing the best team in the country and Payne, Ellis, Bell, Conde, Bayman and Hickton were all said to have acquitted themselves with distinction. Frighteningly, *The Sportsman* considered that the conditions had prevented Preston from playing at their best.

Although Preston lost in the Final to West Brom that year, the following season they won the inaugural Football League without losing a game and lifted the F.A. Cup without conceding a goal. That is a measure of the side Crewe came up against. For Crewe, it was to be an experience which over 100 years later, they have still to savour again.

ON THE SAME DAY...

News: MP's are to raise questions in the House of Commons to ask if recent boxing matches were legal, and if not, if the Government would prosecute both the boxers and the newspapers which reported on these bouts.

Sport: With the expansion of the popularity of Boxing, the great John L. Sullivan is training in England although he is reported to he homesick for the USA.

Entertainment:
The Savoy Theatre under its manager and proprietor R.D'Oyly Carte produces a new Gilbert & Sullivan show, 'HMS Pinafore'.

CRYSTAL PALACE 4
Vs Liverpool 3

April 8th 1990 - F.A. Cup Semi-Final (Villa Park)

Crystal Palace: Martyn, Pemberton, Shaw, O'Reilly, Thorn, Barber, Thomas, Salako, Pardew, Bright, Gray.

Crystal Palace always seem to promise something at the start of a new decade. In 1960 they were climbing out of the 4th Division. At the start of the 70s they were a 1st Division side for the first time. By the dawn of the 80s they were labelled, somewhat embarrassingly as it turned out as the *"team of the eighties,"* by their then manager Malcolm Allison. Now, at the start of the 1990s they were back in the top flight, led by one of the game's best young managers, Steve Coppell. Even so, there were few outside South London who would have bet on them beating the mighty Liverpool. The Anfield-side were F.A. Cup holders and were also striding to yet another League title. Earlier in the season they had hammered Palace 9-0 in a League game at Anfield.

So, as the teams took the stage for the first ever live TV Semi-Final, only the most optimistic gave the Palace team, appearing in the last four for only the second time in their history, much of a chance against the country's top team for the last 25 years, a team who had lost only once in their last 23 outings. It was Liverpool who took the early control of the game. After 13 minutes, McMahon found Rush with a finely timed pass and as Palace vainly appealed for offside, Rush delicately chipped over Martyn to put the Merseysiders ahead. Was that the sign for the floodgates to open? No. Palace held out against the red tide until half-time, and before the break Liverpool suffered a serious casualty, Rush being forced to retire with a hip injury after 39 minutes. If it was a tragedy for the Welshman, then it helped to even things up for the Eagles, for Palace's own hit-man, Ian Wright, had been forced to miss the match through injury.

Just sixteen seconds into the second half, McMahon tried to find Staunton, but Pemberton intercepted. He dashed down the wing and crossed to Salako whose shot was blocked on the line by Staunton. Bright lashed onto the rebound and his well-struck shot cannoned off McMahon's head into the net for the equaliser. Palace were now the better team. A Geoff Thomas effort was saved on the line by Grobbelaar in the Liverpool goal. In 69 minutes a Pemberton free kick caused panic in the normally sound Liverpool defence and Gary O'Reilly took his chance to hit the ball past the 'keeper to put Palace 2-1 up.

The minutes ticked away with the twin spires of Wembley beckoning ever closer but Liverpool were renowned for their never-say-die attitude and with just nine minutes left, they struck. A neatly taken free-kick allowed McMahon to crack home the equaliser. Two minutes later, it looked all over for Palace. Pemberton, one of the most outstanding players on the field, was controversially adjudged to have fouled Staunton. Penalty to Liverpool. John Barnes scored what looked like the winner for Liverpool. Palace resumed on the offensive and with only two minutes left, the Liverpool defence was flailing again, Grobbelaar attempted to punch clear and missed, Staunton tried to head off the line and failed. Gray stepped in to make it 3-3. Even then Palace weren't finished, from a Gray free-kick, Andy Thorn headed against the bar. An enthralling 90 minutes ended with the score 3-3.

In extra time Palace regained the lead. After 109 minutes, Gray's corner was flicked on by Thorn and Alan Pardew, a £7,000 signing from Yeovil, headed over the line. Still it wasn't over. Nigel Martyn had to play the hero with five minutes left when he brilliantly saved a close-range Barnes header. At the end of 120 minutes, the Eagles fans could scarcely believe the result.

Their team of lambs to the slaughter had made the mighty Liverpool the sacrificial victims instead. The 9-0 humiliation was wiped out. Crystal Palace were on their way to Wembley. It was a magnificent match for the 38,389 present and a superb one for the first semi to be seen live on TV. Liverpool couldn't believe what had happened either. The normally erudite Alan Hansen was reduced to cliches by the defeat, *"I am absolutely gutted,"* was his comment on the shock of the season.

Sadly, Palace couldn't quite manage to lift the Cup. Having beaten a Liverpool team just about to surrender their pre-eminent position among English clubs, it was Palace's misfortune to run into the side about to inherit the crown, Manchester United. After a magnificent 3-3 draw at Wembley, they went down 1-0 to the Red Devils in the replay.

Sheffield Wednesday 0 Vs
DARLINGTON 2

January 19th 1920 - F.A. Cup 1st Round

Darlington: Greig, Golightly, Taylor, Dickson,
Sutcliffe, Malcolm, Kirsopp, Lawrence, Healey,
Stevens, Winship.

Darlington had been fortunate to survive the First World War. Financial hardship had almost driven the club to extinction, so the chance to play a famous First Division club in the F.A. Cup was greeted with enthusiasm in the County Durham town. Wednesday (still known at the time as 'The Wednesday'), were struggling at the foot of the table but were still expected to easily despatch the side from the North-East League. Darlington were drawn at home but the tie, scheduled for Saturday January 10th became the first ever game to be postponed at the Feethams ground. Frost, followed by torrential rain forced the game to be re-arranged for the following Wednesday. A crowd of 12,106, just sixty short of the ground record, saw the teams fight out an uninspiring 0-0 draw. So it was off to Hillsborough the next Monday for the replay, with few holding out much hope for the North-East team.

But the Darlington fans weren't downhearted. Over 3,000 travelled for the replay, swelling the crowd to a splendid 52,810. Wednesday, playing against the wind, dominated the early part of the match, with Brentnall, Capper and Brittleton to the fore. Darlington did manage to win a couple of corners before being subjected to some intense Wednesday pressure. But the non-League outfit began to put together some clever moves of their own, even if they did lack a scoring touch. As the Darlington-based *Northern Echo* put it: *"They were certainly not deficient in ability to get the ball somewhere in the vicinity of goal, but as far as getting it into the net, well, they were hopeless."*

An opinion that had to be hastily revised in the 40th minute. Healey forced a corner, Winship slung an excellent cross into the area and in the melee that ensued, Malcolm heel-tapped into the net to put Darlington ahead. Great were the scenes of jubilation among the travelling support. As the *Echo* said: *"There were bugle-calls, wild whoops of delight,"* and singing too. *"Henry the Eighth and women's screams all were mixed up in one discordant medley."*

Conditions worsened during the break. Sleet descended on the ground and continued throughout the first quarter of an hour of the second half. But Darlington were forcing the pace now. Kirsopp and Winship were both denied by Wednesday defender Blair. Goalkeeper Birch made a fine save from a Dickson shot. Then Wednesday resumed the attack. Three times in the same number of minutes, they forced corners. But Darlington held them at bay and the Quakers counter-attacked too. Kirsopp chased a loose ball but was beaten to it by Wednesday defender, McSkimming. But the defender miskicked toward his own goal. Birch ran

on to save but slipped and the ball rolled past him. Agonis-ingly for Darlington it went past for a corner which was cleared.

Then Malcolm won the ball from McSkimming. He sent it forward to Healey who tangled with Blair. Both went down. Birch and Stevens raced for the ball with the inside-left winning. He shot past the 'keeper to make it 2-0. Darlington continued to press and finished the stronger side. They had pulled off a 2-0 win away from home against a First Division side. It would be 55 years before another non-League side could make the same claim. At 9.30 that evening the team arrived back at Bank Top station to be met by a crowd of thousands cheering wildly.

There was to be no more Cup joy for Darlington that year. They were beaten 4-0 at Birmingham in the next round but their magnificent victory over Wednesday had made the football world sit up and take notice of the Quakers. When the Third Division (North) was established two years later, Darlington were founder members and within a few years they had won the title and a place in the 2nd Division. However, after a couple of years they were relegated and they have never achieved such prominence since. Indeed they even lost their League status in the late 1980s, although it was quickly regained. Although they have had the odd success against teams from a higher sphere in both domestic Cups, there has never again been anything like the Monday they beat the Wednesday.

ON THE SAME DAY...

News: A political crisis in France as George Clemenceau resigns as President.

Sport: At the Amateur International trial match at West Ham, 'The North' and 'The South' draw 1-1 in front of only 2,000 spectators.

Entertainment
The big show at the Assembly Picture Hall in Darlington features Tom Mix in 'Treat 'Em Rough', a fair description of what Darlington did to the team from Sheffield.

DERBY COUNTY 0
Vs Juventus 0

April 25th 1973
European Cup Semi-Final 2nd Leg

Derby County: Boulton, Webster, Nish, Powell,
Daniel (Simms), Todd, McGovern, O'Hare,
Davies, Hector, Hinton.

The good people of Derby could scarcely have known what hit them in the late 60s and early 70s. A twin tornado in the shape of Brian Clough and Peter Taylor took over the reins of a club languishing in the 2nd Division and within a few short years turned it into one of Europe's finest. They took over the lead of the 1st Division in their last match of the 1971-72 season and were on holiday in Majorca when news reached them that their rivals had failed to overhaul them, making Derby champions for the first time in their history.

Europe was yet another adventure on the Clough-Taylor roller-coaster and their inexperienced side prevailed against some battle-hardened European veterans. Zeljeznicar Sarajevo, a tough Yugoslav side, were beaten both home and away. Next to fall were the famous Benfica, 3-0 losers at the Baseball ground. Derby's European steel was forged in the atmosphere of the Estadio De Luz in Lisbon where they emerged with a creditable 0-0 draw. In the Quarter-Finals, the difficult Czech team Spartak Trnava were beaten on a 2-1 aggregate, Derby winning 2-0 at home and losing 1-0 away. So now their path to the European Cup Final was barred by one of the most famous names in world football, Juventus, the giants of Turin.

The first leg in Italy was lost 3-1 and bookings to key Derby players Roy McFarland and Archie Gemmill meant that they would miss the return. Some Derby fans had to rub their eyes in disbelief as Juventus stepped out onto the Baseball ground. There was Dino Zoff one of the best custodians in the world. Pietro Anastasi, the most expensive player on the planet. And other world-class players like Causio and Altafini. Just four years previously, these same supporters would have had to have been content with the fare on offer in the English 2nd Division. This was the measure of how far Clough had taken them.

But even though most of the 35,350 present would not have witnessed much in the way of European football, they knew what to expect from an Italian side holding a two goal advantage. And they were right. Derby attacked incessantly and just as surely Juventus defended. Yet in the first half, for all their pressure, Derby never looked like scoring, whereas their opponents, in what few sporadic breakaway attacks they mounted, always looked dangerous. Juventus' years of playing to the *catennacio* system had seen them hone it to perfection.

The pattern continued at the outset of the second half, until the 57th minute. Spinosi was adjudged to have brought down Kevin Hector in the area. Penalty, said Mr Lobo the Portuguese referee. Hinton stepped up to take the kick. One of the best penalty-takers in the land, he looked perfectly calm as he thumped the ball, only to see it slice way off target. It was like watching Jack Nicklaus hit a two-foot putt past the hole and into a bunker. A goal at that stage would have severely unsettled the Italians. Ten minutes later, all hope was lost. Davies, who had been subjected to niggling fouls by the Juventus centre-half Morini all evening, retaliated. He head-butted Morini into the net, his only header on target during the match. Lobo was on the spot and had no hesitation in ordering the Derby man off. Simms was sent on for Daniel in a bid to bolster the forward line, but it was no use. Derby never came anywhere near scoring and the game ended with hundreds of jubilant Italians invading the pitch.

The match later became dogged by controversy as referee Lobo claimed that one of the Italian officials had attempted to bribe him, but despite valid evidence and a campaign in the press, UEFA declined to take any punitive action. Clough later left Derby in acrimonious circumstances. He would get his hands on the European Cup, in 1979 and 1980, but with Nottingham Forest. Derby won the League in 1975 and had one more attempt at Europe's premier club trophy but with no success. They have only occasionally played in the top League in the 80s and 90s, and the night when they stood 90 minutes away from the European Cup Final must seem a long long time ago now.

ON THE SAME DAY...

News: *"Nixon, impatient to air Watergate disclosures,"* is one newspaper's headline. Really?

Sport: Princess Anne is named in the Great Britain side for the three-day event European Championship in the USSR. She will be the first member of the Royal Family to go there since the 1917 revolution.

Entertainment
Most popular TV show of the evening is 'Colditz', the drama based on the notorious wartime prisoner-of-war camp.

DONCASTER ROVERS 10

Vs Darlington 0

January 25th 1964 - Division Four

Doncaster Rovers: Potter, Raine, Meadows, Windross, White, Ripley, Robinson, Booth, Hale, Jeffrey, Broadbent.

To say that Doncaster Rovers have had an unsettled League history is to be charitable. Twice in the first five years of this century they failed to be re-elected and their very first season in the League, 1901-02, remains their best performance when they finished seventh in Division Two. The meagre tally of eight points gleaned in 1904-05 is the joint-lowest of any Football League club. Conversely their 72 points, taken under the two points for a win set-up when winning the Third Division (North) in 1947, remained the highest tally of any League club for nearly 30 years. So Rovers have had their moments, even if they have been few and far between.

By 1963-64 they were in the Fourth Division and not performing all that well, even at that lowly level. Certainly there was little to suggest that their home game with Darlington would be anything more than a run-of-the-mill League clash. There were only 6,150 in attendance at Rovers' Belle Vue ground on a day when conditions were close to perfection, a stiff breeze being the only problem for the players.

It was Darlington who made the first attack. Their debutant, McGeachie, who had left Dundee in controversial circumstances, blasted over the top from six yards out when faced with an open goal. Then the same player wasted another good chance before Rovers got into their stride. After four minutes, Alick Jeffrey split the defence with a cross-field pass. Broadbent cut in and centred low for Booth to supply the finishing touch. Rovers had scored in their first attack. Just three minutes later, Ripley lashed in a shot from eighteen yards which beat Penman in the Quakers goal. In twelve minutes, a Ripley shot was only half-cleared and Hale volleyed home from six yards. 3-0 with less than fifteen minutes played.

Doncaster eased off for the next quarter of an hour before embarking on another goal spree. In 28 minutes, Broadbent took a corner on the left. Hale back-headed to Booth who turned the ball in for the fourth goal. Six minutes later, Robinson dummied Darlington left-back Heavisides and crossed into the area. Hale jumped a distance Dick Fosbury would have been proud of, to head in the fifth. Five minutes from the break, Hale tried a speculative shot from the edge of the eighteen yard box. The harmless-looking shot slipped through Penman's fingers and was over the line before the hapless 'keeper could retrieve it. 6-0 at half-time.

The third-quarter of the game passed uneventfully before Rovers stepped on the pedal again. In 69 minutes, Windross broke through on his own and fired in a left foot shot for number seven. Two minutes later, it was Hale, likewise. He had plenty of time to pick his shot before despatching the eighth. There were eleven minutes remaining when Ripley, always in the thick of the action and the best player on the field, won a tussle on the edge of the penalty area. He walked forward, in possession, as the Quakers defence stood back, and calmly chipped Penman for the ninth. With four minutes to go, Jeffrey cut in from the left, but lost control. Broadbent regained the ball for Rovers and his cross-come-shot beat Penman to notch the tenth goal, making the final score Doncaster Rovers 10 Darlington 0.

The *Doncaster Gazette and Chronicle* praised the local side for recording their highest-ever victory in a first-class match, but, very generously, did not gloat. Nor did they make Rovers out to be a great side. *"Darlington's failings rather than any sustained brilliance on the part of Rovers made this* (win) *possible,"* the paper said, adding that the score should have been no more than five or six in Rovers favour and asserting, *"for a period in the second half, Darlington enjoyed an equal share of the attacking."* But the paper did realise the historical significance of the result, declaring that it was, *"a memorable afternoon for those who like goals, less memorable perhaps for the purist. And for those (if any) who like to appreciate defence in depth, a very sad afternoon indeed."*

For Rovers it was a sign of things to come. Twice within the next five years they lifted the Fourth Division title but they never produced a team capable of staying at a higher level. More than 30 years after their record win, the same can still be said of them.

ON THE SAME DAY...

News: Local Auctioneers and Estate Agents have ridiculed the idea of American-style out of town shopping centres ever catching on in South Yorkshire.

Sport: It's not just Doncaster who are in goalscoring mood. In the Scottish Cup the minnows are flayed alive by the big sides. Scores include: Dunfermline 7 - Fraserburgh 0, Rangers 9 - Duns 0 and Brechin City 2 - Dundee 9. The latter game was 2-2 at half-time!

Entertainment: It's unlikely that the Darlington squad will attend the play at the Gaumont, Doncaster. With a screenplay by Ted Willis and starring Janet Munro, John Stride and Alan Badel, it is entitled *'Bitter Harvest'*.

OFFICIAL PROGRAMME

Saturday, January 25th, 1964

ROVERS v DARLINGTON

Football League Division Four

Price 4d.

After years in the doldrums, Everton were again a major force in English football. Howard Kendall, their manager, who had seemed to be a certainty for the sack in 1984, had answered his critics in the best possible way when his side lifted the F.A. Cup the same year. That win provided the impetus for Everton to go from strength to strength. By the time they arrived in Rotterdam for this match, they had already won the League for the first time since 1970. They were also four days away from a second successive Cup Final. Yet their European achievement has gone largely unlauded. Perhaps because they lost the F.A. Cup Final against Manchester United after this game, perhaps because their League triumph was more highly regarded. More likely, it was because of the Heysel Stadium disaster shortly afterwards in which their city rivals Liverpool were involved.

At any rate, for Everton to appear in a European final was something of a minor miracle. For, of all English clubs who took part in Europe on a regular basis, Everton had by far the worst record. In nine previous European outings, Everton had only once reached as far as the Quarter-Finals. This time, their path was easier. Weak opponents from Ireland, Czechoslovakia and Holland allowed them to enter the Semi-Finals. But a magnificent victory over Bayern Munich silenced those who doubted the Merseysiders Euro-pedigree. 3-1 at home and a 0-0 draw in Germany earned them the right to face Rapid Vienna.

The Austrians had faced sterner opposition to reach the Final. A controversial win over Celtic (when the 2nd leg had to be replayed at Old Trafford) was followed up by successes against Dynamo Dresden and Moscow Dynamo. Both sides appeared to be evenly matched as they stood before the kick-off for a minute's silence in memory of those who had lost their lives in the Bradford fire disaster, a sad reminder of what a tragic year this was for football.

When play did get under way, Everton were the dominant force. Andy Gray and Graeme Sharp's aerial prowess allowed Everton to get on top. Koncel, the Austrian 'keeper was in top form, and he had to be. An early shot from Sheedy tested him and Gray, Bracewell, and Mountfield all went close, but the break was reached without a goal from either side.

In fact, half-time was reached without Rapid forcing as much as a corner. The second period confirmed the pattern of the first, with Everton always in command but finding the Austrian defence a stubborn beast to break down. In 58 minutes, their Scots striking duo took control.

EVERTON 3
Vs Rapid Vienna 1

May 15th 1985 - European-Cup-Winners Cup Final (Rotterdam)

Everton: Southall, Stevens, Van Den Hauwe, Ratcliffe, Mountfield, Reid, Steven, Sharp, Gray, Bracewell, Sheedy.

Sharp intercepted the passback to the keeper, and crossed for Gray to volley home the opening goal via the empty net. Rapid looked a beaten side. Stevens and Van Den Hauwe took the luxurious option of joining the attack. Sharp and Bracewell both went close. Then Konsel made a good save from Steven. After 73 minutes, a corner from the right by Sheedy confused the Rapid defence. Steven, based at the far post, shot past Konsel to make it 2-0. At last, Rapid Vienna decided to attack. In the 82nd minute, Southall made his first serious save of the game, from substitute Gross. With five minutes remaining, Everton's defence was caught out for once and Hans Krankl, dormant for most of the match, took the ball round the 'keeper and scored, to inspire hopes of a late Austrian surge. But, just two minutes later, Sharp held the ball up for Sheedy to get into position. Once Sheedy got the ball, he unleashed a fierce shot which settled the tie at 3-1 in Everton's favour.

Kendall was understandably proud of his men: *"In terms of possession football, you will not see better than that,"* claimed the Everton boss. It was the start of a golden period for Everton under Kendall. Three Cup Finals in succession (although they won only one), two League titles in three seasons, plus this success made them the equal of their old foes from across Stanley Park. But Europe was to see no more of them. English clubs were banned from Europe following the deaths in the Heysel. No-one will ever know if Everton, having finally got the hang of European football, would have been able to defend their crown or even whether they could have gone on to win the European Cup itself. By the time English sides returned to Europe, Everton were no longer as potent a side and Kendall had departed the scene. Although he later returned to the helm at Goodison, it was not with the same success. We can only wonder just how good a side Kendall's eighties Everton might have been.

ON THE SAME DAY...

News: After only three days, the Bradford (Fire) Disaster Appeal has passed the £¼M mark as the nation continues to mourn those who lost their lives.

Sport: Olympic quadruple gold medal winner, Carl Lewis, announces he will run in Britain at the AAA Championships in July.

Entertainment Top TV show of the evening is 'The Lenny Henry Show'.

STADION FEIJENOORD - ROTTERDAM № 80039

A ERETRIBUNE
Finale Europacup v. Bekerwinnaars
WOENSDAG 15 MEI 1985 AANVANG 20.15 UUR

ERETRIBUNE
ZITPLAATS 1e RING
Rij : 1   No. : 24

Dit biljet op aanvraag te tonen
Ongeldig zonder controlestrook

PRIJS f 65,--

KONINKLIJKE
NEDERLANDSCHE
VOETBALBOND

CONTROLE № 80039

STADION FEIJENOORD

15 MEI 1985

Met losse controlestrook géén toegang
S.v.p. NIET op perforatie vouwen

B.V. Nederlandsche Speciaal Drukkerijen, Delft

When *'Old Moore's Almanack'* for 1931 predicted that the F.A. Cup Final would be contested by two teams whose names started with the letter E, it caused little excitement in Exeter. Despite the fact that only the local team and Everton - of all the League clubs in England - fitted the bill. A few began to take notice when Exeter City, in the middle of the Third Division (South) eliminated high-flying Derby County in the third round of the Cup. An away win over Bury in round 4 brought a few more waverers on board, but when another First Division scalp, Leeds United, were accounted for in the 5th round, even the most sceptical of Devonians began to take the Almanack more seriously.

When the draw for the Quarter-Finals (a stage of the tourney not reached by an Exeter team before or since) sent them on the long trek North to Wearside, it appeared that the venerable book of prognostications had got it wrong. Sunderland were one of the biggest names in the country. When the local side scored early on to cheer the vast bulk of the 51,642 in attendance, Exeter's Cup run appeared to be over. But, undaunted, the plucky outsiders refused to lie down. A 75th minute equaliser brought the Roker men down to Devon the following Wednesday for the replay.

It was an inauspicious day for such an important occasion. The rain had poured incessantly all day. But that wasn't enough to deter 21,015 spectators from turning up, a record which stands to this day. The first fifteen minutes gave little for the Grecians supporters to cheer as Sunderland took control. It was Davies, the Exeter 'keeper, who had to prove his worth, and he did, until the fateful quarter-hour mark. Full-backs Baugh and Miller got caught in a mix-up allowing Sunderland's outside-left Connor to shoot, unmarked, perfectly, putting his side ahead. Seven minutes later, there was further disaster for Exeter as clever triangular work saw centre-forward Gurney score a second for Sunderland. Exeter looked dead and buried.

But the First Division side, thinking the hard work was done, eased off. Exeter came more into the match. In 37 minutes, Barber sent forward what looked like a harmless ball but 'keeper Middleton was off his line. In nipped Varco to reduce the deficit to 2-1. Exeter piled forward for the remainder of this half and Sunderland were left to do some pretty desperate defending. They were lucky to get to the dressing room with their lead intact.

Sunderland started the second half as they had the first, on the attack. Inside-left Leonard hit the post. Then Exeter hit back. Houghton robbed the Roker centre-half McDougall and sent Doncaster away on a long solo run, ended only when the winger too smacked the ball against the upright. Exeter were dominating the match when tragedy struck. Totally against the run of play, Sunderland scored when Gurney fed Connor with an unbeatable opportunity. Even now, Exeter refused to give up. *"The Grecians fought like Trojans,"* said the *Devon & Exeter Gazette*, somewhat confusingly. Armfield was fouled. Clarke took the kick, and there was inside-left Purcell to head home a glorious goal. 3-2 down with fifteen minutes to play. The ground heaved with excitement as the huge throng roared their team on.

Exeter attacked again. In a furious goalmouth melee, the Grecians claimed that the ball had passed over the line. The players appealed frantically but the referee stood firm. No goal. Temporarily fazed, Exeter failed to spot a Sunderland breakaway which resulted in the ball lying in the back of the Exeter net for a heart-breaking fourth time. Still, Exeter came forward. Barber tried a

EXETER CITY 2 Vs Sunderland 4

March 4th 1931 F.A. Cup Quarter-Final Replay

Exeter City: Davies, Baugh, Miller, Clarke, Angus, Barber, Armfield, Purcell, Varco, Houghton, Doncaster.

shot but Middleton held it well. The whistle sounded on a game the likes of which had never been seen before in Devon. Charlie Miller, Exeter's captain approached his Sunderland counterpart, McDougall and shook him warmly by the hand. The First Division side had won, but they knew what a battle Exeter had put up.

It was the nearest an Exeter team has ever got to Cup glory and a reminder that the big clubs should never assume that the Grecians will ever be easy opponents. As for Old Moore, he was wrong too. The only other E, Everton, were beaten in the semi-finals by the eventual winners, West Brom.

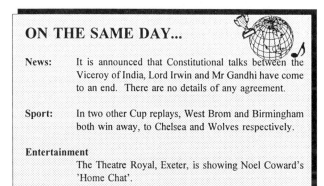

ON THE SAME DAY...

News: It is announced that Constitutional talks between the Viceroy of India, Lord Irwin and Mr Gandhi have come to an end. There are no details of any agreement.

Sport: In two other Cup replays, West Brom and Birmingham both win away, to Chelsea and Wolves respectively.

Entertainment
The Theatre Royal, Exeter, is showing Noel Coward's 'Home Chat'.

The captains - Miller (Exeter) and McDougall (Sunderland)

FULHAM 0
Vs West Ham United 2
May 3rd 1975
F.A. Cup Final (Wembley)

Fulham: Mellor, Cutbush, Fraser,
Mullery, Lacy, Moore, Mitchell, Conway,
Busby, Slough, Barrett. Sub. Lloyd.

For most of their history, Fulham had been regarded as one of the less fashionable of the London clubs. True, they had spent the bulk of the 1960s in Division One, but they had never finished higher than 10th in the table. In the F.A. Cup they had reached four semi-finals but had never progressed to the Final. By 1974-75 they were in their accustomed position in the middle of the 2nd Division. But, in the Cup, they embarked on a promising, if tortuous, run. It took them no fewer than seven matches just to account for Hull City and Nottingham Forest, and three of those games had gone to extra time. It was the 5th round before they grabbed the headlines with a superb away win over Everton. A similar success at the then 1st Division Carlisle propelled them into a last four confrontation with Birmingham City. The midlanders became the third top League side in succession to fall to the Craven Cottagers when Fulham, after a 1-1 draw at Hillsborough, won the Semi-Final replay at Maine Road 1-0, again after extra time. At long last Fulham were at Wembley.

Normally, Fulham wouldn't have been expected to have much of a chance against their 1st Division opponents, West Ham, in the Final, but circumstances conspired to give the lower League side hope that they could pull off a shock result. Firstly, this was only the second ever "Cockney" Cup Final, creating great interest in the capital. Secondly, Sunderland's epic win over Leeds two years previously had given hope to all 2nd Division teams that they could emulate the Wearsiders. Thirdly, there were Fulham's own achievements in already eliminating three top flight sides from the competition. Finally, and for Fulham, most importantly, they had within their ranks two players who already knew that feeling of exhilaration which grabbed Wembley winners. Their captain was Alan Mullery, 35 times capped for England and a former Cup-winner with Spurs. But those hoping for a poetic victory pointed in the direction of Bobby Moore. The man who led England to the World Cup and played a record 108 times for his Country was in the twilight of his career. But it was hoped that he would do for Fulham what he had done for West Ham eleven years previously, and lead them up the famous Wembley steps for a first F.A. Cup success.

For a long time it seemed that it might indeed happen. Mullery and Moore were outstanding in what was a largely disappointing first half. His old club's fast-running wing-halves tried to exploit the veteran's lack of pace with runs from the middle of the park, but the old warrior was too sharp mentally. His covering and passing was as astute as ever. His leadership calmed Fulham. The underdogs won several crucial tackles on the half-way line. Slough tried a shot on goal but Mervyn Day, for the Hammers, saved easily. Lacy fired in a header which caused the 'keeper more trouble. Lacy tried with another header before West Ham made their first proper attempt on goal, Jennings testing Mellor with a header which the Fulham goalkeeper struggled to keep out. Then Moore, with a flash of his old vintage, split the defence with a single pass, sending Busby away. But nothing came of this enterprise. West Ham's Brooking, anonymous until now, burst through on his own. His low cross just failing to find Alan Taylor. Then Taylor landed a header on top of the net. With Billy Bonds beginning to move up into attack for the Hammers, Fulham began to lose the ball. Half-time was reached with the score still 0-0 but with the 1st Division side starting to take control.

Fulham's wily manager Alec Stock attempted to rally his side during the interval but Mellor's nerves began to show early in the second half when McDowell and Taylor went close for West Ham. Mitchell revived Fulham's spirits with a darting run into the box but Day raced out to clear. Then, within four minutes, Fulham's dream collapsed. In 62 minutes, Cutbush, in no danger, allowed himself to be robbed by Holland who sped forward, checked, and shot. Mellor managed to turn the ball away, but only as far as Taylor who fired back in to put the Hammers ahead. In 66 minutes, Paddon's shot was fluffed by Mellor and in the ensuing melee, Taylor scooped the ball home for the second, and final goal. Barret tried to rescue Fulham with a couple of good sprints, but the game was over. Moore summed it up: *"After such a good performance in the first half, it was very disappointing."* But Fulham had given their all. Their fans had every right to be proud of the men who had taken them to the very brink of glory. Sadly, it is a feat Fulham have seldom, if ever, looked capable of achieving again.

ON THE SAME DAY...

News: McNeill's feat would be the headlines in a new newspaper, *The Scottish Daily News*, launched as a workers co-op at the old Daily Express plant in Glasgow.

Sport: Another footballing veteran is more successful. Billy McNeill picks up his seventh Scottish Cup Winners medal as Celtic beat Airdrie 3-1 in McNeill's final appearance for the club.

Entertainment:
No.1 in the charts is the haunting 'Loving You', sung by Minnie Ripperton.

Newport County 0 Vs

GILLINGHAM 1

April 30th 1964 - League Division Four

Gillingham: Simpson, Stacey, Hudson, Arnott, Burgess, Farrell, Newman, White, Francis, Gibbs, Meredith.

Gillingham had already celebrated their first-ever promotion without kicking a ball. Bradford City's defeat by York City the previous Saturday ensured that the Kent side would be playing Third Division football the next season. But this Thursday evening trip to South Wales would give Gillingham something they had only hitherto dreamed of, a trophy to put in their boardroom. Strangely, for a side which was the most successful in the club's history, Gillingham had come in for some unwanted criticism. Unwanted and unwarranted as far as their Chairman, Dr. Clifford Grossmark was concerned. He put it on record that Gillingham FC did not exist primarily to, *"entertain,"* but was, *"a business venture out to succeed."*

It seemed that the fans disagreed with Dr. Grossmark. While Gillingham enjoyed a home average support of 9,900, the best in the Division, only a small band made the journey to Newport to watch what might be history in the making. Two points were essential to take the title. Carlisle had finished their programme and had 60 points. Gillingham needed to win without losing a goal. Carlisle had scored 113 and lost 58. Gills had scored 58 and lost 30. Goal average for Carlisle was 1.948. If Gillingham won, say, by 2-1 or 3-2 then Carlisle would be the champions, 1-0 it had to be, unless Gillingham won by two or more goals, but given their defensive reputation that was asking for a lot.

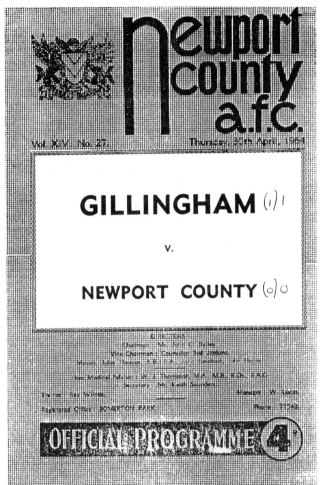

reverted to their tried and tested safety first formula. The goal appeared to knock the heart out of Newport who offered little threat for the remainder of the match. At time up it was the little knot of Gillingham supporters who were entitled to celebrate. Their side had lifted the 4th Division title by a goal average difference of just 0.018.

What should have been a carnival atmosphere was soured by the purists at the *Chatham Standard*, which wrote: *"If Gillingham's promotion bid was agony, then Thursday's all-important championship match was little short of excruciating."* It seems a scant tribute to a side which accomplished something no Gillingham team has done before or since, lifted a League title. For although Gillingham have, on occasion, looked likely to gain promotion to the old Second Division, and have won other promotions, this remains the only time when, at the end of a season, supporters of the Kent club have been able to peruse the League table and find their team sitting at the top of the heap.

Whether it was the pressure of the occasion or the mathematical gymnastics required, Gillingham got off to a nervous start. The defence was its usual reliable self, but their attack was erratic to say the least. One minute it appeared to be all guns blazing in search of victory. The next, defence-splitting passes would find no-one waiting up front. Meredith, Newman and Francis all tried to find a way through but the busiest player on the park was Gills 'keeper John Simpson. Newport, with nothing but pride at stake, tested the custodian, firing in a series of shots which brought off some tremendous saves. The 'keeper made good use of his generous reach to keep the scores level and enthuse the little band of travelling supporters.

But the Gillingham midfield also never wavered. Newman broke away, flicked the ball to Brian Gibb, received the return and sped into the box. In the tussle which followed, Francis got in a shot which put Gillingham in front. Gillingham then

ON THE SAME DAY...

News: Football violence in Kent. Not at triumphant Gillingham, but at Chatham Town, where supporters storm the ground, two of them assaulting the referee, after losing 4-3 to Cray Wanderers in the Aeolian League Cup. They were clearly incensed that their hopes of glory had 'gone with the wind'.

Sport: History is made, not just in Kent, but in other footballing outposts like Cumbria and Devon as Carlisle, Workington and Exeter accompany Gillingham into the Third Division. None of the four successful sides had ever been promoted before.

Entertainment: Dr. Grossmark may have felt that the current No.1 hit reflected the local paper's attitude towards his team. It was Peter & Gordon's 'World Without Love'.

GRIMSBY TOWN 0
Vs Arsenal 1

March 21st 1936
F.A. Cup Semi-Final (Huddersfield)

Grimsby Town: Tweedy, Vincent, Kelly, Hall, Hodgson, Buck, Baldry, Bestall, Glover, Craven, Smailes.

Grimsby Town had a fair side in the 1930s. They had finished 5th in the First Division in 1934-35 and although struggling this season had impressed in the F.A. Cup. They had only drawn 0-0 at Hartlepool in the 3rd round. But their 4-1 replay win gave them the impetus for some pretty impressive results thereafter. 4-0 away to Port Vale in the 4th round, a 3-2 home win against Manchester City in the 5th before a then record Blundell Park crowd of 28,000. An equally-sound 3-1 home win over Middlesbrough in the 6th round was good enough to send Grimsby into the last four for the first time in their history.

With two Second Division sides also in the semi-finals, hopes were high that Grimsby might be on their way to Wembley. Alas, fate intervened in the draw to match Grimsby with Arsenal, mightiest team of the day and three-times League Champions in succession. Filled with house-hold names like Male, Hapgood, Roberts, Copping, Hulme, Bastin and James, Arsenal boasted **nine** internationals in their line-up. But Grimsby were undaunted. They resolved to treat the occasion as a great day out. Those who think that face-painting is a recent phenomenon would be surprised to learn that Grimsby fans turned up for the Huddersfield semi dressed in pierrot costumes in the club colours of black and white with their faces *"made-up in the style of the white-eyed kaffir"* as the *Grimsby Telegraph* put it. Alas, the thirties images of happy fans shaking hands with smiling policemen were somewhat rarer than is generally supposed. The humourless constabulary denied the fancy dress fans access to the ground. All the same, a massive 63,210 assembled in ideal conditions to see the Mariners make their bid for glory.

But it was Arsenal who were quickest out of the blocks. In just two minutes, Hulme's speed carried him clear of two defenders, allowing him to get in a cross which Bowden headed goalwards until Bestall timely cleared. Hulme, again, had the beating of Kelly and sent in a dangerous ball, only for the alert Hodgson to clear. Grimsby recovered their composure. Craven twice attempted shots but they were tame efforts. Glover's shot was better but too high. Arsenal claimed a penalty when Bastin fell in the area but the referee waved play on.

In 19 minutes, the hitherto unseen Alex James showed his mettle. He dribbled through the defence, and passed to Hulme, whose shot was well held by Tweedy. Baldry had a chance for Grimsby but shot wide. Then Bestall was brought down by James just outside the penalty area. But Glover spurned the opening when his free kick ran straight into the defensive wall. Bastin returned to the attack for Arsenal. He drew Tweedy out of his goal and crossed to Hulme, but he failed narrowly to connect. After 38 minutes came the moment Grimsby were dreading. Bowden drew Hodgson to him, then slipped the ball to Bastin who ran through and scored. Grimsby fought back. Wilson, the Arsenal 'keeper, pulled off a brilliant save to prevent

Smailes from equalising. But Tweedy was still called into action. He had to make a great save of his own from a Bowden header before the half-time whistle sounded.

Grimsby must have thought they were still in with a chance as long as they could prevent the Gunners from scoring again. Arsenal realised that as well. They started the second period with Hulme again tormenting the Mariners defence. Then James almost got a second goal, Hodgson clearing at the last. Arsenal's left-winger Beasley got in a good shot. As did Bastin. After 62 minutes he was clean through when Tweedy made a marvellous save. Shortly after, the Grimsby goalie again proved his worth with a one-handed save from Bowden then stopping a point-blank header from Beasley.

With fifteen minutes remaining a great roar went up from the Grimsby contingent in the crowd, when Glover passed to Smailed who sent his shot crashing into the net. The cheers subsided when no goal was awarded. Whether it was handball or offside, no-one was sure. Grimsby still refused to yield. Hall in particular inspiring the team. Bestall was still looking for openings. All ten outfield players had surged upfield in search of the equaliser when Beasley broke away for Arsenal. Again, it was Tweedy to the rescue. The elusive goal didn't come. Grimsby trooped off beaten in what was described as "a fine full-bloodied exhibition of football." Tweedy received a standing ovation from the Grimsby fans. If anything, Grimsby were slightly unlucky. Although they again reached the last four in 1939, Grimsby's great days were coming to an end. Relegated in 1948, they have never again played at the top level, although in recent years they have come close to doing so; inspiring hope that the day may shortly dawn when, once again, Grimsby Town can stand on the brink of F.A. Cup success against the best in the land and play then without fear.

ON THE SAME DAY...

News: Abyssinian troops inflict heavy losses on the Italian invaders in the Ueri Valley.

Sport: England win a close encounter at Twickenham, beating Scotland 9-8 in the Rugby Union International match.

Entertainment:
That tried and tested team of James Cagney and Pat O'Brien are starring at the Tower Cinema in Grimsby in "The Irish In Us."

HARTLEPOOLS UNITED 10
Vs Barrow 1

April 4th 1959 - League Division Four

Hartlepools United: Oakley, Cameron, Waugh, Johnson, Moore,
Anderson, Scott, Langland, Smith, Clark, Luke.

Hartlepool were known by this more cumbersome name until the late 1960s. But they were a similar sort of team, usually struggling near the foot of the League, never quite sure if the next re-election campaign would prove to be the last. 1958-59 was no different. They lay 19th in the first season of the new 4th Division with only 33 points from 40 games. Bottom of the pile were Barrow with just 25 points from the same number of games played. Together, these two teams had conceded a massive 168 goals. So it was no great surprise that this match was attended by only 3,870, the lowest crowd of the day.

But those who did attend were to witness an historic occasion. It didn't look that way at the start. One of 'Pool's few 'Star' performers, Tom Burlison, was injured, so ex-Middlesbrough player Joe Scott was drafted into the side. Burlison, who went on to become a highly influential figure in the TUC and the Labour Party, was forced to watch from the sidelines as the spectacle unfolded.

There was a sombre note at the start as a minute's silence was observed in memory of Jeff Hall, the Birmingham and England full-back, who had died of polio that morning. Once proceedings got underway, it was 'Pool who dominated. After just eight minutes, Clark's 20 yard shot drove into the top corner past the helpless Barrow 'keeper Keys to put the home side ahead. Barrow tried to respond, but 'Pool kept up the pressure. Luke shot wide from 30 yards. Simpson of Barrow almost headed into his own net. In 19 minutes, Keys made a good save from Langland, but the ball was quickly returned into the area where Smith, at the far post, made it 2-0. Smith then found himself clear, only to shoot over both the bar and the stand! Another Smith attempt saw the ball fly halfway between the goal and the corner flag. But, on the half-hour, Simpson's poor back pass landed right on Luke's toe. He scooped up the easiest of chances to make it 3-0.

Four minutes later, Smith headed home from a Luke cross to prompt the *Hartlepool Mail* into a flurry of metaphors: *"It was like a one-horse race with 'Pools cutting through the defence like a knife through butter."* In 38 minutes, Smith notched his third and his team's fifth. Another four minutes, another goal, Scott making it six, three minutes from the break. Even then, Hartlepools weren't finished. Langland, the only forward who hadn't scored, rectified that in the 44th minute to make it 7-0 at half-time. BBC TV were forced to repeat the half-time result, so astonishing did it seem that Hartlepools had scored seven.

Despite more home pressure, it was Barrow who scored first in the second half, through Kemp in 55 minutes. Oakley was then called on to make a fine save from Murray before the 'Pools procession re-started. In 65 minutes, Smith, closed down by the defence, passed to Luke who fired in a beauty to make it 8-1. The crowd were indignant when a good-looking penalty appeal was turned down after Langland was severely tackled by King. Scott and Smith both saw Keys bring off good saves. But with eleven minutes remaining, Moore cleverly found Clark who advanced on goal and shot home the ninth. In 83 minutes, Marsden of Barrow put through his own net. Keys furiously smothered the ball on the line but the linesman ruled that it had gone over. Hartlepools had reached double figures.

That 10-1 win remains their record score. They had beaten non-League St. Peter's Albion by the same score in an F.A. Cup tie in 1923-24 but this was of far greater significance. It helped keep 'Pools clear of the re-election zone, something they would fail to do for the next five seasons. For a team whose only other achievements lie in a couple of promotions, followed by swift relegations, it gave their hardy band of followers a memory which would abide forever among those who were there.

ON THE SAME DAY...

News: The Dalai Lama, fleeing from Tibet in the wake of Chinese invasion, is reported to have reached safety in India.

Sport: Brian Clough got married in the morning but returned to duty at Ayresome Park in the afternoon, scoring in Middlesbrough's 4-2 home win over Leyton Orient.

Entertainment:
After match TV highlights are 'Wells Fargo' on the BBC, or pop show 'Oh Boy' on the new North-East independent channel, Tyne-Tees.

HEREFORD UNITED 2

Vs Newcastle United 1

February 5th 1972
F.A. Cup Round Three Replay

Hereford United: Potter, Griffiths (George 82),
Mallender, Jones, McLaughlin, Addison, Gough,
Tyler, Meadows, Owen, Radford.

Hereford United had already astonished the football world by drawing 2-2 at St. James Park to bring Newcastle to Edgar Street for this replay. Owen had put the Southern League side ahead in just seventeen seconds. McDermott had equalised from a spot kick less than two minutes later. When the Geordies went ahead in 23 minutes, Hereford seemed doomed. But player-manager Colin Addison scored two minutes after that to set the scene for a mouth-watering replay.

The second tie was scheduled for the Monday following the first game and queues waited for hours for tickets. The *Hereford Evening News* plastered a photo of Wembley on their front page with the caption: *"Is this where it will end?"* However, the weather put paid to the game that night. It wasn't until the same day as the 4th round tie were scheduled to be played that the game was able to go ahead. Not that it needed to take place at all as far as the haughty geordies were concerned. Despite making all the right platitudinous noises about respecting opponents etc, Newcastle had already printed tickets for the 4th round tie against West Ham. Len Shackleton, in a newspaper column, described the contest as, *"Sotheby Vs Steptoe & Son."* Shackleton played in the Sunderland team once knocked out of the Cup by Yeovil. He should have known better, for, just like the Steptoes, Hereford were determined to have the last laugh.

But it was Newcastle who started brightest in front of 14,313 spectators. After five minutes, Malcolm MacDonald burst through, forcing Potter to bravely smother the ball. But Hereford meant to show the 1st Division side that they had a fight on their hands. Twice, Tyler had the Newcastle defence back-pedalling. Then Gough shot just wide. With nineteen minutes gone, Newcastle's Craig looked like opening the scoring until Jones headed off the line. Potter brought off good saves from Busby and Hibbitt. But still Hereford battled. Midway through the first half, Tyler forced Geordies goalkeeper McFaul into a double-save. Radford also went close. In 38 minutes, McDermott had the ball in the net for Newcastle but Tudor had fouled Potter. No goal. Just before the interval came a nervous moment. A Hereford clearance fell to Tudor, and he hit the bar. Hibbitt seized the rebound, and, with the goal at his mercy, he too hit the bar. Half-time 0-0.

Hereford played much better in the second half. Mallender shot over the bar from close in. McFaul had to be at full stretch to tip a Tyler shot over for a corner. From this, Mallender headed against the post, with Craig desperately

clearing. It was now that Newcastle's 'Supermac' took a hand, carving out three chances. He rounded Potter then shot wide. His header brought an equally good save from the 'keeper. But his third effort, a header from a Busby cross found the target. 1-0 to Newcastle with only eight minutes to play. Was it all over?

Ronnie Radford provided the answer in 86 minutes. Playing a neat one-two with Owen, he blasted home from all of 30 yards. It was a spectacular strike, and one which was destined to go down in Cup history. Hereford surged forward in extra time and, near the end of the first fifteen minutes, Ricky George took a pass from Tyler, turned, saw the far corner of the net unguarded and shot home. 2-1 to Hereford. The last fifteen minutes saw Hereford grow stronger as the Geordies wilted. Owen and George both came close to scoring a third. The final whistle saw scenes of unparalleled delight as Hereford fans invaded the pitch. Even Len Shackleton was forced to confess that the better side had won. Steptoes 2 - Sothebys 1.

Hereford were the first non-League side to beat a Division One team in a Cup replay since the War and only the third in total. But there was precious little time to celebrate. As thousands of shell-shocked Geordies tore up their 4th round tickets, Hereford faced West Ham at Edgar Street just 48 hours later and achieved a creditable 0-0 draw before losing the replay the following Monday 3-1. But their Cup heroics had gathered the attention of the Football League. After years of trying, Hereford United were voted into the League at the subsequent A.G.M. By August they were a League team.

ON THE SAME DAY...

News: Klaus Atlmann, alleged by France to be Klaus Barbie, the war-time Gestapo Chief in Lyons, is arrested in La Paz, Bolivia.

Sport: Jonah Barington wins the British Open Squash title for the fifth time in six years, after a gruelling 115 minute contest against Australia's Geoff Hunt in Sheffield.

Entertainment:
The post-match TV schedule on BBC-1 is of a traditional vintage, Dr Who, Cliff Richard and Dixon of Dock Green.

HUDDERSFIELD TOWN 3
Vs Nottingham Forest 0

May 3rd 1924 - League Division One

Huddersfield Town: Taylor, Barkas, Wadsworth, Steele,
Wilson, Watson, Richardson, Brown,
Cook, Stephenson, Smith

Huddersfield Town were a comparatively young club. Hailing from a rugby stronghold, the club was established as late as 1908. They joined the 2nd Division in 1910 and gained some success in 1920 when they reached the F.A. Cup Final, losing to Aston Villa and gaining promotion to the 1st Division. But it was the arrival of Herbert Chapman as manager in 1921 which heralded Huddersfield's arrival as a top club. He led them to victory in the F.A. Cup in 1922 and then 3rd place in Division One a year later. Now Huddersfield were in a position to mount a Championship challenge in 1923-24. As the more fancied clubs slipped back, it became clear that the title was on its way to a new home, either in the West Riding, or to South Wales. On the final day of the season the top of the table looked like this:-

	P	W	D	L	F	A	Pts	G.Av.
Cardiff City	41	22	12	7	61	34	56	1.794
Huddersfield T.	41	22	11	8	57	33	55	1.727

If Huddersfield drew, Cardiff could afford to lose 1-0 and still lift the title. If Cardiff drew then Huddersfield had to win by three goals to clinch it. Of course, if Cardiff won, that was it. 20,000 turned up at the Leeds Road ground, willing Chapman's side on to success. They witnessed a tense half, full of scrappy play. But Smith livened up proceedings with a glorious run. He beat two defenders before passing to Stephenson who quickly sent it on to Brown. As Brown was tackled, he touched the ball sideways to Cook who snapped up the chance to put the Terriers in front. Half-time 1-0.

But it was Forest who started the second half the brighter, coming close to equalising. They had virtually nothing to lose. Although on the same points tally as second bottom Chelsea, only an unlikely eleven goal thrashing would send them below the London club who had completed their programme. But, as Forest pressed, it was the Huddersfield fans who cheered. News had just reached the crowd of the half-time score from St. Andrews, where Birmingham and Cardiff were drawing 0-0. The title race was still on.

Buoyed by this news, Huddersfield resumed the offensive. Wilson skied his attempt. Then Watson fired in a cannonball which left a circular mud patch on the crossbar. Richardson sent a corner right over to the far side where Smith returned it to the centre. There was Cook, heading down to make it 2-0. With the Holy Grail of the League Championship right before their eyes, Huddersfield sought out that vital third goal. Wilson dodged past two Forest defenders before slinging the ball out to the unmarked Richardson on the right. He bore down on goal, passing at

the last minute to let Brown touch the ball home. 3-0 and the title was Huddersfield's, providing things stayed as they were at Birmingham.

Now Huddersfield turned on the champagne football. Midway in his opponents half, Steele - *"proceeded to juggle and swerve and feint his way past six or seven of the Forest side,"* according to the *Huddersfield Daily Examiner*. He kept his feet in the slime and mud all the way up to the goalmouth, only to shoot wide. Still, it was the best move of the match. Meanwhile, Taylor, in Huddersfield's goal enjoyed what the local paper called an, *"almost unbroken rest."* Just as well. A goal lost now could prove fatal. But no goals were lost, nor were any more scored. The crowd hung about the ground at the end of the game, waiting to see if their heroes endeavours had been good enough.

What they didn't know was that Davies of Cardiff had missed a penalty. Officials huddled anxiously around a phone in a small room as thousands waited outside. Then came the moment described by the Examiner. *"Then suddenly, the door was flung open and Mr Chapman dashed out with his face one huge smile and shouting "We've won!."* It had finished 0-0 at Birmingham. Both sides had 57 points, but Huddersfield's goal average was 1.81 and Cardiff's 1.79. For Huddersfield, this was the start of their glory days. They lifted the title three times in succession, the first club ever to do so. Before their third title though, Chapman had gone to Arsenal where the feat would be repeated. Sadly, Herbert Chapman died before the accomplishment of that task. Huddersfield Town, where he made his name, have enjoyed little in terms of concrete success since those days. But now, in the 1990s, Huddersfield have a magnificent new stadium. Perhaps it won't be too long before they have a team to match their ground.

ON THE SAME DAY...

News: Ominous news from Germany, where the extreme right make significant gains in the German elections.

Sport: More glory for Yorkshire as Batley beat Wigan 13-7 in the Rugby League Championship Final.

Entertainment:
Acclaimed composer Sir Edward Elgar is appointed Master of the King's Musick.

HULL CITY 2

Vs Arsenal 2
March 22nd 1930 - F.A.Cup Semi-Final (Leeds)

Hull City: Gibson, Goldsmith, Bell, Walsh, Childs,
Gowdy, Alexander, Starling, Mills, Howieson, Duncan.

To many outsiders, Hull City's lack of success over many years is mystifying. Situated in a large conurbation, geographically isolated from other large centres, and with a sports-inclined population, Hull seems ideally placed to be the East Coast equivalent of Merseyside. However, Hull is a city dominated by Rugby League. The football club, founded in 1904, have never played in the top flight, reaching 3rd in the old 2nd Division in 1910 represents the pinnacle of their League achievements.

But in the spring of 1930, it was soccer talk which filled the City as Hull set off on a long run in the F.A. Cup. They overcame stiff opposition in Plymouth, a 4-3 away win over the side running away with the 3rd Division (South) was no mean feat. That was followed by a fine 3-1 win at their own Anlaby Road ground over 2nd Division Champions-to-be Blackpool. It was the 5th round which really made the sceptics sit up and take notice though when Hull travelled to Maine Road and knocked out Manchester City, lying 3rd in the 1st Division, 2-1. A 1-1 draw in the Quarter-finals away to the famous cup-fighters of Newcastle brought out a big crowd for the replay to see the Tigers win 1-0.

Although there were three Yorkshire sides in the last four of the Cup (Huddersfield and Sheffield Wednesday were the others), Hull were drawn to play Arsenal in their semi-final. So it was that thousands travelled west to Leeds to join the 48,000 strong crowd which eagerly awaited the contest between the struggling 2nd Division side from Rugby League country up against the soccer aristocrats from the capital. They saw Hull enjoy a comfortable start. Gibson, in goal, was excellent. Centre-half Childs took control of Lambert and James, Arsenal's feared forwards. But some of the others were both excited and nervous. Play was quick, but also haphazard. Arsenal came close early on, Hulme's free kick headed just wide by David Jack. But Duncan and Howieson carved out an opening for Hull, Arsenal's Parker throwing himself full-length to head clear. Hull, it was said, were employing, *"kick-and-rush methods, combined with grim and earnest tackling."*

After fifteen minutes, Arsenal 'keeper Lewis ran out to kick clear but sent the ball straight to Howieson whose volley dropped under the bar before the desperate 'keeper could get back into position. 1-0 to Hull. Emboldened by this piece of good fortune, Hull continued to press forward. Alexander went on a run. Past Hapgood, past Jones, and eventually past the post. But, with 30 minutes on the clock, Childs moved up. He threaded his way past man after man before releasing the ball to Duncan who accepted the chance, tucking the ball away to give Hull a 2-0 lead. Gibson and Lambert both went close for Arsenal but half-time arrived with the unlikely-looking scoreline intact.

Arsenal were greatly improved after the break, Lambert skimmed the bar. But Hull were still playing well. Alexander forced Lewis out of his goal to parry a shot. But, in 67 minutes, Hulme found Jack who scored from a narrow angle. Sixty seconds later, Gibson brought off a great save from the menacing Hulme. Arsenal powered forward but Hull stayed resolute. Until there were only seven minutes remaining. Cliff Bastin beat Goldsmith in the air, rounded the same player, and drove his shot right into the top of the net. Seven minutes of absolute hell ensued as Arsenal strove for the winner. But Hull held out. At the end they had earned their draw.

The replay at Villa Park the following Wednesday saw Hull again strive manfully but, in truth, their chance had gone. Arsenal squeezed home 1-0 before going on to lift the Cup for the first time by beating Huddersfield in the Final. Hull were left, not only with the memory of how close they had been from Wembley, but also with a relegation fight on their hands which, ultimately, they lost; surrendering their 2nd Division status after 25 years. Since then there have been the occasional flattering noises emanating from the Humber. But, to this day, no side from Hull has come as close to success as that noble bunch of warriors of 1930.

ON THE SAME DAY...

News: It was announced that those unwanted relics from the past, the Poor Law system and the Workhouse are to be abolished.

Sport: British boxer Len Harvey is negotiating for a World Title middleweight bout against Mickey Walker.

Entertainment
At the Hull Palace Theatre the attraction is an Edgar Wallace play: *"The Calendar."*

IPSWICH TOWN 3

Vs AZ67 Alkmaar 0

May 6th 1981 - UEFA Cup Final (1st Leg)

Ipswich Town: Cooper, Mills, McCall, Thijssen, Osman, Butcher, Wark, Muhren, Mariner, Brazil, Gates.

The football world had been taken by storm by Ipswich Town in the early 1960s. In their first-ever season in the top flight they had won the title under the aegis of Alf Ramsey. Although subsequently relegated, Ipswich had returned to the 1st Division and, with Bobby Robson at the helm, had spent most of the 1970s establishing themselves as one of the most feared sides in England. They won many friends through their fluid, attacking game and F.A. Cup success in 1978 was welcomed by lovers of exciting football. Yet that win apart, Ipswich earned a reputation for being the nearly-men of football. In 1981 it seemed that would be their tag again. After leading the League, they lost six of their last eight games to surrender the title to Aston Villa. It was at Villa Park where their F.A. Cup hopes ended in defeat at the semi-final stage against Manchester City. Not the most hopeful of omens as they prepared for their first European Final.

But Ipswich, generalled by their Dutch duo of Thijssen and Muhren, had excelled in Europe. In the Quarter and Semi-Finals, they made the entire continent sit up and take notice as they eliminated St. Etienne and Cologne, winning both at home and away in both ties. Their opponents in the Final were the free-scoring, attractive outfit from Alkmaar, a team not unlike Ipswich themselves. Alkmaar, however, changed their game plan in the first leg. They came content to achieve a 0-0 draw and both Mariner and Gates took some knocks from the tough-tackling Dutch defenders early in the game. But the East Anglian side's own Dutch masters soon took control. Gates and Mariner shrugged off their injuries as well, both going close to goal. 27 minutes had elapsed when Mariner's attempt was handled by defender Hovenkamp. Penalty expert John Wark drove his spot kick low and hard to put Ipswich ahead. Thijssen and Gates had chances as well but half-time came with the score still 1-0 in Ipswich's favour.

The second half was less than a minute old when Ipswich scored again. Thijssen took Wark's pass and his firm shot struck against 'keeper Treytel. Thijssen headed the rebound home to put Ipswich two up. Now the 27,532 fans crammed into the compact Portman Road ground began to sense that history was being made. In 56 minutes, Alan Brazil weaved his way into the box. His cross was met by Mariner's right boot and it was 3-0 to Ipswich. It was only now that the Dutch tried to open up and attack the home side. Peters and Metgod in particular drove them forward but Ipswich were no slouches at defending a lead. They gradually forced the Dutch back, closing the game down. The final whistle signalled a night of celebration in Suffolk. 3-0 was reckoned to be good enough.

So it proved, though not without some scares. Ipswich refused to fall into the same trap as the Dutch had at Portman Road. They attacked the game in the second leg as if it were a home tie. They needed to. A frantic first half in Alkmaar left the Dutch side 3-2 ahead on the night. But those precious away goals ensured that Alkmaar started the second half still needing to score three more times without reply if they were to win the trophy. It was too tall an order, and although the Dutch managed one more strike to make it 4-2 on the night and 5-4 to Ipswich on aggregate, their hopes had gone long before the end. Ipswich's control and assurance had seen to that.

Just as the 1960s had seen the unlikely sight of the League Championship being paraded through Ipswich and the 1970s witnessed the F.A. Cup's presence in the town, so, in the 1980s, the UEFA Cup took up residence in East Anglia. The team which had played just one full League season prior to the Second World War had come a long way.

Sadly the 1990s have yet to see a similar success. But Ipwich's achievements over the past thirty-odd years have been substantial, not the least of which is the fact that they have played the bulk of their football at the highest level domestically, but the greatest of which is surely the lifting of the UEFA Cup.

ON THE SAME DAY...

News: Prince Charles and his bride-to-be Lady Diana Spencer take out an injunction against the broadcasting of calls made to each other from Australia.

Sport: World tennis No.1 John McEnroe is sensationally beaten in the Tournament of Champions in New York by unknown Brazilian Carlos Kirmayr.

Entertainment:
On TV was the programme 'Heroes', a searching documentary on the plight of US Vietnam War veterans made by John Pilger.

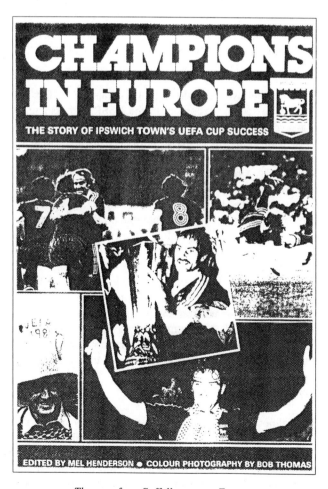

The men from Suffolk conquer Europe.
A celebration of Ipswich Town's 1981 UEFA Cup triumph.

Ferencvaros 0 Vs
LEEDS UNITED 0
September 11th 1968
Fairs Cup Final (second leg)

Leeds United: Sprake, Reaney, Cooper, Bremner, Charlton, Hunter, O'Grady, Lorimer, Jones, Madeley, Hibbitt (Bates).

Manager Don Revie revitalised Leeds in the mid-sixties. They arrived in the First Division in 1964 and took the League by storm; only goal average prevented them from lifting the title in their first season and they lost in extra time in the F.A. Cup Final. But those second prizes proved to be typical of Leeds, the nearly-men of English football. It was the same in Europe too. Leeds reached the Final of the 1967 Fairs Cup but were beaten by Dynamo Zagreb. By the time they made the following year's Final they had, at last, deposited a trophy in the Elland Road boardroom, the League Cup. But that competition did not enjoy the same prestige it does today. To prove that they had truly joined soccer's elite, Leeds had to win something more substantial.

Although this was the 1967-68 tournament, the Fairs Cup Final was held over to the start of the following season. The Yorkshire side's opponents, Ferencvaros from Budapest, were a highly-fancied side. They had won this competition thanks to a Final success over Juventus in 1965 and they had within their ranks several of the Hungarian players who had impressed during the 1966 World Cup. But Leeds had star names too, Cooper, Bremner, Hunter and Lorimer to name but a few. They had one of the winners of the 1966 tourney, Jack Charlton. It was one of their lesser-praised players though - Mick Jones - who scored the only goal in the scrappy home game to give Leeds a lead to protect in Hungary.

Between the two legs the political situation in Eastern Europe worsened. Troops from the USSR and associated Warsaw Pact countries, including Hungary, invaded Czechoslovakia. In a world dominated by the threat of nuclear war, moral outrage was the only weapon the West felt safe in using. As Alexander Dubcek's Prague spring was crushed by the tanks of a Stalinist summer, clubs from Western Europe demanded a re-drawing of the European competitions for 1968-9, adamant that they would not play representatives from those blood-stained states responsible for destroying Czech freedom. For their part, the Eastern teams were happy to withdraw, only neutral Yugoslavia, Romania (who had not been involved in the invasion), and Czechoslovakia stayed in the three tournaments. But it meant that this game, from the previous season, had to go ahead and in the worst of atmospheres. For even if they did not share their rulers enthusiasm for Moscow's actions, most Hungarians felt slighted by the stance of the West against their football teams. 65,000 gathered inside the Nepstadion anxious to avenge this perceived slur.

They almost had something to cheer about early on. Sprake failed to hold a shot from Rakosi, but the reliable Terry Cooper was on hand to clear. Leeds had something of a reputation as a dour, defensive side. And in Charlton and utility man Paul Madeley, they had two of the best defenders in the business.

This pair quickly established themselves with their tackling, interceptions, and, most crucially, their aerial mastery. But Leeds were also out to score too, if they could. Peter Lorimer went close for the Yorkshire side. Leeds were content to counter-attack when they saw a chance and relaxed in absorbing their foes pressure. Ferencvaros were playing excellent, passing, attacking football. But at half-time it was the British style which was in the ascendancy with the scoreline still 0-0.

The Hungarians upped the tempo in the second period. Szoke's shot bounced luckily off Sprake's leg. Varga (later to defect to join Aberdeen), was full of invention. And the magnificent Florian Albert was at his very best. The match was, said the *Daily Telegraph*, "*a classic of its kind.*" Ferencvaros were a, "*fast, fluent and clever Hungarian side who would probably have humbled any other club defence in the world.*" This gives an indication as to how good Leeds were. Their resolute defence continued to defy waves of spectacular attack, till, in the last fifteen minutes, Ferencvaros seemed to give up. Even so, there were still three long minutes of injury time to endure before the whistle finally blew to give Leeds United their first European trophy. Indeed, they were the first British team to win the Fairs Cup.

That success seemed to galvanise self-belief into this Leeds side. Although they were destined to take more runners-up prizes, including both the other European competitions, they went on to lift the English League title at the end of the season; another League triumph, an F.A. Cup win and a second Fairs Cup success were Elland Road-bound before the magic of the Revie years faded. After almost two decades in the doldrums, it took until the 1992 championship-winning side before Leeds again had a team to be proud of. But even that side couldn't match the class of '68, a team capable of beating the most illustrious opponents in the most hostile of conditions, to capture the one prize which had eluded every previous British contestant.

ON THE SAME DAY...

News: Basil D'Oliveira, already banned from playing cricket in South Africa by the apartheid authorities, is now refused permission to even report on the current test series.

Sport: Lester Piggott on Ribero wins the St. Leger.

Entertainment: Yorkshire TV's top evening show is *'Mission Impossible'* - exactly what some faint-hearts thought of Leeds' chances in Hungary!

LEICESTER CITY 1
Vs Wolverhampton Wanderers 3

April 30th 1949
F.A. Cup Final (Wembley)

Leicester City: Bradley, Jelly, Scott, W.Harrison, Plummer, King, Griffiths, Lee, J.Harrison, Chisholm, Adam.

Few gave Leicester City much hope of success in this, their first-ever F.A. Cup Final. Lying 20th in the Second Division as the teams took the field, they were (and remain) the lowest-placed League side ever to play in soccer's showpiece. And with their top player, the scheming Don Revie, out through injury, most neutrals felt that the Cup was already on its way to Molineux.

In perfect conditions, Wolves started off intending to prove the bookies right. Outside-right Johnny Hancocks was the star, orchestrating proceedings. In twelve minutes, he demonstrated his artistry, half-trapping the ball as it fell, before haring around Scott and placing it perfectly for Pye to head the opener. But the threatened floodgates failed to open. Leicester strove manfully at their task, taking the game to Wolves. It seemed that at the very worst they would reach the interval, trailing by that single goal when Wolves struck again. There were only four minutes of the half remaining when Wolves won two successive corners. Hancocks took the second, flighting the ball to Mullen who beat two defenders before passing to Pye who knocked in the second. It looked like the end for Leicester.

But the second half had some surprises in store. Those who think that tactical awareness is a modern invention should have been present at the start of this half. Centre-forward Harrison switched to right wing, winger Griffiths went to inside-right and inside man Lee moved to the centre. The re-shuffle worked almost instantly. Starting in his own half, Adam beat player after player, reaching the Wolves penalty area. He released the ball to Chisholm who went on a shimmying run of his own before passing to the unmarked Griffiths. The impromptu inside-right slammed the ball home to put Leicester right back into the match.

The next 20 minutes witnessed some splendid football from both sides. Chisholm put the ball into the Wolves net but was ruled offside so quickly that the fans never really had time to clear their throats to cheer. Then it was Wolves' turn. Smythe jigged past three Leicester players before making it 3-1. But still Leicester fought doggedly. Goalkeeper Bradley, only playing because of injury to regular McGraw, made several great saves. Chisholm used his tremendous strength to good effect, making many runs on goal. Left-half King looked every bit as good as his opposite number Billy Wright, high praise indeed.

But for all their effort, it was not destined to be Leicester's day. They had proved beyond all doubt that they were in a false position in the League but it was Billy Wright who received the Cup from Princess Elizabeth. The only consolation for Leicester was that they had played their part in one of the best F.A. Cup Finals. One in which, *"the goals were clear-cut and the culmination of brilliant bits of football"* according to *The Observer*.

There was even worse news for the dejected Leicester players and supporters as they headed homewards. Victory for Nottingham Forest in a League game had pushed the Filbert Street men into a relegation place. That would have been the cruellest blow of all. But Leicester rallied to finish the season in 19th, fourth bottom. Leicester returned to Wembley three times in the 1960s and lost all three F.A. Cup Finals they played in. True, they did win the League Cup, but that was in the days when the Final was a two-leg affair. It was 1994 before Leicester broke their Wembley duck, winning a promotion play-off. A far cry from the day nearly 50 years beforehand when a side in fear of relegation to the 3rd Division, took on, and almost bettered the most famous names in the land.

A Leicester attack is thwarted by this well timed tackle from the Wolves defender.

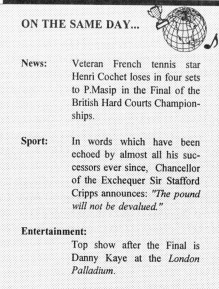

ON THE SAME DAY...

News: Veteran French tennis star Henri Cochet loses in four sets to P.Masip in the Final of the British Hard Courts Championships.

Sport: In words which have been echoed by almost all his successors ever since, Chancellor of the Exchequer Sir Stafford Cripps announces: *"The pound will not be devalued."*

Entertainment: Top show after the Final is Danny Kaye at the *London Palladium.*

LEYTON ORIENT 2

Vs Middlesbrough 1
March 14th 1978
F.A. Cup Quarter-Final (replay)

Leyton Orient: Jackson, Fisher, Roffey, Grealish, Hoadley, Roeder, Godfrey, Gray, Mayo, Kitchen, Payne.

For all their history, little of note has surrounded the East London team Leyton Orient. They are better known for their name changes, from Clapton Orient to Leyton Orient to plain Orient then back to Leyton again, than for any prodigious feats on the pitch. True, they did gain promotion to the First Division in 1962, but their solitary year in the top flight was such a disaster that its best not spoken of around Brisbane Road way.

But it was as unvarnished Orient that they made the football world sit up and take notice of them in 1978. The O's were in the not entirely unknown position of struggling for survival in Division Two when the F.A. Cup rolled round. Wembley was far from the forefront of the players and spectators minds. But the fans perked up after a sparkling replay win away to Division One Norwich City. Promotion-chasing Blackburn Rovers were despatched at Brisbane Road in the fourth round to leave Orient with a home tie against another top League outfit, Chelsea. A goalless draw seemed to have put paid to Orient's chances, but they confounded everyone with a masterly display in the Stamford Bridge replay, winning 2-1.

The draw for the last eight must have brought groans from the Brisbane Road dressing room. Not only would they have to make a 500-mile round trip to Middlesbrough, but the First Division Teessiders were on a roll, they had gone nine games undefeated. But those who knew their football history knew that 'Boro had never advanced beyond this stage of the competition.

Orient arrived at Ayresome Park minus manager Jimmy Bloomfield, who was laid up in hospital. His assistant, Peter Angell, took charge of the side as they threw off the lead weights of their relegation fight and matched Middlesbrough man for man. The bulk of the crowd of 33,426 trooped off home frustrated after a 0-0 draw. But the bookmakers still offered long odds against Orient claiming their third Division One scalp of the Cup. Orient fans agreed. Their best form had been away from home. With just five League wins at Brisbane Road all season, a difficult night loomed ahead.

A healthy gate of 18,501 greeted the teams as they emerged for the Tuesday night replay, and it was just as well they arrived in time, for the match started with a whirlwind performance from Orient. In just six minutes a high cross from Godfrey found Kitchen, who, from twenty yards out, smacked a volley into the net off the post to put Orient in front. Middlesbrough, battling against a fierce wind, were clearly shocked. They were still struggling when Mayo picked up a pass inside his own half and moved quickly upfield. He attempted a shot from twenty-five yards and Boro's Northern Irish international 'keeper, Jim Platt, mistimed his dive, allowing the ball to bounce over his

shoulder into the net. Only twelve minutes had been played and the side lying fourth bottom of Division Two were 2-0 ahead.

Mayo and Kitchen kept 'Boro under constant pressure, dual footballer/cricketer Alan Ramage earning himself a booking for bringing down Mayo. Boro's Ashcroft and Orient's Hoadley clashed and both names went into the book. But Orient were playing with a panache which belied their League position. Middlesbrough didn't get a look-in until they brought on Craig Johnston as a 75th minute substitute. With ten minutes left, David Armstrong scored for Middlesbrough. Now Orient had to hang on, and they did. It was a joyous crowd that celebrated a notable triumph after the ninety minutes had elapsed. "Orient," wrote the Daily Telegraph, had, "out-thought, out-ran, out-gunned" their higher League opponents. As for Jimmy Bloomfield, lying in his hospital bed, there was only one cliche worth repeating: "I'm over the moon" said the Orient boss.

40,000 fans applied for semi-final tickets, such was the effect of Cup fever. But Orient's moment of glory had passed. Although never humiliated, they were comfortably disposed of, 3-0, by Arsenal. But League Division Two status still had to be preserved. A 1-0 win at Cardiff in their last match lifted them clear of trouble and into a comparatively comfortable 14th place. But the division was so tight, that, had they even drawn, O's would have gone down. Nowadays, as the club stumbles from crisis to crisis, it is hard to imagine another team like the class of '78 ever emerging from Brisbane Road. But football is all about dreams, and Orient's fans must believe that not only will their team once again reach the last four of the Cup, next time they might even go on to win it.

ON THE SAME DAY...

News: Israel launches an attack on Palestinian camps in Southern Lebanon.

Sport: The first day of racing's Cheltenham Festival produces an even split, three English and three Irish-trained winners.

Entertainment: Dennis Potter's popular drama series, 'Pennies from Heaven', is the top show of the evening on BBC-1.

LINCOLN CITY 3
Vs Cardiff City 1

April 30th 1958 - Division Two

Lincoln City: Downie, Jackson, Dykes, Green,
Emery, Linnecor, Smillie, Hannah, Harbertson,
Chapman, Withers.

At the beginning of April 1958, Lincoln City's Sincil Bank ground had an air of despondency around it. Lincoln lay bottom of Division Two with just 19 points from 36 matches. Relegation seemed inevitable. The only hope for Lincoln was to win all their remaining games and hope their rivals slipped up. To everyone's astonishment, City proceeded to do just that. Under the wily eye of manager Bill Anderson, Lincoln won five in a row, three away from home, scoring thirteen and conceding just two goals. Even so, as 18,000 fans crammed into the ground for this final game on a Wednesday evening, another victory was a must. Anything else and Lincoln would still go down.

While the fans expected another minor miracle to follow all the others, it seemed that the players exertions had finally told on them. Lincoln were sluggish and it was Cardiff who started the sprightlier. Downie had to be at his best to tip a Hudson shot over for a corner. After twelve minutes, Cardiff's Nugent was clear through when Downie brought off one of the best saves in a long and distinguished career, throwing himself sideways to put the ball out. Three shots from three different Cardiff players came back off defenders before Cardiff won yet another corner. In truth, there was only one team in it. There were 27 minutes on the clock before Lincoln had a proper chance. Chapman passed to Smillie who touched it on Hannah. The inside-right laid it back to Smillie whose shot beat the 'keeper, but was cleared off the line by a Cardiff defender. Then Lincoln burst into life, showing the form that had brought them their five wins. Harbertson shot inches past the post, and Chapman and Smillie both went close with headers. The period ended with the Imps on top but with the score still 0-0.

Six minutes into the second half, Cardiff 'keeper Jones took the ball off Chapman's head. His mighty punt was touched on by a Cardiff player to Nugent, thirty yards from goal. He ran forward, shrugging aside a challenge, and lobbed over the advancing Downie to put the Welsh side ahead. One Cardiff player walked up to Lincoln centre-half Emery and said: *"That's put you into the Third Division."* It appeared as much prophecy as sneer.

Lincoln were in no mood to surrender now. Not after all the hard work of the last month. Withers shot wide when well-placed. Downie was beaten again - this time by a Hudson centre - but Emery headed clear, to the relief of all in the ground. Now the fans redoubled their efforts to help their side. In 69 minutes, Dykes found Hannah who rounded a defender and put over a cross, well out of the 'keeper's reach, for Chapman to hammer in the equaliser. A minute later, Harbertson's shot was tipped over the bar.

Cardiff were still playing well, but Lincoln's sheer determination was beginning to tell. In 74 minutes, Harbertson's pass from the right found Chapman running in. His right-foot shot put Lincoln into the lead. 2-1. But Cardiff came close to ruining things a minute later when Hewitt hit over from close range. With eleven minutes to go, the miracle was complete. Harbertson beat Walsh, just inside the Cardiff half. He body-swerved, sending two defenders the wrong way, and, from at least twenty yards, hit a screamer of a shot which smacked the iron support at the back of the goal before rebounding onto the ground and bouncing up again, before finally resting in the back of the net.

As the final whistle blew on Lincoln's sixth successive win, they had escaped relegation by a single point. The pitch was invaded by enthusiastic youngsters and George Hannah said: *"The tension was worse than Wembley."* The *Lincolnshire Echo* summed it up by saying: *"Not one of the world's greatest showmen could have planned a season's finish so fantastic as this."*

There may not have been much to boast about in Lincolnshire by way of trophies but the locals can take pride in this, surely the most amazing relegation fightback of all time.

ON THE SAME DAY...

News: There are unconfirmed reports of an accidental nuclear explosion in Kamchatka, USSR.

Sport: The 2,000 Guineas is won by 20-1 shot Pall Mall, owned by The Queen.

Entertainment:
The *'Stars of Tomorrow'* are premiered in TV's Carroll Levis Show.

LIVERPOOL 3
Vs Borussia Muchengladbach 1

May 25th 1977 - European Champions Cup Final (Rome)

Liverpool: Clemence, Neal, Jones, Smith, Kennedy, Hughes, Keegan, Case, Heighway, Callaghan, McDermott.

Liverpool had won trophy after trophy in the sixties and seventies. But the one which eluded them, indeed had eluded every English side - bar Manchester United in 1968 - was the European Cup. The supreme title of Champions of Europe was the one the Anfield Reds prized above all. 1976-77 had been yet another glory year for the men from the Mersey. Their League title had been retained and in Europe, where they had twice previously lifted the UEFA Cup, they had at least reached the Final of the big one. And there had been some impressive performances along the way, not least the Quarter-Final victory over the 1976 losing finalists, St. Etienne. Swiss side Zurich had been swept aside in the semi-final with that air of imperious ease instilled into the Anfield players by first Bill Shankly, and latterly, Bob Paisley.

But just four days before the Final in Rome, the first cracks in Liverpool's armour had been exposed. Hot favourites to complete the domestic 'double', they had been beaten in the F.A. Cup Final by Manchester United. So it was with rather less Scouse braggadocio than usual that their supporters awaited this match. Their foes, Munchengladbach, were a class side themselves, and were looking to keep the trophy in West German possession for a fourth successive year by following in the footsteps of triple winners Bayern Munich. Indeed, West Germany were reigning World Champions and had failed to add the mantle of European champions only by virtue of a penalty shoot-out. English football, by contrast, was in one of its periodic downturns, missing out on both World Cups held in the 1970s.

Such a state of affairs might have overawed most clubs, but not Liverpool. They knew that they had already beaten Munchengladbach in the 1973 UEFA Cup Final and, even if playing personnel in both sides had altered somewhat since, that gave them a psychological edge which they were determined to exploit. So it proved in the early stages of the game. Terry McDermott, ably assisted by Case, Kennedy and Callaghan, ran the midfield. But it was still a tough contest. Liverpool's prized forward, Keegan, was well-marked by the wily Vogts and had little opportunity to threaten the Germans. In the Borussia team were players of immense talent like Rainer Bonhof, Uli Stielike, and the Danish star Allan Simonsen. But for once, it was the efficiency of the English side which outshone the individual flair of the Germans, a reversal of the usual stereotype. It was no surprise when the veteran Callaghan robbed Bonhof and sent Heighway free. McDermott demonstrated his cunning by running into the gap to receive the pass from Heighway, striking his shot low and hard into the far corner of the net. Half-time arrived with Liverpool comfortably holding their one-goal lead.

But in the second half, Liverpool almost made the same mistake as Alf Ramsey's England did against a German side in the 1970 World Cup. And in similar circumstances, trying to protect a lead in humid conditions. Liverpool's attempts to conserve energy allowed themselves to be caught out. Case hit a poor pass which was pounced on by Simonsen. The Dane sped into the box and gave Clemence no chance, squaring the match at 1-1. For the next ten minutes, Liverpool came under ferocious attack. The match, and their dreams, looked like slipping away from them when, of all people, Tommy Smith, in the last game of a glorious career, saved the day. From a Heighway corner in the 65th minute, Smith, barely off the ground, hooked the ball home to restore the Reds lead. The calm authority, so typical of Liverpool, was restored to the side. There could only be one winner now. With seven minutes left, Keegan managed to get past Vogts for once. The defender reacted by scything him down. The nerveless Phil Neal struck the penalty away as if he was out on the practice ground. At long last the European Cup was on its way to Merseyside.

Liverpool had won with what the press described as, *"smoothly-skilled intelligent football we had come to believe was a continental monopoly."* The European Cup became an English monopoly for the next few years. Liverpool won three more times, Nottingham Forest twice, and Aston Villa once. Sadly, it all came apart on that horrific evening in the Heysel Stadium. Now, after the restoration of English clubs to European competition, that dominance is long gone. It will be a long time, if ever, before an English team again strides the continental stage the way the Anfield colossus so triumphantly once did.

ON THE SAME DAY...

News: South Moluccan gunmen hold 106 children and 55 adults hostage in two mass kidnappings in the Netherlands.

Sport: Geoff Boycott hits his 30,000th run in cricket.

Entertainment:
TV highlight is the match itself, with *Tom & Jerry* on beforehand, and Andre Previn's *'Music night'* following on BBC-1.

LUTON TOWN 3
Vs Arsenal 2

April 24th 1988 - League Cup Final (Wembley)

Luton Town: Dibble, Breacker, Johnson, Hill, Foster, Donaghy, Wilson, B.Stein, Harford (M.Stein 64) Preece (Grimes 76), Black.

The late 1980s saw Luton Town produce the finest side in their history. They had enjoyed a spell in the First Division in the fifties and played in, and lost, the 1959 F.A. Cup Final. But apart from one solitary term at the top in the seventies, little of note was achieved by the Bedfordshire club until the arrival of David Pleat as manager. Pleat took the club into the top flight and not only did they stay there, they flourished. Pleat's departure to Tottenham left the club in the capable hands of Ray Harford. Luton finished 1986-87 in their best-ever 7th position, and were again in the top half of the table the following season as they charged towards Wembley in the League Cup.

Their path to the Final was not the most difficult ever trodden - Bradford City in the last eight and Oxford in the semi-finals - but it was fully merited. After all, many big clubs had fallen by the wayside at the hands of allegedly inferior opposition. One major side did survive all the way to the Final though, Arsenal. George Graham's team were the holders of the trophy and were among the hottest favourites ever as they took the field for the Final. Perhaps they should have remembered the previous year when Arsenal themselves won as underdogs against Liverpool. With no European place at stake (English clubs had been banned from the continent in the wake of the Heysel disaster), Luton were in the position of genuinely having nothing to lose.

Luton supporters were apprehensive though. There were three 'weak' spots in their team, they thought. Andy Dibble, in goal, was a replacement for the regular custodian Les Sealey, who was out through injury. Ricky Hill was playing his first game since breaking a leg on Boxing Day. Youngster Kingsley Black had just two first-team appearances to his credit. But such worries vanished in the 13th minute when Brian Stein fired Luton ahead. The remainder of the first half was a dour affair. Arsenal came forward. Luton fell back. This pattern was repeated until the half-time whistle. On the rare occasions that Arsenal looked likely to force an equaliser, Dibble proved himself more than equal to the task. After 45 minutes, most fans welcomed the break. It had not been the most riveting of Finals and no-one could have predicted the drama that was to come.

The first quarter of an hour of the second half mostly followed the routine of the first. With no sign of an equaliser coming, Arsenal brought on Martin Hayes as a substitute. Hayes immediately made a difference, carving open the hitherto resolute Luton defence. But, with twenty minutes remaining, Luton still led. The scene was set for one of the most incredible finales that even illustrious Wembley had ever witnessed.

It was Hayes who ignited the match, scrambling in the equaliser from an Alan Smith cross in the 71st minute. Four minutes later, Smith himself scored to put Arsenal 2-1 ahead. It looked like the end for brave Luton. Arsenal's seemingly inexorable drive to victory was apparently confirmed with just nine minutes remaining. David Rocastle sped past Mal Donaghy. The Luton defender brought the Arsenal man down. Penalty! Arsenal, who had missed their previous **five** penalties, entrusted Nigel Winterburn with the task of finishing off the contest. The full-back struck his shot firmly, but Dibble guessed the direction correctly, diving full-length to his left to turn the ball away. The reserve became an instant hero to the Kenilworth Road fans.

Reprieved, Luton stormed back into the match. Sixty seconds later, Arsenal's Caesar allowed himself to be caught in possession and Stein and Black worked the ball to Wilson who headed in to level the game at 2-2. Extra time seemed certain. But, with Dibble and Black having done their bit, it was time for the third member of the supposedly 'weak' trio, Ricky Hill, to enter the fray. Hill sent a lovely pass to Grimes. He, in turn, outpaced Richardson and centred. Brian Stein nipped in front of Winterburn and cracked home a first-time shot seconds before the end of the 90 minutes. The Bedfordshire contingent in the crowd of 95,732 went wild with delight. Luton had won the Cup in the most amazing manner possible. Dibble received the 'Man of the Match' award, and young Black learned that he had been called up into the Northern Ireland squad. But, individual heroics aside, this was a team performance of the highest character, for a team on the verge of defeat to snatch victory in such a thrilling style. A day that will stay in the hearts of Luton fans forever.

ON THE SAME DAY...

News: It was announced that Lord Ramsey, the former Archbishop of Canterbury, had died the day previously.

Sport: Graham Gooch hits his highest score to date, scoring 275 runs for Essex Vs Kent.

Entertainment:
ITV screen *Ian Botham - The Hannibal Test*, as the cricketer, plus elephants, walks over the Alps, raising money for leukaemia research.

MANCHESTER CITY 2

Vs Gornik Zabrze 1
April 29th 1970 - European Cup-Winners Cup Final (Vienna)

Manchester City: Corrigan, Book Pardoe, Doyle (Bowyer), Booth, Oakes, Heslop, Bell, Lee, Young, Towers.

Until the late 1960s, that otherwise memorable decade had been a miserable time for Manchester City fans. Three years spent in the Second Division while their Old Trafford rivals assembled yet another great team was frustrating enough. But even when City forged a powerful side of their own, they still found the shadow of United cast over them. City pipped their great rivals for the League title in 1968 but United went one better by winning the European Cup. City's own initial European excursion proved disastrous, beaten by Turkish side Fenerbache. But the team built by the partnership of Joe Mercer and Malcolm Allison earned plaudits of their own by winning the F.A. Cup in 1969. They had added the third domestic trophy, the League Cup, by the time this match was contested and were clearly a team to be reckoned with.

City's second tilt at Europe had been more successful. Sides of the pedigree of Athletic Bilbao, Lierse, Academica Coimbra and Schalke '04 - not an easy draw among them - had fallen to the Maine Road outfit. Their opponents in the Final, Polish side Gornik Zabrze, were no slouches either, having accounted for Olympiakos, Glasgow Rangers, Levski Spartak and Roma on their way to the Prater stadium in Vienna. It promised to be an intriguing game but, once again, City found themselves over-shadowed, domestically at least, by Old Trafford. Not by United this time, but their rivals ground was in use for the first F.A. Cup Final replay for nearly sixty years, and that was the match that British Television chose to cover the same evening.

Nor was the magnificent Prater looking its best. Just 10,000 supporters, mainly from Manchester, gathered to see a confident start by City. Francis Lee was the first to show. He hit a ferocious ninth-minute shot from close range but Gornik 'keeper Kostka's spectacular leap turned the ball away. Three minutes later and Lee, again, had the ball. From the left, he blasted a drive that Kostka couldn't hold and Neil Young moved in to put City ahead. Their fans fears were alleviated. Their great worry had been that injured hero Mike Summerbee's absence in front of goal would cost them. But now Young, scorer of the only goal in the 1969 Cup Final, had laid those fears to rest.

Malcolm Allison had promised an aggressive approach before the game and that was certainly being borne out. Perhaps a shade too aggressive. For Mike Doyle was badly injured in a clash with Gornik's Florinski. Initially City played with ten men. Only when it became clear that Doyle was in no fit stage to return did substitute Ian Bowyer take the field.

Close to the break, Young found himself free down the middle and tried to dribble round Kostka, only for the Polish goalie to bring him down. Sides in England already knew that it was fatal to concede a penalty to Manchester City. The Poles learnt the same lesson the hard way, as Francis Lee, the most-feared penalty taker in the game, put City 2-0 up at the interval.

City appeared to be coasting to victory when the Poles struck midway through the second half. Their most dangerous player, Lubanski, had been marked out of the game by Heslop, but broke free in the 68th minute to provide an opening for Oslizlo who reduced the deficit to 2-1. It was the only real error in the City defence all evening. Briefly encouraged, Gornik enjoyed their best spell of the match, coming close to equalising. City regained their composure and Young and Lee set up Bowyer with a good chance, only to see the nervous youngster shoot wide. There were no more real chances after that and City were acclaimed by their supporters at the end of the match when the rain-soaked fans gave their heroes a rapturous welcome. It had been an excellent victory. Only those who were there realised that the match had been nowhere as close as the score suggested. Joe Mercer thought that, *"the heavy rain ruined the game."* His Polish counterpart, Michael Matyas, lavished praise on his team's conquerors. *"Manchester City are a great team,"* he said. A view that would be endorsed by those who had travelled to Vienna and by thousands more Mancunians back home.

This should have been the opportunity for City to break free from the spectre of United. The Old Trafford team were entering a serious decline. The chance was there for the Maine Road team to re-establish their pre-war primacy in Manchester. However, it never happened. City came close to further success over the next few seasons but only the 1976 League Cup has been added to the trophy cabinet since then. They remain a club with the potential to be as big as any in the game. For a brief period in the 1960s and 1970s they achieved it.

City join the European elite - Tony Book holds aloft the trophy.

ON THE SAME DAY...

News: The USA, embroiled in the Vietnam War, admit 'incursions' into neighbouring, and neutral, Cambodia.

Sport: Quite a day. Lester Piggott, on Nijinsky, wins the 2,000 Guineas in the afternoon and Chelsea beat Leeds United in the replayed F.A. Cup Final in the evening.

Entertainment: A choice of styles on TV. ITV has the thriller series *'Callan'* starring Edward Woodward, while BBC-1 plumps for comedy with Peter Cook and Dudley Moore in *'Not only but also'*.

MANCHESTER UNITED 4
Vs Benfica 1

May 29th 1968 - European Champions Cup Final (Wembley)

Manchester United: Stepney, Brennan, Dunne, Crerand, Foulkes, Stiles, Best, Kidd, Charlton, Sadler, Aston.

Manchester United and the European Cup is the story of football's Holy Grail. The first English side to enter the competition, they had reached two successive semi-finals. But their chance of success disappeared after a quarter-final tie in Belgrade in 1958 when the flower of a generation was destroyed amid the carnage of a wreck-strewn Munich runway. Their manager, Matt Busby, had considered giving up the game after that horrific night but had been persuaded to carry on, and once again he had built a United side that could stand comparisons with the best.

There had been another semi-final defeat, in 1966, before United embarked on their fourth attempt to lift the greatest prize in club football. No English team had so much as played in a Final, but 1967 saw the Latin stranglehold on the trophy broken by Jock Stein's Celtic, proving that the British game could triumph in the hardest arena of all. United's 1968 campaign started gently with a win over Hibernians of Malta. Stiffer competition in the shape of Yugoslavia's Sarajevo and Polish side Gornik Zabrze were accounted for as United reached their customary semi-final place. A 1-0 Old Trafford lead against Real Madrid hardly seemed enough and when United trailed 3-1 on the night, 3-2 on aggregate, in the Bernabeu stadium, defeat stared them in the face once more. But, in true heroic fashion, the English champions battled back to gain a 3-3 draw and a 4-3 aggregate victory which saw them overcome that semi-final barrier at long last.

With the Final at Wembley, United would normally have expected to start as clear favourites. This wasn't the case. There were those who reckoned the sheer emotion of the occasion would prove too much for a side so cruelly deprived, through injury, of the brilliant Denis Law. A cogent threat lay in the shape of their opponents. Benfica had won the title in 1961 and 1962. They had lost in the Final (at Wembley) in 1963 and again in 1965. They were the most experienced side on the continent. Many of their players were members of the Portuguese team that had thrilled football when finishing 3rd in the 1966 World Cup. And, in Eusebio, they had a player ranked second only to Pele himself; and there were those who proclaimed the Benfica player to be superior.

100,000, almost all supporting United, packed Wembley. Millions more watched on TV. Many of these had little or no interest in football but were moved by the memory of Munich and the sentiment of the occasion to cheer on Busby's side. In Manchester, the doors and windows of the city's pubs were thrown open so that the game could be viewed from the streets. Yet the first 45 minutes saw little to cheer the millions watching. United's fans were strangely, and nervously, silent. The loudest noise was the referee's whistle, and that was in use often enough. Benfica's Cruz made several tackles on George Best. Nobby Stiles, for United, did likewise to Eusebio. In turn, the great Eusebio committed a foul on Pat Crerand, a little akin to a chihuahua biting a rottweiler. Finally, the referee took action, booking Humberto for a foul on Best. By the time the teams reached the dressing rooms, with the game goalless, there had been 31 free kicks awarded, 17 to Benfica, 14 to United.

The second half was a transformation, as the game at last began to live up to its billing. In 55 minutes, Sadler's chip was met by Bobby Charlton's head and United were in front. The game ebbed and flowed in a manner more fitting to Europe's two finest sides. But United - calm confident United - edged ever closer to that elusive triumph. Then, with ten minutes left, Graca hit the equaliser for Benfica. At once the balance of the game altered. Now it was the Portuguese who made all the running. Twice, Eusebio broke away from his markers and twice Alex Stepney was on hand to deny him with magnificent saves. As the signal went for the end of 90 minutes, Benfica were playing superb football. United looked a spent force.

While their fans feared the worst, United set about extra time with a relish. From somewhere deep within they found fresh legs and new resolution. In 93 minutes, Best threw off the shackles imposed on him and picked up a header from Kidd. He avoided a lunging tackle, then, in typical nonchalant style, sauntered round 'keeper Henrique to coolly slot the ball into the net. Almost immediately, United won a corner. Charlton floated it over. The ball bobbed from head to head before Brian Kidd nodded home the third goal. It was Kidd's 19th birthday and a present unlike any other teenager would ever receive. With ten minutes of the first extra period played, Kidd set up Charlton who shot past the 'keeper to make it 4-1, and effectively end the contest. Benfica were numbed by it all. They had little left to offer, a Eusebio shot which Stepney saved with one hand was all the resistance they could muster.

The European Cup belonged to Manchester United at last. No-one could ever bring back those who lost their lives so tragically at Munich but if ever a tribute to those departed can have any sort of meaning, then there could be no finer salute than this. Busby spoke simply but with more depth than the most eloquent of orators when he said, *"I am proud of them all."* His tear-filled eyes bore testimony to the truth of his words. Benfica boss Otto Gloria acknowledged United's triumph, saying: *"The title is in very good hands."*

In Manchester, tears of joy swelled the air in recognition of the achievement of the heroes of the present, and tears of regret spoke volumes in memory of the titans of the past. The repercussions of United's victory were felt in the most unlikely places. Prime Minister Harold Wilson saw his government's majority fall from over 90 to just 18 as MP's ignored the division bell in the House of Commons and stayed on to watch extra time. And, hours later, one solitary fan could be seen, clad only in his underpants, splashing about merrily in the fountains in Trafalgar Square.

Amazingly, six years later, United were in the Second Division. Restored immediately by Tommy Doherty, he, and successors Dave Sexton and Ron Atkinson laboured to bring the League title back to Old Trafford. Without success. It took the arrival of Alex Ferguson to land that honour once more. But for all their achievements of the 1990s, Manchester United still live in the shadow of the class of '68. Their supporters will not be content until the European Cup is on display in the United boardroom once again.

ON THE SAME DAY...

News: 250,000 workers march through Paris demanding the resignation of President Charles de Gaulle.

Sport: Victory for Lester Piggott on odds-on favourite Sir Ivor in the Derby.

Entertainment: After the match and the news, BBC-1 show a play with the unfortunate, (if you were a Benfica fan) title, *'The Loser'*.

One disastrous season in the old Second Division and a Freight Rover Trophy Victory is the sum total of concrete achievements Mansfield Town have garnered since joining the League in 1931. So success in the F.A. Cup is not usually at the forefront of Stags fans minds. But for a brief, glorious period in the late sixties, it was different. Then there were dreams of reaching Wembley in the real thing, not the midweek filler for 3rd and 4th Division sides that eventually saw them arrive at the twin towers in 1987.

MANSFIELD TOWN 3

Vs West Ham United 0
February 26th 1969 - F.A. Cup Round 5

Mansfield Town: Hollins, Pate, Hopkinson, Quigley, Boam, Waller, Keeley, Sharkey, Ledger, Roberts, Goodfellow.

The goal imbued Roberts with unbounded confidence and, almost from the re-start, he dispossessed Billy Bonds. Roberts looked certain to score until a timely intervention from Stevenson saved West Ham. Fired-up Stags bombarded the Hammers goal. Ledger shot narrowly wide from twenty yards. Roberts flicked on to Sharkey in a good position but Hammers 'keeper Ferguson dived to grab the ball from his feet.

Mansfield spent season 1968-69 struggling to avoid relegation to the bottom division. Wins over Tow Law Town and Rotherham United in the F.A. Cup were mere diversions from that arduous task. But a magnificent 2-1 victory over Sheffield United in the third round, followed by a gentle home pairing against Southend United, which the Stags won 2-1, saw talk of Cup glory bandied about the Nottinghamshire town. The draw for the fifth round seemed to put paid to such idle gossip. Stags next opponents at their Field Mill ground were West Ham United, the side of Moore, Hurst and Peters. A cultured, skilful, attacking side, capable of drawing a huge crowd to the game but also capable of inflicting defeat on even the very top sides when their individual flair gelled as a team.

For most of the 21,117 watching, it looked like Mansfield boss Tom Eggleston would have been better concentrating on avoiding the drop, instead of thinking about the Cup, as West Ham tore the Stags apart in the early part of the game. A shot from Lindsay was headed out by Waller. Then Johnny Sissons headed narrowly over. Trevor Brooking set up Harry Redknapp but the forward blasted way over the top. Hollins, in goal, had his work cut out but demonstrated his ability by diving bravely to save from the feet of Geoff Hurst. Martin Peters shot wide, as did Redknapp. Mansfield did threaten a couple of times but the West Ham barrage continued. A cross from Brooking found Hurst in the six-yard box. The usually-lethal England man shot wide when it looked easier to score.

Mansfield boss Tom Eggleston had been enduring agony in the dug-out. But, as the twenty minute mark passed with Hurst's incredible miss, both he and the Stags fans began to feel that the storm may have been weathered. So did the players. Now it was Mansfield's turn to go on the offensive. After 22 minutes, Keeley, Goodfellow and Sharkey combined to take the Hammers defence apart, allowing Dudley Roberts to score for the Stags.

West Ham tried to retaliate. From a Moore free kick on the edge of the area, Peters forced Hollins into making a fine save. Roberts set off on another run for Mansfield but was brought down from behind by Moore, causing the Field Mill crowd to vent their wrath on the England Captain. In 39 minutes, Goodfellow sent over a dangerous-looking cross. Ferguson punched clear from the head of Roberts but the ball travelled only as far as Keeley, who cracked home a superb volley. Half-time arrived with the almost unbelievable scoreline, Mansfield Town 2 - West Ham United 0.

The Stags were still on top in the second half. Roberts headed over. Sharkey's shot was beaten out. Then Ferguson dived at Sharkey's feet and looked to have won the ball, but, somehow, Sharkey won it back and knocked it into the far corner to put Mansfield 3-0 up. Only 49 minutes had been played. The Hammers moved Moore up into attack, a sign of sheer desperation. Bobby Moore may have been the finest defender in the world but as an attacking force he was in the novice class. It was Mansfield who finished in charge. Keeley and Sharkey both went close and the home side might even have had a penalty when Roberts was brought down in the box, but play was allowed to continue. It was a performance unlike any ever seen at Field Mill and Hammers boss Ron Greenwood was generous in his assessment. *"They are a great team,"* said the future England manager. While Geoff Hurst claimed, *"they weren't far short of supermen."* Stags boss Eggleston was more guarded: *"We could be the first 3rd Division side to reach the F.A. Cup Final and get relegated."*

Alas, there was to be no Wembley joy for Mansfield. They gave Leicester City a run for their money in the Quarter-Finals before succumbing 1-0. But they didn't get relegated either. It would be 25 years before their fans witnessed anything similar, when Mansfield knocked Leeds United out of the League Cup. But that was in an earlier round in a tourney which, though important, does not retain the glamour of the F.A. Cup. For Mansfield, their greatest day remains the one when they sent the soccer aristocrats of West Ham, three World Cup winners, et al, spinning out of the F.A. Cup.

The 1968/69 Mansfield Town squad.

ON THE SAME DAY...

News: A major Vietcong offensive is launched against 50 towns and military bases in South Vietnam.

Sport: Champion jockey Josh Gifford is rushed to hospital after falling from a mount at Windsor. But he recovers in time to return and ride the 7-2 winner Jewel of Spring in the last race of the day.

Entertainment: Stars of the children's ITV show *'Do not adjust your set'*, include Eric Idle, Michael Palin and David Jason, amongst others.

MIDDLESBROUGH 1

Vs Manchester City 0
January 13th 1976
League Cup Semi-Final (1st Leg)

Middlesbrough: Platt, Craggs, Bailey, Souness, Boam,
Maddren, Murdoch, Mills, Hickton (Foggon 69),
Cooper, Armstrong.

Middlesbrough supporters regard their side as a big club, one which should be right in the hunt for honours. However, this has rarely proved to be the case. Apart from the Amateur Cup, back in the 19th Century, the major prizes never found a home at Ayresome Park. And, after missing out on top flight football for **twenty** years, 'Boro fans expected great things of the team managed by Jack Charlton when they finally returned to Division One in 1974. With a team containing old heads Terry Cooper and Bobby Murdoch, precocious young talents Graeme Souness, David Mills and David Armstrong, backed up by international 'keeper Jim Platt and a host of other solid professionals, they were entitled to their expectations. And, in 1975-76, it looked like they might achieve them. Middlesbrough embarked on a long League Cup run and, on a passionate night at Burnley, won their way through to their first-ever Semi-Final in a major competition. As they prepared to face Manchester City over two legs, they knew that something special might be on the cards, an all North-East Cup Final. The other last four clash was between Spurs and 'Boro's great rivals Newcastle United.

The mouth-watering prospect brought out a full-house crowd of 35,000 to Ayresome Park on a cold January evening for this game. And those spectators saw a match played at a breakneck pace, with 'Boro doing most of the attacking. John Craggs, one of the best uncapped backs in England, rampaged on the overlap, causing havoc in the City defence. But the burly Craggs wasted the best chance to fall his way when he sliced a volley wide. Mills, Armstrong and veteran striker John Hickton all went close for Middlesbrough. But City seemed to be coping well with the relentless pressure. A Souness free kick put giant City 'keeper Joe Corrigan in trouble, full-back Barrett hooking the ball against his own bar in a desperate attempt to clear. Cooper's follow-up hit the post, with 'Boro players screaming that it had crossed the line. Their frantic appeals came to nothing, the linesman's flag stayed studiously down.

For over an hour City frustrated the Middlesbrough charge. But in 66 minutes, centre-half Stuart Boam moved down the right flank, passed to Cooper then sped quickly to receive the return, heading on to Hickton. The big hitman cracked an instant right-foot shot past Corrigan from fifteen yards to give 'Boro the goal that had looked like it would never come. Three minutes later, Hickton, the tireless workhorse who had run all night, was substituted by Alan Foggon. After nearly 450 matches for the club, he left the field to applause as loud as any heard before.

'Boro made only occasional breaks thereafter, fearful of losing a goal. They were content to protect their lead, an attitude typical of Charlton's sides but one which, though it may work well in the League, is potentially dangerous in cup-ties. Although the 'Boro fans roared their appreciation of their team's 1-0 win, Manchester City did not appear too disconsolate as they headed for the dressing room.

That guarded optimism proved to be an accurate assessment of how things would go in the second leg. For once, 'Boro proved unable to defend to their usual standards. City scored early on and eventually overran the Teessiders 4-0 before going on to beat Newcastle in the Final. For Middlesbrough, it was the first time they ever got close to one of the game's really big prizes. True, they did win the Anglo-Scottish Cup the same season and finally played at Wembley in the ZDS Cup in 1990, as well as reaching another League Cup Semi-final in 1992, when they lost narrowly to Manchester United. But that great, untapped Teesside potential still lies bubbling under, waiting to explode. One day, perhaps, it will.

ON THE SAME DAY...

News: Two Provisional IRA terrorists are blown up by their own bomb in Belfast.

Sport: The F.A.'s Match & Ground Committee recommends that kissing and cuddling by players after a goal is scored, and gestures to the crowd, should lead to a charge of bringing the game into disrepute.

Entertainment: BBC-1's *Play for Today* is an instant classic, Mike Leigh's *Nuts in May*.

MILLWALL 1
Vs Sunderland 2

April 10th 1937 - F.A. Cup Semi-Final (Huddersfield)

Millwall: Yuill, E.Smith, Inns, Brolly, Wallbanks, Forsyth, Thomas, Burditt, Mangnall, McCartney, J.R.Smith.

Third Division (South) side Millwall played like a team possessed in the F.A. Cup of 1936-37. They had already done well to reach the fifth round when they produced a brace of victories which stunned soccer. First, they beat Derby County, runners-up in the League the previous season and in 4th place this time round. That home win was followed by another, also at The Den. This time their victims were Manchester City, the team destined to win that year's League title. Millwall had reached the Semi-finals of the F.A. Cup. Old supporters could recall 1900 and 1903 when the club had advanced to the same stage while in the Southern League. But this was the first time that a team from Division Three had progressed so far in the competition.

Having disposed of the Champions-elect, Millwall found that their path to Wembley was barred by the reigning Champions, Sunderland. Fearsome they may have been, but Sunderland had never won the F.A. Cup, a fact that gave Millwall cause for hope. The choice of venue for the tie was controversial. Huddersfield may not have exactly been next door to Roker Park but the Yorkshire ground was undoubtedly an easier place to travel to for the Wearside fans than it was for those from London's docklands. In the days before the motorway, an arduous journey awaited Millwall's supporters, but, although outnumbered, there were still plenty of them among the 62,813 who greeted the two teams as they walked out for the match.

There was almost a goal in the first minute when Sunderland's Gurney broke through and fired in a strong shot. But Yuill was equal to the task, bringing off a great save. Millwall's tackling was quick and direct. And it had to be against a talented Sunderland combination. After ten minutes, Millwall began to come into the match in their own right. Inns booted the ball a long way downfield. McCartney headed on to Mangnall who pulled the ball down, and drove an unstoppable shot straight into the net. The Sunderland defence and 'keeper had no chance. With their first serious attempt of the match, Millwall were in front. Wembley beckoned.

Sunderland's Gurney tried to bring his side back into the game but shot wide from a good position. Generally though, Millwall were coping well, preventing the Roker men from building attacks. They were faster to the ball than the Northerners, thanks mainly to Inns, who was outstanding in defence. The game was almost interrupted by the crowd. Pressure of numbers forced the fans onto the track but the police managed to keep them back.

At length Sunderland began to force a series of corners. One of these, in 29 minutes, produced a shot from Roker hero Raich Carter. Yuill pushed it out for what looked like another corner but Gurney, from an angle that looked impossible, somehow managed to squeeze the ball in for the equaliser. Sunderland upped the tempo with Carter testing Yuill twice more with good attempts which produced equally fine saves. But Millwall could attack too. Mapson, the Sunderland 'keeper, missed a Thomas corner which was cleared off the line. Then Burditt found himself free with the goal at his mercy, but, incredibly, missed. The break was reached with the honours even at 1-1.

Millwall's early second half attacks were met with a vigorous Sunderland response. Yuill tipped a Burbanks shot over then, twice more, had to make saves from the same player. The Champions were getting on top, and winning a lot of corners. A Carter header saw Yuill beaten for once, but the danger was cleared. His opposite number, Mapson, had only one free kick and one shot to save in the entire half. But, with only a few minutes left, and just as it looked that Millwall would earn a replay, a header from the hitherto quiet Gallacher beat Yuill to give Sunderland the lead, and the match.

Millwall fans invaded the pitch, but not with the venomous intent associated with them latterly. This time they wanted to demonstrate their appreciation of their heroes who had fought so gallantly. None more so than Yuill, who was chaired off the pitch by the Lions fans. Sunderland went on to lift the Cup for the first time, but their hardest match had come from Millwall, the Lions who were the pride of the lower Leagues. Other Third Division outfits have reached the semi-finals since then, but none have won through to the Final. It seems increasingly that none ever will. Even if they do, Millwall's place in history is assured, the first 3rd Division team to play in an F.A. Cup semi-final.

ON THE SAME DAY...

News: Government troops advance against Franco's forces on the Madrid front during the Spanish Civil War.

Sport: Preston claim the other Cup Final place, beating West Bromwich Albion 3-0.

Entertainment:
On a night when the top radio show is *'Music Hall'*, starring Tessie O'Shea, Sir Thomas Beecham attacked the BBC monopoly of the airwaves at the AGM of the National Federation of Music Societies.

NEWCASTLE UNITED 3

Vs Ujpest Dosza 0

May 29th 1969 - Fairs Cup Final (1st leg)

Newcastle United: McFaul, Craig, Clark, Gibb, Burton, Moncur, Scott, Robson, Davies, Arentoft, Sinclair (Foggon 70).

Newcastle United made their European debut in the 1968-69 Fairs Cup, but by rights they should never have ventured from British shores. Only a combination of the most freakish circumstances allowed their name to go forward as England were granted four places for the first time. United had struggled to retain the 1st Division place they had regained in 1965. Finishing 10th in 1968 with 41 points from 42 games meant mid-table security but hardly seemed the launch pad for a tilt at Europe. However, both Manchester clubs took part in the European Cup and 7th place West Brom were the Cup-Winners Cup entrants. Three prospective Fairs Cup entrants, 5th placed Everton, Spurs (7th) and Arsenal (9th) were all ruled out of contention by the 'one club, one city rule', giving United their chance. Few expected them to make anything of it.

But when over 46,000 turned up to see Newcastle carve out an impressive 4-0 win over a Feyenoord side that would win the following year's European Cup, the Geordies took to Europe the way they once loved the F.A. Cup. So, although Newcastle did little better in the League than in 1968, in Europe they were transformed. And they had to be. Seldom, if ever, can a side have had such a rough baptism in continental competition. After safely negotiating Rotterdam, losing 2-0 for a 4-2 aggregate win, their next stop was Lisbon. The famous Sporting Club were strong favourites but Newcastle earned a 1-1 draw away before winning the home leg 1-0. It then took the away goals rule for them to overcome Spanish giants Real Zaragoza before comfortably despatching another Portuguese team, Setubal, in the last eight. A defiant 0-0 draw at Ibrox in the semi-finals set the scene for a famous 2-0 win over Rangers at St. James Park, a victory marred by the attempts of some Scottish supporters to get the game abandoned with a pitch invasion when their side went two down.

So it was that the rookies from the North-East ended up facing crack Hungarians Ujpest Dosza in the Final. A full-house 60,000 crowd gathered, in some trepidation, for the match. For Ujpest had eliminated the holders, Leeds United, and Leeds were running away with the English League. Nor had Ujpest lost a match in the competition, while United's progress was dependent on their fortress of St. James. Two draws and three defeats being the results on their travels. A resounding home victory was imperative, if they were to have a chance.

Wyn Davies and Bryan 'Pop' Robson tried hard to find a way through the wily Magyar defence. But, even when they threatened the goal, the 'keeper, Szentimihalyi, was on top form. The custodian's name may have sounded exotic to the Geordie crowd, but it's English translation, St. Michael, was probably labelled on their underwear. And although at times, it may have seemed that the 'keeper was flying by the seat of his pants, more than an hour elapsed with the game still goalless. That was when the United fairytale arrived. After 63 minutes, Tommy Gibb flighted a free kick into the crowded penalty area. Davies pounced but shot against the goalie. Following up was Newcastle skipper Bobby Moncur whose left foot shot landed in the corner of the net. The Scottish international had been eight years at St. James, and this was his first goal in a competitive match. It took him just eight more minutes to get his second. Moncur picked the ball up in midfield, played a one-two with Arentoft before lashing the ball home from eighteen yards. With six minutes remaining, Tyneside went wild. A move forged between Arentoft and Scott ended with the latter making it 3-0. The fans invaded the pitch, but, unlike the semi-final, this was a good-natured, joyous occasion. Manager Joe Harvey was jubilant, telling reporters, *"I think we've got one hand on the Cup now."* His Hungarian counterpart, Lajos Baroti, refused to concede anything, saying, *"We can still win."* With players in his team like Fazekas, Dunai and the feared Ferenc Bene, the second leg was anything but a formality.

So it proved. By half-time United were 2-0 down and one slender goal ahead on aggregate. But the incredible Moncur scored again to restore calm to Newcastle. The Geordies, unchanged from the first game, hit two more through Arentoft and substitute Foggon to win for the first time on continental soil. The *News of the World* summed it up. Newcastle's victims were from the, *"Debrett of European football."* It was the, *"miracle of Tyneside."* Joe Harvey returned with the Cup in his hands and led the airport crowd in an impromptu rendition of 'Blaydon Races', the Geordie anthem. Newcastle had won Leagues and Cups in the past, but, never in history had such a low-placed team taken apart the cream of the continent.

ON THE SAME DAY...

News: Traffic grinds to a halt in Paris as thousands cheer and sound their horns when the prototype Concorde 001 flies over the Champs Elysee on its way to the Paris Air show.

Sport: The North-East's cricketing hero, Colin Milburn, had ten stitches removed after losing his left eye in a road accident the previous weekend.

Entertainment: A sporting evening of a sort. Match highlights from St. James followed by the *World Amateur Ballroom Dancing Championships* in the BBC-1 menu.

NORTHAMPTON TOWN 4

April 17th 1965 - Division Two

Northampton Town: Harvey, Foley, Everitt, Leck, Carr,
Kiernan, Walden, Martin, Brown, Hunt, Robson

Re-organisation of English football in 1958 had placed Northampton Town in the 4th Division. They had won promotion from that sphere in 1961 and two years later lifted the Third Division title, sending them into the Second Division for the first time. A year spent consolidating in mid-table was followed by this magical term when the Cobblers were up among the front-runners from the word go. The tantalising prospect of becoming the first team to climb from the bottom division to the top, and to do it inside four years, drove them on. They jockeyed with Newcastle for pole position but were aware that the chasing pack could still destroy the dream. Gradually though, the rest fell away. Come Good Friday 1965, and a defeat for 3rd placed Bolton at leaders Newcastle, and the prize was almost within reach. The following day saw Northampton travel to Bury, knowing that if they won and Bolton failed to take both points from Rotherham, then the Cobblers had arrived in the top League.

But Bury needed the points too if they wanted to retain a Division Two spot. So, an exciting game was in prospect for the 6,800, including a good Northampton contingent, who turned up at Gigg Lane. Bury took the early initiative, Carr sliding along the mud to foil Alston. Harvey checked Eastham's progress before Bury's Griffin shot just over the bar. But, in their first attack, Northampton scored. Walden's flick to Brown was squared to Kiernan, who belted in a powerful drive off the post from twenty yards. Only five minutes had been played. In fourteen minutes, Brown tried a shot which struck off Bury 'keeper Harker's leg and dropped under the bar to put the Cobblers two ahead.

Bury fought back. Durrant shot over the diving Harvey to make it 2-1 with 21 minutes gone. A Lindsay shot looked like equalising before flying inches past the post. Then came a dangerous corner which Carr rose to clear. Northampton were looking ropey, the effects of their hard season were beginning to tell on them.

But Carr's composure began to translate itself to his colleagues. The storm was weathered and Northampton resumed the offensive. In 39 minutes, Martin restored their two-goal advantage. Half-time proved a welcome respite. The Cobblers re-started the better side, their covering was more secure. The defence were determined to do nothing silly, now that their prize was in sight. Martin added a second goal of his own, making it 4-1. Northampton left the Gigg Lane field to the ringing cheers of their fans while waiting for news of Bolton. In the dressing room, manager Dave Bowen phoned the BBC. Upon hearing that Bolton had only drawn, he turned to his players and said simply,

"you are up." The dressing room erupted into wild scenes of delight, quickly joined in by the waiting fans and by the thousands back home. Northampton had achieved what many doubted possible.

Huge crowds turned up to see their heroes at Northampton's two remaining home games at the County Ground; 19,718 saw a 3-1 win over Plymouth on Easter Tuesday, and 20,660 turned up to see Portsmouth veteran Jimmy Dickinson's last League appearance in a 1-1 draw the following Saturday. It wasn't enough to catch Newcastle though, as the Geordies finished a point ahead to take the title.

Sadly, Northampton's stay at the top was destined to be limited. Though not disgraced, they struggled all season, a 4-2 home defeat by Fulham before the County Ground's record gate of 24,523 in late April 1966 proved decisive, as the Craven Cottagers finished two points ahead of Northampton. By 1969 the Cobblers were back in the bottom division. With odd exceptions that is where they have stayed. But with the reality of a brand new ground (something mooted as far back as 1965) it may be time for Northampton to go on the march once more.

ON THE SAME DAY...

News: Deposed Soviet leader, Nikita Khruschev is reported to have spent a quite 71st birthday at his Moscow home.

Sport: Real Madrid win the Spanish League for a record fifth successive season.

Entertainment:
Althrop, near Northampton, the home of Earl Spencer, is open to the public over the Easter weekend. Admission 3/6 (17½p). No stilettos are allowed, a rule not adhered to later in life by his then four year old daughter, Lady Diana.

Norwich City should have entered Europe long before the 1993-94 season. A spate of high League finishes in the late 1980s, would normally have been enough to see the Canaries establish themselves as regular continental contenders. But Norwich's high spots were hit at the time when English clubs were exiled from Europe following the Heysel Stadium disaster. So it was that they had to wait until they finished a highest-ever 3rd in 1992-93, before they could enter the lists abroad.

Vitesse Arnhem were their first opponents in the UEFA Cup and three second half goals at Carrow Road proved to be good enough as Norwich earned a 0-0 draw in the Netherlands. There next foes were in a different class entirely. Bayern Munich had a European pedigree stretching back nearly thirty years. Five times European Cup finalists, winning three in a row in the 70s, former Cup-Winners Cup winners, perhaps the only comfort for the Euro-new boys from East Anglia lay in the fact that the UEFA Cup was the one competition in which Bayern had yet to reach the Final. But with world class players like the Dutchman Jan Wouters and Germany's World Cup-winning captain, Lothar Matthaus in their ranks, few expected an upset.

Certainly not in the first leg, for Bayern had never been beaten by a British team on Bavarian soil. And Norwich were missing Ekoku and Polston, two of their most influential players. But Bayern boss Uli Hoeness warned his club's supporters that Norwich were no pushovers. And thirteen minutes into the game he was proved right. Newman's centre was poorly dealt with by Matthaus and Jeremy Goss cracked home a right-foot volley, stunning most of the 28,500 crowd into silence. But an injury to Robins upset the Canaries. His replacement, Sutch, soon proved himself in action. He was sent through by Prior and forced international 'keeper Aumann to touch his shot into the side-netting. Then the Bayern custodian blocked a good header from Butterworth. With each minute that passed, Norwich grew in confidence. After half an hour, Ian Crook's free kick rose over the defence and Bowen stole in to head home from six yards. 2-0 to Norwich, a sensational scoreline.

Bayern Munich 1 Vs
NORWICH CITY 2

October 19th 1993
UEFA Cup Round Two (1st Leg)

Norwich City: Gunn, Prior, Culverhouse, Butterworth, Newman, Fox, Crook, Goss, Bowen, Sutton, Robins (Sutch 15)

Now Bayern were forced to come at them. And they did so with some style. Nerlinger saw his attempt blocked by Butterworth. In 40 minutes, Bayern pulled one back. Jorginho's cross was met by Nerlinger and he headed, bullet-like, past Bryan Gunn. A daunting second half lay in store for Norwich.

Bayern were desperate to equalise. They were experienced enough to know that a two-goal triumph in Norfolk was a tall order. Valencia's shot was well held by Gunn. Then a header from the same player brought out a diving save by the Scotland 'keeper. Try as they might, Bayern could not force a way through. At the end of 90 minutes, Norwich had achieved what on many occasions Liverpool, Everton, 'Spurs, Rangers and others had been incapable of, winning in the Olympic Stadium, Munich.

There was still the second leg to play but Norwich manager Mike Walker fired off a triumphal message to the beaten Germans, *"I hope that when Bayern come to Norwich they will be frightened to death of us."* That was possibly stretching things too far, but the 20,829 who saw Norwich clinch their place in the next round with a 0-0 draw certainly knew their team was in command all the way. The third round brought an equally famous name, Inter Milan, to Norfolk, but a Dennis Bergkamp penalty in the first leg in Norwich and another Bergkamp strike in Milan were enough to separate the teams as Inter went on to win the UEFA Cup. One month after defeat in Milan, Norwich were rocked by Mike Walker's defection to Everton. Their promising season ended in mid-table and with the loss of top players like Ruel Fox and Chris Sutton, followed by relegation in 1995, what seemed like the start of a European era in East Anglia now looks more likely to have been a brief, but exhilarating interlude.

ON THE SAME DAY...

News: Benazir Bhutto becomes Prime Minister of Pakistan for the second time.

Sport: Garry Kasparov retains his world chess champion title after a one-sided series against Britain's Nigel Short.

Entertainment: The 23rd series of *'A Question of Sport'* starts on BBC1.

The final whistle, and Norwich City have beaten Bayern Munich in the Olympic Stadium.

NOTTINGHAM FOREST 1
Vs Malmo 0

May 30th 1979 - European Champions Cup Final (Munich)

Nottingham Forest: Shilton, Anderson, Clark, McGovern, Lloyd, Burns, Francis, Bowyer, Birtles, Woodcock, Robertson

Stuck in the Second Division, Nottingham Forest appointed the controversial, but brilliant, Brian Clough as manager in 1975. With his long-time assistant, Peter Taylor, alongside him, Clough began to fashion a team which would rival, then eclipse, the one he had built at Derby. Squeezing into a promotion spot in 1977, he then signed England 'keeper Peter Shilton and was rewarded as his Forest side swept to the League Championship in their first season back at the top. With a League Cup victory into the bargain, Forest began their assault on Europe in good heart. Forest had only two brief sojourns into Europe in the 1960s to their name. And there was no great expectation of a lasting continental adventure this time when they were paired with the reigning European champions, Liverpool, in the first round.

Forest though, were virtually unbeatable by English sides at this time, going 42 League matches without defeat from November 1977 - December 1978, and they built a 2-0 1st leg lead at their City Ground before eliminating the holders by virtue of a 0-0 draw at Anfield. AEK Athens and Grasshoppers Zurich were swept aside with ease as Forest reached the semi-finals. But a 3-3 draw at home to German champions Cologne placed their quest in jeopardy. Clough, the master tactician and motivator, knew otherwise. His charges won 1-0 in Germany to reach the European Cup Final at their first attempt.

Their opponents, the Swedish side Malmo, were not highly-rated. But, under the astute leadership of English boss Bob Houghton, they had performed creditably in becoming the first side from their country to reach any European Final. As Monaco, Dynamo Kiev, Wisla Krakow and Austria WAC, all beaten by the Swedes, would testify. And Forest had to face the Final in Munich's Olympic Stadium deprived of the services of two of their leading players. Both Martin O'Neill and Archie Gemmill had to miss the match as a result of injury. Clough had an ace up his sleeve though. Apart from remoulding his team to take account of the missing stars, he had signed Trevor Francis, British football's first million-pound transfer, from Birmingham City with one intention in mind, to bring the European Cup to Nottingham..

So it was that Forest, in their first season in the competition, were overwhelming favourites and Francis made his European debut at the highest level of all. But it didn't look good at the start. The normally-reliable Kenny Burns casually mis-hit a back-pass in ten minutes and Kindvall pounced. But the striker, a European Cup winner with Feyenoord in 1970, shot straight into Shilton's arms. It was a dreadful error and an amazing let-off for Forest. The shock stung Forest into action. They began to play more like English champions. And Francis was everywhere. There couldn't have been a blade of grass on the pitch which didn't feel the imprint of his boots. He even helped out in defence. Twice though, Francis weaved his way through the Swedes but his final passes came to nothing.

Bowyer sent a long ball to Francis which was knocked on to Anderson. The lanky defender crossed to Robertson who hit his shot well, but saw it deflected by Malmo's Roland Andersson for a corner. Malmo tried to snatch the lead on the break. In 40 minutes, the menacing Kindvall lifted a cross beyond Shilton's head. Luckily for Forest, there was no other Swede in sight. Seconds from the interval, the game came alive. Bowyer sent Rovertson away on the left. The winger beat two defenders and crossed to the far post. And there was Francis. The striker had run all of thirty yards to reach the ball. He headed home superbly to give Forest a 1-0 half-time lead.

Forest refused to sit back. Robertson created havoc with his runs in the second half. As did Francis. McGovern drove his men forward but Malmo coped. Forest's finishing was poor. The Swedes though rarely threatened the Forest goal and when they did, Forest were equal to the occasion. McGovern sprayed a long pass to Francis. He took off down the byline then sent the ball back into the middle for Robertson to shoot. The Scottish international, with plenty of time, reacted too quickly and the shot hit the post. It was the last of the action, 60,000 voices acclaimed Forest as European champions. It had never been a classic match but European Cup Finals seldom are. In 1975, Forest asked Clough to take them back to Division One. No-one could have dreamt that four years later, they would be hailed as the best in Europe. For Nottingham Forest, who went on to retain their trophy the following year, had done little of note in the era B.C. - 'Before Clough'. In taking a middle-ranking side to the summit of the game and keeping them there for over a decade, Clough ensured himself legendary status at the City Ground and set his successors a task it will be difficult, if not impossible, to achieve - to equal the record of Brian Clough.

ON THE SAME DAY...

News: Torrential rain causes havoc in Southern England, with London, Southampton and the West Country the worst affected.

Sport: Kerry Packer, whose World Series Cricket had caused a breakaway in the game, signs a 'peace' deal with the Australian Cricket Board.

Entertainment: ITV screen *The Derby Stakes'*, a history of the famous race one week before the running of the 200th Derby.

NOTTS COUNTY 4
Vs Bolton Wanderers 1

March 31st 1894 - F.A. Cup Final
(Goodison Park)

Notts County: Toone, Harper, Hendry, Bramley, Calderhead, Shelton, Watson, Donnelley, Logan, Bruce, Daft.

Notts County had been one of the pioneers of English football. Having been founded in 1862, they are the oldest Football League club and were among that select group of twelve which founded the League in 1888. Even then, however, they never ranked among the giants of the game. Their best year was in 1890-91 when they finished 3rd in the League and reached the F.A. Cup Final, losing 3-1 to Blackburn Rovers. Finishing 14th out of 16 in 1893 forced County into a 'test match' for their 1st Division place, which they lost 3-2 to Darwen. Thus, 1893-94 saw them line up in Division Two.

While regaining top status must have been County's priority, a bit of Cup success would not go amiss. Victories over 1st Division Burnley and fellow 2nd Division outfit Burton Swifts took them into a Quarter-final clash with rivals Nottingham Forest. County sprang one of the surprises of the tournament by eliminating their 1st Division foes 4-1 after a 1-1 draw. They gained revenge for that 1891 defeat with a semi-final win over Blackburn Rovers, thus earning the right to play Bolton in the Final.

Bolton's own path to the final had been somewhat fortuitous. Liverpool, Small Heath and Newcastle may have all been in the top four of Division Two, but Bolton's wins over them were expected nonetheless. The only top League scalp to be taken was that of The Wednesday in the semi-final; and they, like Bolton, were struggling to keep out of the bottom three.

But, having disposed of three of the lower League's top four, Bolton were expected to polish off the survivor of that quartet in the Final, played at Everton's Goodison Park for the first time. County, though, didn't see things quite like that and, once Calderhead made a timely clearance in Bolton's opening attack, it was the lower division side which gained the upper hand. Donnelley, in particular, putting on a virtuoso display of dribbling which had the Bolton defence reeling. Then Watson burst down the right before shooting over the bar. County turned the screw, firing in three more shots in two minutes as Calderhead hit the bar, then both Bruce and Logan saw their efforts saved by Sutcliffe in the Bolton goal.

The East Midlands side would not be denied though. When a Donnelley shot hit the post, Watson was on hand to net the rebound. 20 minutes played and the outsiders were in front. Ten minutes later there was further joy for the Nottingham supporters. The nomenclaturally-challenged Daft combined with Bruce to set Logan up for a shot which Sutcliffe could do little about. 2-0 to County. The Lancastrians rallied but it was Notts County who finished this half the stronger, almost scoring a third when Watson burst through again, only to be denied by Sutcliffe.

Bolton started the second half in a more determined fashion but the County defence, with Calderhead in command, withstood the onslaught well. On the hour mark, County broke out of defence and Logan's swiftly-struck shot sailed through Sutcliffe's hands for the third goal. Just three minutes later, Logan ran clear of the Bolton backs and slid his shot past Sutcliffe's reach to make it 4-0. The Cup was well and truly won. County continued to pour men forward, Daft nearly added a fifth, and Donnelley produced a fine run and shot. The whistle was just about to blow when Cassidy provided Bolton with the most meagre of compensations to make the final score 4-1.

As the County fans in the crowd of 37,000 feted their gallant heroes, thousands more back in Nottingham assembled outside newspaper offices in the city to hear the joyous tidings, providing a rapturous reception from afar. Notts County had not only won the F.A. Cup they had done so in style, the first Second Division team to win the trophy.

County failed to regain their top flight status that season, losing 4-0 to Preston in a test match. But they did go back up in 1897 and between then and 1926 enjoyed a periodic existence in the top sphere. A long decline followed which was not arrested until the 1980s, since when County have again sporadically tasted first class football. But, setting aside minor divisional titles and promotions and flings in Anglo-Italian tourneys, their finest hour remains that experienced over 100 years ago, a day which witnessed, *"another example of the caprice of fortune,"* according to *The Sportsman*, the leading journal of the time.

ON THE SAME DAY...

News: Chester housebreaker Thomas Burns appealing against a 12 month jail sentence said he was drunk at the time and remembered nothing. The Recorder said that drink could blamed for many things, but not for *"breaking into an office with three crowbars, and some chisels, wheeling a 3-cwt safe to the end of the yard and nearly smashing it open"*!! The appeal was dismissed.

Sport: The Amateur Athletics Association's AGM savagely criticised cycling as an example of veiled professionalism.

Entertainment:
Top event in Drury Lane is *'Carmen'* by Bizet.

OLDHAM ATHLETIC 0
Vs Nottingham Forest 1

April 29th 1990 - League Cup Final
(Wembley)

Oldham Athletic: Rhodes, Irwin, Barlow, Henry, Barrett, Warhurst, Adams, Ritchie, Bunn (Palmer 66), Milligan, Holden.

Apart from a brief spell just before and shortly after the First World War - when they played in the First Division and reached the semis of the 1913 F.A. Cup - Oldham Athletic had spent their time in the lower reaches and had certainly never had cause to provide employment for trophy engravers. Indeed, from 1935-1974, they had spent just one season at Second Division level. Two men changed all this. Firstly there was Jimmy Frizzell, the manager who led them back into Division Two and kept them there. He was followed by Joe Royle. By 1989-90, Royle had fashioned a side capable of challenging for promotion to the top league and one which also emerged as feared cup fighters.

In the F.A. Cup, the Latics won a marathon tie against Everton in the fifth round and then knocked out Aston Villa in the sixth. In a live televised Semi-Final, they thrilled the nation with their performance in a stirring 3-3 draw with Manchester United over 120 minutes, and took the Old Trafford giants to a further two hours before losing 2-1 in the replay. But it was in the League Cup where they excelled. Home and away wins over Division Two leaders Leeds United marked them out as dangerous opponents. Then came a piece of history from Oldham striker Frankie Bunn as he hit six goals - a competition record - against Scarborough in the third round. When reigning League Champions Arsenal were bundled out of the tournament, 3-1 at Boundary Park, Oldham fans began to sense that something special was on the cards. A fighting 2-2 draw against the Le Tissier-inspired Southampton - away - set up another Boundary Park glory night when the Latics won the replay 2-0.

But not even the most optimistic Oldham supporters could have expected the first leg of their Semi-Final to end with the score Oldham 6 West Ham 0. Rampant Latics relaxed at Upton Park, losing 3-0, but the result was never in doubt. The night they took the Hammers apart was the night they booked their ticket to Wembley.

Facing Oldham in the Final were Nottingham Forest, the League Cup specialists. Brian Clough's side had already won the tourney three times and were the current holders. History was on Oldham's side - for the past two years the holders had got to the Final again, only to lose. Against Oldham was weariness. This was their **19th** cup-tie of the season. And all those games had started to have an effect. This was Latics **ninth** match in April. They had dropped out of contention for promotion. It was less than three weeks after the heartbreak of their defeat by Manchester United.

But Oldham appeared fresh enough at the start of the game. Used to their artificial surface at Boundary Park, they adapted well to the famous Cumberland turf of wembley. Henry and Milligan were outstanding. Earl Barrett though, was the hero of the hour.

His reading of the game, his speed and his tackling was superb. Forest's strike pair of Clough and Jemson were effectively shackled by Barrett. It was almost as if he was taunting Forest, so much was he in command. And Oldham looked good in attack too. Andy Ritchie, who had scored in every round, threatened to continue that run in the 20th minute, with a 25 yard shot which brought out an acrobatic save from Sutton in the Forest goal. Half-time was reached with the honours even at 0-0.

But three minutes into the second half tragedy struck. Nigel Clough spotted a gap which Jemson ran into. His shot was poorly hit but bounced off Rhodes, and Jemson could hardly avoid scoring from the follow-up. Oldham tried to recover but their lack of penetration, matched by Forest's sturdy defence, saw moves break down well before the Latics were in a threatening position. After 69 minutes though, came a real chance. Palmer produced a header aiming for the corner of the net which saw Sutton bring off a magnificent dive to knock clear. The alert 'keeper managed to push the ball away just before the on-rushing Adams could make contact. It was Oldham's first direct attempt on goal since Bunn's 20th minute shot.

Disappointed, Latics could produce no more. But it was a tribute to them that the Man of the Match award was given to a defender in the winning team - Des Walker. Joe Royle left the pitch arm in arm with Brian Clough. It had been that rare sort of Final - a friendly affair. Oldham were desperately unlucky to lose. Seldom can a team have performed so outstandingly over a season, only to end up with nothing to show for their efforts.

But Oldham's reward came the following year when they won the Second Division title, returning to the top after 68 years. For three years, and against every expectation, they held their place. Relegation in 1994, followed by the departure of Joe Royle to Everton, means that it may take some time to revive the Boundary Park glory days. But Oldham fans can take comfort in the fact that their club's greatest moments are not only within recent memory, they are positive proof that a 'little' team can live alongside the big boys.

ON THE SAME DAY...

News: U.S. students rehearsing a Shakespeare play in a wood, are arrested by police who thought they were Devil Worshippers.

Sport: Stephen Hendry beats Jimmy White 18-12 to become the youngest-ever World Snooker Champion.

Entertainment: 350 youngsters are treated for hysteria and fainting at a *New Kids on the Block* concert in Brighton.

OXFORD UNITED 3
Vs Queens Park Rangers 0

April 20th 1986 - League Cup Final
(Wembley)

Oxford United: Judge, Langan, Trewick, Phillips,
Briggs, Shotton, Houghton, Aldridge,
Charles, Hebberd, Brock.

Known as *Headington United* until 1960, Oxford United only joined the League in 1962. A run to the last eight of the F.A. Cup in 1964 (the first 4th Division side to progress so far) and a spell in the 2nd Division between 1968 and 1976, were all that they could boast of until taken over by Robert Maxwell. His name may not elicit much praise these days, but it was under Maxwell that Oxford made an impact on the game. Led by manager Jim Smith, Oxford completed a remarkable double triumph in 1983-84 and 1984-85, winning both Third and Second Division titles. But it was under Maurice Evans and his assistant Ray Graydon, that Oxford embarked upon their great League Cup run.

A home win over Newcastle in the third round was followed by a similar triumph over the Cup holders Norwich City. There was another home success against Portsmouth before Oxford won a hard-fought two leg Semi-Final against Aston Villa. Having reached a major final for the first time in their history, Oxford were - not surprisingly - the underdogs. They were still involved in a battle to stay in the top flight so their opponents, the more comfortably placed QPR, led - ironically - by Jim Smith, were strong favourites to lift the prize.

90,396 spectators must have wondered why they had bothered turning up at Wembley, so tedious was the first half-hour. Both sides adopted a tentative approach, the most abundant quality on display being nervousness. But, as a pattern developed, it showed Oxford taking charge. Hebberd, Phillips and Houghton began to boss the midfield. Five minutes from the break, Aldridge set up Hebberd on the edge of the six-yard box. Hebberd snapped up the easy chance to send Oxford into the dressing room with a 1-0 advantage.

Oxford started the second period in much more confident mood. In 51 minutes, Ray Houghton beat the QPR offside trap, passed to Hebberd, accepted the return, and placed the ball beyond the reach of Barron in the Rangers goal. QPR's substitute Rosenior tried to put them back into the match, but it was 72 minutes before the London side produced a shot on goal, when Judge was equal to the task, tipping a long range effort from Dawes over the bar. Oxford kept up the pressure at the other end. The normally reliable John Aldridge spurned two good chances.

With four minutes remaining, Hebberd sent John Aldridge away once more. His shot was put out by Barron, but Jeremy Charles was right in position to follow through for Oxford's third.

At 3-0, it was the biggest win in a Wembley League Cup Final. And, for once, the citizens of Oxford could truly celebrate a victory won on dry land. But it was a success destined never to be built on. True, Oxford managed to the avoid relegation which had afflicted Norwich after winning the trophy the previous year, but they were denied entry into Europe - a consequence of the five year ban on English clubs imposed post-Hysel. And with the declining interest of the Maxwell family, compounded by later revelations about their business methods, Oxford sunk back into relative obscurity. Their battle to stay at the top level ended in relegation in 1988.

For some players - like Aldridge and Houghton - it was the passport to big-money transfers and international success. For others, like Malcom Shotton, it was the highlight of a career and a fond memory to recall as he ended his playing days in the twilight zone of Ayr United. For Oxford supporters, it was an event to savour, but one which even the most incurably optimistic must ever doubt will come again.

PETERBOROUGH UNITED 2

Vs Arsenal 1

January 30th 1965 - F.A. Cup Round 4

Peterborough United: Duff, Cooper, Birks, Crowe, Rankmore, Orr, Barnes, Conmy, Dougan, Deakin, McNamee.

Founded only in 1934, Peterborough United joined the League in 1960. They made an immediate impact, running away with the 4th Division title - top scorer Terry Bly notching a post-war record 52 League goals. They were comfortably settled in Division Three, challenging occasionally for further promotion, by early 1965. To be drawn at home to Arsenal in the fourth round of the F.A. Cup was undoubtedly the biggest ever event to take place at their London Road ground. For although Arsenal had been going through a rough time by their own high standards, the side managed by Billy Wright retained enough charisma to persuade 30,056 spectators to cram into Posh's ground.

They saw a first half in which the Third Division side took most of the credit but also saw enough of Arsenal to suggest that the Gunners old defensive resilience was as strong as ever. And on the rare moments when they took the offensive, Arsenal possessed skilful players like Armstrong and Eastham who could take advantage of any weakness in the Posh line-up. Indeed, the home crowd was stunned into silence when an Eastham corner allowed Radford to fire in a left foot shot which gave the Gunners an undeserved interval lead.

Despite increased Arsenal pressure after the break, Peterborough held firm. Duff in goal, was superb. Posh skipper Vic Crowe urged his team forward. In 72 minutes, Barnes sent the ball to the one undoubted star in this otherwise unsung Peterborough side - Derek Dougan. The mercurial Northern Ireland star who had shocked many by dropping down to this level so early in his career, was in fine form. As the *Peterborough Advertiser* put it: *"He shrugged off Ian Ure like an unwanted overcoat,"* before shooting past the advancing 'keeper Burns, to equalise.

It was all Posh now. Arsenal mounted a rare attack in the 85th minute, but it was to prove their undoing. Rankmore headed clear to Deakin. He laid the ball off to McNamee who put it out to Barnes on the left. Barnes centred right through Frank McLintock's legs and there was McNamee running in. And the man who had cost just £75 from the ranks of the Scottish Juniors drew back before carefully shooting past Burns.

McNamee's shot provides the winner for the Posh.

All hell broke loose in the ground. Peterborough's fans had seen nothing like it. Now it was Arsenal who tried to salvage something. They threw nine men into attack. Skirton drove in a piledriver, magnificently saved by Willie Duff. And it was Duff to the rescue again, this time from Eastham. There was no time for anything else. The final whistle blew on a victory which proud Peterborough would never forget. The most famous name in English football had been humbled by a side less than five years in the League, with two Scots - Duff and McNamee - and the Irish Derek Dougan taking most of the credit.

As the Posh trooped off the pitch, left back Birks refused to accept what had happened. *"I just can't believe it,"* he told Vic Crowe. Crowe responded with the wisdom of an Owl: *"Of course you can. Just believe in yourself, the rest is easy."* Nor was that the end of it. A record gate of 30,096 saw the Posh take on Swansea in the fifth round. And, after two games, it was Peterborough who entered the last eight. The dream died in a 5-1 defeat at Stamford Bridge and more woe was to be visited on Peterborough three years later. By then Dougan had departed, back on his way to the top of the game. Peterborough were demoted back to the 4th Division for financial irregularities. Their golden era (they had also reached the League Cup Semi-Finals in 1966) was at an end. It was the 1990s before the good times returned to London Road when they reached the First Division (old Second Division) finishing as high as tenth in 1993 before relegation the following season. But to this day, the most memorable side Posh have ever had, was the one assembled by manager Gordon Clark, the one which sent mighty Arsenal tumbling out of the F.A. Cup.

ON THE SAME DAY...

News: After a week of nationwide mourning over the death of Winston Churchill, the wartime leader is buried at Bladon, Oxon..

Sport: Days after ten football players were jailed for match fixing, *The People* which first exposed the scandal, claims that 90 more have got away with it.

Entertainment: Top film at the Odeon, Peterborough is *"Roustabout"* starring Elvis Presley.

PLYMOUTH ARGYLE 0
Vs Watford 1

April 14th 1984 - F.A. Cup Semi-Final
(Villa Park)

Plymouth Argyle: Crudgington, Nisbet, Uzzell, Harrison,
Smith, Cooper, Hodges, Phillips, Tynan, Staniforth, Rogers.

Since joining the League in 1920, Plymouth Argyle had achieved little of note. They had bobbed up and down between the second and Third Divisions, rarely looking as if they could climb to the top. In the F.A. Cup they had never progressed beyond the 5th round. The nearest they had come to success was to reach a couple of League Cup Semi-Finals. But, in 1983-84, under manager John Hore, Plymouth set off on a trail of F.A. Cup glory.

Admittedly, their progress to the fifth round went little noticed outside of Devon. Southend United, Barking, Newport County and Darlington were their victims. It had been a kind draw for Argyle up to that point, but when Plymouth were drawn away to West Bromwich Albion, that looked like the end of their run. Argyle had other ideas, and a second-half strike by experienced forward Tommy Tynan, enabled them to pull off a shock victory over the First Division side, putting Argyle into the last eight for the first time. A home tie against a Derby County side heading for relegation from division two appeared to offer them a fair chance of further progress, but a 0-0 draw in front of 34,365 at Home Park looked to have scuppered their hopes. But again, Argyle showed their fighting spirit away from home, winning 1-0 at the Baseball Ground. Amazingly, Plymouth had reached the Semi-Finals of the Cup.

Their form in the League had suffered as a result. So, when Argyle set out to face First Division Watford at Villa Park, there was a very real possibility that they could reach Wembley and end up in the Fourth Division in the same season. Fear of relegation was the last thing on the minds of the 20,000 plus who had made the long trek to Birmingham in Argyle colours, swelling the crowd to 43,858. The thought of a slightly less wearying outing to the twin towers of Wembley dominated their thinking.

And they saw an entertaining start. Both sides looked confident pressing forward, but their respective defences were distinctly dodgy. After five minutes play, Crudgington flapped at a corner and was relieved to find Watford's Reilly too slow to take the chance offered to him. Three minutes later, Plymouth carved out an opening. Rogers's cross to Smith was knocked on to Nisbet, whose shot flew just wide of the post. Then, with Watford 'keeper Sherwood in trouble and their defence stranded, Smith hit his shot just over the bar. The game was being played at a furious pace and it was Watford who now took up the attack. John Barnes sped up the park before crossing to Reilly, who was more alert this time. The big striker tucked the ball away to put Watford 1-0 up with 13 minutes on the clock.

Callaghan and Barnes were impressive on the wings for Watford, as were Reilly and Mo Johnston in the centre. Plymouth's options were thus severely restricted, but they battled gamely to the interval, keeping the match still in the balance. In the second half, Plymouth started brightly. Gordon Staniforth broke past Sinnott and fired in a good looking attempt. Unfortunately for Argyle, Watford's Price was on hand to head clear for a corner.

The pace of the game inevitably slowed down for a while, the only action of note being a shot from Watford's Taylor which went narrowly wide. As the game drew to a close, Argyle launched one final attack, Hodges' shot going agonizingly past the post. The whistle blew to the sound of Plymouth being applauded by the Watford fans. That was of little compensation to John Hore, who summed up the day saying, *"it's a very empty feeling I have."*

Plymouth had come so close to being the first Third Division side to play in the F.A. Cup Final. Alas, luck deserted them on the day, for no-one watching could have concluded that there were two divisions between the sides. Fortunately, Argyle rallied sufficiently well to avoid relegation. Their life since has reverted to the usual pattern of bouncing between the two middle divisions, although latterly a drop to the third. But Devonian memories are strong. One day, they believe, Plymouth Argyle will mount another serious F.A. Cup campaign. And this time they will go all the way.

ON THE SAME DAY...

News: The actor Sir Ralph Richardson, who died the previous October, has left an estate valued at over £1 Million in his will.

Sport: The 17 years old South African runner Zola Budd, wins her first race in Britain.

Entertainment:
Another fine actor, Ian McKellen, appeared at the National Theatre for the first time in *'Venice Preserved'*.

PORTSMOUTH 5
Vs Aston Villa 1

May 6th 1950 - Division One.

Portsmouth: Butler, Hindmarsh, Ferrier, Spence,
Flewin, Dickinson, Harris, Reid, Thompson,
Phillips, Froggatt.

Portsmouth were far and away the most successful of the teams which joined the League after the First World War. By 1927, they had reached the First Division, where they stayed for more than 30 years and they lifted the F.A. Cup in 1939. Owing to the onset of the Second World War, they were to retain the famous trophy for seven years. Post-war Portsmouth saw the legendary Jack Tinn end his 20 year managership of the club in 1947, to be replaced by Bob Jackson. And it was Jackson who led them to the League championship in 1948-49. The following season saw one of the most tremendous tussles ever to take place for the destination of the title. Almost half of the clubs were in contention at one time or another. The bald statistics show a meagre four points separating the top seven clubs. But as the final game of the season approached, the race was down to three, Sunderland had 50 points, Wolves had 51 but leading, also with 51 points and with a superior goal average, were Portsmouth the reigning champions. Ninety nervous minutes beckoned for the followers of the leading trio.

Pompey's fans had more reason to worry than the others. The side which faced Aston Villa was an unfamiliar line-up. Injuries to three first-teamers plus the suspension of the popular Jimmy Scoular might have been expected to have made for a tentative start. But the bulk of the crowd of 42,295 needn't have fretted, for within 20 seconds of the kick-off, Thompson had the ball in the back of the Villa net. That settled the crowd, but not the team. Villa tried to claw their way back into the match and 1-0 was too slender a lead to protect. In 26 minutes though, Pompey resumed the attack. Harris' shot was blocked by Rutherford in the Villa goal but Reid, Portsmouth's outstanding player, quickly nipped in to put the home side two up.

Even now, Villa refused to lie down. They fought back strongly. Dorsett made a fine run, culminating in a pass to the well-placed Edwards who back-heeled the ball for what looked like a certain goal. Butler threw himself full-stretch to fingertip the ball away to safety. Half-time was reached with the two-goal cushion intact.

If the first 45 minutes had seen Portsmouth snatch a somewhat lucky lead, then the second period saw them perform like true Champions. Three minutes into this half, Reid took a direct free-kick from twenty yards out and blasted the ball past Rutherford for their third goal. With 72 minutes gone, a superb shot from Thompson notched the fourth. Shortly after, Reid claimed his hat-trick, and Pompey's fifth. It was only now that nervous Portsmouth officials could admit to themselves that the title was staying

where it was. With twelve minutes to go, they ran up the Championship flag. Villa, reduced to bystanders in the second half, received a consolatory penalty a minute from the end which Dorsett converted to make the final score Portsmouth 5 Aston Villa 1.

Wolves had won 6-1 and Sunderland had triumphed too. But it meant nothing. Pompey's far superior goal average meant that they had won the League title two years in succession. And their fans knew it. Thousands broke the police cordon so that they could dance in delight on their beloved Fratton Park pitch. Team captain Reg Flewin addressed the masses thronged on the pitch. But the crowd bayed for their hero, the suspended Jimmy Scoular, before they would leave. At length, Scoular, who had been watching from the stand, came down to speak to the fans. Only then did the ecstatic thousands depart to continue their celebrations elsewhere.

Those fans deserved to celebrate. No-one would have guessed then, but, for Portsmouth, the glory days were over. There were some more high League finishes, but Pompey never again looked like a title winning side. And years of struggle ended in relegation in 1959. Two years later, they were in the Third Division. Since then, they have spent just one solitary term in the top flight, in 1987-88. They even suffered the ignominy of dropping into the Fourth Division in the late 1970s. Most galling of all, for Pompey fans, has been the emergence of Southampton as the premier South Coast side. Like many other clubs, Portsmouth have the potential to do more. If few expect them ever to celebrate back-to-back title wins again, then a place in the Premiership, at the very least, is what Pompey fans would most like to see.

ON THE SAME DAY...

News: Purges in Czechoslovakia as the army is re-modelled along Soviet lines.

Sport: Warrington beat Widnes 19-0 to win the Rugby League Challenge Cup for the first time since 1907.

Entertainment:
Top London play is 'A streetcar named Desire' at the Aldwych Theatre, starring Vivien Leigh.

PORT VALE 1
Vs West Bromwich Albion 2

March 27th 1954 - F.A. Cup Semi-Final

Port Vale: King, Turner, Potts, Mullard, Cheadle,
Sproson, Askey, Leake, Hayward,
Tomkinson, Cunliffe.

Port Vale have one of the oddest histories of any League side. Original members of the Second Division back in 1892, they failed to be re-elected in 1896, returned two years later, resigned from the League in 1907, came back to take over the expelled Leeds City's fixtures in 1919, and even found themselves moved between the Third Divisions North and South more or less at random. They have never played in the top division but have, on occasion, managed to sustain a position just below that level.

In the early 1950s, big changes took place at the club. They moved from their Recreation Ground to Vale Park in 1950 and appointed Freddie Steele as Manager the following year. By 1953, he had assembled a side which lost out for promotion by a single point. The next year saw Vale run away with the Third North title, but it was in the F.A. Cup that they demonstrated their mettle, eliminating First Division sides like Cardiff and Blackpool, then winning away to Third South team Leyton Orient to become the first team from the Third North to reach the last four of the F.A. Cup.

Vale's opponents for a place at Wembley were West Brom. At the time, they stood top of the table and were being tipped as the first 'double' winners of the 20th century. But Vale had lost just three times all season and were confident about their chances, even if the rest of the footballing world had written them off. Both sides brought huge supports with them, the gate amounting to 68,221. And they saw Vale hold their own after an early Albion flurry. Turner and Sproson were commanding in defence. Roy Sproson was to become the epitome of the loyal servant. Having signed for Vale in 1949, he was still playing for them in the early 1970s.

Having weathered the early storm, Port Vale began to come into the game themselves. A Cheadle free kick set up a sweet move, Hayward heading on to Cunliffe, who passed to Askey on the wing. Askey crossed for Tomkinson to power in a header, only for Heath in the Albion goal, to make the save. Another Vale attack almost ended in an own goal from Albion's Dugdale. On the rare occasions when Albion forced the pace, Vale's defence lived up to the club's nickname, the Valiants. There were five minutes remaining in the half when Vale attacked once more. Cunliffe sent the ball into the penalty area and from the ensuing scramble, it was Vale's Leake who won possession, knocking the ball over the line. The League leaders were stunned going in at the break, but Vale were value for their lead.

West Brom had to go on the offensive in the second half, but Vale still held firm. For the first quarter of an hour, nothing got past the defence. The Third Division team looked Wembley bound, but after 61 minutes came disaster. A cross from Dudley saw both Allen and Nichols jump for it. Vale's keeper King, seemed momentarily distracted. He took his eyes off the ball for a split second and Albion had equalised. Eight minutes later, Cheadle up-ended Albion's Lee in the penalty box. Ronnie Allen didn't miss many penalties and he made no mistake with this one to give Albion the lead.

Many teams would have conceded there and then, but not this fighting Port Vale team. They battled back, putting in a final flourish that had West Brom reeling. In 85 minutes, Cunliffe shot just past the post. Sixty seconds later and Leake actually got the ball into the net, only to be given offside. Right up to the final whistle, it was Vale on the attack. But when that whistle came, it was West Brom who had reached the Final. It had been a lucky escape for the side which would go on to win the Cup, but miss out on that elusive double, ending up in second place in the League. Albion Manager Vic Buckingham summed it up perfectly when he said this match was, *"our toughest game of the season."*

Port Vale have had a chequered history since then. But they know that the vagaries of the draw mean that every club looks forward to a good run in the F.A. Cup. Maybe it's time they repeated, or surpassed, the efforts of the team of '54.

ON THE SAME DAY...

News: At a wreath-laying ceremony in Australia, The Queen wears white gloves as a precaution against polio.

Sport: Royal Tan is the 8-1 winner of the Grand National, but four horses die during the race, the worst tally ever.

Entertainment: Even the best can have flops. J.B.Priestley's *'The White Countess'*, comes off stage after just five nights.

PRESTON NORTH END 3
Vs Wolverhampton Wanderers 0

March 30th 1889 - F.A. Cup Final (The Oval)

Preston North End: Mills-Roberts, Haworth, Holmes, Drummond, Russell, Graham, Gordon, Ross, Goodhall, Dewhirst, Thomson.

Preston North End were the great 'Invincibles' of the 19th century. They had already established the all-time F.A. Cup scoring record the previous season with a 26-0 victory over Hyde, but had lost in the final to West Bromwich Albion. In the inaugural Football League in 1888-89, Preston romped through the season unbeaten, winning the title by eleven points. In the F.A. Cup, no-one could even score against them let alone beat them, as Bootle, Grimsby Town and Birmingham St George's all found out to their cost, vanquished by proud Preston. In the last four, there was the sweet taste of revenge with a 1-0 win over West Brom. Now came the chance to not only lift the Cup for the first time, but the opportunity to do the 'Double' and set a target for all other sides to this day.

A huge (for the time) crowd of 22,000 assembled at the Oval for the match, the kick-off having been delayed until 4.00 p.m. to allow people to watch the University Boat Race first. And, initially at least, they witnessed an even encounter. Russell and Dewhirst were prominent for Preston, but it was Wolves who made the early chances. Their forward Brodie took a pass from the left and shot narrowly over the bar. Preston retaliated with a direct free-kick from Thomson which was touched away by Wolves 'keeper Baynton. But Wolves were slightly ahead on points, Knight hitting the post with a fiercely struck shot. Another Wolves surge was broken up by Gordon's intervention. His pass found Ross who ran and shot, only to see the ball rebound off the bar. Dewhirst was quick to follow-up and stabbed the ball home to give Preston the lead in 15 minutes.

Thus inspired, Preston forced Wolves onto the defensive. After 25 minutes, Goodall and Ross combined well, the move ending with a shot from Ross which Baynton let slip, to put Preston two ahead. North End kept up the pressure, Dewhirst almost grabbing a third. But at half-time, they had to be content with a 2-0 lead.

The second half saw a contrast of styles with Wolves, *"individual rushes and long kicks,"* as one paper put it, being outclassed by Preston's *"short passing and combination attacks."* But Wolves, just like the first half, produced all the early pressure as they tried desperately to get back into the game. Hunter shot over the bar. A Fletcher free kick was just wide of the target. Then Knight shot too high. But this Preston side, schooled by the famous Major Sudell, knew how to absorb all this. At length, they returned to the attack. A Gordon shot was cleared by right back Baugh. The same player saw another attempt kicked away by Bayton. Then Gordon set off down the flank. His cross was met by Dewhirst. The inside-left's effort was blocked by Baynton, but only to Thomson, who gladly accepted the chance to tuck away the third goal.

Preston dominated affairs until the final whistle but without adding to their tally. Full-time saw a pitch invasion by jubilant Lancastrian fans. Back in Preston, thousands had gathered outside the local newspaper offices and at 5.55, there came a mighty roar, heard throughout the town, as news arrived of their side's triumph. League Champions, now Cup winners. Unbeaten in the League, no goals conceded in the Cup. An achievement which would stand forever.

Preston retained their League title the following season and won the Cup again in 1938. But, several runners-up spots in both League and Cup not withstanding, the record of the 1889 team stands unparalleled. Other teams have won the double, the cup has been won without a goal being lost, but no side has ever come close to equalling the records set by the old invincibles. Today, as Preston languish in the lower reaches of the League, it is difficult to conceive of them ever returning to top flight soccer, last seen at Deepdale in 1961, let alone aspire to the greatness of old. But their place in football's history has long been assured.

The original F.A.Cup.

QUEENS PARK RANGERS 3

Vs West Bromwich Albion 2

March 4th 1967 - League Cup Final (Wembley)

Queens Park Rangers: Springett, Hazell, Langley, Keen, Hunt, Sibley, Lazarus, Sanderson, Allen, Marsh, Morgan.

Until the mid-1960s, Queens Park Rangers were a club of almost total anonymity. With the exception of four years in Division Two, they had spent their entire life in the Third Division. That dull image changed during the course of a single 90 minutes play at Wembley in 1967. Led by the management team of Alec Stock and Jimmy Andrews, QPR were running away with the Third Division title. And the performances of Rodney Marsh were attracting attention from bigger clubs. So, while promotion was a virtual certainty, Rangers allowed themselves the luxury of a cup run in the League's own competition.

Never previously past the second round, QPR safely negotiated ties against Colchester, Aldershot and Swansea before turning on the style in a 4-2 home win over First Division Leicester City. Second Division opposition in the shape of Carlisle United were beaten in the last eight and another Division Two side, Birmingham City, were comprehensively despatched 7-2 on aggregate in the Semi-Finals. Rangers had reached Wembley.

No-one outside West London gave them much hope in the Final. Their opponents were First Division West Bromwich Albion, the League Cup holders. But this was a special occasion. For the first time the Final was being played at Wembley, and with a European place at stake. Rangers were the first side from the Third Division ever to play at the famous stadium, and they carried the hopes of small clubs everywhere as they stepped out to the tumultuous roar made by 97,952 voices. But it was the top League side who looked the better. QPR seemed clumsy, out of place even. Clive Clark, an ex-QPR player, caused most of the damage; being ably supplied by Doug Fraser, Bobby Hope and Jeff Astle. Tony Hazell found the task of marking Clark difficult and the Albion player had the freedom of the wing in the tenth minute, when he took a pass from Fraser and sped in to give Springett no chance. It seemed a matter of how many Albion would win by.

Clark could make chances too. He set up Astle, but, for once, the West Brom hit-man was off target. Next, Clark floated over a beautiful cross to an open goal, with no-one there to take advantage. Then he was through himself, only to stumble at the crucial moment. QPR had little to offer by way of reply, only Lazarus looked remotely dangerous. West Brom's (and Clark's) pressure had to tell. And it did, with a flowing move involving Fraser, Kaye and Brown, which left Clark with all the time in the world to score the second. At half-time the match looked to be effectively over.

QPR had no option but to open up in the second half and try to go out with some dignity. Morgan and Keen both forced Albion 'keeper Sheppard into making saves. The same pair combined on the hour mark to give QPR some hope. Keen's free kick was headed firmly by Morgan past Sheppard to reduce the deficit. Clark opened up QPR again, but the chance went begging. That raid apart, the nature of the game had changed, and, appropriately, Lazarus was involved in the Rangers rebirth. He sent the ball to Marsh, who was beginning to find his best form. Marsh, *"jinked, spurted, stopped and strolled,"* according to the late John Arlott. He weaved his way through a five-man defence, then fired in a right-foot shot low off the left hand post to equalise.

West Brom were shattered by this turn of events, their stroll to victory was becoming a nightmare. And worse was to follow. Hunt and Sheppard both challenged for a long through ball. The 'keeper fell on the ball just as Hunt kicked it. It bounced off Sheppard's chest to be tapped in by a QPR player with just nine minutes remaining. The scorer? Who better to round off this sporting comeback from the dead than Mark Lazarus?

The Third Division team had triumphed. Sadly, UEFA ruled that only sides from a country's top division could enter the Fairs Cup, so QPR's European dream was (temporarily) shelved. They were promoted again the following season and, although relegated immediately, QPR have spent the bulk of their time since playing in the top flight. They have come close to winning both the League and the F.A. Cup and have played in Europe too. Nowadays, it is hard to think that this club was ever a Third Division outfit. The trophy they won at Wembley bulleted QPR out of obscurity and into the spotlight they have enjoyed ever since.

ON THE SAME DAY...

News: Senator Edward Kennedy calls for peace in Vietnam.

Sport: France beat Great Britain 23-13 in a Rugby League international at Wigan.

Entertainment:
Top new film is the latest in a long-running series, *"Carry on, don't lose your head."*

READING 0 Vs Cardiff City 3

March 26th 1927 - F.A. Cup Semi-Final (Wolverhampton)

Reading: Duckworth, Eggo, McConnell, Inglis, Messer, Evans,
McDonald, Johnston, Davey, Richardson, Robson.

Members of the League only since 1920, Reading won the Third Division (South) title in 1926. They settled down comfortably in a mid-table slot in the Second Division and launched a challenge for the F.A. Cup which delighted the Elm Park fans. Reading safely negotiated the first two rounds before coming up against the big guns. Drawn against Manchester United in Round Three, the Royals created a sensation by eliminating the First Division side after three tough encounters. They followed up that triumph with a home win over Portsmouth who were second top of Division Two. The next round brought Third Division opposition in the shape of Brentford to Elm Park. It also brought an attendance record which stands to this day, 33,042 turning up to see Reading win 1-0. That result put them into one of the most unlikely of Quarter-Finals draws; only **two** First Division sides remained in contention alongside **five** from the Second and one from the Third (South). Reading travelled to fellow, Second Division side Swansea and brought off a fine 3-1 victory. They were in the last four and anything, even winning the Cup itself, was now possible.

But the two First Division survivors, Arsenal and Cardiff, had both made it through as well, and it was further Welsh opposition that the draw threw up Reading's way. But the Royals fans were convinced their team was Wembley-bound and many made the trek to Molineux where they brought the attendance up to 39,476. They saw Cardiff start the livelier and Eggo had to be at his best to break up the Welsh attack. Reading soon got into their stride, forcing Cardiff's Irving to head back to his own goal, and injuring himself in the process. But it was end-to-end stuff at this stage of the game, with neither side able to establish mastery over the other. Cardiff's Davies came close, shooting just over the left post. Then Robson and Richardson combined well for Reading on the left, Richardson's shot forcing Cardiff 'keeper Farquharson to tip the ball away for a corner. McDonald's kick was well-placed but Cardiff cleared the danger.

Now it was Cardiff's turn to take the offensive. Davies made a smart run on goal but the reliable Eggo was on hand to clear. A surge by Cardiff's McLachlan was stopped by Inglis. Messer prevented another attack from gaining shape, but the pressure was now constant and Reading were being badly stretched. Eggo was finally beaten, by Ferguson, and his low shot along the ground beat Duckworth to put Cardiff ahead in the 27th minute. Reading responded vigorously but the Cardiff defence held firm. The First Division side resumed their own barrage. McLachlan sped along the touchline, eluded Eggo, and crossed almost from the corner flag. Wake rose above the defence to head home Cardiff's second. With just 35 minutes played, Reading faced an uphill struggle.

The Royals had played well enough but had made few direct chances for their forwards. They did the bulk of the attacking in the second half but rarely troubled Cardiff. After 65 minutes, Ferguson won the ball for Cardiff near the centre circle. Challenged by McConnell, he drew back, side-stepped the defender and ran on before firing home a tremendous shot for the best goal of the game. Reading battled away gamely, even though they knew their cause was lost. They finally beat Farquharson in the 89th minute but even that effort was cleared. But even a 3-0 defeat was no disgrace against the side who went on to become the only team to take the F.A. Cup out of England. *The People* paid tribute to Reading the next day, describing the match as: *"The wonder team's farewell."*

Reading spent only a few more seasons in the Second Division before relegation. Never again have they performed so well in the F.A. Cup. But, after a long spell in the doldrums, the 1980s saw a revival of the Royals fortunes when they returned to Division Two after an absence of 55 years. Though they didn't stay long, there was renewed hope for the future when they reached the same level (now the re-named First Division) in 1994, and after finishing runners-up were deprived of a place in the Premiership in a Wembley thriller against Bolton.

Almost Wembley. But Reading's brave F.A.Cup run comes to grief in the Semi-Final

ON THE SAME DAY...

News:
Charlie Chaplan and his second wife Lita Gray are to divorce.

Sport:
The refurbishment of Hampden Park is completed a week before the Scotland Vs England international match, the new capacity is 130,000.

Entertainment:
After being seen by over two million people in a remarkable run of 851 performances in 105 weeks at the Drury Lane Theatre, *'Rose Marie'* is being replaced by a new production - *'The Desert Song'*.

ROCHDALE 0

Vs Norwich City 3

April 26th 1962 - League Cup Final
(1st Leg)

Rochdale: Burgin, Milburn, Winton, Bodell, Aspden, Thompson, Wragg, Hepton, Bimpson, Cairns, Whitaker.

Rochdale, home of the Co-op Pioneers, comedian Mike Harding and Rochdale Hornets Rugby League club. Football has always had to struggle to find the limelight in the Lancashire town. Although Rochdale joined the League in 1921, they have never unduly worried sportswriters looking for a back page headline. They spent the entire lifetime of the Third North as members, qualified for the re-formed Third Division in 1958 on goal average and were promptly relegated in their first year. Yet just three years later they reached a national Cup Final, the first - and to date the only - Fourth Division side ever to do so.

The Football League Cup was established in 1960-61 with many of the big clubs looking down their noses at the competition. But the smaller clubs immediately recognised its value. Rochdale entered the 1961-62 tournament hoping for a financial bonus, to even think of reaching the Final would have been akin to madness. In the opening round, they drew away to Second Division Southampton and won the Spotland replay 2-1. A 4-0 home win over Doncaster Rovers brought Second Division Charlton to Spotland in the third round, and another fine display resulted in a 1-0 victory for Rochdale. A fourth round bye was followed by another home tie, a 2-1 win over York City. Almost unnoticed outside their home town, Rochdale had reached the Semi-Finals.

It was in this round that Rochdale grabbed the media attention at last. They faced First Division Blackburn Rovers over two legs and shocked their big-name foes with a 3-1 home win. In the second leg, Rochdale fought gallantly, losing just 2-1, to win 4-3 on aggregate. The knockers could be safely ignored. Rochdale were in the Final, on merit.

In those days the Final was also a two-leg affair. So not only were Rochdale in a Cup Final, that Cup Final was coming to Rochdale. And their fans responded to the magnificent achievement of the manager Tony Collins and his team. Instead of the usual 3,500 or so, 11,123 turned up to watch Rochdale do battle with Second Division Norwich City.

Hepton made an early run for Rochdale but was intercepted. That first-minute dash was followed by third-minute disaster. Norwich's Punton put over a cross which eluded the defence. He found Derek Lythgoe. Lythgoe totally mis-hit his shot, but, even so, it still rolled through Burgin's legs. 1-0 to Norwich. Rochdale thought they had equalised in the 15th minute when top scorer Ron Cairns netted. Unfortunately, for the 'Dale, the referee detected handball on Cairns' part. Three minutes later came another body blow. Bill Punton again set things in motion with a pass to Scott. In turn, he found Lythgoe. This time there was no need for luck as Lythgoe rounded the approaching Burgin before despatching his second goal.

Rochdale responded well, launching a series of attacks, but front-men Cairns and Bimpson found it tough going against the East Anglian defence. Indeed, when Burton sent Mannion away, it looked like it might be three for Norwich. But Mannion screwed his shot wide. Half-time came with the score still Rochdale 0 - Norwich City 2.

In the second half, Norwich relaxed and let Rochdale come at them. Aspden, Milburn, Bodell and Thompson all moved forward as the Fourth Division side battled gamely to retrieve something from the match. The best chance fell to Colin Whitaker six yards out. Amazingly, he contrived to hit the corner flag! It was that kind of night for Rochdale. The tie was effectively sealed in the 85th minute when Mannion's cross found Punton at an awkward angle. Punton's shot was inch-perfect. 3-0 to Norwich. Rochdale had been, *"outclassed in a first 45 minutes of agony,"* according to *'Scrutator'* in the *Rochdale Observer*. With Whyke and Richardson replacing Wragg and Hepton, the second leg was a closer affair, Rochdale forcing Norwich 'keeper Sandy Kennon into several breathtaking saves. It wasn't until fifteen minutes from the end that Norwich scored the only goal of the game for a 4-0 aggregate victory. Football League Secretary, Alan Hardaker, who attended the Spotland game, paid tribute to Rochdale, saying: *"That they reached the Final was a feat in itself."*

Hardaker was right. Rochdale achieved something that no other Fourth Division side has ever been able to do, play in a national Cup Final. So, although the best Rochdale have done since is to spend five years in the old Third Division in the early 70s and enjoy a run to the last sixteen of the F.A. Cup in 1990, their supporters can look back with pride to the time when a Cup Final was played at Spotland.

ON THE SAME DAY...

News: One of the paper's comments, with astonishing prescience, on the 13-year old Prince Charles: *"Didn't he look grown up. I suppose we shall be hearing about his girlfriends next."*

Sport: Salford youngster John Virgo wins through to the Semi-Finals of the Boys Snooker Championship in London.

Entertainment:
Ratings figures show that Prince Philip's first TV appearance, on *'This Week'*, was only the 8th most popular programme. No.1 is *'Coronation Street'*.

ROTHERHAM UNITED 6

Vs Liverpool 1

May 2nd 1955 - Division Two

Rotherham United: Quairney, Selkirk, Warner, Marshall, Jordan, Williams, Grainger, Pell, Farmer, Guest, Wilson.

On the last day of April 1955, Rotherham United lay just two games away from the First Division. But the scramble for promotion was so tight that, even at this late stage of the season, no fewer than **five** clubs were still in with a chance of grabbing one of the two spots available. The table looked like this:-

	P.	W.	D.	L.	F.	A.	Pts.	G.Ave.
1. Luton Town	41	22	8	11	85	53	52	1.6037
2. Stoke City	41	21	10	10	69	44	52	1.5681
3. Rotherham U.	40	24	4	12	88	62	52	1.4193
4. Birmingham	40	21	9	10	85	44	51	1.9318
5. Leeds United	41	22	7	12	67	52	51	1.2884

Rotherham had won their last **seven** League matches but surprisingly lost 1-0 at Port Vale. Luton won 3-0 at Doncaster to virtually guarantee themselves one of the promotion slots. Leeds won 3-1 and leapt into second place, while Birmingham kept their hopes alive with a 2-2 draw at Liverpool. Stoke, in a promotion place in the morning, lost 2-0 at Plymouth and slumped to fifth, and out of the reckoning. Rotherham knew that victory over Liverpool on the Monday would take them above Leeds and Birmingham. It would eliminate the West Yorkshire club from contention and put pressure on the Brummies. What they couldn't do was guarantee promotion for themselves. Both Birmingham and Luton had far superior goal averages (then used to determine placings when teams were level on points). Rotherham would have to beat Liverpool 17-0 to better Luton's goal average.

The defeat at Port Vale had an effect on the crowd. At 17,868 it was nowhere near as large as expected for this crunch match. But manager Andy Smailes was a happy man as he watched Rotherham pile on the pressure in the early stages of the game. The Millers had three or four chances early on before Liverpool tried an attempt of their own, Rowley blasting over the bar from six yards. Rotherham continued to pound forward. Wilson's shot unluckily hit off a defender. Guest, Wilson and Pell all forced Liverpool 'keeper Rudham into some good saves. Then Guest lobbed over 'Pool's Campbell and shot on the volley, only to see the ball strike another defender and bounce harmlessly away. Finally, a Guest centre was met with a confident header from Pell and Rotherham were in front at last. It had taken them 37 minutes to break down the stubborn Liverpool defence. Grainger was brought down in full flight for what looked like a penalty, but the referee awarded only an indirect free kick. Undeterred, Guest touched the kick on to Marshall. He found Wilson who slotted home the second. Pell scrambled the ball into the net just before the break but offside was given against him. The Millers had to be content with a 2-0 interval lead.

The one-way traffic continued in the second half. Rudham saved well from Wilson, then tipped over an effort from Farmer. A Guest shot from 35 yards found Rudham barring the way again. Then Pell's attempt swerved narrowly wide. But after 62 minutes a Warner free kick eluded the defence, and Grainger nodded in the third. But Rudham was back to his best to deny a Farmer header. A Wilson shot from an awkward angle saw the 'keeper make his first mistake as he fumbled the ball over the line for the fourth. A throw-in found Guest who headed to Wilson, and the winger whipped in the fifth. Rudham brought off two more great saves before a Selkirk pass allowed Wilson to score the sixth. With thirty seconds to go, Billy Liddell netted for Liverpool to make the final score Rotherham 6 - Liverpool 1.

Only good goalkeeping and bad luck prevented Rotherham from running up a record tally. The *South Yorkshire and Rotherham Advertiser* said that the, *"stay-aways missed a season's classic."* Rotherham were back in the promotion frame, but to stay there they had to hope that their local rivals Doncaster Rovers could deprive Birmingham of victory two days later. That game witnessed the odd sight of thousands of Rotherham fans travelling to Doncaster to become honorary Rovers supporters for the day. To no avail. Birmingham won 5-1. By the narrowest of margins, Rotherham had been denied promotion to the First Division. Had there been three points for a win in 1955, Rotherham's 25 League victories would have won them the Second Division title. Present Football League rules would also have seen them triumph by virtue of being top scorers. Alas, such things were not considered in 1955.

Rotherham have done little of note since that historic near-miss, reaching the very first League Cup Final in 1961 being their most noteworthy achievement. Their 1954-55 campaign gives them some claim to the tag of the team who should have played in the First Division - but never did.

ON THE SAME DAY...

News: An unofficial dispute in the coal industry brings out 80,000 South Yorkshire miners on strike.

Sport: Bobby Wilson is called up into the British Davis Cup team against Austria.

Entertainment: The Rotherham Hippodrome's film is *'Martin Luther'*, starring Niall McGinnis.

SCARBOROUGH 3

Vs Coventry City 0

October 7th 1992
League Cup Round Two (Second leg)

Scarborough: Ford, Thompson, Mudd, Lee, Hirst,
Curran, Ashdjian (Wheeler 64), Himsworth,
Mooney, Foreman, Jules.

Although they had been in existence since 1879 it took almost 100 years for Scarborough to make any sort of mark in football, winning the F.A. Trophy three times in the 1970s. They won the Vauxhall Conference in 1987 and were rewarded by becoming the first side to be automatically promoted to the Football League. A couple of good initial seasons was followed by a downturn in the team's performances, and five years after entering the League they were firmly marked out as one of the game's 'also-rans.' Nor did they possess an impressive record in the cups. They had never made the third round of the F.A. Cup since joining the League and had never been past the same stage in the League Cup. The early enthusiasm of supporters was wearing away as League football became less of a novelty. And when they were drawn against Premiership side Coventry City in the 1992-93 League Cup, few gave the side - managed by Ray McHale - any chance of causing an upset.

'Boro lost the first leg at Highfield Road 2-0. Although not disgraced, it seemed too much to expect the tie to be turned round at the McCain stadium and only 2,663 bothered to turn up for the second leg. They saw Mooney fire in a couple of shots which were easily dealt with by Coventry custodian Steve Ogrizovic. Mark Jules slung over a pair of dangerous crosses but, all in all, Coventry were well on top. Phil Babb fired just wide after 23 minutes and a Smith effort brought out a good save from Stuart Ford in the 'Boro goal. It looked like it was only a matter of time before Coventry increased their lead. A McGrath lob in 33 minutes forced Ford to dive backwards to tip the ball over the bar. Rosario headed wide for Coventry when in a good position. Scarborough were coming under intense pressure and escaped, somewhat luckily, to the dressing room with the score still 0-0.

What McHale said to his charges is unknown but it must have been a potent message, for the second half was an entirely different affair. Lee robbed Babb in front of the penalty area and the ball broke to Mooney. The striker ran on and beat Ogrizovic to put 'Boro ahead on the night and just one goal behind on aggregate. Scarborough were now running the show but they failed to capitalise on their chances. Ogrizovic was beaten by a cross from Mooney, but both Foreman and Hirst failed to reach the ball. Babb retaliated for Coventry with a fine shot which produced an equally good response from Ford. 'Boro again pushed forward, but with time running out, it looked like Coventry had escaped.

Thompson humped a long ball over the defence in what looked like one last desperate 'Boro charge. Pearce tried to clear but struck the ball only as far as Foreman. He turned and shot into the left hand corner of the net to send the 'Boro fans wild. 2-0 on the night, 2-2 on aggregate. There were 90 minutes on the clock. Scarborough had forced extra-time, or so it seemed. But battling 'Boro weren't finished yet. In the third minute of injury time, Mooney chased after a long ball, only to be elbowed by Atherton. Himsworth floated the free kick into the penalty area and Hirst soared above everyone, heading home an incredible third goal for Scarborough. The team which was lucky to be level at half-time had produced a magical second-half performance, culminating in that dramatic 93rd minute winner. Club chairman Geoffrey Richmond summed it up as, *"The greatest night in our history."*

He was right. Scarborough produced another memorable performance in the next round, beating Plymouth Argyle, to reach the last 16 of the competition. That brought the mighty Arsenal to the Yorkshire Coast. And 'Boro made the Gunners fight all the way for their 1-0 triumph which carried the Londoners forward on their path to an eventual domestic cup 'double.' But Scarborough have slipped back in the last few seasons. Now the battle is to keep League football at Seamer Road. In a short League career, they have contributed much to the game. It is a battle they deserve to win.

ON THE SAME DAY...

News: Chancellor of the Exchequer, Norman Lamont, faces the Tory Party conference, just weeks after the debacle which saw Britain forced to leave the ERM, and with the pound seriously devalued.

Sport: After Scarborough, the performance of the evening comes from Derby County who overturn a first-leg 1-0 deficit by beating Southend United 7-0 in their League Cup tie.

Entertainment: Yet another re-run of cult 1960s TV show *'The Prisoner'* is the evening's Channel 4 highlight.

Newcastle United 1 Vs
SCUNTHORPE UNITED 3

January 25th 1958
F.A. Cup Round Four

Scunthorpe United: Hardwick, Sharpe, Brownsword, Marshall,
Horstead, Bushby, Marriott, Waldock, Davis, Haigh, Jones

To the uninitiated, Scunthorpe United are simply the repository of one of football's 'trick' questions; Name the three eventual England captains who once played for Scunthorpe? The answer being, Ray Clemence, Kevin Keegan and (the 'trick' one) Ian Botham. But in the early part of their life as a League club, Scunthorpe & Lindsey United - to give them the name they carried until 1958 - enjoyed a rise in their fortunes which, if not quite meteoric, was at least in the jet travel class. They only joined the League in 1950 and in their eighth season were running away with the last-ever Third Division (North) title. They also progressed to the fourth round of the F.A. Cup but their chances of going any further were rated at virtually zero when they were drawn away to face Newcastle United.

Scunthorpe had never ventured past the fourth round. Their previous best in the competition had been a three-match epic tie against Portsmouth in 1954, which the Iron had eventually lost, though not before being compensated with a record 23,935 attendance at their Old Showground home. Newcastle, were the cup-fighting aristocrats of the fifties, three times winners between 1951-55. And although the Geordies were struggling to keep their top flight status, they were fancied by many to add a fourth F.A. Cup win to that impressive haul.

St. James Park presented a grim visage to the arriving Scunthorpe players. Not only was it a forbidding citadel in its own right but, covered with ice, water, mud and snow, it was as inhospitable as any football ground can be. The pitch was, however, deemed playable. And Scunthorpe proved that decision to be correct as they set about Newcastle with a determination which masked the two divisions gulf between the sides. Scoular and Mitchell, the home side's star performers, were marked out of the game. McMichael was mastered by Marriott. After 25 minutes gritty play, Scunthorpe appeared to have taken a shock lead through Waldock, but the linesman's flag signalled offside. Waldock tried again, only to see 'keeper Ronnie Simpson slither successfully in the water to hold the shot. With Bushby marshalling his men superbly in defence on the rare occasions Newcastle threatened, even at this early stage of the game the Geordie supporters must have felt that a shock was in the offing.

That threat became reality almost right on the half-time whistle when a Marriott corner found Haigh with the time to tuck away the opening goal. The 3,000 Steelworkers fans who had braved the hazardous journey north spent the half-time break singing the praises of their heroes.

But Newcastle hadn't forged their Cup reputation out of nothing. After the break they launched a wave of attacks on the Scunthorpe goal. A Mitchell corner gave Paterson the opportunity to equalise with Brownsword vainly hooking the ball away after it had already crossed the line. With forty minutes still to play, few would have backed Scunthorpe now. But, just five minutes later, the Geordie majority in the crowd of 39,407 were stunned into silence when Davis out-jumped McKinney to head Scunthorpe back in front. Newcastle attacked furiously, but they produced only one genuine chance when the normally-reliable Len White missed a sitter.

With fifteen minutes to go, Scunthorpe ventured forward again. Jones centred and Newcastle's Paterson miskicked completely, allowing Davis to nip in and score a third. The ecstatic centre-forward celebrated by, *"performing a Maori war dance,"* as the *Scunthorpe Evening Telegraph* joyously put it. An overconfident Newcastle had failed to adapt to conditions which are not exactly unknown in the north-east. There were no more goals and Scunthorpe's 3-1 victory gave their travelling support cause for lengthy celebrations. All 3,000 of them, it seemed, danced in a circle outside Newcastle's Central Station and hundreds continued to jig all the way back to Scunthorpe. England's cup kings had been humbled on their own turf by one of the League's youngest clubs.

Scunthorpe lost in the fifth round, 1-0, in a hard-fought tussle at home to Liverpool. But they duly went on to lift the Third (North) title by a seven point margin. Four years later, they stood at the very gates of the First Division, but eventually settled for fourth spot in Division Two, their best League placing ever. With the exception of another run to the fifth round of the F.A. Cup in 1970, there has not been a lot of success since and their Old Showground was left for Glanford Park in 1988. The memory of that sensational cup win still lives on however, in the minds of all those who were there to see it.

SHEFFIELD UNITED 1

Vs Sunderland 0

April 2nd 1898 - Division One

Sheffield United: Foulkes, Thicket, Cain, Johnson, Morren, Howard, Bennett, Cunningham, Hedley, Almond, Priest.

Just three years after their 1889 formation, Sheffield United joined the newly-created Division Two. They finished second top and thanks to victory in a 'test' match, gained promotion to the top sphere. Within a few seasons they had assembled a team capable of taking on the best in the land. Their line-up contained two of the greatest players of the late Victorian era; the 20 stone-plus goalkeeper, 'Fatty' Foulke and brilliant wing-half Ernest 'Nudger' Needham. As Easter 1898 approached, the Blades were top of the League, in line to bring the title to Yorkshire for the first time. With three games to play they led with 36 points. One point behind, and with a game in hand were Sunderland, the most feared side in the country. And Sheffield United's next match was at home to .... Sunderland. The scene was set for a titanic struggle.

United started the match with some trepidation. Victory would make them the clear favourite for the flag, but defeat would almost extinguish their chances. And they were below strength. Regular first-teamers Gaudie and McKay were out injured and the famous Needham was absent on England duty - no question of postponements due to a national call-up in those days. Sunderland had their regular first eleven on display and, with the wind at their backs, should have capitalised on their advantage. But it was United, roared on by 25,000 partisan Yorkshire voices, who made the better start. They contained the Roker men's charge and carved out several chances of their own.

Sunderland gradually came back into it and both Leslie and Saxon brought out some fine saves from Foulke. The big 'keeper has gone into the record books under his sibilantly-challenged surname, but contemporary reports always referred to him as Foulkes. Bennett ran the show for the Blades, setting up Priest, Almond and Hedley with chances which were well saved by Sunderland's own famous goalkeeper, Scottish international Ned Doig. Half-time arrived with the game still goalless and both sides with everything still to play for.

The Blades used the wind to their advantage rather better than their opponents had. In the first 25 minutes of the half, Sunderland crossed the half-way line just once. But, with Doig in such superb form, United found it difficult to break through. They knew how much hinged on the match, a draw would leave Sunderland with the best chance of the title. But Sunderland held out until fifteen minutes from the end. Priest's corner was met by Johnson who shot through a crowd of players to find the target. The goal created, *"a scene of excitement which has scarcely been paralleled even in Sheffield,"* according to contemporary newspaper *The Sportsman.*

Sunderland tried to come back but their defensive efforts left them tired. Sheffield United had little to worry about for the rest of the match. And but for Doig the score would have been much heavier. The win sparked off scenes of celebration which continued until six days later, Good Friday, when the Blades went to Bolton and won 1-0 while a demoralised Sunderland lost by the same score at home to Bury. Now it was official, Sheffield United were the Champions of England for the first time. The title came to Sheffield, indeed to Yorkshire, for the first time. And if 'Nudger' Needham felt bad about missing the crucial game against Sunderland, he had the mighty compensation of scoring the goal at Bolton which officially secured the Championship.

For the Blades, this was part of a golden era when they finished runners-up twice in the League and appeared in three F.A. Cup Finals, winning two of them, all between 1897-1902. There were further Cup wins in 1915 and 1925. They were relegated in 1934 after 41 years in Division One. Since then, a losing Cup Final in 1936 has been their best achievement. The past 60-odd years have seen them bouncing around the Divisions, never spending more than seven consecutive seasons in the top division and even ending up in Division Four in the early 1980s. The club which became Yorkshire's first English Champions remain one of the great enigmas of the game.

At 6'-2" and 22 stone, Billy 'Fatty' Foulkes was a remarkably agile goalkeeper and an expert at saving penalties.

SHEFFIELD WEDNESDAY 2

Vs Wolverhampton Wanderers 1

April 18th 1896 - F.A. Cup Final (Crystal Palace)

Sheffield Wednesday: Massey, Earp, Langley, Brandon, Crawshaw,
Petrie, Brash, Brady, Bell, Davis, Spikesley

Sheffield Wednesday (or The Wednesday as they were known until 1929) had already played in one F.A. Cup Final, losing to Blackburn Rovers in 1890. They had joined the League in 1892, being elected straight into Division One, and soon established themselves in that company. In the Cup they had reached the Semi-Finals in 1894 and 1895, losing both games. And when they eliminated reigning League Champions Sunderland in the second round of this season's competition, another long run was on the cards. Everton were next to fall, then Bolton were overcome after a Semi-Final replay to take them through to an eagerly-awaited Final against Wolves.

The Midlands side had already tasted Cup success in 1893 so a tough game was anticipated. There was also a new trophy to play for, the original one having been stolen from a Birmingham shop window the previous September. It was no surprise therefore when a new record crowd of 48,836 assembled at the Crystal Palace for the Final, and they saw one of the most sensational starts ever. Wednesday kicked off by charging down the left. They lost the ball but managed to force a throw-in. The throw was received by Petrie who played a long ball to Brash. He made a brief run before crossing to left-winger Spikesley. The winger hit a low, quick shot into the net to put Wednesday ahead with less than a minute played.

The scorer has gone into history as 'Spiksley' but the papers of the day referred to him as 'Spikesley', one of the many confusions surrounding names from this era. Wednesday swarmed over Wolves immediately after the goal, attempting to kill the game off as soon as possible. Crawshaw and Brandon joined the attack and both came close to adding to Wednesday's lead. But the opening period of this match had further sensations to give. Wolves humped a free kick into the Wednesday goalmouth and their left-winger, Black, with his back to goal, launched a scissors-kick straight into the net. 1-1 with only eight minutes on the clock.

The fiery approach was continued by both teams. Spikesley was in great form for Wednesday, prompting move after move. Wolves came back through inside-left Wood who actually got the ball in the net but was clearly offside. A midfield tussle between Spikesley and Wolves right-back Baugh, ended with the Wednesday winger in possession. He fired in a magnificent shot which went in off the right hand post before goalkeeper Tennant had any time to react. 2-1 to Wednesday with only twenty minutes played. The Yorkshire club maintained their dominance until the interval but without adding to their lead.

Wolves were better in the second half. Right-winger Tonks shot over the bar, but Wednesday came back at them. Bell forced Tennant into a good save. There was more drama from a free kick. Wolves left-back Dunn sent a drooping shot into the net. But the kick had been indirect and no-one else had touched the ball. No goal. At the other end, Crawshaw's free kick was flighted on by Bell's good header, only to be fisted away by Tennant. Crawshaw was inspiring Wednesday but Wolves were stringing some neat passes together. Massey found his services called on; twice in the same number of minutes he had to punch clear. Wolves kept pressing but Wednesday were resolute. The whistle finally sounded on an historic triumph. For the very first time the F.A. Cup was on its way to Yorkshire.

Wednesday were to repeat their triumph in 1907 and 1936. Twice they won League Championship 'doubles', in 1902-03 and 1903-04 and again in 1928-29 and 1929-30. But Wednesday were more noted for their regular 'yo-yo-ing' between the top two divisions, an unfortunate habit which ended up in relegation to the Third Division in 1975. Recent years have seen a Hillsborough revival with the winning of the League Cup in 1991 and their 'double' Cup Final defeats in 1993. They have certainly won enough over the years to make selecting their greatest day a difficult task. But, although there is now no-one alive who can remember it, the day the F.A. Cup first came to Yorkshire must have been very special indeed.

ON THE SAME DAY...

News: Fresh discoveries are made in the Bunyip Gold Fields of Western Australia.

Sport: World Billiards Champion J.Roberts gives a series of exhibition matches. Despite giving opponents a 7,000 points start, he is still first to reach the winning target of 21,000 in every game.

Entertainment: The post-match variety show at the Crystal Palace includes clowns, acrobats, singers, the band of the Grenadier Guards and a comic pantomime from the famous Fred Karno Troupe.

SHREWSBURY TOWN 2

Vs Ipswich Town 1

February 13th 1982 - F.A. Cup Round Five

Shrewsbury Town: Wardle, King, Johnson, Cross, Griffin, Keay, Tong, McNally, Atkins, Biggins, Bates.

Football success and Shrewsbury Town are not synonymous. The Shropshire club only joined the League in 1950 and for almost 30 years there was little to celebrate. Promotion from the 4th Division in 1959 and 1975. A Semi-Final appearance in the inaugural League Cup in 1961. Arthur Rowley completing his League record 434 goals while with the Shrews. A man who went out in a coracle to fetch balls blasted out of the ground. And a ground, Gay Meadow, which became subject to increasing schoolboy sniggering throughout the 1970s. That all changed during the reign of Graham Turner as manager. Appointed in 1978, Turner led the Shrews to a Third Division title in 1979. He also led them to the Quarter-Finals of the F.A. Cup for the first time, courtesy of a largely fortuitous draw and a giant-killing fourth round win over Manchester City. Three years later, Shrewsbury were established in Division Two and the prospect of another Cup run beckoned.

Keeping Shrewsbury at Second Division level on average gates of less than 5,000 was an achievement in itself. Cup success was the icing on the cake. Port Vale and Burnley were both beaten before Shrewsbury faced the toughest possible task. In a competition where favourites had fallen like ninepins, they were drawn at home to Ipswich Town. The East Anglian side were UEFA Cup holders, and right in the hunt for the League title. Shrews had the memory of the Manchester City match to inspire them but the City side they had knocked out in 1979 had been accustomed to such blows and they were nowhere near the class of Ipswich.

Bobby Robson's team had injury problems however. But these were not apparent in the early stages of the game as Ipswich tore into the Shrewsbury defence. For most of the first fifteen minutes, the First Division side looked a different class until Shrewsbury received a stroke of luck no-one could have expected. Fourteen minutes had elapsed when the ball bounced off the referee's head straight into the path of Wayne Biggins. Ipswich's Scottish International, John Wark, decided to take no chances, even though Biggins was 25 yards from goal. He promptly fouled the Shrewsbury man. King's chipped free kick found Cross. Ten yards out, he coolly fired a low shot past Cooper in the Ipswich goal to give Shrewsbury the lead totally against the run of play.

Shrewsbury were fired up now and it was the home side which took command. In 24 minutes, McNally neatly dispossessed Mick Mills and sent Bates clear. His low cross was met by Biggins, whose shot deflected off Osman for a corner. Tong's kick was knocked backwards by Keay to the far post where it was met by Jake King. Playing only his second match after a nine-match lay-off, King gleefully headed in the second goal.

The bulk of the 13,965 crowd roared on the Shropshire side. Ipswich were clearly rattled. Their game fell to pieces as Shrewsbury continued to dominate. With all their fluency gone, it was Ipswich who appeared to be the lower division club. The homesters played like a First Division team. Not until Mich D'Avray replaced Mills in the 75th minute did Ipswich threaten again. D'Avray took a pass from O'Callaghan and beat Wardle to make it 2-1. That inspired a late Ipswich fightback but Shrewsbury were in no mood to surrender. They clung on tenaciously to the final whistle.

With five Second Division clubs through to the last eight and, of the three First Division survivors, only Spurs from the top half of the table, every single team left - Shrewsbury included - thought they could win the Cup. Unfortunately for the Shrews, they were drawn away to Leicester City. Their away form was poor and although at half-time it was 2-2, Leicester, inspired by young striker Gary Lineker, ran out 5-2 winners at full-time. Thus ended Shrewsbury's best hope of bringing the F.A. Cup to Shropshire. No other Second Division side was satisfied either, Spurs eventually lifting the trophy.

Shrewsbury spent a decade in Division Two, being relegated in 1989. Three years later, they ended back in the lowest Division. Winning the new Third Division in 1994 may herald a revival for football in Shropshire. If the Shrews could last for ten years in the old Second Division in the 1980s, then they must surely be capable of reaching the new First Division before the end of this century.

SOUTHAMPTON 1

Vs Manchester United 0

May 1st 1976 - F.A. Cup Final
(Wembley)

Southampton: Turner, Rodrigues, Peach, Holmes, Blyth, Steele, Gilchrist, Channon, Osgood, McCalliog, Stokes. Sub: Fisher.

Southampton had been a major force in football at the turn of the century, reaching (and losing) two F.A. Cup Finals in 1900 and 1902. But until promotion to the First Division in 1966, their League record had been largely anonymous. After relegation back to Division Two in 1974, it looked like their brief flirtation with life at the top was over. 1975-76 was to dispel that idea entirely. Under manager Lawrie McMenemy, Saints developed a side carefully blended with skill, youth, experience and talent as they stormed to Wembley in the F.A. Cup Final.

Some thought that the traditional cup element of luck had been handed out in generous measures to Southampton. For after an extra time third round victory at Villa Park, Saints never again faced First Division opposition before the Final. That would be doing them an injustice. They produced a fine home win over Blackpool in the fourth round, then produced a fighting draw away to promotion-chasing West Brom before winning the replay 4-0, with Mick Channon bagging a hat-trick. A hard-fought away win over Bradford City sent them into the Semi-Finals where they faced Crystal Palace. Although in the Third Division, Palace were strongly fancied to make the Final and the Stamford Bridge venue favoured the London team more than Saints. But Southampton's experience won through, with two second half goals pointing them down the Wembley way.

The Final was a different proposition. Manchester United had knocked out First Division outfits Leicester, Wolves and reigning League Champions Derby on their way to Wembley and, under Tommy Docherty, were one of the most exciting teams in the land, lying third in the table a year after promotion. Saints were predicted to be the onlookers at the coronation of Docherty's Cup Kings.

McMenemy, though, was at the height of his tactical prowess. And he devised a plan to bring the Cup to the South Coast. They stopped United from using their attacking full-backs and neatly interposed a man between Gordon Hill and any potential pass the flying winger may have had on his mind. McCalliog and Gilchrist made long passes to good effect. Even so, it was United who made the first real chance in eleven minutes when Pearson, with his back to goal, turned and passed to Hill. Turner raced out smartly to block. Daly was next to test the 'keeper but Turner saved with ease. Hill tried a shot which was deflected past the post by Blyth. After 33 minutes, Saints, growing in confidence, almost carved out the opener. McCalliog sent a lovely through pass to Channon, but the striker hesitated long enough for Stepney in the United goal to position himself for the save. United were still coming forward but Rodrigues effectively stifled Hill, and McCalliog, Steele and Holmes neutered the Old Trafford Midfield threat. At half-time it was Saints who were the happier with the 0-0 scoreline.

The second half saw McIlroy and Coppell provide the service lacking from Hill. Coppell made chances for Pearson and Macari but both efforts were well off target. Then McIlroy headed against the post. United brought on McCreery for Hill but the switch made no difference. Channon's runs and Osgood's dribbling were beginning to have an effect for Saints. From a good position, Rodrigues sliced his shot. A neat one-two between Channon and McCalliog saw the former go close. Twice, Stokes, one of the lesser-known names in the side shot over the bar.

With seven minutes remaining, McCalliog - the best player on the pitch, and one determined to make up for the disappointment of having played in the Sheffield Wednesday side that had lost the 1966 Final after holding a 2-0 lead - deftly passed to the unmarked Stokes. He evaded Greenhoff's lunge, then hit the ball past the diving Stepney to record his name in the folklore of Southampton for evermore. While United defenders flocked round Osgood and Channon, they had ignored Stokes. The goal punished their contempt.

As Saints fans celebrated their success, McMenemy downplayed their role as giant-killers: *"Ability won it for us, it wasn't a surprise,"* said the big Geordie who, before the match, told his players *"Never mind if the Queen is watching, if there's danger, belt the ball into the Tyne."* A feat surely beyond even the most powerful of players. *"Good luck to them,"* said a sporting Docherty. He, and everyone else, knew that the Second Division side were worthy winners.

Two years later Southampton returned to the top Division. They lost a thrilling League Cup Final in 1979 and reached a League best by finishing runners-up in 1984. The Saints of the early 80s were regulars in Europe too. They have proved that Southampton deserves a Premiership club. Their status in the game derives from that magical moment when McMenemy's Second Division battlers brought home the F.A. Cup.

Bury 0 Vs

SOUTHEND UNITED 1

May 4th 1991 - Division Three

Southend United: Sansome, Austin, Hyslop, Martin,
Scully, Locke (Powell), Clark, Butler, Ansah,
Benjamin, Angell (Cornwall)

Founded in 1906, League members since 1920, Southend United had never played above Third Division level. When they were relegated - for the fifth time - to Division Four in 1989, few could have predicted the transformation the club would undergo in just two years. But former Chelsea hero David Webb took the Shrimpers to heights undreamed of in their past. First, there was promotion back to the Third, and achieved at the first time of asking. Then came the magnificent run of 1990-91 when Southend, after the first few games, were never out of the top two places. Division Two beckoned. Victory over Bury would confirm Southend's historic move up.

Preparation for the match was vital. Southend flew to the North-West for the game, an unaccustomed luxury, but an indication of how seriously Webb took this game. For Bury too had something to play for, they needed a win to keep their play-off hopes alive. The crowd, at 4,254, was not particularly large but it contained 1,500 Blues fans, all anxious to see history in the making. Instead, they witnessed a somewhat tentative first half, with both sides reluctant to take risks. The match was enlivened by two attempts from Andy Ansah, both narrowly wide. That was the signal for Southend to move forward. A Hyslop cross six minutes from the break was just missed by Angell. Then, almost on the point of half-time, came a disaster for Southend. A challenge from Scully on Bury's Lee which should have earned him a booking, saw him sent off instead. Even though the half ended goalless, Southend seemed to be the side with the greater problems to face.

It wasn't just that they had to play for 45 minutes with ten men. The Shrimpers were facing a swirling wind against foes with their tails up. Martin dropped back and he and Clark formed a staunch defensive pairing. But Bury's extra man began to prove decisive in their forward probes. With fifteen minutes to go, Bury's Robinson unleashed a thirty yard thunderbolt which Sansome bravely fisted onto and over the bar. From the corner, Valentine produced a header that looked a winner all the way, until Sansome, somehow, managed to turn it over the top.

The 'keeper's efforts inspired his team-mates. In 82 minutes, Ansah sent over a cross to Ian Benjamin. He turned quickly and lashed the ball into the Bury net to ignite a dance of delirium from the travelling band of Shrimpers supporters. Bury were left floundering, with no time to come back. Southend held on easily to ensure victory and promotion. After 85 years in existence, they had reached the Second Division.

But, in victory, there was still sourness. Chairman Vic Jobson scorned a civic reception. A long-running dispute with the local authority led him to claim that the local council undermined sport in Southend. Dave Webb concentrated on the task in hand. *"This is our little Everest,"* he said, referring to the fact that he still wanted to win the Third Division title. But just one point from their final two games robbed Southend of that opportunity, Cambridge snatching the title by a point.

The Shrimpers found the going tough in the higher sphere. But they have, if not thrived, at least survived. Proof that their 85 year wait was not in vain. And when they look at the success of a side like Wimbledon, who is to say that Southend will not, one day, play in the Premiership?

ON THE SAME DAY...

News: Yugoslavia is reported to be on the brink of break-up and civil war.

Sport: Defeat at Nottingham Forest ends Liverpool's title hopes but manager Graeme Souness vows his team will be Champions next season.

Entertainment:
BBC-1 shows the 36th Eurovision Song Contest.

STOCKPORT COUNTY 13
Vs Halifax Town 0

January 6th 1934 - Division Three (North)

Stockport County: McGann, Vincent, Jenkinson, Robinson, Stevens, L.Jones, Foulkes, Hill, Lythgoe, Stevenson, Downes.

Originally formed under the name Heaton Norris Rovers by members of a congregational chapel, Stockport County joined the Second Division in 1900. They failed to be re-elected in 1904, regained their place the next year, were relegated in 1921, promptly regained their Division Two status in 1922, only to lose it again in 1926. In 1933-34 they were bidding for promotion, lying 2nd in the table as they prepared to face Halifax Town. No-one could have known that history was going to be made in Stockport that day.

Halifax were in 5th spot and must have fancied their chances of taking at least a point from this Edgeley Park Encounter. Instead they were to enter the record books for all the wrong reasons. After just eight minutes the Yorkshire side were a goal behind when Hill took a pass from Lythgoe and fired high into the net. Six minutes later the same player scored from close in. But Halifax's stand-in 'keeper Milton was having a superb game. He saved good efforts from Downes, Lythgoe and Foulkes, earning himself the applause of the County fans in the process. At half-time Stockport led by those two early goals.

But Stockport fans were far from certain of even claiming the points at this stage. There was a powerful wind, in Stockport's favour in the first half. Resuming against it, as the *Stockport Express* said, *"doubts were expressed in some quarters as to whether the two-goal lead was sufficient to gain the day."* Within five minutes though, Lythgoe had made it 3-0. Sixty seconds later Hill added the fourth, and two minutes after that came a Vincent penalty for the fifth. Scarcely had the supporters time to draw breath when Foulkes scored the sixth, in 57 minutes. Two minutes later it was Downes' turn to get on the scoresheet. A further two minutes and Stevenson got the eighth. It took four minutes before Downes made it nine but the same player made up for his tardiness by adding a tenth - and his own hat-trick, sixty seconds later. There were still 24 minutes to play. Stockport had scored eight times in the space of 21 minutes. Unaccountably, it was not until the 79th minute that Lythgoe made it eleven.

With four minutes to go Stevenson grabbed the twelfth, equalling the League record. Two minutes later Downes scored number thirteen, making Stockport the record holders, the first team ever to score that number in a League match. The local paper praised County's *"unselfishness."* Lythgoe, *"in particular, being most generous in his distribution of the ball."* And some of the goals were really special: *"Downes, on one occasion, screwing the leather off the goal-line and landing it in the net, to the astonishment of the youthful goalie."* With the exception of the penalty, every goal came from a forward and every forward scored, the final tally reading: Downes(4), Hill(3), Lythgoe(2), Stevenson(2), Foulkes(1), Vincent(1 pen).

Stockport failed to win promotion that year, finishing 3rd. They did go up in 1937 but lasted just one season in Division Two. They have never reached those heights since, although a play-off defeat at Wembley in 1994 for a place in the new First Division brought new hope to a club which has been in the doldrums for far too long. As for their record, it has never been beaten. Tranmere scored thirteen against Oldham in a Third (North) game in December 1935 but they also conceded four goals. County found their efforts matched by Newcastle in 1946 when the Geordies beat Newport County 13-0 in a Second Division match. But the proud claim of having been the first team to score thirteen goals in a League match is one which can never been taken away from Stockport County.

ON THE SAME DAY...

News: It was announced that Herbert Chapman, manager of Arsenal and formerly of Huddersfield Town, and the greatest manager of the times, is dead.

Sport: It is a day dominated by International trials; for all Four home Countries in Rugby Union, for England at Hockey and for both Oxford and Cambridge in Rowing.

Entertainment: 10 years old Margarita Heifetz astonished the Moscow Conservatory by conducting Schubert's Unfinished Symphony, Tchaikovsky's fifth and also music by Rimsky-Korsakov. She also played Chopin waltzes on the piano, as well as some waltzes she had composed herself.

The team that the scored the lucky 13 - players only: (Back) Vincent, McGann, Jenkinson, Stevenson. (Middle) Foulkes, Hill, Stevens, Lythgoe, Downes. (Front) Robinson, Jones.

STOKE CITY 2

Vs Chelsea 1

March 4th 1972 - League Cup Final (Wembley)

Stoke City: Banks, Marsh, Pejic, Bernard, Smith, Bloor, Conroy, Greenhoff (Mahoney), Ritchie, Dobing, Eastham.

Indelibly associated in the public mind with the incomparable Stanley Matthews, Stoke City have had a chequered history. One of the original founders of the Football League, they lost their League place after just two seasons. Quickly re-elected, they suffered the indignity of having to resign from the League for financial reasons in 1908. Re-joining after the First World War, Stoke even sank as low as the Third Division (North) in the pre-Matthews era. After a twenty year run in Division One they spent a decade (1953-63) in the Second Division. It was under manager Tony Waddington, and with the returning veteran Matthews in the side, that they returned to the top grade in 1963. Matthews played on till he was 50, becoming the first playing footballer to be knighted.

Waddington had a reputation for signing players thought to be past their best and rejuvenating them. Such was the case with the side of 1971-72. Peter Dobing and George Eastham were both considered past their prime but played some of their best football in Stoke colours. Others, like Pejic, Smith and Greenhoff were nowhere near the veteran stage and players of note in their own right. And there was Gordon Banks, quite simply the finest goalkeeper in the world. So it was no great surprise when this Stoke side reached the F.A. Cup Semi-Finals for the first time in the 20th Century in 1971 and repeated the feat the next season. On both occasions they lost to Arsenal after a replay. But prior to their 1972 Semi-Final, Stoke launched themselves on a fabulous run in the League Cup.

Southport and Oxford were eliminated in the early stages before Stoke conquered Manchester United in a three-game epic. A Quarter-Final away win over Bristol Rovers sent them into a last-four tussle with West Ham. Ostensibly over two legs, it took four games to separate the sides in a series of matches which produced some of the best football the League Cup has ever seen. The end result was that Stoke City, for the first time in their 109 year history, had reached a major Cup Final. Their opponents were Chelsea, cup specialists, having won the 1970 F.A. Cup and the European Cup-Winners Cup in 1971. A fascinating Final lay in prospect.

A full house crowd of 100,000 saw Chelsea start confidently yet within five minutes Stoke were in front. Dobing took a long throw which Bonetti, blocked by Osgood, could only punch half-clear. Eastham curled the ball back into the area. Conroy failed to connect and Dennis Smith's shot was blocked. The ball bobbled around the box before Conroy got his head to it to open the scoring. Chelsea weren't fazed by this setback. Twice, Chris Garland threatened danger. He was put through by Osgood before being brought down by Bloor just outside the penalty box, then received an inch-perfect pass from Charlie Cooke before being brought down again, this time by Pejic. Ritchie burst through for Stoke but was stopped by Hollins. It was a flowing game, worthy of the occasion. Cooke flighted the ball over to the near post and Garland got the header in, but Bloor cleared for a corner. Seven minutes from the break it was Garland again, with a shot which saw Banks produce his best to save. Cooke found Webb. His shot was blocked but Osgood, lying on the ground, hooked in the equaliser. An entertaining half ended 1-1.

Chelsea's frantic first half efforts seemed to have worn them out. Stoke took command of the game as the second period wore on. After 73 minutes, Conroy beat Harris and sent a long pass on to Ritchie. The striker headed down to Greenhoff whose shot was parried away by Bonetti. But only as far as Eastham. The 35 year old, who had only returned from South African football in October 1971, neatly slotted home from an angle. Now Chelsea threw caution aside, moving Webb up into attack. Baldwin headed just over in 82 minutes. A point blank Osgood header saw another of Banks' wonder saves. Ritchie counter-attacked for Stoke, Houseman heading off the line. With seconds to go, Garland was clear through. Out came Banks with a brilliant block. This wonderful game ended with Stoke City the 2-1 victors. After 109 years, one of the game's top prizes was at last on its way to the Potteries.

Stoke had richly deserved their triumph and their players were as emotional as their fans. *"For me this ranks alongside England's World Cup win,"* said Gordon Banks as he picked up the only winners medal of his domestic career. Eastham was more light-hearted: *"I don't like to score, normally. It embarrasses the rest of the boys."* Waddington was the master of the understatement: *"I am satisfied with the way things went,"* was his comment.

The Potteries have never experienced a day like it, neither before nor since. Stoke were relegated in 1977 and although they came back up two years later, further relegation in 1985 was the prelude to a spell in the Third Division. Now back in Division One (new style), their supporters believe that Stoke is a big enough place to deserve a team in the Premiership and regular challenges for honours. A look at the teamsheet for their League Cup success reveals the kind of talent they will have to lure to the Victoria Ground before those days ever return.

SUNDERLAND 1

Vs Leeds United 0

May 5th 1973 - F.A. Cup Final
(Wembley)

Sunderland: Montgomery, Malone, Watson, Pitt, Guthrie, Horswill, Kerr, Porterfield, Hughes, Halom, Tueart.

Five times League Champions before the First World War, Sunderland were one of the giants of Football's early era. But with only a 1936 title and a 1937 F.A. Cup win since then, they had sunk into mediocrity. Embroiled in scandal, their proud boast of never having been relegated came to an end in 1958. They hovered between the top two divisions, seemingly too good for the Second and perennial strugglers when in the First. By 1973 they were again a Division Two side and an ordinary one at that. Yet the first few months of that year were to produce a legend on Wearside comparable to anything that had gone before and unequalled since.

Their early Cup performances were hardly inspiring, wins over Notts County and Reading after replays taking them into the fifth round. It was here that the legend began to take shape. A 2-2 draw away to First Division Manchester City, Summerbee, Lee, Marsh et al, was the prelude to a magnificent 3-1 Roker replay triumph. Over 100,000 watched the two games. Another 50,000 plus turned up to see the home win over Luton which took the Roker side through to the last four. At Hillsborough they defied the odds in spectacular fashion with a 2-1 win over an Arsenal team seeking their third successive Cup Final. Now it was Wembley and Leeds United, the F.A. Cup holders, 3rd in the League and on their way to the European Cup-Winners Cup Final. No Second Division team had won the F.A. Cup for 42 years. Surely this particular fairy tale was destined for an unhappy ending?

But this Cup Final had caught the public imagination like no other since the time of the 'Matthews' Final. And, outside the environs of West Yorkshire, there were few who were not willing Sunderland to Victory. Perhaps only their bitterest rivals on Tyneside and Teesside begrudged the Wearsiders their chance of glory. Elsewhere, everyone became an honorary Rokerite for the day.

Sunderland set out to harry the Leeds midfield, to prevent them from controlling the match. Dick Malone, considered to be the weak link, emphatically disproved this theory by mastering Eddie Gray. Malone relished appearing in front of 100,000 at Wembley as only a player brought up on playing in front of crowds one hundredth of that size at lowly Ayr United can. Bremner and Giles found themselves policed out of the match by Porterfield and Horswill. Leeds were rattled after thirteen minutes when Hughes shot narrowly over the bar from 25 yards. A minute later a Giles run saw neat passing to Reaney then Clarke. But the striker hesitated just long enough for Dave Watson to rescue the day. Hunter beat Halom and found Lorimer with his cross. But the lethal-footed Scot crashed the ball into the side-netting.

Sunderland were capable of mounting attacks of their own. Horswill drove just wide from 20 yards with 'keeper Harvey beaten. Clarke tried again for Leeds but the immaculate Watson barred his progress. On the half-hour Gray at last got a shot in but was wide. Sixty seconds later Porterfield sent a 30-yard pass to Kerr. Seeing Harvey off his line, Kerr attempted to chip him but the 'keeper recovered to tip the ball over the bar to give Sunderland their first corner. Hughes sent it to the far post, Halom knocked it back and Porterfield cushioned it on his left thigh before volleying home with his weaker right foot. Sunderland were now in command, Leeds made just one good move before the interval when Madeley split the defence, but, once more, Watson had the measure of Clarke. Half-time saw the almost unbelievable scoreline, Sunderland 1 - Leeds 0.

Leeds attacked furiously at the start of the second half. But Montgomery and Watson were usually in command. Montgomery did fail to hold a Bremner drive but Malone reacted promptly, clearing the danger. Horswill, Tueart, Porterfield and Guthrie all had chances or half-chances for the Wearsiders, relieving the pressure. But Roker hearts leapt into their mouths in the 55th minute when Watson brought down Bremner in the box. Fortunately the referee waved play on. In 64 minutes came the moment that ensured Jim Montgomery would never have to put his hand inside his pocket in a Sunderland pub ever again. Lorimer crossed from the right to beyond the far post. Clarke angled his header to perfection but there was Montgomery, twisting and turning in mid-air before diving to parry the ball away. Even then it seemed Leeds must score, for the ball landed at Lorimer's feet five yards from the open goal. Lorimer hit it hard and fast but somehow Montgomery was up off his knees, punching the ball up onto the underside of the bar before it bounced down to be cleared.

Leeds must have known at that point that nothing was going to beat Montgomery, or Sunderland, that day. They poured ten men into attack but Sunderland comfortably repelled them. The Cup was theirs and manager Bob Stokoe raced across the pitch like an Olympic sprinter to embrace his players at the end. *"Three months ago we were Second Division nobodies,"* said Stokoe, *"now we are known by all."* Captain, Bobby Kerr, told of his astonishment at lifting the trophy, *"I was in such a daze when I took the Cup from the Duchess of Kent that I slipped down the first three or four steps on the way down. But the Cup wasn't dented."* Thousands of Roker fans danced in jubilation in Trafalgar Square, without a single arrest being made. Hundreds of thousands, many who had never seen a football match in their lives before, took to the streets in the North-East. They had every reason to celebrate. Sunderland had shown that fairy tales can have a happy ending.

The Roker team failed to capitalise on their success. Three times since they have won promotion to the top flight. Twice they have gone straight back down. Their best spell was in the early '80s when a five year fight against relegation ended in the double agony of the drop and a League Cup Final defeat in the same season. There has even been the ignominy of a spell in the Third Division to endure. Everybody knows that Wearside can support a side at the very top level. But with just that 1973 success to show for nearly the past sixty years, how much longer will it be before they have a team to match the fans?

ON THE SAME DAY...

News: Lord Longford complains to the IBA over a Bob Monkhouse sketch which portrays the peer as Don Quixote chasing a stripper into a womens lavatory.

Sport: Another outsider triumphs. Mon Fils, ridden by Frankie Durr, is the 50-1 winner of the 2,000 Guineas.

Entertainment: Appropriately for Sunderland, the top film in London is *"That'll be the day."*

Swansea City (Swansea Town until 1970) spent the bulk of their first 60 years of League membership in the Second Division with occasional dips down into the lower regions. In the 1970s they were languishing in the Fourth Division when along came the inspirational John Toshack as manager, player-manager at first. Toshack led Swansea to promotion in 1978, then repeated the trick twelve months later. After a year's consolidation in Division two, Tosh produced his real magic when he guided Swans to 3rd place, edging Blackburn for promotion on goal difference. In just three years they had risen from the bottom division to the top. But this was a level Swansea had never played at before. Critics said that Toshack's, and Swansea's, big test would come on the day First Division football arrived at their Vetch Field ground.

That day dawned on August 29th 1981 and Swansea was buzzing with excitement. 23,489 turned up, filling the ground almost to capacity. Leeds may have been a shadow of the side which bestrode the continent a decade previously, but they were still a big draw. Those Welsh heroes of yore, John and Mel Charles, took their seats to watch Mel's son Jeremy make his First Division debut. And when a mighty roar rent the South Wales air after just five minutes, none shouted louder than the famous brothers, for it was Jeremy who scored Swansea's first goal in the top grade. A dream start for Charles and Swansea.

But all good dramas need a touch of the unexpected. So it proved here when another Welshman, Carl Harris of Leeds, earned the enmity of his countrymen by setting up Scottish international Derek Parlane to equalise after 26 minutes. Now it was Leeds who were in control. Dai Davies, in goal, had to be at his very best to turn a Graham header onto the post. The 'keeper proved equally alert in stopping a 20 yard drive from Kevin Hird. Half-time arrived with the teams still deadlocked at 1-1 but with Swansea the more apprehensive.

Toshack's team were not lacking in experience though, as many promoted clubs often are. Only four players were making their First Division debuts and two of these, Hadziabdic and Rajkovic, were Yugoslav internationals. Jeremy Charles and Robbie James aside, this was a side packed with players who had been the distance. And it was one such, Bob Latchford, who turned this game round in less than ten minutes, to make it a day Swans fans would never forget.

Latchford, playing his first League game since the previous November, fired Swansea back in front just one minute after play resumed. In 50 minutes he left defender Paul Hart and 'keeper John Lukic helpless to make it 3-1. And in 55 minutes a Latchford header earned him his hat-trick. The players had been back on the field for precisely nine minutes and thirteen seconds. Leeds must have been sick of the sight of Latchford, for two years before, he had scored a treble against them while with Everton.

SWANSEA CITY 5
Vs Leeds United 1

August 29th 1981 - Division One

Swansea City: Davies, Robinson, Hadziabdic, Rajkovic, Irwin, Mahoney, Curtis, R.James, L.James, Charles, Latchford.

Swans were rampant now. Mahoney and Charles ran the midfield. Irwin and Rajkovic were solid in defence. Neil Robinson marked Peter Barnes out of the game. And Leighton James and Alan Curtis showed great flair in attack. The icing on the Swans cake came in the 70th minute when Curtis, taunted by Leeds fans as a reject, sliced through the Leeds defence to make it 5-1, a scoreline unthinkable before the kick-off. Some Leeds supporters reacted with their customary good humour by raining bottles, firecrackers and coins down upon the police after Curtis scored.

Despite this huge victory, Mel Charles singled out Dai Davies for praise, saying it was, *"the finest goalkeeping display I have ever seen from a Swansea player."* Curtis was ecstatic. *"If the gates had opened, they would not have caught me. I would have been half way down Mumbles Road,"* was his reaction to scoring the fifth goal. It was a magnificent start to a fine season for Swansea. Always up with the leaders, they eventually finished in sixth place. Normally this would have been good enough for a UEFA Cup spot, but as members of the Football Association of Wales and as previous contestants under that banner in the Cup-Winners Cup, Swansea were deprived of a UEFA cup place, settling instead for their traditional passport to the continent, the Welsh Cup.

Swansea's stay at the top was destined to be brief. Relegated after two seasons, they fell straight through to the Third Division. Two years later they were in the Fourth Division. The fall was as dramatic as their rise. In 1978 they were in the Fourth. By 1981 they'd reached the First. In 1983 they were in the First. By 1986 they were back in the Fourth. Perhaps, one day, Swansea will again soar to the top. It's an unlikely thought now, but no more unlikely than it was in February 1978 when John Toshack was appointed manager.

ON THE SAME DAY...

News: A portrait of the Princess of Wales, hanging in the National Portrait Gallery is damaged by a man with a knife.

Sport: In the 6th Test Vs Australia, England's Geoffrey Boycott sets a new world record of 61 Test 50s, overtaking Colin Cowdrey.

Entertainment: As Swans top the League, Welsh singer 'Shakin' Stevens is dislodged from the top of the charts when his 'Green Door' is replaced by Scots rocker Aneka and 'Japanese Boy'.

SWINDON TOWN 4

Vs Leicester City 3

May 31st 1993 - Promotion Play-off Final
(Wembley)

Swindon Town: Digby, Summerbee, Bodin,
Hoddle, Calderwood, Taylor, Moncur (Hazard 88),
McLaren, Mitchell, Ling, Maskell (White 78).

Swindon Town supporters know all about Wembley truimph and heartbreak. In 1969 they had overcome Arsenal to win the League Cup as a Third Division side. And in 1990, with Ossie Ardiles at the helm, they had won the first ever Wembley play-off for a First Division place by beating Sunderland. But Swindon never took their place in the top sphere. Penalised by the authorities for financial irregularities, they were originally relegated to the Third Division, a punishment later reduced on appeal to non-confirmation of their move up. Many thought that Swindon's only chance of bringing top class football to Wiltshire had gone.

They had reckoned without the indomitable spirit of the players and the fans. Determined to right what they viewed as a monstrous injustice, Swindon again reached a play-off spot in 1993. Now managed by player-boss Glenn Hoddle, they eliminated Tranmere Rovers to win the right to face Leicester City for a place in the F.A. Premiership.

The 73,802 spectators present witnessed an even and exciting game. But both sides seemed capable of neutralising each other's threats and the game, for all its excitement, remained goalless as the half-time whistle approached. Then, with 42 minutes played, Maskell played a lovely back-heel to Hoddle. Still one of the best shooters in the game, the player-manager slammed the ball home from 15 yards to give Swindon a precious interval lead.

Maskell was again in the forefront of the action after the break. Two minutes after the restart, he played a one-two with Moncur, then despite being in an awkward position, Maskell took a leaf out of the Glenn Hoddle textbook by slamming a great shot into the right-hand corner of the net. Swindon could almost smell the Premiership now. In 54 minutes the referee overruled his linesman's decision on a Leicester goal-kick and awarded a corner to Swindon. Summerbee's kick found Moncur who moved forward into the penalty area. He released the ball to Taylor who slipped it past Leicester 'keeper Kevin Poole. 3-0 up and surely Swindon were home and dry?

Not quite. Leicester retaliated immediately, a Walsh shot rebounding off the post for Julian Joachim to reduce the deficit. But, at two goals to the good, there were precious few prepared to bet against Swindon. Inside sixty seconds the situation was transformed. 68 minutes had been played when Leicester mounted another attack. Walsh beat Fraser Digby to the jump to make the score 3-2. One minute later, Mike Whitlow put Steve Thompson through. Thompson made no mistake, finding the right-hand corner of the net to equalise. All bets were now off.

With only seven minutes remaining, extra time was looming when Swindon and controversy walked hand in hand again. The referee adjudged that a challenge from Poole on Swindon substitute Steve White was a foul and awarded a penalty kick. Up stepped Paul Bodin. The Welsh international made no mistake as he crashed the ball home to put Swindon 4-3 ahead. Hazard came on as a late substitute for Moncur as the seconds ticked away. The whistle eventually blew on one of the most amazing games that even Wembley had ever seen, and Swindon Town, three years after they thought they'd done it, were in the big time at last.

Even as the celebrations started back in Wiltshire, storm clouds were gathering over Swindon once more. Glenn Hoddle's name had already been linked with the manager's job at Chelsea. At a civic reception for the club, Hoddle stayed studiously silent about his future. There was a petition mounted, pleading with him to stay. Photos of Hoddle emblazoned with the words 'Don't go Glenn' were brandished in their thousands by supporters. All to no avail. Just four days after Wembley, Hoddle took over at Chelsea.

John Gorman replaced Hoddle but the damage had already been done. Despite recruiting experienced players like Terry Fenwick, Brian Kilcline, Andy Mutch and Jan-Aage Fjortoft, Swindon struggled in the Premiership from the word go. It was sixteen games before they won and they ended up bottom, having conceded 100 goals. After all the heartbreak endured in reaching the top, it was a sad end to the Swindon adventure. A second successive relegation in 1995 ended all hope that the Wiltshire club might make a quick return to the top flight.

There has been little in the history of Torquay United to excite their devoted Devonian fans. Since joining the League in 1927, they have never played above Third Division level. The 1951-52 season saw them struggling near the foot of the Third Division (South) when Swindon were the visitors to Plainmoor in early March. The fixture appeared to be just a routine game. What unfolded before the eyes of the 7,523 present was to go down in Devon folklore...

TORQUAY UNITED 9

Vs Swindon Town 0

March 8th 1952 Division Three (South)

Torquay United: G. Webber, Topping, R. Calland, D. Lewis, E. Webber, Towers, Shaw, Marchant, Northcott, Collins, Edds.

has seen has been a few promotions from the Fourth Division, though one of these was a play-off success at Wembley in 1991 - a ground also visited by the Devon side when they made the Sherpa Van Trophy Final in 1989. But concrete success still eludes this club from one of football's out-posts. Such memories of success that they do have are made all the more precious by their rarity.

Swindon, also near the bottom, made the early running before Torquay's Lewis tried a shot which was easily saved. Northcott's powerful header for the homesters was also well held by Uprichard in the Swindon goal. But after ten minutes Torquay took the lead. Northcott received the ball from a Towers throw-in and knocked it back to Edds who left Uprichard floundering in the Plainmoor mud as he scored the opener. Northcott continued to maraud, leading the line with distinction and often being fouled by the Swindon defence. Edds hit a shot just past the post. Swindon weren't out of it though and Torquay's 'keeper, George Webber, had his work cut out, twice having to dive full-length in the mud to make saves. Another Swindon attack saw Calland clear off the line.

But it was Torquay who were on top and they proved it five minutes from half-time. Topping sent Shaw away on the wing. He crossed to Collins who headed home the second goal. Then, just seconds from the interval, Shaw beat Swindon's May and crossed to Northcott. The striker rounded off a fine 45 minutes by heading in the third goal. Five minutes after the restart, Edds centred, Uprichard fell awkwardly, failing to collect the ball, and Collins knocked in the forth. Uprichard was clearly dazed and had to leave the pitch. 4-0 down and reduced to ten men, left-back May went into goal with some trepidation.

May's fears were confirmed in 61 minutes. Shaw put Marchant through. The inside-right passed the ball about a foot off the ground to Northcott. The centre-forward **dived** to head in the fifth. Northcott then turned provider, centring for Marchant to head the sixth in 70 minutes. Three minutes later, Collins scored the seventh from a Shaw pass. But May was actually performing well in goal. Under a non-stop bombardment, he pulled off several stunning saves. The damage had already been done though, and late in the game, Shaw and Edds added to the Wiltshire side's agony to make the final score an unbelievable Torquay United 9 Swindon Town 0 - Torquay's record League victory.

True, Torquay faced ten men, including a stand-in goalkeeper, for most of the second half. But it would be wrong to detract from their famous win as they had already scored four in the first 50 minutes. But even as they celebrated their triumph, Plainmoor was touched by tragedy. Regular right-half, Hugh Brown, a former Scottish international, missed the Swindon game thanks to an injury sustained at Crystal Palace the week before. (Although this hasn't stopped supposed 'reference' books from listing him as playing against Swindon.) Brown was given the shock news that he would have to quit the game. At 31, his career was over.

Sadness at Brown's misfortune apart, this game provided memories to warm many a cold winter night. Nine goals, four of them headers, every forward scoring, Northcott's header from twelve inches off the ground. And those memories have been needed. Torquay, buoyed by their record win, climbed up the table to midway. Over the past forty-odd years though, the best Plainmoor

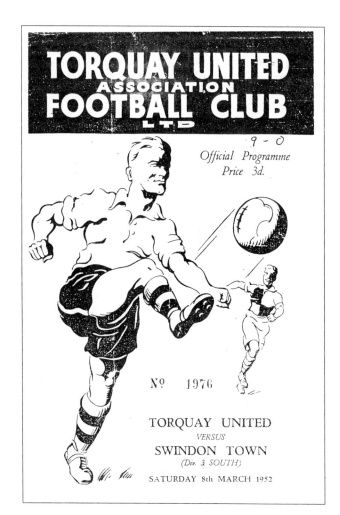

TORQUAY UNITED ASSOCIATION FOOTBALL CLUB LTD

9 - 0

Official Programme Price 3d.

Nº 1976

TORQUAY UNITED
VERSUS
SWINDON TOWN
(Div. 3 SOUTH)
SATURDAY 8th MARCH 1952

TOTTENHAM HOTSPUR 5
Vs Atletico Madrid 1

May 15th 1963 European Cup-Winners Cup Final (Rotterdam)

Tottenham Hotspur: Brown, Baker, Henry, Blanchflower, Norman, Marchi, Jones, White, Smith, Greaves, Dyson.

Tottenham Hotspur's history is littered with success. League Championships, domestic Cups and European triumphs are all there in abundance in the record books of White Hart Lane. But most Spurs fans would agree that it was the team of the early 1960s that produced the club's finest era. In 1961 they became the first team in the 20th Century to do what many thought to be impossible - win the domestic 'double' of League and Cup, equalling the points record in the process. But that triumph has been allowed to overshadow, wrongly in this author's opinion, their night of glory in Rotterdam two years later. It is that peculiarly British insularity which makes us regard victory over domestic opposition as being somehow greater than triumph on a foreign field. The Spurs players of the time knew better. The incomparable Danny Blanchflower, skipper of the double-winning side voiced his fears just after that historic success when, speaking of Spurs European hopes, he said; *"I think we may find it difficult. Playing against foreign teams in strange lands will be a new experience for some of our youngsters. Real Madrid, for example, are thoroughly conditioned to world travel. But it will be a fine experience."*

So it proved. Tottenham's European debut saw them stage several fine performances before narrowly losing in the European Cup Semi-Finals to the holders, Benfica. But they retained the F.A. Cup, qualifying for an attempt on the Cup-Winners Cup in 1962-63. Their first opponents were Glasgow Rangers. The Scottish side boasted the proud record of having been the only British side to reach the Final of this competition and were on their way to another Scottish League triumph. But Spurs brushed them aside, winning at both White Hart Lane and Ibrox for a stunning 8-4 aggregate success.

A comfortable 6-2 aggregate win over Slovan Bratislava, Spurs winning their home leg 6-0, sent them through to the Semi-Finals where another double victory, 5-2 on aggregate, over Yugoslavia's OFK Belgrade, booked their ticket for the Final against Atletico Madrid. If not quite as illustrious as their city rivals Real, Atletico were still a formidable side in their own right. In their only European Cup campaign, they had lost in the Semi-Finals to Real, but only after a play-off. And they were the holders of the Cup-Winners Cup, having triumphed over that competition's inaugural victors Fiorentina in a replay. Put simply, Atletico were a team who had bowed only to their great foes from the Bernabeu stadium while Spurs were from a country that had **never** won a European trophy. It was no surprise that the Spaniards were the favourites to retain their crown.

The odds against Tottenham increased before the kick-off when their tigerish half-back Dave Mackay failed a fitness test. So it was no great surprise to the 25,000 present in Rotterdam when the English team made a nervous start. But Spurs were managed by one of the shrewdest men in the game, Bill Nicholson. And Nicholson had taught his charges to respect their rivals but not to fear them. With Atletico failing to capitalise on that initial Tottenham hesitancy, Spurs began to realise the wisdom in their manager's attitude. With sixteen minutes gone, Marchi fed Bobby Smith. The bustling Smith passed to Cliff Jones out on the wing. Jones roared past Rodriguez and crossed for Jimmy Greaves - the most lethal predator in English football - to drive the ball home. 1-0 to Spurs. 33 minutes had gone when Greaves turned supplier. The 'keeper failed to cut out a Greaves centre. The ball flew across the goal area, to be put back in by Dyson. Smith knocked it back to John White. With no hesitation, the Scottish international whacked it into the roof of the net. Half-time arrived with Spurs holding a 2-0 lead.

If Tottenham thought it looked easy, they received a rude awakening at the start of the second half. Atletico attacked from the off. Just two minutes into the action and Collar's centre found the unmarked Adelardo. His shot was punched away. Unfortunately for Spurs, the fist in question belonged to Henry rather than' keeper Bill Brown. Collar struck home the penalty to reduce the deficit to 2-1. For the next fifteen minutes, Atletico were in charge as Tottenham defended desperately. The game was still in the balance when Spurs broke out of the trenches. Dyson picked the ball up on the left and curled it goalward. The wind floated it over the despairing grasp of Atletico 'keeper Madinabeytia and landed it just under the bar to restore Tottenham's two-goal lead.

Shocked by this turn of events, the Spaniards simply collapsed. A Dyson centre allowed Greaves to make it 4-1. Then Dyson, the man of the match, ran fully 25 years through the middle to score the fifth. 5-1 it stayed. A scoreline even the most dedicated of Spurs fans could scarcely have dreamed possible before the match. Mackay leapt up off the bench at the end to embrace his team-mates while the 4,000 Spurs fans in the crowd roared their appreciation. The match referee, the experienced Leo Horn, said; *"You could send this side anywhere in the world and be proud of them,"* adding that Spurs were the best British team he had ever seen. After a decade of despair, starting with England's 6-3 and 7-1 thrashings at the hands of Hungary, at last English football had a team worthy of ranking with the best.

But Bill Nicholson's men contained the seeds of tragedy in their moment of glory. The great John White was killed by lightning on a golf course little more than a year later. Dave Mackay was to fight a battle against cruel injuries all his playing days. The personal problems of Jimmy Greaves became well-chronicled over the years. And the sad decline of Danny Blanchflower brought tears to the most hardened of men.

Nor, on the pitch, has it been constant success for Spurs. They have won more cups and have triumphed again in Europe. But there was also relegation in the 1970s and the Venables-Sugar dispute which rocked the club to its foundations. But, in the latter half of the 1990s, Spurs again look more like the cavalier team of old. They may well go on to great things. But one thing they can't do, the one thing no team can do, is to replace the team of 1963 in the record books. That night in Rotterdam saw Spurs make football history - the first British team to win a European tournament. It is a record they richly deserve.

ON THE SAME DAY...

News: Some of that old-fashioned Southern hospitality is meted out to British journalists covering Civil Rights demonstrations in Alabama. Locked up for hours without charge and denied permission to phone the British Embassy, the party of reporters are eventually freed, and describe Alabama as a police state.

Sport: Rugby Union chiefs are to take action to end the scandal of hooliganism by touring rugby clubs.

Entertainment: Before the match highlights on T.V., viewers have a choice of 'Z-Cars' on the BBC, or 'Rawhide' on ITV.

TRANMERE ROVERS 3

Vs Aston Villa 1
February 16th 1994
League Cup Semi-Final (1st Leg)

Tranmere Rovers: Nixon, Nolan, McGreal, Hughes, Garnett, Brannan, Nevin, O'Brien, Irons, Malkin, Aldridge.

For over a hundred years, Tranmere Rovers were regarded by the outside world as simply the little team from the 'wrong' side of the Mersey. While Liverpool and Everton battled for the game's major honours, the Birkenhead club struggled to get any share of the limelight at all. Apart from the oddity of winning the Welsh Cup in 1935 and spending one forlorn year in the Second Division, their history was one of fighting for survival in the nether regions of the League.

The arrival of John King as manager in 1987 changed all that. Within two years he had steered Rovers out of Division Four. Two more seasons and he had taken them into Division Two, renamed Division One in 1992. King's team wasn't just concerned with staying at this level either. With talented players like Scotland's Pat Nevin and Irish international John Aldridge in the side, Rovers consistently finished in one of the play-off spots; never quite making it into the Premiership.

They were also never regarded as a team worth having a flutter on in Cup competitions. That curious Welsh episode aside, Tranmere made no impact on the game's prizes. Again King changed this. There was success in the Leyland DAF competition in 1990 at Wembley and a runners-up place in the same tourney the following year. But that was a 'mickey mouse' cup. The real glory lies in the F.A. Cup and the League Cup. And in 1993-94, Tranmere set off on an exhilarating run in that latter tournament.

Victories over Oxford and Grimsby were no more than expected. Premiership strugglers Oldham Athletic were thought to provide a sterner test in the fourth round but three second half goals sent them crashing out of the Cup. Rovers fifth round opponents were fellow promotion contenders and League Cup specialists Nottingham Forest. A stiff test but one Rovers passed with flying colours by drawing 1-1 at the City Ground and winning the replay 2-0 at their own Prenton Park. For the first time they had reached the last four of a major competition.

If they were to return to Wembley in a 'proper' Cup Final though, Tranmere would first have to overcome Premiership outfit Aston Villa. Interest in the clash was immense. Rovers more than doubled their average League gate with a capacity crowd of 17,240 passing through the Prenton Park turnstiles for the first leg of the Semi-Final. But it was an apprehensive crowd. With Dean Higgins and Tony Thomas suspended, Rovers defence looked vulnerable. It meant call-ups for reserve John McGreal and veteran Mark Hughes.

Rovers decided that the best form of defence is offence. They attacked right from the off. After just five minutes, Pat Nevin, in his 100th match for Tranmere, sped down the right flank. Villa failed to clear his cross and Ian Nolan swept in to knock the ball past 'keeper Bosnich and in off the underside of the bar for a rare - and most welcome - goal. Villa were rocked by the directness of Rovers approach and it was the home team that kept the initiative. Midway through the half they struck again, Mark Hughes justifying his selection when he volleyed home following a Rovers corner. Considering that Hughes had hit just nine League goals in over 250 matches for Rovers and Nolan had a solitary League goal to his credit, it is little wonder that the faces of the Villa players told their own story of devastation.

But Villa possessed the determination that is characteristic of Ron Atkinson's sides. A Stauanton free kick was tipped over the bar by Eric Nixon as Villa won four corners in two minutes. But Rovers remained steady. Half-time arrived with them still 2-0 ahead. Villa stepped up the pace in the second half, Dean Saunders twice missing from good chances. Aldridge, who had been effectively shackled by international team-mate Paul McGrath, broke free and timed his run perfectly to meet a through ball from Irons. His first effort hit the post but Aldridge pounced on the rebound to put Rovers three up with eleven minutes to play.

On the stroke of full time, the hitherto invisible Dalian Atkinson hit a half-volley from the edge of the area which found the net. Did that late goal give Villa a chance? According to manager Ron Atkinson they had.... *"no hope if we play like that again. Tranmere have given a top-class performance."* High praise indeed. Rovers fans left Prenton Park believing that Wembley was in their grasp.

But roared on by most of the 40,593 crowd at Villa Park, two goals from Teale and Sauders had restored parity by the 23rd minute of the second leg. When Bosnich committed a professional foul six minutes later, he should have been sent off. The 'keeper escaped punishment but Aldridge scored from the spot to restore Tranmere's lead. There were no more goals until two minutes from the end when Dalian Atkinson struck again, denying Rovers a deserved triumph and taking the game into extra time.

With no more goals in the extra half-hour, it was down to penalties. And it was here that Bosnich displayed his worth, saving three as Villa edged through 5-4 in the shoot-out. It was an injustice for Rovers that the efforts of a man who should not even have been on the pitch, should deprive them of a richly-deserved crack at treble-chasing Manchester United in the Final. That prize was Villa's and they took it, going on to beat United. But the world of football can be a cruel one and, just months after his team's success, Villa boss Atkinson found himself the victim of the sack.

It was a shattering blow for Rovers but they picked themselves up to qualify for another play-off attempt, losing narrowly to Leicester City. 1995 brought another play-off defeat, this time by Reading. Prenton Park remains a ground full of optimists though. The supporters know that the past few years have been the best in their club's entire history. They remain confident that one day, in the not too distant future, they will welcome Liverpool and Everton to their ground as Premiership equals.

Tranmere take the lead against Villa in their epic Cup duel.

WALSALL 0
Vs Liverpool 2

February 14th 1984
League Cup Semi-Final (2nd Leg)

Walsall: Green, Caswell, Mower, Shakespeare, Brazier, Hart, Rees, Brown, O'Kelly, Preece, Summerfield.

For most people Walsall's place in football history was earned by their sensational victory over Arsenal in the F.A. Cup in 1933. While that tie was probably the biggest single upset of the inter-war years, the Saddlers reward was a next round knockout at Maine Road. For Walsall it was the highlight of a humdrum League existence which began in the inaugural Second Division in 1892 when they were known as Walsall Town Swifts. Twice failing to gain re-election, they left the League at the dawn of the 20th Century, returning after the First World War. Since then they have spent a not-so-grand total of three seasons (1961-63 and 1988-89) in the old Division Two, so the importance of that historic Cup triumph should not be underestimated. But, in 1983-84, as a Third Division side, Walsall played Liverpool at their then ground, Fellows Park, needing a victory to take them to Wembley, a prospect undreamt of at the time of their elimination of Arsenal.

Walsall's path to the Semi-Finals was far from easy. They had to overturn an away defeat at Blackpool just to get past the first hurdle. A fine double win over Second Division Barnsley earned some respect for the side managed by Alan Buckley. Another Division Two team - Shrewsbury Town - were knocked out at Fellows Park in the third round, allowing Walsall to equal their previous best in the competition. The fourth round draw must have brought back memories to Fellows Park old-timers. Arsenal! This time at Highbury. On November 29th 1983 the Saddlers proved that giant-killing lightning could strike twice, even if separated by 50 years. Trailing 1-0 at the interval they struck with second half goals from Mark Rees and Ally Brown to send the stunned Gunners - Jennings, Sansom, O'Leary, Woodstock, Nicholas **et al** - reeling out of the competition.

In a season of shocks, three teams from Division Three had made the last eight. And it was another of these - Rotherham United - that Walsall faced next. In a thrilling game at Millmoor, Walsall triumphed 4-2 to reach a major Semi-Final for the first time in their history. Few could have given them any chance against Liverpool. The Anfield team were enjoying a run of success which surpassed even their own previous standards. They were about to win the League for a third successive season - the first time any team had done so since the 1930s. Already League Cup winners thrice, they were looking towards an unprecedented fourth successive Final. And, for good measure, they were also about to win the European Cup for the fourth time.

Yet it was 'no-hopers' Walsall who emerged the moral victors in the first leg at Anfield. Ronnie Whelan scored in each half for Liverpool but twice Walsall equalised, through a Phil Neal own goal and a late strike by substitute Kevin Summerfield. By the time the teams ran out at Fellows Park, Walsall really believed they could win it. And so did their fans among the 19,591 present. But although Walsall started brightly, it was Liverpool who notched the opening goal when a David Hodgson centre was headed in by the lethal Ian Rush after thirteen minutes.

But Walsall's determination simply grew despite this setback. David Preece drove the side on, reminding them they had come back from behind twice at Anfield. The acclaimed pair of Graeme Souness and Mark Lawrenson had their work cut out to prevent the Saddlers from scoring. Liverpool were relieved to make the dressing room with their narrow advantage intact. Eight minutes into the second half and with Walsall doing all the pressing, Liverpool managed to break out defence. Whelan's shot was beaten out by Ron Green but Whelan snapped up the rebound to put his team two ahead.

At this point, a terrace wall collapsed under the sheer pressure of the fans. Supporters were forced onto the pitch. Thirteen minutes of total confusion followed, with many wondering if the game would be abandoned. Seventeen spectators were taken to hospital but, fortunately, there were no serious injuries. When the teams re-emerged, Walsall continued to take the game to their foes but their efforts were wild. Their composure was lost as they desperately tried to force a way through. Rees, Brown, Shakespeare and O'Reilly all had chances in the last fifteen minutes but none were taken. A disappointed Alan Buckley still reckoned his players had done themselves proud - a view Liverpool manager Joe Fagan was happy to endorse.

Walsall had been desperately unlucky to lose the tie. Their subsequent history has not been so glorious. Promotion to Division Two in 1988 was actually the catalyst for a slide down into the Fourth just two years later. It looks like being a long time before another Walsall side gets to within 90 minutes of a major Cup Final.

When Graham Taylor arrived as Watford manager in 1977, any suggestion that the club would play in European competition just six years later would have been laughed at by even the most die-hard of Hornets fans. Three Second Division season in the early 1970s and a solitary FA Cup Semi-Final appearance were the best achievements in more than 50 years of League membership. But Taylor, aided by Watford's football-mad Chairman, rock star Elton John, built, in record time, a team capable of challenging the best both at home and abroad.

The first stage in Watford's remarkable rise was the Fourth Division title in 1978, finishing eleven points clear at the top. Runners-up spot in Division Three the following season ensured a second successive promotion. Watford then paused for breath, taking three more years before completing their rise to Division One. The wait was worthwhile, for in their first ever season at top level, Watford finished in second place; meaning that Vicarage Road would host European football a little more than five years after it had been a Fourth Division ground.

Watford could scarcely have asked for a tougher continental baptism. Kaiserslautern were a highly-experienced West German outfit. This was their fifth successive season in the UEFA Cup. They had reached one Semi-Final and two Quarter-Finals previously. They had never lost in the first round. They had easily beaten the only English opposition they had ever faced - Stoke City. The had internationals of the quality of Briegel, Brehme, Allofs and the Swede, Nilsson in their ranks. By contrast, Watford were new boys from England, with only one player, 19 year old John Barnes, that their foes might have even heard of. Yet Watford performed admirably in the first half, 1-1 being the interval score. Experience won the day in the second period, the Germans scoring twice to take a 3-1 lead to England. Watford's European excursion looked bound to be a short break rather than an extended tour.

The tie brought 21,457 curious spectators to Vicarage Road to see an unfamiliar line-up. Injuries forced Taylor to re-jig his side, giving 19-year old Ian Richardson an unexpected first team debut. Four minutes after the kick-off, the unknown teenager was the toast of the crowd. Picking up a header from the other teenager - Barnes - Richardson held off a challenge before driving past 'keeper Reichel to give real hope to his team-mates.

WATFORD 3
Vs Kaiserslautern 0

September 28th 1983
UEFA Cup Round One (2nd Leg)

Watford: Sherwood, Palmer, Rostron, Jobson, Terry, Bolton, Callaghan, Richardson, Gilligan, Jackett, Barnes.

The Germans were attempting a man-marking system but even this early in the game, it wasn't working. Barnes, Richardson and Nigel Callaghan were just too fast for their markers. With just nine minutes played, Reichel attempted to punch clear but the ball came back off German defender Melzer for an own goal. Watford had not only eliminated the deficit within ten minutes, thanks to the away goals rule they now led.

Although not playing well, Kaiserslautern still posed a threat. A goal would change everything. Briegel and Allofs remained a danger and it was Allofs who burst through in 42 minutes but then shot weakly straight at the back-pedalling Sherwood. Watford's territorial advantage continued in the second half but they were still prone to a sudden break by the German side. Nilsson's header put Geye through. But his shot hit Sherwood on the chest and bounced over the bar. In 67 minutes Watford settled affairs. A low cross from Jobson on the right found Richardson. The youngster became the hero again, firing over Reichel to make it 3-0 on the night, 4-3 on aggregate. Graham Taylor was jubilant at the end. *"This may be the most important win in Watford's history,"* said the manager, adding, in what sounded like a prophecy, *"it may be the greatest result of my managerial career."*

It proved to be another memorable season for Watford. They pulled off a fine win in Bulgaria after extra time in the next round before losing to Sparta Prague. Domestically, they reached a first-ever FA Cup Final, losing 2-0 to Everton. For both Ian Richardson and Watford this was to be their glory hour. The youngster never hit such heights again and the Hornets, after a few years in mid-table, were relegated in 1988. Taylor too, although subsequently manager of Aston Villa, England and Wolves has never enjoyed the success of those heady days at Vicarage Road.

ON THE SAME DAY...

News: Gordon Getty, worth 2.2 billion dollars, is reckoned to be the richest man in the U.S.A.

Sport: In the Cup-Winners Cup, Glasgow Rangers beat Maltese side Valletta 10-0 for an 18-0 aggregate success.

Entertainment: Before the game, fans could watch veteran soap opera 'Crossroads'.

The scoreboard records the achievement

WEST BROMWICH ALBION 2

Vs Preston North End 1

March 24th 1888 F.A. Cup Final (The Oval)

West Bromwich Albion: Roberts, Aldridge, Green, Horton, Perry, Timmins, Woodhall, Bassett, Bayliss, Wilson, Pearson.

West Bromwich Albion, founded in 1879 as West Bromwich Strollers and changing their name two years later, benefitted from the legalisation of professional football in 1885 and their impact on the F.A. Cup in the seasons immediately thereafter was considerable. The reached the Final in 1886, taking the superb Blackburn Rovers to a replay before losing to the triple-winners. 1887 saw them reach the Final again, losing to Aston Villa. The next year saw Albion charge to their third successive Final. But it looked like they would be treble losers, for their opponents were Preston, the most feared combination of the day. Preston actually asked to have their picture taken with the trophy before the game, reckoning that they would be covered in dirt after the match, spoiling the photo. The referee, the famous Major Marindin, refused the request, asking *"Had you not better win it first?"* Such arrogance from the Lancastrian side only served to provoke the Midlands team to greater efforts to ensure that for once they did not leave the Oval empty-handed.

West Bromwich fielded seven players taking part in the Final for the third time, but when the game got under way at 3.33p.m., it was one of their 'new boys', Billy Bassett, who was first to show promise. Four minutes into the game, he forced Preston 'keeper, the quaintly-named Dr. R.H. Mills-Roberts to fist a clearance. The goalie had to make a further save from Bassett, and also from Perry, before Preston got into their stride. But when they did, Preston showed the 19,000 crowd - a new record - what they were capable of. Goodall broke through but Roberts made a fine save. Preston forced three successive corners, two of which brought attempts on goal from Dewhurst and Drummond that Roberts gamely stopped.

Having survived that onslaught, Albion attacked again - Woodhall's effort being saved by the 'keeper. Woodhall was through again, in the eighteenth minute, but elected to pass to Bayliss. The centre-forward made no mistake, giving the underdogs the lead. Albion enjoyed a brief spell of ascendancy after this but the 'keeper and his backs easily repelled their further attacks. Preston stormed back into the match but apart from a Dewhurst shot which was well saved, their shooting was wild. Until the last five minutes of the half. Then Drummond, Goodall and Dewhurst all tested Roberts. But to no avail. Albion led 1-0 at the break.

Seven minutes into the second half, Preston's pressure was finally rewarded. A Goodall header was held by Roberts but he was bundled over the line, the ball still in his hands, by Dewhurst. Under the rules prevailing, the goal was given. Things looked grim for the midlanders. For a long spell they were confined to their own half and Villa were reckoned to have had ten good chances to Albion's one.

That was of no account though, in the 77th minute, when Albion resumed the offensive. Timmins punted the ball up to Bayliss who laid it off to Woodhall to his right. Woodhall attempted a shot through a ruck of players. The ball deflected off Bassett's knee and went in off the post. Preston were stunned, unable to cope with this surprise reverse. Bassett took control for Albion and they ended the game well on top. After two losing Finals, the Cup was theirs at last. This was a victory which can be compared with Sunderland's over Leeds 85 years later, so great was the sensation it caused. Albion later travelled to Scotland to play Scottish Cup winners Renton for the title of 'Champions of the World' but lost.

Albion became founder members of the Football League later the same year and eventually became League Champions in 1920. They have lifted the F.A. Cup on a further four occasions since 1888, most notably as a Second Division side in 1931. They have vacillated between the top two divisions for many years, even having to endure a spell in Division Three in the early 1990s, a far cry from their predecessors of a century previously. But West Brom. are one of those clubs whose supporters believe they belong at the very top of the game. That was certainly the position they enjoyed when winning their first F.A. Cup more than 100 years ago.

ON THE SAME DAY...

News: Llantwit Vardre School Board in South Wales has barred married women from teaching in its schools - an attitude condemned in the press as 'unchivalrous'.

Sport: An exhibition boxing bout by John L. Sullivan in Liverpool causes controversy. For the champion has shaved off his famous moustache, making many think they are watching a fraud.

Entertainment: The Pantomime season ends with the final performance of *'Puss in Boots'* at the Drury Lane Theatre.

WEST HAM UNITED 2
Vs TSV Munich 1860 0

May 19th 1965 European Cup-Winners Cup Final (Wembley)

West Ham United: Standen, Kirkup, Burkett, Peters, Brown, Moore, Sealey, Boyce, Hurst, Dear, Sissons.

For many years West Ham United were simply a footnote in the history books - losing Cup Finalists in the first Wembley Final. But if mention of Wembley brought a grimace to the faces of long-standing Hammers fans, the 1960s saw them come to regard the place as almost a second home. Hammers had followed up that initial walk down Wembley way with nine years in Division One until relegation in 1932. That remained their only spell in the top flight until they lifted the Second Division title in 1958. Their manager, Ted Fenton, was succeeded by Ron Greenwood in 1961 and he quickly assembled a talented collection of players at the Boleyn Ground. The breakthrough came with F.A. Cup success in 1964 - the first major honour to go Upton Park way. It also sent the Hammers into Europe.

Hammers had only one player acclimatised to the rigours of continental football - England captain Bobby Moore (though Peters and Hurst were soon to join him in the national side). But they survived their baptism well, winning 1-0 away to La Gantoise and drawing with the Belgian side at home. That was followed by a tough tie with Czech side Spartak Sokolovo. West Ham needed their 2-0 home leg lead, losing 2-1 in Prague to win 3-2 on aggregate. The Quarter-Finals brought a well-deserved double over Swiss team Lausanne, 2-1 away and 4-3 at home. But it was the Semi-Finals which saw the Hammers come of age, beating Real Zaragoza 2-1 at home and claiming a 1-1 draw in Spain against the reigning Fairs Cup holders - a vastly experienced side.

The Final had been earmarked for Wembley before the start of the competition - a dry run for the 1966 World Cup Final. So Hammers were delighted to make the short trip across London to the scene of their previous year's success. Their opponents, TSV Munich, were also European novices but fine victories over Porto, Legia Warsaw and Torino had established their right to a place in the Final.

They were a formidable side, the youngest player was left-winger Rebele, 22, the oldest Yugoslav 'keeper Radenkovic, 30. The average age was just over 25. Right wing pair Heiss and Kuppers were German internationals while right-half Bena was a Yugoslav cap.

The match was a 100,000 sell-out with the receipts of £76,000 constituting a new record for a floodlit game. And it was an engrossing affair for the fans to enjoy. Kuppers, Grosser and skipper Brunnenmerev, aided by Rebele were happy to take the game to West Ham whenever they could. They brought the best out of defender Luttrop was well as Radenkovic. It was a fairly even first half but there was one crucial difference between the sides - Bobby Moore. The England skipper was at the peak of his form. He was the main reason for West Ham's transformation from mediocrity to magic.

Prompted by Moore the Hammers gradually wore down the Germans, establishing command of the game. Yet, twenty minutes from the end, it was still goalless. It was then that Boyce made a crucial interception, drew left-back Kohlars to him, then slipped the ball to Alan Sealey. In an instant, Sealey - not even a first team regular - cracked the ball into the roof of the net. Two minutes later, Moore curled a free kick into the penalty area. In the midst of a mess of players, it was Sealey who reacted first, scoring his - and the Hammers - second. Little wonder that he somersaulted and danced all the way back to the half-way line. It was all West Ham now. Sissons hit both the post and the bar. Dear had a 'goal' disallowed. Sissons, Hurst and Sealey all missed easy chances but it didn't matter. The Liverpool chant of 'Ee, ay, addio, we've won the Cup' was adopted by the Eastenders for the evening. Cars drove all night, their horns blaring away, with fans on the bumpers and climbing on the backs of every vehicle in sight. And above it all came the sound of 'I'm forever blowing bubbles,' as the Hammers fans celebrated a magnificent performance - a European trophy in the club's first season in Europe.

The team that won was a remarkable one. No fewer than nine of the players had come through the ranks at West Ham. Standen, signed from Luton and Sealey from Leyton Orient being the exceptions. And, apart from Kirkup and Hurst, every player was born in the Greater London area. Hurst, Moore and Peters returned to Wembley in 1966 to pick up World Cup winners medals. For Moore and Hurst it was their third title at the ground in three seasons. And, on every occasion, Bobby Moore had captained the side. A truly incredible feat.

If West Ham didn't quite capitalise on their success to the extent of joining the game's elite, they did carve out a reputation as one of the most skilful and enjoyable teams to watch. They have also spent the bulk of their time since 1965 in the top division and lifted the F.A. Cup on two more occasions (once while actually in Division Two). They were never able to repeat their European success, losing in the Semi-Finals in 1966. They reached the Final again in 1976, losing a wonderful match 4-2 to Anderlecht and maintained their fine record by reaching the last eight in 1981. But, even if they achieve European success again, it would be stretching the imagination too far to believe that West Ham could ever field an eleven to compare with that of 1965, let alone produce another Peters or Hurst. They will certainly never find another Bobby Moore.

EUROPEAN CUP WINNERS' CUP
FINAL TIE
TSV MÜNCHEN 1860
V
WEST HAM UNITED
MAY 19th 1965 WEMBLEY Kick-off 7.30 p.m.
OFFICIAL PROGRAMME · · · ONE SHILLING

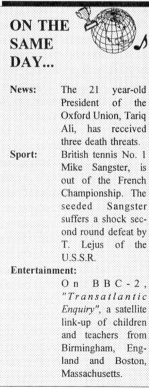

ON THE SAME DAY...

News: The 21 year-old President of the Oxford Union, Tariq Ali, has received three death threats.

Sport: British tennis No. 1 Mike Sangster, is out of the French Championship. The seeded Sangster suffers a shock second round defeat by T. Lejus of the U.S.S.R.

Entertainment: On BBC-2, "Transatlantic Enquiry", a satellite link-up of children and teachers from Birmingham, England and Boston, Massachusetts.

WIGAN ATHLETIC 0
Vs Leeds United 2

March 15th 1987
F.A. Cup Quarter-Finals

Wigan Athletic: Tunks, Hamilton, Knowles,
Hilditch, Cribley, Beesley, Lowe, Thompson,
Campbell, Jewell (Butler 75), Griffiths.

There had been a League team in Wigan after the First World War but Wigan Borough resigned from the League in 1931. Wigan Athletic were formed a year later with the express aim of regaining League status. It was a campaign that lasted nearly half a century. It took a string of successes against League clubs in the F.A. Cup to batter down the League's door, Wigan finally being accepted in 1978. It took them just four years to gain promotion to the Third Division and by 1986, when Ray Mathias took over as manager from Bryan Hamilton, Latics were in a strong position. A single point stood between them and the Second Division in 1985-86, so it was a confident side which adorned Springfield Park the following season.

Wigan were again in the forefront of the promotion battle but, appropriately, it was the F.A. Cup, where they had performed with such distinction as a non-League team, which brought them to the attention of the nation once more. It started off quietly enough with wins over Lincoln, Darlington and Gillingham taking them to the fourth round. The game which re-established the flame of cup-fighting came with a 1-0 home win over Norwich City - fifth in Division One - which set up another home tie with Second Division Hull City. Latics won that game as well, by 3-0. Suddenly they were in the last eight. The draw paired them with Leeds United, then near the top of Division Two, again at Springfield Park.

The game took place on a Sunday with the crowd limited to 12,500. Every ticket was sold, with some Leeds fans paying up to £50 to make sure of admission. There was a fierce wind in Wigan's favour in the first half, and, with Leeds missing four regulars, there were strong grounds for believing that Latics could extend their long unbeaten run and reach the Semi-Finals. But both Campbell and Thompson failed to cash in on opportunities from around the six yard mark. Campbell then tried again, with a header this time, which hit the upright and bounced harmlessly away. Top scorer, David Lowe, carved out a good opening for Thompson which was spurned. But the pressure continued to come from Wigan's direction. A shot from Griffiths was blocked by the legs of Leeds 'keeper Mervyn Day. And a similar stop by Day prevented Thompson from opening the scoring. Towards the end of the first half, Edwards and Ritchie both missed opportunities for Leeds. The break came with the scoreline still 0-0. It had been Wigan's half, but those late Leeds chances looked ominous.

Although Wigan started the second half strongly, conditions were now in the Yorkshire team's favour. In 58 minutes

Leeds forced two quick corners, the second of which was only half-cleared. Stiles lashed out from 20 years to beat veteran 'keeper Roy Tunks and put Leeds in front. Wigan tried to battle back but it was in vain. Sixteen minutes from the end, Micky Adams surged forward for Leeds, ending his run with a fierce shot from 25 yards which left Tunks with no chance. 2-0 to Leeds and Wigan's Wembley dream was over.

"There were a few tears in the dressing room," said Ray Mathias, before adding, in philosophical mood, *"We had enough chances. But we've had a great run and enjoyed every single second of it."* That was more than could be said for the thousands of ticketless Leeds fans milling around outside the ground. Because of trouble in previous cup-ties, their allocation was only 2,000 tickets. Those restrictions meant that the crowd was the lowest for a post-war Cup Quarter-Final, some 250 less than Wimbledon's gate the same day. But it took in over £40,000 in receipts, a Wigan record to this day.

Latics still had promotion in their sights. They bettered their previous points tally by two but still ended up fourth for the second successive year. This was the season the play-offs were introduced, but that did Wigan no favours. Holding a 2-0 half-time lead, they were beaten 3-2 by Swindon at Springfield Park. A 0-0 draw away was a sour end to a year which had promised so much. Wigan haven't got near such heights again, being relegated to the bottom division in 1993. But for a short, glorious period back in 1987, it looked like the Latics might end up in the old Second Division... and bring the F.A. Cup with them.

ON THE SAME DAY...

News: A new international survey claims that Switzerland is the best country to live in, and Mozambique the worst.

Sport: Payne Stewart's victory in golf's Hertz Classic gives him his first win on the U.S. tour.

Entertainment:
On BBC-1, *'The World of UB40'* is not a documentary on the reggae band, but a look at how long-term unemployment is affecting people

WIMBLEDON 1
Vs Liverpool 0

May 14th 1988
F.A. Cup Final (Wembley)

Wimbledon: Beasant, Goodyear, Phelan, Jones, Young, Thorn, Gibson (Scales 63), Cork (Cunningham 56), Fashanu, Sanchez, Wise.

The rise of Wimbledon is a modern fairy tale. Winning election to the League in 1977, they were in the First Division nine years later. Yet their rise is even more dramatic than it sounds. For Wimbledon spent their first six years in the League bouncing up and down between the bottom two divisions. They won the Fourth Division title in 1983, were promoted straight through to the Second Division and, two years later, arrived in the First. When they reached the last eight of the F.A. Cup in 1987, it was the furthest they had ventured in the competition. Wembley seemed to be just a memory of their amateur days, indeed they won the Amateur Cup there in 1963. A quarter of a century after that triumph, no-one would have bet on Wimbledon getting to Wembley again.

The Dons astonished everyone by their performances in the top flight. Sixth in their first season, they finished a comfortable seventh in 1988 under manager Bobby Gould. If their style of play earned them criticism, then there was also a fund of goodwill towards them from those who liked the idea of a team like Wimbledon competing against the big outfits. They gave hope to every small club in the land. But their run in the F.A. Cup in 1988 would have confounded the dreams of even the most romantic of fans.

Struggling Second Division West Brom at home and Mansfield away were easy enough passages to the fifth round. But when they knocked out Newcastle 3-1 at St. James Park, everyone took notice of Wimbledon. A home win over Watford - doomed to relegation - before 12,228 sent them into the Semi-Finals. That crowd was a good one for Wimbledon's Plough Lane ground, but it was even lower than Wigan's tie with Leeds the year before, setting a new post-war low for a last eight tie. Many thought their run would end against Luton in the Semi-Final, but Wimbledon carved out a hard-won 2-1 success at White Hart Lane. Meanwhile in the other Semi-Final, Liverpool (1st in the League) beat Nottingham Forest (3rd) in what most thought to be the 'real final'.

So, if the Dons dream was to end in success, they would have to beat the most accomplished side in the country. Liverpool were looking for another 'double' to add to their 1986 success. Few outside London SW19 would have wagered against them. The capacity gate of 98,203 weighed up the arguments. Liverpool's first Cup win in 1965 was the same year as Wimbledon first played in the Southern League. When the Reds brought home the European Cup in 1977, Wimbledon were just about to be elected to the League. The Liverpool squad cost over £8m to assemble. Wimbledon's was £650,000. Wimbledon's average home gate since they joined the League was 4,179. Over the same period, Liverpool's was 38,459. It seemed a foregone conclusion.

And Liverpool started as if they wanted the whole business out of the way before half-time. But despite all their pressure they found it difficult to get past Dave Beasant in the Dons goal. Peter Beardsley thought he had done so when he chipped the 'keeper but the referee had already blown for a foul on Beardsley by Thorn. Naturally, the Anfield fans felt the advantage should have been given. Beardsley tried again. As did Houghton, Aldridge and even Alan Hansen. But Beasant, playing out of his skin, was equal to them all. His best save came in the 25th minute. Beardsley passed to the unmarked Houghton who centred for Aldridge to pick up. Aldridge side-footed what looked like an easy goal. Beasant, diving the wrong way, somehow managed to knock the

ball up with his leg then palm it away. It was a brilliant save and one which demonstrated that Wimbledon had a real chance. With Beasant in this kind of form, anything was possible.

They made their own chances too. A Wise centre ended with Fashanu shooting just wide. Then a Wimbledon move down the left was ended by a foul on Phelan. Wise directed the free kick to the near post and there was Lawrie Sanchez, nipping in between Nicol and Ablett, to head into goal. 36 minutes played and Wimbledon were ahead. Another Wise centre saw Grobbelaar fumble the ball but Gibson shot over the var. The half ended with Wimbledon up 1-0. And what had been feared would be a dirty match hadn't turned out that way. Apart from one incident between Jones and McMahon, two of the most robust in the business, it had been a clean game.

Ten minutes after the restart, it looked bad for the Dons. Aldridge picked up a pass from Beardsley. Goodyear intercepted with a slide-tackle, knocking the ball away. It looked like Aldridge had fallen over Goodyear's legs, but a penalty was given. Aldridge, with eleven spot-kick goals to his credit already this season, stepped up to hit penalty number twelve. He struck a good shot to the left hand post, but Beasant hurled himself in the right direction to tip it away. It was the first penalty to be saved in a Wembley F.A. Cup Final.

Wimbledon knew then it was their day. Liverpool brought on Johnston and Molby but made no further impact until two minutes to go when Nicol went close with a diving header. That was their last chance. The beautiful summer afternoon ended with the name of Wimbledon on the Cup - the most unlikeliest winners ever. And it was their hero, Dave Beasant, who went up the steps first, as captain, to receive the magnificent trophy.

Wimbledon's win didn't take them into Europe, English clubs were still serving the post-Heysel ban. But it did prove that romance and the F.A. Cup are still inextricably linked. And Wimbledon, though not repeating that success, have kept themselves at the very top in the English game - an achievement which has not received the credit it has been due in certain quarters. The Dons continue to confound both supporters and critics alike from their ground-share with Crystal Palace. When bookies list Cup odds these days, the name of Wimbledon is always prominently featured. And, unless Wycombe Wanderers or Middlesbrough win the F.A. Cup some day, Wimbledon will remain the only team to win the Amateur Cup and also the main professional prize.

ON THE SAME DAY...

News: Newly re-elected as President of France, Francois Mitterand calls a general election which his Socialist Party is expected to win.

Sport: Steffi Graf loses just one game and 25 points in beating compatriot Claudia Kohde-Kilsch in her 41 minute 6-1, 6-0 win in the German Open Tennis Championship.

Entertainment: On TV after the match: another bunch of alleged no-hopers who end up winning in the end. BBC-1 screens the film version of 'Dad's Army'.

WOLVERHAMPTON WANDERERS 2

Vs Tottenham Hotspur 0

April 24th 1954 Division One

Wolverhampton Wanderers: Williams, Stuart, Wright, Slater, Shorthouse, Flowers, Hancocks, Broadbent, Swinbourne, Wilshaw, Mullen.

Founder members of the League, Wolverhampton Wanderers had known bad times as well as good. Three times F.A. Cup winners, they had also spent more than a quarter of a century out of the top class. Either side of the Second World War saw them re-established as one of the best teams in the country. Yet, with the exception of the F.A. Cup in 1949, no silverware adorned the Molineux trophy room. There were fears that Wolves would always lose their nerve at the end of the League's long slog. On only two occasions since 1936 had they finished outside the top six and the number of times they narrowly failed to land the title was astonishing. Runners-up in both 1938 and 1939. Deprived by a single point in 1947. Beaten on goal average in 1950. They had finished third in 1953, three points off the pace. And the next season saw a fierce battle between Wolves and their deadly local rivals West Bromwich Albion for the Championship.

Albion had led for long stretches and had looked like they might even win the elusive 'double'. But Wolves had shown a determination lacking in their previous campaigns. As the teams approached their final games, Wolves had their noses in front:

	P	W	D	L	F	A	Pts	G.Av
1 Wolves	41	24	7	10	94	56	55	1.678
2 West Brom	41	22	9	10	85	60	53	1.417

Manager Stan Cullis and his side knew that they stood on the threshold of victory. Only a heavy defeat coupled with an equally heavy Albion victory could prevent them from winning the title. But Wolves had had last-day disappointments before. No-one was taking anything for granted. The 44,055 inside Molineux were every bit as anxious to know how Albion were doing against Portsmouth as they were to see Wolves win the day.

The players were palpably nervous, fearing to venture out of midfield in the first few minutes. Spurs tried to capitalise, Walters forcing Williams to his knees to stop a shot. Wolves first attempt saw Swinbourne fire wide. From 30 yards, Flowers attempted a shot which was also wide. Wolves won their first corner after eleven minutes. Spurs 'keeper Ted Ditchburn could only palm the ball away to Slater. He powered a drive at goal but the Spurs defence cleared off the line. Slater's shot had given Wolves the confidence they were lacking. And it was Slater who started a good move in the 18th minute. He slipped the ball to Hancocks who sent Mullen away on the left. He cut the ball back across goal to Swinbourne who headed home the opener.

Wolves were in the driving seat now. Ditchburn had to be at his best to stop Swinbourne from adding to his tally, then saved on the line from Hancocks. Spurs refused to lie down though. Both Walters and Dunmore went close for them. Then Walters had the ball in the net. It was clearly offside but the referee hadn't seen the linesman's flag. Surrounded by furious Wolves players, the referee eventually spoke to the linesman before signalling no goal. This incident inspired Wolves. Up till the break they rained in shots on goal. Ditchburn brought off a great save from Swinbourne in the 37th minute and then tipped a Wilshaw effort over the bar. Half-time arrived with Wolves still ahead by a single goal. The news from Fratton Park was encouraging too. 0-0 at half-time.

Wolves dominated the second half, playing like the Champions they knew they would shortly become. Broadbent and Wilshaw both going close to adding to their lead. After 69 minutes, Stuart set Broadbent off on a run. He passed to Mullen who earned a throw-in. Mullen took the throw, sending the ball to Wilshaw who played it quickly back to Mullen. The winger crossed and there was Swinbourne, in a repeat manoeuvre, heading in the second goal. There were those on the terraces who swore that the cheers could have been heard down at Fratton Park. Ditchburn made two flying saves late in the day from Wilshaw and Swinbourne but the damage had already been done. News that West Brom had lost 3-0 was the icing on the cake for the delighted Molineux faithful. Stan Cullis gentlemanly refused praise after the match. *"The credit belongs to the players,"* he said, modestly. After so many near-misses, Wolves were the Champions at last.

For skipper Billy Wright (who didn't have much to do in this game) and his men it was the breakthrough they had searched for. Two more titles arrived in 1958 and 1959. The F.A. Cup was won in 1960 when one solitary point prevented Wolves from doing the 'double'. There have been many ups and downs at Molineux since those days, most notoriously the infamous years of 1983-1986 when Wolves fell from First to Fourth Divisions in successive seasons. The rebirth has taken a long time. But as the century draws to a close there is greater optimism about the future at Molineux than for many years. Whatever that future holds, it is difficult to envisage it being quite as good as those golden days of the 1950s, when the 'nearly-men' of English football finally shook off that unwanted tag and embarked on a run of unparalleled success.

WREXHAM 1
Vs Anderlecht 1

March 17th 1976 European Cup-Winners Cup Quarter-Finals (2nd Leg)

Wrexham: Lloyd, Evans, Fogg, Davis, May, Whittle, Tinnion, Sutton, Lee, Ashcroft, Griffiths.

Founded in 1873, Wrexham are the oldest club in Wales. They joined the Third Division (North) as founder members in 1921 and led a largely undistinguished life thereafter. But they hold an advantage over most clubs of similar status - as a Welsh side they are eligible for entry into Europe by means of winning the Welsh Cup. In 1972-73 they did just that, beating Zurich before losing to Hajduk Split on away goals only. 1975-76 saw Wrexham return to the European scene with a team shrewdly assembled by manager John Neal which was also fighting for promotion to Division Two.

Neal's side proved adept at conjuring victories over supposedly superior opposition. Djurgårdens of Sweden and Polish side Stal Rzeszow both fell to the Welsh battlers. With big names like Celtic, Eintracht Frankfurt and West Ham still involved in the competition, it was a team to rank alongside those names that Wrexham drew in the Quarter-Finals. With players like Van der Elst, Coeck and the Dutch duo Haan

and Rensenbrink, Anderlecht were the favourites to win the trophy. But Wrexham performed admirably in the away leg, losing just 1-0 to give real hope that they could pull off a famous victory at the Racecourse ground.

19,668 turned up to cheer on their heroes. They saw a first 45 minutes in which Wrexham worked hard, dominated the play, but failing to make any clear-cut chances. The Belgian team had played in Europe every year since 1964 and were past masters in the art of protecting a lead away from home. Anderlecht appeared to be taking over in the second half, thinking the tie was already won when big Billy Ashcroft ran through their defence. He passed to Tinnion who laid it off to Sutton. He set up Stuart Lee who knocked the ball in at the far post, sparking off jubilant scenes on the terraces. Wrexham were level with half an hour to play. The next few minutes saw the Belgian 'keeper Ruiter out of position, Lee fired over the bar. A second goal at this stage could well have been decisive but somehow Anderlecht survived.

At 1-1 on aggregate the game looked bound for extra time. But Anderlecht steadied their nerve and came back at Wrexham. It was still delicately balanced with fifteen minutes to go when Rob Rensenbrink stole into the penalty box and blasted an unstoppable shot past Brian Lloyd. Under the away goals rule Wrexham now needed to score twice in the last quarter of an hour. Sadly, even notching another one was a task beyond them. They were beaten by a team which went on to win the trophy that year, reach the Final again in 1977 and win it again in 1978. That was the mark of the opposition that evening when a Third Division side almost reached the last four of the Cup-Winners Cup. Defeat, but not disgrace, on a night of pride and passion for Wales.

Two years later, Wrexham lifted the Third Division title, spending four years in the old Second Division, their best placing being 15th in 1979. In Europe they have played host to famous names like Roma and Manchester United. They eliminated the famous Porto and lost on away goals to Zaragoza. But never again have they come within touching distance of the Semi-Finals, a distinction which remains with the side of '76.

WYCOMBE WANDERERS 4
Vs Preston North End 2

May 28th 1994 Promotion Play-off (Wembley)

Wycombe Wanderers: Hyde, Cousins, Crossley, Creaser, Titterton,
Carroll, Reid, Ryan, Guppy, Thompson, Garner.

Like Wimbledon before them, Wycombe Wanderers were an amateur club, previous winners of the Amateur Cup, graduating through a series of Leagues to the Isthmian League. They enjoyed success at that level and won promotion to the Conference in 1987. Wembley triumphs in the F.A. Trophy followed in 1991 and 1993. The latter success being accompanied by a fifteen points winning margin in the Conference which saw them gain admission to the League.

Undefeated in their first six League games, Wycombe quickly established themselves at the higher level. Indeed, it was December before they lost away from home. Much of the credit was given to manager Martin O'Neill who had turned down an approach to succeed Brian Clough at Nottingham Forest. By January Wycombe were in second place. It was asking too much of the League newcomers to maintain that position and a poor run at the end of the season, failing to win any of their last five matches, left them in fourth spot, one below the automatic promotion positions. It was a creditable achievement, reflected in a rise in attendances from the average 4,602 during the Conference-winning season to 5,448 this term.

Wycombe's placing sent them into the play-offs. Ironically their first game was at Carlisle where their first ever League fixture had been played the previous August. A 2-2 draw that day was converted to a 2-0 victory this time and a 2-1 home win before 6,265 at Adams Park provided Wycombe with another ticket to Wembley - this time with a place in the Second Division (old Third Division) as the prize.

Their opponents were Preston North End, a side seeking, if not quite a return to the glory days, then at least a measure of respectability by escaping from the bottom division. They would also bring the bulk of the spectators down from the North as well. A further counter against Wycombe was the fact that since automatic promotion had been introduced, only Darlington, a former League club, had won promotion in their first League season. Many felt that Wycombe's amazing climb was about to be brought to an end.

There were at least 25,000 Lancastrians among the crowd of 40,109 and they saw a tentative opening half hour before Preston drew first blood. A dramatic overhead kick from Bryson in 32 minutes giving them the lead. But Wycombe's success had been founded on a resilient spirit and less than a minute later Steve Thompson levelled the proceedings. In what was turning into an explosive contest, Preston regained the lead through Raynor in 37 minutes and reached the interval with their advantage intact.

With only two minutes of the second half gone, veteran striker Simon Garner added to the 190 League goals he had amassed in a distinguished career, when he punished the hesitant Preston defence. Ten minutes later Dave Carroll scored to put Wycombe in front for the first time. Preston weren't finished though. Less than twenty minutes remained when a powerful header from Whalley rebounded off 'keeper Paul Hyde's chest. But the superbly organised Wycombe defence cleared the danger.

Preston's own defence was rather less well drilled. One minute later Carroll received the ball at the end of a four-man move and ran past three defenders, turned and shot home off the post to make it 4-2. There were only eighteen minutes to go and Carroll's second goal had killed off Preston. The League's newest side had vanquished the first-ever Champions at football's most famous ground. It was a fitting way to earn promotion. Preston manager John Beck was magnanimous in defeat, saying: *"Justice was done".* O'Neill was understandably delighted. *"Everything we have tried to do at this club has come right today,"* was his summation.

For Wycombe it was a thrilling climax to an unforgettable first season. And their performances since suggest that the summit of their League ambitions may not yet have been reached.

ON THE SAME DAY...

News: After 20 years in exile, Nobel Prize-winning author Alexander Solzhenitsyn returns to his native Russia.

Sport: It's just not Cricket. Accusations fly that Ball-tampering is rife in the game.

Entertainment:
Ten years after his death, a tribute is screened in honour of Eric Morecambe.

Manchester United 0 Vs
YORK CITY 3

September 20th 1995
Coca-Cola (League) Cup Round Two (1st Leg)

York City: Kiely, McMillan, Hall, Pepper, Tutill, Barras,
Murty, Williams, Barnes, Peverell (Baker 66), Jordan.

For centuries York ranked as England's premier city outside London but it's football team could scarcely claim such status. York City have rarely hit the football headlines. True, they had been the first League team to amass 100 points in a season. They had played at Wembley in one of the welter of third-rate tourneys which sprung up in the 1980s. They had, in the '70s, spent two seasons in the old Second Division. In 1985 they had knocked Arsenal out of the F.A. Cup. But by 1995 it would be fair to say that their greatest moment had been forty years earlier when they became the only Third Division side to be mentioned as possible Cup Finalists. In 1955 they reached the semi-finals of the F.A. Cup and drew with Newcastle, leaving the Final billed as Newcastle or York Vs Manchester City. Sadly for York they lost the replay.

But a midweek match at Old Trafford in September, 1995, provided an occasion to overshadow even that achievement. They were supposed to be simple cannon fodder for Manchester United. The Old Trafford side had won five League games on the trot and lay joint top of the Premiership. True, they rested certain key players for this match and others, like the injured Andy Cole and the suspended Eric Cantona, were unavailable. But their line-up still looked far too formidable for a York side which had won just once this season - and that thanks to a Swansea own goal the previous Saturday. Players like Parker, Irwin, Sharpe, Pallister, McClair and Giggs were battle-hardened men of international stature. Youngsters like Neville and Beckham had already demonstrated their talents against the best in Europe. York - second bottom of the new Division Two - should, on the face of it, have stayed on their own side of the Pennines.

But it was York who attacked furiously from the kick-off. For the first twenty minutes Pilkington, in the United goal, spent his time coping with nervous back-passes from his defence. But then Lee Sharpe and Ryan Giggs turned on the style. Their wing marauding provided McClair with a chance which he headed firmly towards goal. Dean Kiely - the York custodian - reacted superbly to tip the ball over the bar. A superb flick-on by Giggs again gave McClair a scoring chance, but this time he headed weakly. It looked simply to be a matter of time before United scored.

Then, in 24 minutes, the game turned upside down when a well-hit shot from Paul Barnes flew unerringly past Pilkington into the corner of the net to put York in front. A dumbfounded United lost their pattern after this setback, trooping off disappointed at the break. Six minutes into the second half Barnes burst through the defence only to be brought down by United's debutant centre-half McGibbon.

The offender was shown the red card and York awarded a penalty. Barnes showed no trace of nerves as he despatched the ball safely home. Just two minutes later, a Nigel Pepper cross saw Tony Barras climb above everyone else to head in the third. The bulk of the 29,049 crowd were stunned into silence. On came substitute Steve Bruce in an attempt to salvage something for United, but it was too late. York themselves were reduced to ten men with a quarter of an hour remaining when Paul Baker - who had only been on the field for nine minutes - was sent off for a second bookable offence. Even then United could not respond. 3-0 it stayed - a sublime performance from York and an unbelievable result. United seldom lost at home, it was rare for them to concede three goals and rarer still for them to lose by such a margin. 'Anoraks' all over the country pored over musty record books to find out when such a thing had last happened as the small, but ecstatic, band of York supporters sang all the way home.

Two weeks later, a packed Bootham Crescent was witness to an incredible night of emotion as York held fast against a determined United onslaught. Despite losing 3-1 on the night, York triumphed 4-3 on aggregate to take their place in the third round and confirm the historic upset of the previous fortnight.

ON THE SAME DAY...

News: The European Court rules in favour of Jean-Marc Bosman and declares it illegal for football clubs to demand transfer fees from players out of contract.

Sport: Dynamo Kiev are thrown out of the Champions League and barred from Europe for three years after attempting to bribe the referee in their game against Panathinaikos.

Entertainment: The BBC's ambitious series *Peoples Century* reaches its second episode, with eyewitness testimony from survivors of the First World War.

Potential. That was the word most frequently over-used when talking about Aberdeen's first 75 years of existence. Founded in 1903, the Dons were reckoned to be the side most capable of mounting a challenge to Scotland's Old Firm. With a big population area and no local rivals, untouched by the religious bigotry which disfigured Scottish football in Glasgow, and, to a lesser extent, Edinburgh and Dundee, capable of generating big crowds, there was no doubt that they had the potential. What they never did was to achieve it. One League title, two Scottish Cups, two League Cups - the same tally as might be expected from an ordinary provincial club. Then along came Alex Ferguson as manager.

Building on an already talented squad, Ferguson took Aberdeen to heights previously undreamed of. They won the League title in 1980 and two years later won the Scottish Cup. The same season saw them advance past the first two rounds of European competition for the first time in eleven attempts, including a marvellous triumph over U.E.F.A. Cup holders Ipswich Town. But it was the following season, 1982-83, which was to see the Dons emerge as a side which could live with the European elite. An impressive 11-1 aggregate victory over Swiss side Sion in the preliminary round of the Cup-Winners Cup was followed by a hard-fought 1-0 success against Dynamo Tirana. When Lech Poznan of Poland were beaten 2-0 at Pittodrie and 1-0 in Poland, the Dons had reached the last eight in Europe for the first time.

It was the Olympic Stadium in Munich which was the venue the night the Dons came of age in Europe. A superb 0-0 draw against Bayern brought the famous German team to Pittodrie where, on a night of emotion rarely seen in that douce setting, Aberdeen won 3-2. They overwhelmed their Belgian opponents Waterschei 5-1 at home in the Semi-Final, losing the return leg 1-0 - their first loss in the tournament. All that remained was for the Dons to travel to the Ullevai Stadium in Gothenburg to take on the mighty Real Madrid in the Final.

The Dons side, if not battle-hardened in Europe, did contain experienced international performers. Leighton, in goal, was as good a 'keeper as Scotland had fielded for many years. McLeish and Miller were the regular central defensive paring in the national side. And Gordon Strachan was... well, simply he was Gordon Strachan, a bundle of energy packed into a small but surprisingly strong frame. A runner, a dribbler, a playmaker. A man with magic in his boots. Against all that was the fact that this was Real Madrid's **eleventh** European Final. If they were no longer the great side of the fifties, the Spanish outfit were still one of the most feared names in the game.

But before 17,804 spectators on the rain-soaked Swedish pitch, it was the Scots who were first to show. Three minutes into the game and a Strachan cross gave Black a chance which he smashed off the bar. Three minutes more and it was Strachan again. He whipped in a cross which McLeish headed down for Black to nip in and score. Stung by this setback, Real started to move forward. But Miller and McLeish were equal to the task. With one exception. A bad back pass by McLeish allowed Carlos Santillana to run in on goal. Leighton had little alternative but to bring him down. Juanito scored from the penalty. The Dons lead had lasted just nine minutes.

Apart from that, the threat posed by Santillana and the brilliant, if moody, German, Uli Stielike, was safely contained. It was Aberdeen, with the outstanding Strachan, ably backed by Simpson and Cooper, who called the shots. Half-time saw the match still delicately poised at 1-1.

ABERDEEN 2
Vs Real Madrid 1

May 11th 1983 European Cup-Winners Cup Final (Gothenburg)

Aberdeen: Leighton, Rougvie, McMaster, Cooper, McLeish, Miller, Strachan, Simpson, McGhee, Black (Hewitt 87), Weir.

The second half saw Black and McGhee cause problems for the Real defence. Dutch star Johnny Metgod had his work cut out stopping the Dons and was never able to go forward himself. On the wing, Peter Weir came more into the game as the Dons made chances. A shot from Strachan was stopped by 'keeper Augustin's body. A Black header was tipped over the bar. Both those efforts were a result of Weir's crosses. Near the end of the 90 minutes, Black received a kick when heading over and had to be replaced by Hewitt. The first period of extra time left the teams still level. With eight minutes of the second extra period remaining, Weir set McGhee free down the left. His cross was met by the diving head of substitute Hewitt who placed the ball unerringly inside the far post to regain the lead for Aberdeen. There was no way back for Real. The Cup-Winners Cup was on its way to Pittodrie.

"I'm so pleased for the city and for all our fans", said Willie Miller. His boss was more exuberant. *"We slaughtered them,"* said Ferguson. *"This is the greatest moment of my life."* Ten days later, Aberdeen won the Scottish Cup again. They took the Cup for a third successive year in 1984 and added the League title as well. The Championship was retained in 1985 and both domestic Cups were won the following season. In Europe the Dons reached the last four in the defence of their trophy and the Quarter-Finals of the European Cup in 1986. It was an unprecedented run of triumph for the club. But it ended when Alex Ferguson left for Manchester United in 1986.

The only silverware to be displayed at Pittodrie since then came with another domestic Cup 'double' under Alex Smith's management in 1989-90. Aberdeen have grown used to second prizes and early knockouts in Europe. Their disastrous 1994-95 season suggests that even this modest level of success may now be beyond them. Alex Ferguson brought the city the greatest period the club had ever known. The night they won the Cup-Winners Cup was the pinnacle of success. It also established a yardstick by which all his successors at Pittodrie are now judged. A hard, if not impossible, act to follow. But, as we all know, they have the potential.

ON THE SAME DAY...

News:	Yelena Bonner, wife of Soviet dissident Andrei Sakharov, says her husband wishes to leave the U.S.S.R.
Sport:	Olympic Decathlon Gold Medallist Daley Thompson takes advantage of new rules concerning amateur athletes and advertising by signing a three-year contract with Fabergé.
Entertainment:	
	On BBC-1, the last in the current series of *"Dallas"*.

AIRDRIEONIANS 2

Vs Hibernian 0
April 19th 1924
Scottish Cup Final (Ibrox)

Airdrieonians had joined the Scottish League's Second Division in its second season in 1894-95. Elected to Division One after winning the Second division title in 1903, they had enjoyed a modestly successful existence. But the years shortly after the First World War saw an improvement in their fortunes. League Runners-up in 1922-23, they held the same position the following season. And it was no mere team of provincial journeymen who entertained the fans at Broomfield Park. Included in the Airdrie team were two of the great stars of the time - Hughie Gallacher, later to become a legend on Tyneside, and Bob McPhail, who was to end up a Rangers all-time great.

But their League form took time to rub off on the Scottish Cup. Since their first entry in 1881-82, the best Airdrie had managed was to reach the Semi-Finals in 1905, losing to Third Lanark. However, the early 1920s saw a clutch of so-called smaller clubs - Kilmarnock, Partick Thistle and Morton - all win the trophy. So there was hope for all. And it was one of those previous winners - Morton - who were Airdrie's first victims in the 1923-24 tourney when the Diamonds won 4-2 at home before a crowd of 10,000. A similar crowd saw a 4-0 home win over St. Johnstone before Airdrie pulled off a most satisfying 5-0 away triumph over Lanarkshire rivals Motherwell. But their Quarter-Final tie against Ayr United was a seemingly interminable affair. 1-1 at Broomfield. 0-0 at Somerset Park after extra time. 1-1 at Ibrox after another bout of extra time. By the time Airdrie eventually overcame their Ayrshire adversaries 1-0 in another Ibrox game, the teams had played for **seven hours**. By comparison, their 90 minute Semi-Final win over Falkirk at Celtic Park saw the game just fly past.

Airdrie had made the Scottish Cup Final at last. But even though they were five League places above their opponents, Airdrie were not the favourites. Hibs had not only played, and narrowly lost, in the 1923 Final, they were fielding the identical eleven who had come so close on that occasion. Hibs experience was reckoned to give them the edge.

But Cup Finals don't always go by the book. The 65,000 inside Ibrox Stadium were astonished to find that it was Hibs who were the more nervous side. Early in the game, centre-half Miller needlessly conceded a corner. Reid took the kick and the unchallenged Preston headed goalwards. Despite 'keeper Willie Harper's despairing dive, Russell made sure the ball found the target. Only four minutes had been played.

Hibs tried to respond but Dick and McQueen were too strong at the back. And Hibs inside-right Dunn picked up a knock which left him limping badly. Airdrie attacked again. Seeing the 'keeper off his line, Reid shot from the wing. Harper looked beaten but he ran backwards, keeping

Airdrieonians: Ewart, Dick, McQueen, Preston, McDougall, Bennie, Reid, Russell, Gallacher, McPhail, Sommerville.

his eye on the ball, and tipped it over one-handed. A magnificent save from the Scottish International. With 37 minutes played, the weakened Dunn back-heeled to right-back McGinnigle at the corner flag. But the Hibs man was too slow to move and Bennie seized the opportunity to flight over a cross which Russell headed home. 2-0 at half-time and it was the Lanarkshire supporters who were in full voice.

They never had reason to stop singing in the second half, despite Hibs attempts to come back into the match. Except for one incident, when McQueen appeared to have brought down Hibs inside-left Halligan. Referee Tom Dougray pointed to the spot. Ewart rushed out to speak to Dougray. The referee walked over to his linesman and, to the relief of the Airdrie fans, awarded a goal-kick. Hibs were finished after this and Airdrie dominated the rest of the match. Gallacher was always alert and probing, moving Airdrie forward. McPhail shot on the run but Harper made a fine save. It didn't matter. The Scottish Cup was Airdrie's. A success they roundly deserved.

Those were the great days for Airdrie. They finished League runners-up four times in a row, never quite managing to lift the title. But a side like Airdrie cannot expect to hold on to the Gallachers and McPhails. They had to sell their stars to balance the books. Airdrie spent most of their time in the old First Division without really challenging for honours. Since the establishment of the Premier Division they have only rarely played at that level. Though further, losing, Cup Finals in 1975, 1992, and 1995 brought a taste of success to Broomfield again. They even played, briefly, in Europe. As they prepare for life in a new purpose-built stadium, Airdrie know that their best chance of future success lies in a return to a sensible number of clubs in Scotland's top division. No change and they will never prosper.

ON THE SAME DAY...

News: Ramsay McDonald addresses the Independent Labour Party Conference at York for the first time as Prime Minister.

Sport: A crowd of 5,000 see Hawick win the Border Rugby Sevens.

Entertainment
Children's comic 'The Rover', costing 2d. is a best-seller, featuring football stories like 'Whirlwind Jack Whizzes It Through'.

ALBION ROVERS 2
Vs Kilmarnock 3

April 17th 1920 Scottish Cup Final
(Hampden)

Albion Rovers: Short, Penman, Bell, Wilson, Black, Ford, Ribchester, James White, John White, Watson, Hillhouse.

A runners-up spot in Division Two in 1914 was all that Albion Rovers had to show for over thirty years of endeavour. Shortly after this they were reduced to the minor ranks when the Scottish League decided to operate one division only during the First World War. The Second Division was not re-instated until 1921-22 but two seasons prior to that, the big clubs needed one more side to make up the numbers and Rovers, surprisingly, got the nod. So it was that Albion Rovers became the only team in Britain to reach a Cup Final while lying rock bottom of the entire League.

For Rovers found the transition to the top division painful, but the Cup was another matter. Hitherto, they had never even reached so much as a Quarter-Final. 1919-20 was a different story entirely. In fact their progress to the last eight could scarcely have been made easier, although Rovers contrived to do it the hard way. They took two games to beat non-League Dykehead, received a walk-over when Huntingtower scratched, and then needed another replay to dispose of Edinburgh minnows St. Bernard's. But when they eliminated Aberdeen to reach the Semi-Finals, the town of Coatbridge was abuzz.

In the last four they met Rangers, and Rovers shocked all of Scotland by holding their mighty rivals to a 1-1 draw at Celtic Park. The replay also finished drawn - this time goalless. It was the third game which provided the almost unbelievable result - Albion Rovers 2 Rangers 0. In their first season in the top flight - and as the bottom club - Rovers had reached the Cup Final.

Along with Final opponents Kilmarnock, Rovers helped provide another oddity - this was the occasion when both teams in the Final played a man short for the whole 90 minutes. John Short being the Rovers goalie and Mattha Shortt the Killie right-half. But this Final was special in another way. It was the first Cup Final since 1914 and supporters were desperate to return to normality after the War. The S.F.A., in what was laughingly termed their wisdom, thought that the two provincial Finalists would struggle to amass 50,000 at the gate. Imagine their shock when the gates were closed with a record 95,000 inside and several thousand more locked out.

Rovers were still massive underdogs but they started nervelessly. James White and Ribchester combined, the latter latching onto a cross which Killie full-back Hamilton failed to cut out. Ribchester passed to Watson who netted after just five minutes play. Rovers felt the strength of the Ayrshire side after that and spent most of the rest of the half on the defensive. Yet apart from conceding an equaliser to Willie Culley in 15 minutes, they held firm. 1-1 at the interval and it was still anybody's Cup.

Kilmarnock started the second half the way Rovers started the first. Shortt joined the attack and put the Ayrshire side ahead two minutes after the restart. Rovers didn't take things lying down though. They steamed forward themselves. The next three minutes saw frenetic activity in the Kilmarnock goalmouth. Watson was brought down but no penalty was given. The same player saw an attempt blocked by 'keeper Blair's feet. Then a long cross found Hillhouse who beat Blair to equalise in the 50th minute.

Rovers saw their hopes dashed ten minutes later when J.R. Smith (who would also score in the first Wembley Cup Final) fired an unstoppable shot to restore Killie's lead. Rovers did try to come back but Kilmarnock ended the game well on top. Nevertheless it was a magnificent achievement to reach the Final itself and a wonderful dream come true for James White who had been playing Junior football just three weeks before the Final. And Rovers were a sporting club too. Club President Hugh Thom said: *"We don't deny Kilmarnock credit of their victory, they deserved it."*

Amazingly, Rovers reached the Semi-Finals again the next year and once more faced Rangers. This time they were beaten 4-1. They made a few Quarter-Final appearances in the 1930s but have never progressed so far since. In the League, they lasted just one more year in the top flight after automatic promotion and relegation was introduced. In the 1930s they twice returned to the top division and did so, briefly, after the Second World War. Since then they have remained in the basement except for 1989-90 when, following their Second Division Championship season, they played in the First Division.

For the last few seasons Rovers have struggled to survive, usually finishing near the bottom of the League and sometimes playing in front of crowds of fewer than 200. As they now prepare for life stadium-sharing with Airdrie, perhaps a new start will herald an improvement in Rovers fortunes.

ON THE SAME DAY...

News: Lord French announces his resignation as Viceroy of Ireland.

Sport: The post-war boom in crowds continues. 6,000 see Cowdenbeath beat Lochgelly 4-0 in the Penman Cup, a local competition.

Entertainment: The big film at Glasgow's City Picture House is *"The Convert"*, staring W.S. Hart.

ALLOA ATHLETIC 2
Vs Celtic 3

August 19th 1922
Scottish League Division One

Alloa Athletic: Thomson, Orrock, McGregor,
Ford, McInally, Wood, Forrest, Dunn, Burns,
Craig, Quinn.

Formed in 1883, Alloa Athletic played in regional Leagues up until the First World War. In 1921 the Scottish League re-established a Second Division and Alloa joined that set-up. With just one promotion place available, Alloa exceeded their fans wildest dreams. They romped home a massive **thirteen** points clear of second-place Cowdenbeath. Willie 'Wee' Crilley scored 49 League goals, a club record which stands to this day. It was a truly historic season - Alloa became the first team to win automatic promotion in Scottish football. Crowds nudged the 4,000 mark. But everyone connected with the Clackmannanshire club knew that the top division would be an entirely different proposition.

The League fixtures threw up the most difficult start that Alloa could have envisaged. Away to Rangers in midweek, followed by Celtic at home on Saturday. Alloa lost 2-0 at Ibrox. Their supporters were undaunted. An estimated 15,000 squeezed into Recreation Park for the visit of the Glasgow giants. And they were not disappointed. The Wasps spent the first fifteen minutes running Celtic ragged. Their ex-Celt inside-left Craig opened the scoring with a fierce shot on the quarter-hour mark which Bhoys 'keeper Shaw saw coming but had no earthly chance to save. Alloa had announced their arrival in the big time.

Alloa kept the lead for ten minutes until Celtic were awarded one of those dubious penalties for which the Old Firm are renowned or reviled, depending upon one's allegiance. It was a crowded area and no-one could be sure if the offence was from handling or from obstruction. But a penalty was given nonetheless. McStay levelled from the spot. There were no more goals in the first half but Alloa had done enough to earn the half-time cheers they received.

Celtic started the second period in better shape. Needless handling by Alloa's Burns gave the Celts a free kick. McAtee took it, sending the ball to Cassidy who scored - or did he? The Alloa players were adamant that the Celtic man had handled the ball. They protested to the Referee. At length the official decided to consult his linesman. Consternation for Alloa, jubilation for Celtic. The goal stood.

A few minutes later, Cassidy set up Gallagher for Celtic's third goal - and their first without any hint of controversy. Alloa stormed back. Burns was fouled by Shaw. Now it was Alloa's turn for a spot-kick. Wood blasted home. 3-2 with five minutes to go. Alloa, with Craig in great form, battled like furies for a precious point, but it was not to be.

They had lost, but in circumstances which made Scottish football sit up and take note. It had taken a dodgy penalty and a dubious goal to subdue the fighting Wasps.

It was to be a tough season for Alloa, which ended in relegation. It was the only time they played a full season at Scottish football's top level. Promoted again in 1939, they played just five matches before the outbreak of the Second World War and were placed in the lower division at the end of the conflict. The new set-up established in 1975 gave clubs like Alloa the opportunity to reach the intermediate level of the First Division. It's a chance they have taken on four occasions but they have never survived for long in that company.

Nor have the Cups brought any glory to Recreation Park. The Wasps have never progressed beyond the Quarter-Finals in either of the domestic knockout competitions. It looks like being a long time - if ever - before Alloa again entertain Glasgow's big two in League competition.

ON THE SAME DAY...

News: The Prime Minister, David Lloyd-George, is to receive £90,000 for his war memoirs.

Sport: The cricket season finishes with Aberdeenshire's draw at Stirling good enough to clinch the Scottish County Championship.

Entertainment
Doing the rounds of Scottish theatres is *'Mary Rose'*, a new play by Sir. J.M. Barrie.

ARBROATH 36
Vs Bon Accord 0

September 12th 1885
Scottish Cup Round One

Arbroath: Milne, Salmond, Collie, Milne, Rennie, Robertson, Crawford, Petrie, Marshall, Tackett, Munro.

Arbroath, founded in 1878, had already made one piece of Scottish Cup history before this auspicious day in September 1885. In the previous year's competition, they had sensationally beaten Rangers 4-3 in the fourth round. The Glasgow team famously protested that they had been *"beaten on a back green,"* an allusion to the dimensions of Arbroath's Gayfield park. The S.F.A. ordered a replay which Rangers won 8-1.

For this year's competition, Arbroath were scheduled to face Bon Accord, an Aberdeen side, away from home but their rivals generously agreed to play at Gayfield. The match kicked off in a torrential downpour. It was Bon Accord who got proceedings under way but almost immediately the ball was back in their own half. Receiving the ball from a throw-in, Crawford scored the opener for Arbroath. It soon became apparent that the deluge wasn't just falling from the sky - it was raining goals as well. The first half saw reporters desperately trying to keep an accurate tally of scorers and goals - it happened so fast that describing the goals was impossible. By half-time Arbroath were winning **15-0**.

The second period saw more of the same. All told the ball crossed the Bon Accord line on **forty** occasions but four of these were disallowed. Bon Accord had just one shot all afternoon but Collie cleared easily. The official count at the end was **36-0**. Arbroath played with six forwards and all their goals came from their front men - and every forward scored. Petrie led the way with 13, followed by Munro 7, Crawford 6, Robertson 6, Marshall 2, and Tackett 2. The **Scottish Umpire** was stating the obvious when, in its account of proceedings, it said of Bon Accord: *"Their backs, especially the goalkeeper were worse than useless."*

The local **Arbroath Herald** declared: *"It is believed that the score piled up by the Maroons is unequalled in the annals of football."* So it was and so it stays - the world record score in a first-class competition. But a thought must be spared for Dundee side, Harp. On the same day they led their opponents, Rovers, from Aberdeen, 16-0 at half-time and ran out 35-0 winners. Their game had kicked off at 3.25p.m. Arbroath's at 3.30p.m. For a mere five minutes, Harp were the World record holders!

On account of the weather only a small crowd witnessed this historic match. How small we don't know. But given that the attendance at the re-played game with Rangers was 2,000 then only a few hundred - at best - can have watched the slaughter of Bon Accord.

Arbroath produced some more excellent results in the competition, beating Forfar Athletic 9-1 and East End, from Dundee, 7-1 before losing 5-3 away to Hibernian And how Aberdonian teams must have hated travelling to Arbroath. Another Deeside outfit, Orion (one of the predecessors of the modern Aberdeen F.C.), were beaten 20-0 at Gayfield in the next season's Scottish Cup, then 18-0 the season after that!

But for all their heroics, the Red Lichties never really did that well in the Cup. It was to be 1947 before they reached the Semi-Finals for the first (and to date last) time. Their League Cup tally reads the same - one unsuccessful Semi-Final. They joined the Scottish League in 1921 and for a few seasons before the Second World War held First Division status. Two more post-war promotions were short-lived but Arbroath returned to the top sphere in 1972.

At the time of re-organisation in 1975 they were still a First Division club. But their path has been a largely down-hill one ever since. Arbroath have stood and watched while near-neighbours Brechin, Forfar and Montrose - traditionally 'smaller' sides - have enjoyed their day in the sun. Arbroath's turn will surely come again. They are capable of reaching a place in the First Division. And they have their World record - something it is unlikely any team will ever deprive them of.

ON THE SAME DAY...

News: An Anglo-Russian agreement has been reached on the Afghan border, ending the risk of war.

Sport: The first ever S.F.A. Football Annual is published - priced 6d. (2½p.)

Entertainment: Showing at the Theatre Royal, Dundee is *"Kindred Souls,"* described as a, *"farcical comedy."* Not unlike Arbroath's game against Bon Accord.

The Arbroath Guide.
SATURDAY, SEPTEMBER 19, 1885.

FOOTBALL.

FOOTBALL NOTE.—The Arbroath play off their Cup tie with the Bon Accord to-day, at Gayfield The following players will represent the home team, and should have little difficulty in carrying their club into the second round of the Scottish competition:—Milne, (goal); Collie and Salmond, (backs); Rennie and Milne, (Captain), (half-backs); Munro, Tacket, Marshall, Petrie, Crawford, and Robertson, (forwards).

ARBROATH *v.* BON-ACCORD (ABERDEEN).—The meeting of these teams in the first round of the Scottish Cup Ties was expected to end in an easy win for the Arbroath, but few anticipated the farce enacted at Gayfield last Saturday. The Bon-Accord had the good grace to save a journey to the Arbroath men by electing to play off the tie at Arbroath, and punctually to time both teams appeared on the field. It would have been difficult to choose a stronger team out of the Club than that representing the Arbroath. Winning the toss, Milne, the Arbroath captain, chose to defend the east goal, and then began the most amusing football match ever seen in Arbroath. There could scarcely be said to have been any play shown on the part of the Bon-Accord, and from the beginning of the game the goals began to accumulate at an alarming rate, Petrie opening the account with two in succession, and Marshall immediately adding another couple. After Munro had put on the fifth goal a slight rest in the reckoning occurred, the Aberdeen men somehow managing to keep the ball for a short time near mid-field. Then the Arbroath forwards seemed to get thoroughly into the fun of the game, and before the call of half-time had scored other ten goals. After the thirteenth goal had been got, the Aberdeen forwards had a momentary encounter with the backs near the Arbroath goal, but this was the only time they got away from their own territory. The second half was simply a repetition of the first, five goals being registered within the first fifteen minutes, and sixteen during the other thirty minutes. In the course of this half, however, the Bon-Accord were within an ace of scoring, the only

AYR UNITED 0
Vs Rangers 2

April 4th 1973 Scottish Cup Semi-Finals
(Hampden)

Ayr United: Stewart, Wells, Murphy, McAnespie, Fleming, Filipi, Doyle, Graham (Campbell), Ingram, McLean, McCulloch.

Scottish football is forever being told that certain teams are too small to prosper on their own and that they should amalgamate. Airdrie and Albion Rovers, Dundee and Dundee United, even Hearts and Hibs. Apart from the fact that the last thing supporters want is for deadly local rivals to merge, those same pundits ignore the singular lack of success achieved by (until the arrival of Caledonian Thistle in the League in 1994) the only club formed by such a move.

Ayr United were established in 1910 as a result of the merging of Ayr and Ayr Parkhouse. They gained First Division status in 1913 and spent most of the inter-war period in the top division, if seldom reaching the higher echelons. After the Second World War it was a different story. Between 1946-1969, Ayr spent just four seasons in Division One and lived constantly in the shadow of neighbours Kilmarnock. In the Scottish Cup a handful of Quarter-Finals was the best they could manage.

The arrival of the flamboyant Ally McLeod as manager changed all that. After gaining promotion again in 1969, Ayr managed to stay in the top flight, and began to move into the top half of the table. McLeod built a talented side. David Stewart was a superb 'keeper. Full-back 'Spud' Murphy was a tigerish performer and a fans favourite. Johnny Doyle was a top quality winger, Alex Ingram an ace goal-getter and George McLean brought the experience garnered at Rangers and Dundee to Somerset Park.

The 1973 Cup campaign started with gentle draws. Inverness Thistle and Stirling Albion were both beaten at Somerset. But it was the Quarter-Final tie away to Partick Thistle which put McLeod's men on the map. Against the team which had sensationally won the previous term's League Cup, Ayr ran out 5-1 winners. Their Firhill triumph proved that they were a threat to anyone. It also took them into the last four of the Cup for the first time ever.

51,815 turned up at Hampden Park on a Wednesday night in April to see Ayr do battle with Rangers for a place in the Final. Normally Rangers would have been overwhelming favourites, but the Ibrox side hadn't won the trophy since 1966 and McLeod had convinced both players and fans that Ayr had a real chance. When Ingram headed into goal in the first minute there was, momentarily, bedlam among the United fans. Alas for them their striker was clearly offside, though McLeod would later argue about the decision. That initial flourish aside, Rangers soon took control. But the 'Honest Men' defended admirably until five minutes from the break. A long ball was touched on by 'Gers Alex McDonald. Derek Parlane and Alex McAnespie raced for the ball, the Ibrox striker getting there first to hit it straight past Stewart to give Rangers the interval lead.

With Campbell on for Graham in the second half, Ayr began to hit back. Rangers were coming under some pressure when the tie was turned by John Greig. The Rangers skipper hit a pass which *"would have been envied by Crerand or Netzer,"* as **Hugh Taylor** wrote in the **Daily Record** the next morning. Greig's pass sent Tommy McLean away down the right. Ayr's defence was nowhere as McLean crossed. It was a replica of the opener as Parlane and McAnespie tussled to meet it. Again it was the Rangers man who was successful as he shot home the second goal.

Parlane immediately rushed to receive the adulation of the fans - and was booked for so doing, the first time any Scottish player had his name taken in this way. Wells, Doyle and McCulloch tried to rally Ayr but they were never really in the hunt. The game ended 2-0. It remains the nearest Ayr United have come to playing in a Scottish Cup Final. They were beaten by Hearts in a Quarter-Final replay the next season but in the more than twenty years that have elapsed since, Ayr have made the last eight on just one occasion.

They were founder members of the Premier Division in 1975 but the part-time outfit lasted just three years at that level. They have even spent time in the Second Division. Once more eclipsed by rivals Killie, the night Ayr stood just 90 minutes from the Cup Final must seem like a dream from another age.

ON THE SAME DAY...

News: Uproar over claims that **25% of secondary schoolchildren** have used **illegal drugs**.

Sport: Roberto Duran will have his boxer's licence suspended by the New York State Athletic Commission and be stripped of his World Lightweight title unless he defends it against Scotland's Ken Buchanan within 90 days.

Entertainment
Tonight's ITV highlight is a new series of *'Special Branch'*.

BERWICK RANGERS 1
Vs Rangers 0

January 28th 1967 Scottish Cup Round One

Berwick Rangers: Wallace, Haig, Riddell, Craig, Coutts, Kilgannon, Lumsden, Reid, Christie, Dowds, Ainslie.
Sub: Rodgers.

Berwick Rangers, established as far back as 1881, played on the English side of the border, and competed in the Scottish Cup for many years. Whilst in the 'C' Division of the Scottish League, they recorded some notable Scottish Cup triumphs over higher placed opposition. In 1952 they eliminated Alloa, and the following year they knocked out Dundee United in a Tannadice replay. But 1954 was their best year. They hammered Ayr United 5-1 at home then humiliated First Division Dundee 3-0, also at Shielfield. That success earned them a Quarter-Final trip to Ibrox where the 'big' Rangers beat the 'wee' Rangers 4-0, but Berwick left with a healthy cheque from their cut of the 60,245 gate.

Alas, joining the Second Division in 1955-56 appeared to coincide with the demise of Berwick as a cup-fighting side. Up until 1966-67 they never beat another League club in the Cup. They did though continue to have the odd joust with their larger namesakes. Rangers from Glasgow visited Shielfield for a Scottish Cup tie in 1960 winning 3-1. And there was an identical scoreline in 1963-64 in a League Cup Semi-Final clash at Hampden. By 1966-67 Berwick were no more than a mid-table Second Division side. In the Cup they swept aside non-league Vale of Leithen 8-1 then recorded their first triumph over League opposition since Dundee, beating Forfar 2-0 to reach the First Round proper.

Once more they found their opponents were Glasgow Rangers. The Ibrox team were at the top of the League and on course to reach the European Cup-Winners Cup Final. What chance did the Border side possibly have? The sceptics had reckoned without the inspiration and tactical wisdom of the Shielfield player-boss, goalkeeper Jock Wallace. But at first the match threatened to become a goal feast for the Glaswegian contingent among the 13,283 present. Berwick made a quiet start and the two Willies - Johnston and Henderson - soon had control of the flanks. But Alex Smith and Jim Forrest both decided to have an off-day at the same time. Only George McLean seemed to operate with any fluency as a target man. Playing in typical McLean style he was described as: *"shooting high, wide and occasionally straight."* Henderson tried to force the pace, beating Ainslie and Riddell before crossing only to find Haig well placed to clear. Indeed Haig and Coutts seemed unconcerned about the number of corners they conceded. A header from Smith flew over the top. It simply seemed a matter of time before the Ibrox giants scored.

But having survived the early onslaught, Berwick took the initiative themselves - Lumsden firing wide. Berwick's quick tackling unsettled their famous foes - exemplified by Riddell neatly dispossessing Henderson. The Glasgow side came powering back. Johnston beat two, but Smith fired over from a good position. Then Wallace cut out a dangerous Henderson cross, before making a good save from Johnston. After 20 minutes, the Glasgow side had forced eight corners. Lumsden broke away to set up Christie but his shot was weak.

Wallace - with plenty to do - saved from Henderson, then Smith fired over the top once more. A Sammy Reid shot for Berwick forced Norrie Martin, the Ibrox 'keeper, to make a fine save. Reid and Dowds' passing was troubling the 'Gers. In desperation they brought full-back Johansen into the front line, but he was no more effective than the strikers, also shooting over. With 32 minutes played, Dowds passed to Reid, accepted the return and stroked it on to Christie. He sent the ball into open space where it was picked up by Sammy Reid. Steadying himself, Reid shot in off the post. The stadium exploded. Berwick were ahead. Two minutes later, it was nearly two when an Ainslie pass found Christie. But, with only the 'keeper to beat, Christie shot weakly, straight at Martin. In a last-ditch first-half attempt, John Greig carried the ball upfield before firing inches past the post. Half-time arrived with the miraculous scoreline: Berwick Rangers 1 Glasgow Rangers 0.

For the first ten minutes of the second half, Berwick were on top, almost making it 2-0. Then the Glasgow side stormed back at them. Wallace brought off great saves from a Forrest header and Greig lob. In the last twenty minutes it was all Rangers, Glasgow version. Wallace dived at Forrest's feet then saved from Henderson. With Johnston injured, on came Davie Wilson, who'd hit a hat-trick in the 1960 clash between the teams. There was to be no repeat of that this time. McLean and Forrest both went close before Wallace saved quite magnificently from a McLean header. Berwick were still fighting gamely and desperation set in in the Ibrox ranks. Three minutes from the end a Forrest shot hit Alex Smith. The final whistle blew to ignite scenes never seen at Shieldfield before or since. The whole town appeared to be on the pitch to congratulate their heroes. The Berwick Advertiser stated it was: *"The shock of the century, Berwick's most glorious day."*

That was a fair assessment. There has never been a Scottish Cup shock quite as big as this one. It brought renewed respect for Berwick and Jock Wallace. For the mighty Rangers, it was the end of the line for some of their expensive stars. Berwick travelled to face Hibernian in the next round, losing narrowly, 1-0, in front of almost 30,000, so great was the desire to see the men who had humbled the haughty 'Gers. Wallace went on to coach the Glasgow club to some of their greatest triumphs in the '70s. This was the win which established his name as a coach.

For Berwick, life has been quieter since that famous day. They met Rangers again in 1978, but lost 4-2 on that occasion. Their main Cup highlight coming in 1980 when they reached the Quarter-Finals and held a George Best-inspired Hibernian to a 0-0 draw, losing the replay 1-0. The new set-up in 1975 helped Berwick to spend a couple of years in the First Division. But any real hope of glory has to lie in the Cup, Who knows, maybe a repeat of that wonderful day that rocked Scottish football with the score **Berwick Rangers 1 Glasgow Rangers 0.**

Reid (not in picture) scores the historic goal.

BRECHIN CITY 1
Vs Meadowbank Thistle 1

May 7th 1983
Scottish League Second Division

Brechin City: Neilson, Watt, Reid, Leslie, Hay,
Simpson (Mackie 55), Campbell, Elvin, Fleming
(Graham 65), Stewart, Paterson.

Although founded as far back as 1906, Brechin City led a peripatetic existence in the Scottish League. They were members of the short-lived Third Division in the 1920s, returned to regional level, then joined Division Two. After the Second World War they played in the Twilight Zone of the 'C' Division, which they won in 1954 to return to Division Two. But success and Brechin seldom walked hand-in-hand. The regularly finished bottom of the League. Even when the three divisions format was established, Brechin, initially, failed to benefit from it. It was the arrival of Ian Fleming as player-manager in October 1982 which sparked off Brechin's burst for glory.

Fleming was vastly experienced, having played for Kilmarnock, Aberdeen, Sheffield Wednesday and Dundee. His debut marked the beginning of a 14-game unbeaten run which saw Brechin climb from mid-table to a promotion position. Indeed, in his 28 League games in charge this season, Fleming saw his team lose just twice. Gradually, Brechin began to pull clear of the pack, and in their third last game of the season, they had the double satisfaction of beating local rivals Forfar, to secure promotion for themselves and knock Forfar out of contention.

The following week saw Brechin play Meadowbank. The Edinburgh side were on the brink of stepping up too - a point would clinch their First Division ticket. Given the respective goal differences, a draw would make Brechin Champions. To mark the occasion, women, and children under nine were let in free, swelling the crowd to 1,600. Not many by most standards but Brechin is a small place and that turnout represented a fair proportion of the local citizenry. It was their biggest crowd of the season.

They saw their local heroes make a magnificent start. Campbell forced a corner. Elvin took it. Fleming back-headed to Leslie who headed home. There were just 43 seconds on the clock. The setback seemed to inspire Meadowbank. Neilson made two good saves, fisting away a Ford free kick and blocking a Lawson shot. Thistle's Adrian Sprott flighted the ball right across the face of goal, but there was no-one there waiting. Brechin weren't going to let their gala day be spoiled though. Fleming headed narrowly over, then Paterson tried a lob which was easily held by Meadowbank 'keeper McQueen. At half-time it was still 1-0.

Seven minutes into the second half, Meadowbank injected some tension into the game by equalising. Sprott's shot hit the bar and rebounded to the unmarked Lawson who had the simplest of tasks to prod the ball in. Brechin reacted furiously. A Stewart header was turned round the post. A 20-yard drive from Mackie was saved by McQueen. The 'keeper also had to be alert to prevent efforts from Paterson and Elvin. Stewart and Campbell also saw shots blocked. But Meadowbank almost snatched victory at the death when a Godfrey header was cleared off the line by Mackie.

That was the last action before the whistle blew for Glebe Park to witness a highly rare event - a pitch invasion. Hundreds swarmed all over the turf in celebration of the capturing of the Second Division flag. At last Brechin were to experience life outside the basement of the Scottish League. They finished 5th in their first season in the First Division - 15th of all Scotland's teams - their highest ever placing. Relegation struck in 1987 but Brechin again won the Second Division title in 1990. This time they lasted just one season in the First. They've been back up since but, again, without being able to stay. It took Brechin nearly 80 years to achieve the triumph of 1983. Their supporters will be praying it won't be another 80 before they find a team to match that side.

ON THE SAME DAY...

News: The Sunday Times admits that the *'Hitler Diaries'* they have been publishing are a forgery.

Sport: Nick Faldo wins a three-way play-off to lift the French Open golf title. It's his first national title as well as his first continental win.

Entertainment
ITV screen a tribute to retiring Liverpool boss Bob Paisley while the *'Millionaires Club'* in Brechin has become the unlikely setting for top nights out with regular appearances by big-name DJs.

CALEDONIAN THISTLE 5
Vs Arbroath 2

August 13th 1994 Scottish League Third Division

Caledonian Thistle: McRitchie, Brennan, McAllister, Hercher, Scott, Andrew, Lisle, McKenzie, Noble, Bennet, Robertson.

Football has a long pedigree in Scotland's Highland capital. Inverness Thistle were formed in 1885 and Caledonian a year later. Both clubs took part in the Scottish Cup from 1890-91 onwards, and together with teams like Citadel and Clachnacuddin, developed a rivalry as intense in its own way as any in the Scottish League. The Highland League started up in the 1890s under the auspices of the S.F.A. but separate from the Scottish League. Although the top Highland clubs occasionally sought admission to the League and performed with distinction in Scottish Cup ties, it was felt (by the League clubs) that the distances involved precluded meeting with Highland sides on a regular basis in League competition.

By the 1990s, advances in road and air transport (although sadly not in rail) rendered such arguments redundant. The Scottish League decided to admit two new sides for the 1994-95 season. Inverness sides had long been aware that amalgamation would increase their chances of acceptance by the League. So, of the three remaining teams, Clachnacuddin opted to stay with the Highland League while Caledonian and Thistle decided to merge.

Not without problems though. Caley were the bigger of the clubs and many Thistle supporters felt they were being presented with a takeover rather than a genuine merger. Opposition from both sets of fans was widespread but the lure of the League won the day. The merged club easily won the ballot for admission to the League, another Highland team - Ross County - winning the other place. But the disputes continued right up to the new season and beyond. Diehards from both camps refused to transfer their loyalty to the hybrid outfit who would play at Caley's Telford Street Park, at least until the construction of a new stadium. Wrangles about club colours were eventually overcome as the new club prepared to make its debut in the League.

Managed by former U.S.S.R. international Sergei Baltacha, the new team emerged to the acclaim of the 2,000 or so fans who had decided to look to the future rather than the past as Scottish League football finally arrived in Inverness in the shape of a visit from Arbroath on the opening day of the 1994-95 season. And the team didn't disappoint the Highland fans. After only thirteen minutes play, Alan Hercher, left unmarked at a corner, scored the first-ever League goal in Inverness. In 31 minutes it was Hercher again who had the fans extolling the praises of the new boys when he drove his shot low into the net. Hercher struck again before the break, turning in another corner. Less than 45 minutes played and Alan Hercher had made history. Not just the first League hat-trick of the season, not just the first hat-trick for the merged club, but the first treble in their first League match, and all before half-time.

The Highlanders celebrations looked to be premature during the second period when Arbroath came back strongly. Craig Farnan reduced the deficit, then John Reilly knocked in a second to leave Caley Thistle just 3-2 ahead. It was now that Highland pride and grit were called for. And that was exactly what the players provided. A magnificent lob from Paul McKenzie after 71 minutes made it 4-2 for the newcomers. Then, with thirteen minutes remaining, Wilson Robertson scored to round off a tremendous opening day. Caledonian Thistle 5 Arbroath 2. Baltacha could scarcely have dreamt of such a start.

Unfortunately the merger problems came back to haunt the club. And, as it became clear that promotion to the Second Division would be more difficult than that first day suggested, the supporters started staying away - some games drawing less than 1,000 at the gate. There are problems which still have to be resolved and they need to be done so quickly. For there can be little doubt that a single Inverness club, backed by the supporters, has the potential to reach the First Division at least. Perhaps even the Premier League.

ON THE SAME DAY...

News: Germany seizes its biggest-ever haul of plutonium from thieves arriving from Moscow.

Sport: Reigning British Open Golf champion Nick Price is five strokes ahead of the field at the halfway stage of the U.S. PGA.

Entertainment:
Top film is the live action version of *"The Flintstones"*.

When Jock Stein took over the reins at Celtic in early 1965, he inherited a team going nowhere. Since their foundation in 1888, Celts had been one of the giants of the Scottish game. But during the inter-war period they were eclipsed by Rangers and after the Second World War they fell behind sides like Hearts, Hibs, Aberdeen, Dundee and Kilmarnock as well. There was a talented squad of players at Parkhead at the time of Stein's arrival, but the motivation necessary to succeed had to come from the boss. Stein had proved himself as a manager during his spells at Dunfermline and Hibs and within a few weeks of accepting the job at Celtic Park, his impact was sufficient for Celtic to win the Scottish Cup for the first time in eleven years.

The following season saw Celtic win the League title for only the second time since the war and paved the way for their debut in the European Cup. It may have been their first attempt at the club game's most senior prize, but the Bhoys were already battle-hardened in Europe, having twice reached the last four of the Cup-Winners Cup. The only significant signings made by Stein were strikers Joe McBride and Willie Wallace, but Stein's effect on the side and their free-flowing football won them admirers all over the continent as they disposed of Zurich and Nantes in the early rounds - winning all their games. Their reaction to defeat was tested in the Quarter-Finals after losing the first leg away to Vojvodina in Yugoslavia. But the resilient Celts battled back to win 2-0 at home, 2-1 on aggregate. In the Semi-Finals, where no fewer than **eight** previous British challenges (including three Scots) had come unstuck, Celtic took a 3-1 first leg lead against Dukla Prague. For the only time in the tournament, Stein changed his game plan, relying on a sturdy defensive performance to obtain a 0-0 draw in Czechoslovakia. For the first time, a British side had reached the European Cup Final.

Their opponents were Inter Milan, bidding for their third triumph in four seasons in the competition. They were a star-studded side. Sarti in goal with Burgnich and Facchetti in front of them presented an awesome defensive line-up. Corso, Domenghini and Guarneri were players of distinction at the peak of their careers. And the brilliant Mazzola led the line. But both sides were hampered by injury, Celtic missing the prolific McBride, Inter the incomparable Spaniard, Luis Suarez.

All told, the Italian team cost over a million pounds in transfer fees. The eleven assembled by Celtic contained eight home-grown players. And the three signings - Simpson (£2,500), Auld (£12,000) and Wallace (£27,000) - cost a mere £41,500. No wonder most of the 60,000 crowd in Lisbon for the Final thought the game a formality for Inter. But 10,000 of those had travelled from Scotland, intent on seeing history made. And the locals - whose own Sporting Club also played in green-and-white - soon rallied to the Scots cause.

Celts started brightly enough but disaster struck in only seven minutes. Cappellini was through in a good position when he was brought down by McNeill. It was a blatant penalty and Mazzola made no mistake from the spot. That appeared to be it. Inter were the masters of **catenaccio** and to give them the lead so early in the game appeared to be suicidal. They would sit back, absorb the pressure, and hit on the break.

But Celtic actually raised their game, Lennox and Auld orchestrating sweet moves. Auld smacked a shot against the bar, then Sarti saved well from Gemmell. But at half-time the Italians still led.

CELTIC 2
Vs Inter Milan 1

May 25th 1967
European Champions Cup Final (Lisbon)

Celtic: Simpson, Craig, Gemmell, Murdoch, McNeill, Clark, Johnstone, Wallace, Chalmers, Auld, Lennox.

The second half saw Celtic claims for a penalty when Burgnich appeared to handle but the referee ignored their appeals. With 62 minutes gone, and Celtic still dominating the game, their full-backs decided to take on the forwards job. Gemmell passed to Craig, then accepted the return before unleashing a right-foot thunderbolt straight into the back of the net. There was an explosion of green-and-white everywhere. Inter's coach, Helenio Herrera, held his head in his hands, weeping. His side either didn't know how to combat this reverse, or Celtic simply wouldn't let them. Whatever, it was the marauding Scots who controlled the game, raining down shot after shot on Sarti's goal.

But with five minutes left, it was still 1-1 when Bobby Murdoch ripped the heart out of the Inter defence and fired in a low, hard shot. Stevie Chalmers stuck out his knee to deflect it into the net. 2-1 to Celtic and no time for Inter to recover. The full-time whistle saw Celtic supporters take over Lisbon while hundreds of thousands back in Scotland - supporters of all Scottish teams - took to the streets in a spontaneous display of national pride. Liverpool manager Bill Shankly embraced Stein, telling him: *"John, you are immortal."*

Celtic's dominance was overwhelming: Two goals scored, the bar struck twice, thirteen shots saved, seven blocked, nineteen wide or high, a massive **43** attempts on goal. Inter - for whom Sarti, Burgnich and Facchetti were outstanding (and had to be) - had only one penalty scored and just two shots saved. It wasn't just a victory for Celtic, or Scottish, or even British football. It was a magnificent success for football as it should be played - as an attacking game.

The Celts returned with the European Cup to a rapturous welcome from 60,000 at Parkhead. 200,000 more lined the streets from the airport to the ground. They all believed that what had been done once could be done again. Sadly for Celtic, it was not to be. They remained supreme in the domestic game, winning nine championships in a row. But in Europe they lost to Feyenoord in the 1970 Final and fell at the Semi-Final hurdle on another two occasions.

But they havn't made the last eight in the European Cup since 1980, nor have they played in the competition since 1986-87, owing to the fact that Rangers now dominate Scottish football even more comprehensively than Celtic did in the sixties and seventies. It may be a hard lesson for Celtic fans to take, but their 1967 triumph resembles more of a giant-killing act as each year passes. Their success at European level might just be comparable to Raith Rovers victory over Celtic in the 1994-95 Scottish League Cup Final - a one-off. If that is so then a bleak future lies ahead. For Celtic supporters will not be content until their team rules the European roost once more.

CLYDE 4

Vs Motherwell 0

April 22nd 1939 Scottish Cup Final
(Hampden)

Clyde: Brown, Kirk, Hickie, Beaton, Falloon, Weir, Robertson, Noble, Martin, Wallace, Gillies.

Clyde have always played in the shadow of the Old Firm. Their old Shawfield ground - half in Glasgow, half in Rutherglen - attracted more spectators to dog racing meetings than football matches. Against such a background, survival is an achievement in itself, success almost unthought of. But although never threatening to do very well in the League, Clyde - and others like them - always harboured dreams of holding aloft the Scottish Cup. On two previous occasions they had reached the Final only to lose. In the last season before the outbreak of the Second World War it was a different story.

Home victories over St. Johnstone and, after a replay, Dundee, booked a trip to Ibrox in the third round of the Cup. Even the most dyed-in-the-wool supporter of the 'Bully Wee' couldn't have expected the result that day - Rangers 1 Clyde 4. 63,000 saw one of the biggest upsets of the decade. Thus emboldened, Clyde squeezed past another Glasgow rival - Third Lanark - in the Quarter-Finals, winning 1-0 at Shawfield. Forced to travel to Edinburgh to face Hibernian at Tynecastle in the last four, Clyde fashioned another single-goal triumph to take them into the Final after a 27-year absence.

Their opponents, Motherwell, had already lost two Finals in the 1930s and their 1932 League title win was the only such success outside the Old Firm between 1904-1948. But they were past their best by the time of this match and many inside the 94,779 crowd thought that the time had come for Clyde - the only one of the six Glasgow clubs not to have won the Cup - to engrave their name on the trophy.

Motherwell had the wind behind them but failed to capitalise on their advantage. After a bright opening spell, they became bogged down in midfield and when they did get through they found Brown in superb form in the Clyde goal. With half an hour gone, Robertson won possession for Clyde. He sprinted down the line and passed to Wallace. The inside-left swerved past 'Well centre-half Blair and belted a rising shot high into the net from twelve yards. Motherwell retaliated, forcing five corners in four minutes, but Brown dealt with them easily. 'Well appealed for a penalty when striker Mathie was impeded on the goal-line, but Clyde were awarded a free kick. Then it was Clyde's turn to cry foul when Martin was brought down in the area but again no penalty was given. Clyde retired at the break, ahead by that single goal and now clearly favourites to win the tie.

In Clyde's first attack of the second half, Motherwell appealed for offside. Play stopped and 'Well 'keeper

Murray picked up the ball and gently rolled it out to where he thought the free kick would be taken. Blair made to pick it up but Clyde's Martin hadn't heard any whistle.

He trapped the ball and shot home. Referee Webb gave the goal. With forty minutes still to play, it was clear that Motherwell were a beaten side. They managed just one serious attempt when Mathie found himself shooting at an open goal. Hickie raced back to clear just in time.

Late in the game, Clyde emphasised their dominance. From the left, Gillies passed to Noble. His first shot was blocked by Murray but Noble pounced on the rebound to put Clyde three up. Straight from the kick-off, Clyde were on the attack again. Noble sent over a knee-high cross for Martin - on all fours - to head in the fourth. 4-0 was an emphatic scoreline and worthy of Clyde's approach to the game. For the first time in their history, there was call for the use of an open-top bus. From Rutherglen to Bridgeton Cross the victorious eleven travelled to the adulation of thousands lining the route. At last Clyde had won the Cup.

Owing to the War, the Scottish Cup stayed at Shawfield for eight years. And when it did leave, it wasn't gone for good. Clyde were an infuriating team in the fifties, bouncing up and down the two divisions like a yo-yo. But in both 1955 and 1958 they won the Scottish Cup again - a proud record. But demolition and slum clearance dispersed their support and by the 1980s Clyde were in the new Second Division, watched by a few hundred each week and struggling to survive. They lost the use of their ground and had to share with Partick and Hamilton until a 6,000 capacity all-seated stadium was built as Cumbernauld. It is a brave move to transplant a team to a new location but Clyde had no real alternative if they wished to survive. Their move is one which will ensure that their name lives on in the Scottish game, even if recapturing their past success is the Scottish Cup remains a remote prospect at present.

ON THE SAME DAY...

News: Britain and France have started negotiations for an anti-Nazi pact with the U.S.S.R.

Sport: The English Second Division is in line for its most exciting end ever. With between one to three games to play, no fewer than **eight** clubs still have a chance of winning one of the two promotion spots.

Entertainment: The big show at the Glasgow Empire is *'Band Wagon'* starring Arthur Askey and Richard Murdoch.

CLYDEBANK 0

Vs Celtic 2
April 14th 1990 Scottish Cup Semi-Final
(Hampden)

Clydebank: Gallacher, Dickson, Rodger (Smith), Maher, Sweeney, Crawford (Caffrey), Harvey, Davies, Eadie, Rowe, Kelly.

Before the 1960s, Scottish League football had existed for less than twenty years in Clydebank. The original club was hit badly by the depression in the shipbuilding area and gave up the ghost in 1931. More than 30 years later, the Steedman brothers, in control of Falkirk-based East Stirling, merged their club with Clydebank Juniors and for one season League football returned under the auspices of E.S. Clydebank. The experiment was a failure though and East Stirling returned to Firs Park in 1965, leaving Clydebank - and the Steedmans - playing against reserve and third elevens in the Combined Reserve League. Two years later they won election to the Second Division and the present-day Clydebank F.C. took up their place in the League.

The early years were not successful, but the introduction of three divisions in 1975 proved to be beneficial to Clydebank as the club won promotion from Second to Premier divisions in successive seasons. They failed to retain their place at the top, although they again secured Premier status briefly in the 1980s. It was clear that a town bereft of League football for a generation had formed strong loyalties to other clubs - notably Rangers and Celtic. Clydebank played regularly to gates of just over 1,000.

Nor was the Scottish Cup an avenue to success either. In almost a quarter of a century of competition, Clydebank had made the last eight just twice. The 1989-90 tournament saw them embark on run which was as welcome as it was unexpected.

It started off gently enough with an away win in front of less than a thousand at Albion Rovers. Then came a difficult tie with 1987 Cup winners, Premier side St. Mirren. Bankies forced a draw at Love Street and, before more than 6,000, turfed the Buddies out of the Cup at Kilbowie. The draw for the last eight was kind to Clydebank - pairing them with Second Division Stirling Albion. Even so, it still took two games to dismiss the lower League side, the replay being held at Falkirk's Brockville ground, on account of Stirling's artificial surface being ruled invalid for Cup ties. But the prize was worth all the struggle - a place in the Semi-Finals for the first time, and a tie at Hampden against Celtic. Clydebank were now just ninety minutes away from the Scottish Cup Final.

Bankies sounded an optimistic note before the kick-off. *"Sweeney, Davies and Harvey all have a 100% record at Hampden,"* said Ian Steedman, referring to a youth tournament the trio had played in some years previously. *"How many Celts can say that?"* Steedman's humour was designed to calm the nerves of both players and the hardy contingent of Bankies fans among the 34,768 crowd. It may not have been a huge turnout, but there were more people in Hampden for this match than attended at Kilbowie in a season.

With a strong wind, driving rain and heavy mud, conditions ensured the match would be no classic. Both midfields struggled to cope. Bankies at least had the excuse of nerves. For their illustrious opponents there could be no such mitigation. Clydebank enjoyed the best of the opening exchanges but after ten minutes, Jim Gallacher could only palm out a shot from Wdowczyk to the lurking Andy Walker. The striker accepted the chance and Bankies were a goal down and forced to chase the game.

Bankies gave Celtic some worries but rarely looked capable of penetrating the Parkhead rear. The second half saw more enterprise from Clydebank. At just 1-0 down, anything was possible. Late in the game a Joe Dickson free kick sailed over Celtic 'keeper Bonner's head and bounced around invitingly in the area. Paul Sweeney was first to react but his shot hit the post. With Bankies trying to force their way down the right hand side in search of the equaliser, Walker pulled over to the left for Celtic and sent a daisy-cutter past Gallacher to wrap the tie up. At 2-0 down and only five minutes remaining, there was no way back for the brave Bankies.

It remains the closest Clydebank have ever come to real glory. And, as a side which will always struggle to pull in many through the gate, they do not have the purchasing power to compete with the top clubs. Nor can they hold on to their best players for very long. The Scottish Cup remains Clydebank's best chance of success in the game. Having reached the last four once, there is hope that one day they may make the Final itself.

ON THE SAME DAY...

News: Huge metal pipes, bound for Iraq, which were seized earlier in the week on Teesside, continue to cause controversy. *"Probably only a pipe,"* says Whitehall. *"Of course it's a gun,"* retort Customs Officers.

Sport: Twice-winner Alex Higgins is beaten 10-5 by Steve James in the first round of the World Professional Snooker Championship.

Entertainment
A big attraction is *'Glasgow's Glasgow'* a massive exhibition forming part of Glasgow's Year of Culture. It has 50 screens, 30 TV channels and more than 2,000 items of interest.

COWDENBEATH 1
Vs Rangers 3 (after extra time)

September 21st 1949 Scottish League Cup Quarter-Final (2nd Leg)

Cowdenbeath: Moodie, Hamilton, Cameron, Menzies, Holland, Durie, McGurn, Mackie, Armstrong, Reid, Dick.

Cowdenbeath had been a potent team at one time. From 1924-34 they played in the Scottish First Division and often finished in the top half of the table. But they never had any real success in the Scottish Cup. Even now, after more than 100 years of trying, the best they have managed is a solitary Quarter-Final appearance in 1931. The Scottish League Cup - established after the Second World War - seemed a better bet. In this competition, the Second Division sides were arranged into four sections, guaranteeing four of the last eight would be from the lower echelon.

In the 1949-50, season, Cowdenbeath won their section for the first time, accounting for Ayr United, Morton and Alloa. Their reward was a two-leg tie against all-conquering Rangers. Just 1,000 Cowden fans made the Saturday trek to Ibrox where their voices were lost among the 29,000 present. They witnessed history in the making. Falling a goal behind, Cowdenbeath struck back to reach half-time level at 1-1. Sensationally, they took the lead early in the second half, only for Rangers to equalise. Then, after 67 minutes, the Fife side scored again. Rangers couldn't come back and the 3-2 triumph was the first time Rangers had been beaten at Ibrox by a Second Division side. It also guaranteed a full house at Central Park the following Wednesday for the return leg.

At 25,586 it was a record crowd which greeted the teams as they took the field. And Cowden showed that the atmosphere wasn't in the least bit intimidating as they coolly suppressed the early Rangers cavalry charges. Cameron and Holland were confident at the back, Dick played the home team out of defence and Durie's tackling worried the Ibrox men. A Hamilton free kick set up a siege of the Rangers goal as Cowden set about some attacking of their own. The ball was cleared, but only to Cameron who punted it back into the area. Rangers' Sammy Cox fell as he attempted to clear. The ball fell to Menzies who swiftly brought it under control before cracking a 25-yarder into the net. 1-0 to Cowdenbeath on the night, 4-2 on aggregate. The Fifers in the crowd sent wild with delight. And Cowden continued to hold the upper hand. The celebrated Willie Waddell was superbly marshalled by

Cameron. The defender even had time to join the attack himself, shooting over the bar. The crowd cheered *"every kick, every tackle, every try"* that Cowdenbeath produced, according to the local paper. When Willie Woodburn pushed McGurn to the ground, those same fans howled for a penalty. But in vain. At length, Rangers began to come more into it. For the last twenty minutes of the half, they dominated proceedings but the home side reached the break with their lead intact.

It was still all-out action from the 'Gers at the start of the second half. Five minutes into this period, Rae's pass was headed down by Williamson to Cox. His first time shot levelled the match at 1-1 and reduced Cowden's lead to a single goal. Williamson hit the post then actually got the ball into the net, but his effort was disallowed. Moodie was magnificent in goal, making splendid saves from Cox and Rutherford. As the game entered the final fifteen minutes, it looked like the Fife team had weathered the storm. They even resumed attacking the Rangers goal. Armstrong just missed from a McGurn pass. Then a Reid shot landed not too far away from the target. An Armstrong free kick found Menzies whose shot took a deflection off a defender to go over the bar.

With two minutes to go, Findlay 'scored' for Rangers. The 'goal' was given by the Referee before his linesman told him it was offside. Cowdenbeath breathed again. It looked like they had won a famous victory, and their fans were getting ready to celebrate when a Rutherford header finally beat Moodie to take the game into extra time. There had been only fifteen seconds of normal time left. The deflated homesters continued to battle gamely but, twelve minutes into the extra period, Cox burst through to score, making it 3-1 to Rangers and 5-4 for the Glasgow side on aggregate. Valiant Cowdenbeath had come so close to triumph, the failure was all the more bitter.

Cowdenbeath have not made much progress in the League since those days. There was one season in the old Division One in 1970-71 and a single term in the new First Division in 1992-93. They usually play before a couple of hundred diehards as they attempt to climb out of the basement of Scottish football. Their League Cup record has been better though. In 1959-60 they knocked out county rivals East Fife to reach the Semi-Finals. Alas, they were given a going-over by Hearts, losing 9-3. And in 1970-71 they were back in the last four, losing 2-0 to Rangers at Hampden. Although, statistically, those appearances may rank higher than the 1949 match, they lack the sheer drama and tension of that almost-glorious night when Cowdenbeath came within fifteen seconds of beating Rangers. A Rangers side, it must be said, which went on to complete the first ever domestic 'treble'. That is a measure of how gallant the Central Park class of '49 really were.

COWDENBEATH FOOTBALL GAZETTE

Souvenir
Programme
PRICE—3d

SWORD'S | A NICE

Cowdenbeath Football Gazette—EDITORIAL.

There is only one thing in our minds to-day, and that is the great achievement of our team on Saturday by going to Ibrox and bringing off a 3-2 win.

Very few in Cowdenbeath and less in Glasgow thought we were able to bring off a win at Ibrox. Football experts outside Cowdenbeath were quite sure in their own minds that Cowdenbeath would return from the game three or four goals down, and one went the length of writing that there was something wrong with the arrangements that made such a one-sided match possible as it was only a waste of time. ...DENBEATH

Published by W. Pritchard, 46 High Street, Cowdenbeath, and Printed by Given & Paton.

Dumbarton were one of the early giants of Scottish football. They played in the inaugural Scottish Cup and within less than ten years had won the trophy. Joint winners (with Rangers) of the first Scottish League Championship, they lifted the title in their own right the following year. Decline followed after those successes. The left the League but later returned and gained re-entry to Division One. But in the very first season of automatic promotion and relegation, the Sons lost their top flight status. By 1971-72 they were still in Division Two.

1972 was a significant year in Dumbarton's history. The town was celebrating the 750th anniversary of being granted a royal charter by King Alexander II, it was the centenary year of Dumbarton F.C. and it had been exactly 50 years since they had last played in Division One. But the team assembled by manager Jackie Stewart was a good one. Experienced players like Charlie Gallagher, formerly of Celtic and Davie Wilson, (ex-Rangers), augmented by home-grown players like Colin McAdam and Kenny Wilson had brought them to the very brink of promotion. But defeat at home to St. Mirren the Saturday prior to this midweek clash with Berwick had knocked them from top of the table to fourth:

		Pld.	Pts.	G.Diff.
1	Arbroath	36	52	+30
2	Stirling Alb.	36	50	+38
3	St.Mirren	36	50	+37
4	Dumbarton	35	50	+36

With the others having finished their programmes, Dumbarton needed a draw to ensure a place in the higher sphere and end that barren half-century. Two points would secure the title. If ever their ground needed to reclaim the title of 'fatal Boghead', bestowed on it in the 19th Century, it was now.

Ironically, the crowd of 9,980 who assembled at Boghead for the Berwick game was the largest League attendance in all their Division Two years. It was as if the town's sense of history led it to believe that the good times were about to return at last. Just three minutes into the game, that perspective was endorsed by the team. A chip from Gallagher allowed Coleman to head the opener.

DUMBARTON 4
Vs Berwick Rangers 2

May 3rd 1972 Scottish League Division Two

Dumbarton: Williams, McAdams, Wilkinson, Jensen, Bolton, Graham, Coleman, C. Gallagher, McCormack, K. Wilson, D. Wilson. Sub: Anderson.

Dumbarton swarmed all over the Border side. But, in Berwick's first serious attack, a superb solo effort from Coyne levelled the scores. Many a side would have fallen prey to nerves at that point, but the Sons had the players with the necessary savvy to handle the situation. Composure regained, they set off in pursuit of victory once again. With 30 minutes played, Gallagher's low, fierce shot from 25 yards made it 2-1, a lead Dumbarton held till the interval.

Twelve minutes into the second half and Gallagher fired in a replica of his earlier goal. The Sons were coasting now. A McCormack header in 67 minutes made it 4-1. Berwick had little to offer, even less after Tait was sent off for fouling Davie Wilson. But Davidson did reduce the leeway with a goal for Berwick three minutes from time. Not that the Dumbarton fans were bothered. The final whistle was the scene for an emotional pitch invasion as the supporters relished the prospect of their team - reduced to 'C' Division level in the fifties - jousting at Ibrox and Parkhead after such a long absence.

Jackie Stewart praised Charlie Gallagher, *"What a player, what a team, what a night,"* said the boss. Gallagher was delighted too. *"At Parkhead we were expected to win. This is something different. It's just great,"* was his comment. Chairman Robert Robertson went even further, claiming: *"I see no reason why we can't be the third force in Scottish football."*

That was asking a bit much from players earning £12-15 per week. The Sons survived in the top League. But the 1975 reconstruction placed them in the middle division. The have managed just one season in the Premier since its inception and have even had to play in the bottom League on occasion. Short of winning one of the Cups, it is difficult to believe that there will ever be another night in Dumbarton quite like the one which ended their 50-year exile from the big time.

DUMBARTON'S FOURTH GOAL . . . and Berwick keeper Willie Wilson and right half Peter Brown can only watch as Kenny Wilson heads home his 42nd goal of the season.

ON THE SAME DAY...

News: Lord Wheatley proposes local authority licensing of football grounds in his report into the Ibrox disaster of 1971.

Sport: 23 year-old boxer Jim Watt wins the British Lightweight title, stopping Tony Riley in 12 rounds.

Entertainment
On BBC-1, another repeat of *'Star Trek'*, just as the Sons embark on their own trek, boldly going where no Dumbarton side had gone for half a century.

" Steady on — let the ' champers ' settle . . . time enough to take on Celtic next season . . ."

Dundee had little to show for almost 70 years in the Scottish League. They had won the Scottish Cup in 1910 and recorded back-to-back League Cup victories in the early fifties. But for a city of its size, this was scant return indeed. The supporters expected the team to be at the forefront of the Scottish game. There had even been the humiliation of relegation in 1938, after **leading** the League for a long stretch. Regaining their place in Division One after the war, Dundee had almost won the flag in 1949. Needing to win their final game, they were beaten at Falkirk by a Bairns side managed by Bob Shankly, allowing Rangers to snatch the title. Until 1961-62 that remained the closest they had come to success in the Championship.

The Dens Park side were now managed by the man who had destroyed their title dream at Brockville - Bob Shankly. And the team he built on Tayside was a talented one indeed. The defence had the super-cool Alex Hamilton at right-back and the commanding Ian Ure at centre-half. Up front, the talents of Hugh Robertson, Andy Penman and Alan Cousin were superbly complemented by the goalscoring feats of Alan Gilzean. With the veteran Gordon Smith still an inspirational force, this was a team to be reckoned with, more than half the side earning Scotland caps at some stage during their careers.

Dundee had looked likely to run away with the League in the early part of the season, but stumbled, allowing Rangers to take over at the top. A sensational burst of form during the run-in (Dundee had won five and drawn once during their previous six games) allowed the Dens Parkers to get their noses back in front as the final lap approached. Once again they went into the final match away from home as leaders. This time though, they needed just a point to clinch the flag. Their opponents - St. Johnstone - had their own reasons for wishing to prevent a Tayside triumph. They were lying 14th in the 18-club division and were aware that if they lost and the three teams immediately below them all won, then they would go down.

So the scene was set for a tension-filled day and a bumper crowd at St. Johnstone's Muirton Park. 26,500 attended to see a derby game played in an atmosphere unlike any other between these old rivals. It was Saints who enjoyed early supremacy but, during the opening twenty minutes, they forced Pat Liney into action just once. Having absorbed the Saints pressure, Dundee at last broke out of defence through Wishart. He sent the ball to Gilzean. The striker passed to Smith on the wing. The veteran easily trapped the ball, then waited and watched. He noticed that Gilzean had kept running and flighted over a cross for Gilzean to head past Saints 'keeper Taylor. 1-0 with 24 minutes played. Saints huffed and puffed but the break arrived with Dundee's precious lead intact.

The second half saw the Dens men in charge. Bobby Seith sent a long, curving pass to Gilzean. He won a tussle with the centre-half, got the ball, went past defender McFadyen,

St. Johnstone 0 Vs
DUNDEE 3

April 28th 1962
Scottish League Division One.

Dundee: Liney, Hamilton, Cox, Seith, Ure, Wishart, Smith, Penman, Cousin, Gilzean, Robertson.

rounded Taylor and scored with 59 minutes played. Saints resorted to some desperate tackling but to no effect. In 67 minutes, a sweet move saw Robertson pass to Cousin who sent it on to Gilzean. He drew the defence to him before releasing the ball to the unmarked Andy Penman. Penman's shot cracked off the underside of the crossbar and into the net. That was it. Dundee were the Scottish League Champions.

St. Johnstone's worst nightmares came true as their rivals all won and they were relegated by 0.08 of a goal. For Bob Shankly and his players it was a truly remarkable success. They had used just fifteen players all season - the smallest squad ever to win the title. And Gordon Smith became the first player to win Scottish League medals with three different clubs, having previously triumphed with Hibs and Hearts. Even more incredibly, he achieved this unique feat without ever playing for Rangers or Celtic.

The 22 miles from Perth to Dundee was one long queue of horn-blowing vehicles as the team returned home for the celebrations. Champions of Scotland at long last, Dundee looked good enough to stay at the top for years to come. Unfortunately for Dundee, the title was the peak of their achievements, not the beginning. They reached the Semi-Finals of the European Cup the next year and the Final of the Scottish Cup the year after that. But top players deserted Dens Park. Ure and Gilzean headed south to Arsenal and Spurs. Penman signed for Rangers and others departed too. There was another Euro Semi-Final in the Fairs Cup in 1968 and a League Cup win in 1974, but the advent of three divisions saw Dundee struggle to stay in the Premier. Relegation has been their fate all too often. Especially galling for their fans, has been the end of their ascendancy in the city. For over eighty years they were the top Tayside team. They have lost that role to Dundee United since the foundation of the Premier Division. There are still those who believe that, given success, Dundee are still the 'natural' top dogs on the Tay. For over twenty years now their playing record suggests otherwise. Dundee certainly have the potential to rise again and re-emerge as a major force in Scottish football. But winning the League, as they did in 1962, remains, for now, a distant dream.

ON THE SAME DAY...

News: Nurses march to Trafalgar Square in protest at a 2½% pay offer. Despite being threatened with disciplinary action, they wear their uniforms during their protest.

Sport: Ipswich Town's 2-0 home win over Aston Villa gives them the English League title in their first season in Division One.

Entertainment
After the excitement of Muirton Park, there's another epic at Dundee's Capital Cinema - 'Spartacus', starring Kirk Douglas.

For many years Dundee United were condemned to live in the shadow of their near-neighbours Dundee. Four short seasons in the top division was all they could boast of by the dawn of the 1960s. Manager Jerry Kerr took them up, kept them up and transformed them into a competent First Division force. His work was continued - and improved upon - from the 1970s onwards by Jim McLean. And, for the first time, silverware found its way to the Tannadice trophy room with two successive League Cup wins in the early 1980s. Those successes were topped by the most spectacular triumph of them all in 1983. Winning their final match of the season, away to rivals Dundee, won the League Championship for United and entry into the European Cup.

Their European pedigree was already impressive: in their very first contest back in the sixties they had eliminated Fairs Cup holders Barcelona, winning both home and away. And in the two seasons prior to their European Cup campaign, they had reached the last eight of the U.E.F.A. Cup, with some pretty impressive triumphs along the way. 5-0 at home to Borussia Munchengladbach. 5-2 away to Monaco. And a 2-0 away win over PSV Eindhoven. So Europe held no fears for Dundee United.

Their campaign started with an easy enough tie against Maltese side Hamrun Spartans. That was followed by a superb demolition of Standard Liege. 0-0 in Belgium, 4-0 at Tannadice. They came from behind against Rapid Vienna to win on away goals in the Quarter-Finals. United had reached the last four, 21 years after their city rivals had achieved a similar feat. But, whereas on that occasion, Dundee were soundly beaten by A.C. Milan, now there was a genuine feeling that United could make the Final. To do it they would have to beat Roma, champions of Italy and studded with star names like Tancredi, Di Bartolomei, Conti and Graziani, as well as the Brazilian pair Cerezo and Falcao. It would be a tough task but McLean was renowned as one of the best coaches in the game and United players like Malpas, Gough, Hegarty, Narey, Bannon and Sturrock were no strangers to the big occasion. Tannadice was full to capacity with the bulk of the 20,543 crowd cheering on the Scots.

United started well with Milne producing a near-perfect free kick from the right to the near post. Sturrock failed to provide the simplest of touches needed to score. But that seventh minute near miss showed the Italians that they had a battle on their hands. The pattern of the game was what was expected in European ties - United dominating in terms of possession and chances, and Roma content to lie back in defence and try to score on the break. And they almost did. Chierico floated over a cross which Graziani headed against the bar. At half-time the game was still goalless - a moral victory for Roma.

The Tangerines upped the tempo in the second half. In 48 minutes a Gough cross was missed by the defence. Bannon's shot hit off a defender and broke to Sturrock. He touched the ball back to Dodds who struck home from eight yards to give United the lead. Then, on the hour mark, Sturrock, on the left, switched the ball inside to Stark. He unleashed a spectacular shot from 30 yards which gave Tancredi no chance. United piled on even more pressure. A Milne shot was deflected for a corner. Then a header from Hegarty was tipped over the bar by Tancredi. At 2-0 the tie was far from over but Roma knew they would have to be at their very best to overcome United in the second leg.

The match in Rome was a controversial affair. Milne missed a

DUNDEE UNITED 2
Vs A.S. Roma 0

April 11th 1984 European Champions Cup Semi-Final (1st Leg)

Dundee United: McAlpine, Stark, Malpas, Gough, Hegarty, Narey, Bannon, Milne, Kirkwood, Sturrock (Coyne), Dodds.

sitter at 0-0 which would have ended everything. Two goals from Pruzzo squared the tie at the break. A penalty in the 58th minute allowed Di Bartolemei to put Roma in front. Even then a goal from United would have taken them through to the Final, in the same stadium, courtesy of the away goals rule. They couldn't score however, losing 3-0 on the night, 3-2 on aggregate. After the match, doubts began to be expressed as to how legitimate their defeat was. While they could have no quibble with the penalty, some of the decisions were questionable, to say the least. Rumours circulated that the whole tie had been less than above board. Sanctions later imposed by U.E.F.A. were to be of little solace to a United side convinced that they should have played in the European Champions Cup Final.

It wasn't the end for United in Europe though. In 1987 they became the only Scottish side to play in the U.E.F.A. Cup Final which they lost to Gothenburg. Domestically, after six losing Finals in twenty years, they won the Scottish Cup in 1994 under the short-lived reign of McLean's successor, Ivan Golac. Just twelve months later they were relegated - after 35 years in the top division.

As they enter a phase of rebuilding, there will be arguments over what really was Dundee United's greatest moment. Many will plump for winning the League on the ground of their arch-rivals. Others will opt for winning the Scottish Cup in their seventh Final. Some will suggest the U.E.F.A. Cup Final. It is because of those doubts over the legitimacy of their defeat that I have selected the game against Roma. In that match Dundee United took on a team of supposedly world-class capabilities and roundly defeated them. They never got to play in the European Cup Final, but they certainly deserved to.

ON THE SAME DAY...

News: Sarah Tisdall, jailed for leaking Cruise missile documents to the press, is moved from Holloway to an open prison near Maidstone.

Sport: A record six British teams - Aberdeen, Dundee United, Liverpool, Tottenham Hotspur, Manchester United and Nottingham Forest - take part in the Semi-Finals of the three European tournaments.

Entertainment
Top music show for children - 'Razzmatazz', starts a new series with Boy George, Eurythmics, the Thompson Twins, and Spandau Ballet all in the line-up.

European Cup — Semi-Final, First Leg
WEDNESDAY, 11th APRIL, 1984
Kick-off 7.30 p.m.
Official Programme 1983-84 Season No. 29 PRICE 60p
versus
A. S. ROMA
MATCH SPONSOR BALLANTINES

West Bromwich Albion 0 Vs
DUNFERMLINE ATHLETIC 1

February 19th 1969 European Cup-Winners Cup Quarter-Final (2nd Leg)

Dunfermline: Duff, W. Callaghan, Lunn, Fraser, Barry, Thomson, Robertson, Paton, Edwards, Renton, Gardner.

Until the arrival of Jock Stein as manager, Dunfermline Athletic were one of Scotland's minnows, only occasionally playing in Division One and constantly fighting against relegation when they did. Stein changed all that with the side which won the Scottish Cup in 1961. His work was continued by his successors, firstly Willie Cunningham, and then George Farm. The Pars narrowly lost the 1965 Cup Final (to Stein's Celtic) and were deprived of the League title by a single point. But throughout the 1960s they were a major force, not just in the Scottish game, but in Europe as well. When they lifted the Scottish Cup again, in 1968, they were seasoned European competitors, anxious for another crack at the Cup-Winners Cup.

Cypriot side Apoel of Nicosia were hardly challenging opposition and were swept aside 12-1 on aggregate (including a 10-1 East End Park victory) in the first round. Olympiakos were a different proposition in the next round and Dunfermline needed every single goal from their 4-0 first leg win to advance, losing 3-0 in Greece. Their survival earned them the right to play F.A. Cup holders West Bromwich Albion in the last eight. As usual when English and Scottish clubs are thrown together in Europe, the English press regarded the tie as a formality. With players like Tony Brown and Jeff Astle, plus their own caledonian contingent of Doug Fraser, Bobby Hope and Asa Hartford, the midlands side were expected to coast comfortably into the Semi-Finals. Those same English reporters had forgotten that Dunfermline had eliminated Everton from Europe when that team were running away with the English League. They reckoned that Albion, having survived trips to Bruges and Bucharest, would find Fife little more than a pleasant outing.

In the first leg it appeared the English scribes were right. Despite the presence of a 22,000 crowd, the Pars never really got going. Albion came content to leave with a 0-0 draw and that was exactly what they achieved. Surely it was beyond the Fifers to triumph at the Hawthorns? It wasn't just the English press who wrote Dunfermline off. They travelled south with scarcely anyone outside Fife expecting them to win.

There were 32,269 inside the ground at the kick-off and at least 30,000 of those had midlands accents. The pitch was cement-hard with sand swirling up off it into a gale. Yet Dunfermline started positively. Winning a free kick for obstruction on the edge of the area, Alex Edwards tried a shot. It bounced back to Edwards off a defender and he lifted it high to Pat Gardner. A header flashed past 'keeper Osborne inside the right-hand post and Gardner had given Dunfermline the lead in just two minutes.

The complexion of the tie had altered completely. Under the away goals rule, West Brom now had to score twice without further loss. The Pars brought all their European experience to bear, retreating into defence and denying Albion space. Marshalled by the superb Roy Barry, they looked impregnable. It wasn't until two minutes from the break that West Brom had an attempt on goal. From a free kick just outside the area, Tony Brown smacked the ball with all the venom at his command. Willie Duff got a hand to it but failed to stop it entering the net. But before the Baggies celebrations could get under way, the Referee signalled no goal. The alert official had noticed Jeff Astle sneaking into an offside position before the ball was struck.

West Brom piled on the pressure in the second half and Dunfermline were happy to knock it anywhere - as long as it was out of danger. With 73 minutes played, Brown broke through and then from eight yards out, belted the ball over the bar. Four minutes later, another of Albion's Scots, Dennis Martin, had an opportunity from just six feet. Somehow Duff's foot managed to turn the ball round for a corner. That was their last chance. Dunfermline had pulled off one of the finest victories ever by a Scottish club on English soil. The three substitutes on the bench - including a certain Alex Ferguson - conratulated the heroes on the pitch.

There were immediate celebrations at East End Park. 7,000 Fifers watched the game on closed circuit TV screens. The wind tore a hole in one screen, the projector didn't start on another, depriving supporters of seeing the goal, and the sound connection was pulled out of the third as fans turned to watch the remaining screen. None of it mattered a jot. The Pars had done it - against all the odds.

It was the end of the road though. A home draw against Slovan Bratislava in the Semi-Final was a bridge too far for Dunfermline to cross and they lost the away leg 1-0. They played in Europe one last time the next season, losing in the third round of the Fairs Cup to Anderlecht on away goals. Two years later they were back in Division Two. Dunfermline stayed in the doldrums for a long while. They failed to qualify for the first Premier League and had to endure spells in the Second Division before a revival came about in the 1980s when they at last made the Premier. Undaunted by quick relegation, they returned at the end of that decade for four seasons back at the top, during which time they reached the League Cup Final, only to lose to Hibs. They remain one of those teams which could prosper in a more sensible set-up. But as long as Scotland has a top League of 10 or 12 clubs, it will be Dunfermline's lot to either be fighting for a place in the top flight or battling to stay there. Without major reconstruction, there will be no more European nights at East End Park for a long time to come.

ON THE SAME DAY...

News: The High Court issues a writ against Ringo Starr, preventing him from letting John Lennon and Yoko Ono use his flat for *"Illegal, immoral or improper purpose."*

Sport: Celtic earn a creditable 0-0 draw away to AC Milan in the last eight of the European Cup.

Entertainment
BBC-1 has 'Cilla' with guests Cliff Richard and Dickie Henderson. This show is typical of its time and could just as easily be called 'Dickie' with guests Cliff and Cilla, or 'Cliff' with guests Cilla and Dickie.

EAST FIFE 4
Vs Kilmarnock 2 (after extra time)

April 27th 1938 Scottish Cup Final Replay (Hampden)

East Fife: Milton, Laird, Tait, Russell, Sneddon, Harvey, Adams, McLeod, McCartney, Miller, McKerrell.

East Fife served notice on Scottish football that they were Cup-fighters of top quality when they reached the 1927 Final as a Division Two side, just six years after joining the Scottish League. They lost on that occasion but won promotion to the top League in 1930. Their spell at the top lasted just one season and the men from Methil returned to Second Division obscurity until 1937-38 when another thrilling Scottish Cup run was produced.

They eliminated fellow Division Two sides Airdrie and Dundee United before rocking the Scottish game with an away replay victory over 1937 Finalists Aberdeen. Another away replay win - this time against county rivals Raith Rovers - set them up for a Semi-Final clash against yet another Division Two team - the now defunct St. Bernard's. It took three clashes at Tynecastle to separate the sides but the Fifers eventually emerged triumphant, ready to do battle in a Final few thought they could win.

For, while East Fife may have had a comparatively easy route to Hampden (Aberdeen were the only Division One side they faced), the same could not be said of their opponents - Kilmarnock. Killie had knocked out Celtic at Parkhead, demolished county rivals Ayr United 5-0 at Somerset Park, then beat Rangers 4-3 in a thrilling Hampden Semi-Final. Yet the Ayrshire club were struggling against relegation, and playing so many games in a short space of time had led to injury problems.

A crowd of just over 80,000 saw a disappointing game. McLeod gave East Fife the lead after 17 minutes but McAvoy equalised for Killie eight minutes later. Nerves were showing on both sides and it was little surprise that they were forced to return to Hampden four days later to settle affairs.

The second match was a spectacle of the highest order. John Harvey of Hearts appeared for East Fife in place of the injured Herd at left-half. It would be Harvey's only appearance for the club. And 92,716 turned up for the game - a huge crowd considering the absence of the Old Firm from the occasion.

The early stages belonged to Killie but East Fife did manage to test the opposition in ten minutes when, following a McKerrell corner, Miller saw his header tipped over the bar by 'keeper John Hunter. In sixteen minutes, Russell broke away and passed to McKerrell. The winger hit his shot hard, high and true. Just as in the first match, East Fife were ahead. But, also like the first game, Killie soon equalised. Right-winger Benny Thomson was brought down in the area in the 20th minute. Thomson took the penalty himself to make it 1-1. There was worse to come for the Fifers. Six minutes later, Killie's Felix McGrogan went on a solo run, beating three defenders, evading Milton's lunge, and shooting the Ayrshire ahead for the first time in the tie. And that was how it stayed until half-time.

Kilmarnock had several players hobbling at the start of the second half and East Fife seized their opportunity. In 57 minutes, a McKerrell corner was headed on by Miller. McLeod beat Hunter to the ball and scored with an overhead kick. It was East Fife who were now in the driving seat and Russell went close with a long-range effort. As did Miller from closer in. In extra time, Kilie tried one last sortie. A McGrogan shot was blocked by Milton's right leg. McGrogan sent the rebound back into the area where Thomson headed over. The injured Killie player McAvoy lobbed back to his 'keeper. Hunter's clearance was poor, only going as far as Miller. He made no mistake from twelve yards, firing East

Fife back in front five minutes int the second extra period. Four minutes later, McKerrell put the icing on the cake with his own second and East Fife's fourth. For the first (and to date, only) time a side from outside Scotland's top division had won the Scottish Cup.

Manager Dave McLean and his heroic troops were saluted by the Scottish press. It was, said 'Brigadoon' in the Daily Record, "the best final since 1920" (when, ironically Kilmarnock were the winners) and "the greatest fight since Bannockburn." Killie had the consolation of winning their fight against the drop. East Fife returned to their Bayview ground with the greatest knockout prize in the Scottish game.

The Fifers continued to cause shocks in Cup-ties. They won the League Cup as a Second Division side after the war and went on to become the first side to win that new trophy three times. They spent ten glorious years in the First Division and returned there for a brief spell in the 1970s. Today, they struggle to entice a four-figure crowd through their turnstiles on a regular basis, but their reputation as Cup giant-killers persists - the lasting legacy of that famous team of 1938.

ON THE SAME DAY...

News: The Daily Record heralds the forthcoming Empire Exhibition in Glasgow and makes history by producing a special edition with colour pages.

Sport: Pasch (5-2 fav) is ridden to an easy 2,000 Guineas victory by Gordon Richards.

Entertainment: Non-football fans are catered for on Scottish Radio with live commentary on the all-Perth Ice Hockey game between the Panthers and the Black Hawks.

Official Programme OF THE CUP FINAL EAST FIFE v KILMARNOCK HAMPDEN PARK MOUNT FLORIDA · GLASGOW SATURDAY 23rd APRIL, 1938 KICK-OFF · · 3 p.m. PRICE 3D

Programme for the first match - there was no issue for the replay.

EAST STIRLINGSHIRE 1

Vs Alloa Athletic 0

August 18th 1965 Scottish League Cup Section Eight.

East Stirlingshire: Gray, Miller, McQueen, McGregor, Craig, Laird, Hamill, McDonald, Gerrard, Gillespie, Jones.

Although they joined the Scottish League at the turn of the Century and were, at the time, the leading club in Falkirk, East Stirlingshire were soon supplanted by their eponymous local rivals. They even spent time in the short-lived Third Division but recovered to win the Second Division title in 1932. They lasted just one season in the top flight and after the Second World War ended up in the 'C' Division. Rejoining Division Two in 1955 provided them with a new lease of life and by 1963 they had again won promotion to the First Division. Just as in the '30s though, one season was all they could manage at that level.

The following season the club were moved to Clydebank by their owners, the Steedman brothers, where they performed under the name of ES Clydebank. Naturally, this did not go down well with their die-hard fans who felt that the club had lost its identity. Legal battles took up most of 1964-65 and for a long time it looked like football would never return to Firs Park. Eventually, however, 'Shire supporters were successful. ES Clydebank was split into its two component parts and East Stirling returned to the ranks of the League. The first match back at Firs Park was this League Cup tie against Alloa.

The town of Falkirk celebrated the return in style. At 5.00 a reception was held in the club rooms. At 6.40 Muirhead Pipe Band - reigning World Champions - led a parade of supporters, the Boys club, the Ladies committee and ex-players to the ground. Thousands turned out along the route to cheer. The 3,000 or so who actually paid to get in to the match may have thought that the pre-match entertainment was better than what followed, at least as far as the first half was concerned.

For it was a lacklustre 'Shire out on the pitch. Hamill, re-signed just 48 hours before this game, was the best player, but his crosses were easily blocked by the Alloa defence. The best chance of the half fell to Alloa in the 25th minute. Rogerson tried a lob which bounced awkwardly before being tipped over by Gray. Half-time was reached without the goals of either side ever looking in serious danger of being breached.

'Shire's attack was struggling, though their defence was sound. It had to be. In the 65th minute a shot from Alloa's Walker beat Gray but McQueen was on hand to clear off the line. And the left back was perfectly positioned to do the same thing in 77 minutes following an attempt by Alloa's Marshall. It looked like being a disappointing homecoming until five minutes from the end when Dave McGregor - 15 yards from goal - slammed home a low shot for the only goal of the game. A good result to restart on but Chairman Jimmy Middlemass was happy just to be back at Firs Park. *"14 months away from the ground,"* he said, *"it's a miracle - a miracle."*

The Falkirk Herald was more critical. It accused the forwards of hesitancy, *"particularly centre-forward Gerrard. The bulky centre-forward arrived at Firs Park with a reputation as a goal-scorer, but he has an awful lot to learn. Most of Shire's moves broke down because of his slowness in thought and action."* A harsh verdict on a man who would go on to become a well-known businessman in Hong Kong and who later delighted in regaling the Far Eastern press with tales of his days at Firs Park, where he said he was treated as *"half-idol, half-slave."* When word of this got back to Scotland, Gerrard ended up becoming a minor celebrity in the Scottish press - more column inches being devoted to his reflections in retirement than had ever been written about him in his prime.

Apart from a couple of years in the new First Division, East Stirling have remained largely in obscurity, though they did reach the Quarter-Finals of the Scottish Cup in 1981 - a full 90 years after they had last done so. The miracle is that they are there at all. The proximity of the town to Glasgow and Edinburgh plus the fact that Falkirk receive the support of most locals means that it will always be a fragile existence at Firs Park. But 'Shire fans can look back with pride on August 1965. That was when loyalty to the team was shown in an exemplary fashion by those who refused to let the club die. Not many teams return from the grave. East Stirling - thanks to their tenacious band of followers - did precisely that.

ON THE SAME DAY...

News: Mrs. Winifred Zakim, of Bournemouth, applying to evict her husband Harris from their home, complains of his *"excessive sexual demands."* The Judge refuses her application, noting that her husband is 66 and has diabetes.

Sport: The Scottish League Championship flag is unfurled at Rugby Park, Kilmarnock, at the home side's League Cup tie against Partick Thistle.

Entertainment The Falkirk Odeon has The Beatles in *'Help!'*

Falkirk joined the League after neighbours East Stirling but made much the bigger impact. Entering the Second Division in 1902, they were in the First three years later. Three years after that they were runners-up in the League, a position they reached again in 1910. And sandwiched in between those League near-misses was a Scottish Cup Semi-Final appearance. The Edwardian era saw the Bairns emerge from non-League obscurity into one of the most powerful outfits in the land.

FALKIRK 2
Vs Raith Rovers 0

April 12th 1913 Scottish Cup Final (Celtic Park)

Falkirk: Stewart, Orrock, Donaldson, McDonald, Logan, McMillan, McNaught, Gibbons, Robertson, Croal, Terris.

With the wind behind them, Raith looked set to equalise early in the second half but their shots came from too far out to seriously trouble Falkirk. Rovers dangerous centre-forward Martin was controlled by Falkirk pivot Logan and this allowed winger McNaught to get into the game. He lobbed the ball square across and there was Logan running in to shoot into an empty net - the otherwise excellent McLeod being posted missing at a crucial stage of the game.

The crowning glory of this remarkable rise came in the Scottish Cup in 1913. Falkirk were given a first round bye but after that they never faced an easy tie. It took two games to dispose of Morton before the Bairns pulled off one of their finest ever results - a 3-1 away win over Rangers. A tricky home tie against Dumbarton was safely negotiated next, leading to a 1-0 Semi-Final success over tournament favourites Hearts. With Raith Rovers winning the other Semi-Final, it meant that the 40th Scottish Cup Final would be contested by two teams playing their first Final.

45,000 turned up at Celtic Park - a sharp rebuff to the many sceptics who thought such a pairing would have little appeal. Falkirk quickly established supremacy, displaying no sign of the nerves which afflicted Raith at the start of the match. McLeod, in the Raith goal, was in top form though and he defied the Bairns for the first twenty minutes. Then Rovers full-back Cumming stumbled while tackling Gibbons. Croal seized possession and nipped in between the backs. His shot was palmed out by McLeod, but only as far as Robertson who headed in the opener. Raith came more into it after this setback. But they threw away chances to equalise. Stewart made some fine saves and Orrock and Donaldson were generally on top of things, but when Rovers did get through, Gourlay missed an open goal. Falkirk's lead held till the break.

There were still forty minutes to play but the Cup was Falkirk's already. If anybody looked like scoring, it was the Bairns. They didn't manage to pierce the Raith rearguard again, however, but their supporters were more than content - the Scottish Cup was on its way to Falkirk.

Arriving back by special train, the team found themselves beseiged by their fans. A brass band played *"See the Conquering Hero comes"* as they stepped onto the platform. All traffic was suspended in the High Street to allow the team to be met by Provost Bogle. He filled up the Cup with champagne and toasts were drunk until well into the early hours. Falkirk had travelled far in a short while. Now they were one of the most feared teams in the country and the proud holders of the Scottish Cup.

After the First World War, Falkirk slipped back in the Scottish rankings. Although spending virtually all their time in the old First Division, it was another 44 years before the local engravers got the call from Brockville when the Bairns won the Cup again in 1957.

Falkirk nowadays are one of those teams too big for the First Division but always fearful of the Premier. They recovered from enduring a spell in the new Second Division but need League reconstruction if they are to seriously pursue the game's big prizes. But, almost forty years having elapsed since their last Cup win, who knows? Maybe it will soon be time for that engraver to start working again.

- Falkirk - Scottish Cup Winners 1912-13 -
(Back): J.Drummond, A.F.Carmichael, W.Nicol, R.Waugh, C.Chapman
(Middle): G.Drummond, M.Gibbons, J.Morrison, A.Stewart, T.Logan,
J.Donaldson, J.McMillan, J.Rattray, A.Brown. (Front): R.C.Liddell,
S.McDonald, J.Robertson, R.Orrock, R.Terris, R.Hamilton, J.McNaught, J.Croal.

ON THE SAME DAY...

News: Suffragette leader, Mrs. Pankhurst, very weak from her hunger strike, is released, on licence, from Holloway Prison.

Sport: The wrestler, Martin Breedis, from Riga, known as *'Hammerfist'*, is on a tour of Scotland. His speciality sideshow is to drive a six-inch nail through a deal board three inches thick - with his hand!

Entertainment:
"The very essence of Oriental sorcery" is promised at the Glasgow Empire from Han Ting Chien, the great Chinese Wizard and his troupe of magicians, jugglers and acrobats from Peking.

FORFAR ATHLETIC 0
Vs Rangers 0

April 3rd 1982
Scottish Cup Semi-Final (Hampden)

Forfar Athletic: Kennedy, Bennett, McPhee, Brown, Brash, Allan (Porter), Gallacher, Farningham, Hancock, Leitch, Clarke (Watt).

Joining the League in 1921, Forfar Athletic were always one of Scotland's 'Cinderella' clubs. Spells in the old Third Division and the 'C' Division were the only relief from a monotonous existence in the lower reaches of Division Two. The 1975 reconstruction gave clubs like Forfar a new lease of life. Finishing 26th out of 38 would be enough for promotion. That renewed impetus paid off in the Cups too. Forfar reached the last four of the League Cup in 1977-78 and actually led Rangers 2-1 with seven minutes to go, eventually losing 5-2 in extra time. But their Scottish Cup record was abysmal - a solitary Quarter-Final in 1911 was the best they could lay claim to. 1982 saw that change.

It wasn't the most auspicious of Cup runs to begin with. A first round bye was followed by an away win over fellow Second Division side East Fife. But when Forfar drew away to First Division Hamilton then won the Station Park replay they were in the last sixteen for the first time in twelve years. Their opponents, Hearts, were at the lowest point of their history - stuck in the First Division - but they were still expected to easily dispose of Forfar. When the Loons returned from Tynecastle 1-0 winners, it ranked as one of the biggest upsets of the '80s. Hampden Park was their next destination and a 2-1 win over Queen's Park, also a First Division side, which took them to the Semi-Finals for the first time. The Loons deserved their new exalted status. After all they had beaten three teams from a higher division - two of them on their own ground.

The Semi-Final was meant to be different. Even though the Rangers of 1982 can't be compared to the sided of the late '80s, they were expected to trample Forfar into the Hampden dust. Forfar manager Alex Rae and his side took inspiration from that League Cup contest of a few years previously while most pundits were certain that lightning couldn't strike twice. Keeping count of the Rangers goals seemed to be the hardest task for those in attendance. The gulf between the two clubs can best be expressed by their contrasting attitudes to the crowd of 15,878. For Rangers, it was a disaster.

One of the lowest gates to watch a Semi-Final. To Forfar it was on a par with the numbers who watched them during an entire season. And the 11-1 against outsiders started rather well. They were helped by the fact that Rangers were truly awful. The Ibrox men won plenty of free kicks but showed how bereft they were of imagination by continually pumping high balls to Colin McAdam. Brash and Brown were immaculate in the air and easily snuffed out any threat from this tactic.

The former Rangers and Scotland 'keeper Stewart Kennedy proved his worth too, palming the ball away from McDonald's feet when a goal seemed likely. Kennedy made just one mistake in the entire half - failing to come out for a Redford cross, he allowed Gordon Dalziel a free header. Thankfully for Kennedy and Forfar, Dalziel headed over the bar. At the interval it was still 0-0. The second half, thought the Rangers fans, would be a different story.

They were right too. But not in the manner expected. It was Forfar who took up the pace. A McPhee free kick was knocked on to Gallacher who flicked the ball to Porter. He fired in a shot which 'keeper Stewart just managed to scramble round the post. With eleven minutes to go another McPhee free kick reached the unmarked Brash. Alas for Forfar, he headed way over the top. There were only three minutes left when Porter found himself free in the area, only to be pulled down by Davies. The referee looked long and hard before waving play on - a not uncommon occurrence for teams playing one of the Old Firm. The 90 minutes elapsed with Rangers being booed off the pitch, just as had happened at half-time. By contrast, the Forfar bench leapt onto the pitch to embrace the heroic Loons. *"Forfar fully deserved a replay,"* said 'Gers boss John Greig. Ah, but did Rangers? With seven corners to Forfar and six to Rangers, it could hardly be said that the little team had played for a draw. Alex Rae was upbeat: *"I feel we should have won,"* he said, before adding *"it's a great day for the town."*

So it was. But unfortunately there was to be no repeat, Rangers winning the replay 3-1 before losing to Aberdeen in the Final. But Forfar built on their achievement. Two years later they ran away with the Second Division title, finishing sixteen points ahead of East Fife. Their total - 63 - is a two points for a win record for a 39-game season. It led to eight seasons in the First Division before relegation in 1992. Forfar have started the journey back from the bottom once more. No longer are they the laughing stock of Scottish football. The memories of 1974-75 with just one League win all season have been banished by the fresher thoughts of Cup-fighting glory. And if they had been awarded that late penalty then who knows where it would all have ended?

Rangers' Redford gets the better of Gordon Leitch

ON THE SAME DAY...

News: Foreign Secretary, Lord Carrington, and Defence Secretary, John Nott, face the sack over the Argentinian invasion of the Falkland Islands.

Sport: Grittar (7-1 Fav) wins the Grand National. Only eight of the 38 entrants complete the course.

Entertainment
Top new film is Agatha Christie's *Evil under the Sun*, a Poirot story starring Peter Ustinov and Maggie Smith.

HAMILTON ACADEMICAL 0
Vs Celtic 0

April 8th 1911 Scottish Cup Final (Ibrox)

Hamilton Academicals: J. Watson, Davie, Millar, P. Watson,
W. McLaughlin, Eglinton, J.H. McLaughlin, Waugh,
Hunter, Hastie, McNeill.

Hamilton Academical had joined the League in strange circumstances - taking the place, and the record, of Renton after the start of the 1897-98 season. In 1906 they were elected to Division One where they performed creditably, if without great distinction. Their Scottish Cup record was dreadful though. Having competed regularly since the 1870s, they had yet to progress as far as the last eight. A 1-0 away win over Third Lanark and a 3-1 replay win over Johnstone altered that. For the first time Accies were mentioned among the ranks of possible Cup winners.

Their chances improved further with a 2-1 home success over close rivals Motherwell. That brought them the holders, Dundee, in the Semi-Final. This was the last year when the semis were played on the ground of the first team out of the hat and home advantage was a crucial factor in Hamilton's 3-2 win. After years in the Cup wilderness, Accies were in the Final.

They faced a Celtic side brimful of experience. No fewer than six of their team had played as far back as the 1904 Final. This was also the side which had won six League titles in a row. But they were now in decline, having slipped to fifth in the League. If ever there was a time when Hamilton could beat them it was now. Or it could have been, if Accies hadn't suffered from an attack of Cup Final nerves. With a fluky wind and strong sunshine, it was never going to be a classic match, but the performances of both sides on the day ensured that it would rank as one of the worst Finals ever.

The Centre-halves, McAteer of Celtic, and Hamilton's W. McLaughlin were on top of their game, even if no-one else was. They dominated proceedings to such an extent that there wasn't a single clear-out chance of a goal in the whole 90 minutes. True, Hamilton's Waugh displayed some clever ball skills but he couldn't be expected to dribble round the entire Celtic defence on his own. J.H. McLaughlin also did well for Accies as did full-back Davie who had a solid, dependable game. Celtic found immense difficulty in controlling the ball and the 45,000 crowd went home disappointed after the 0-0 draw.

I had been so bad that the Scottish Referee said that *"the football would have discredited two junior clubs."* The fans thought so too - just 25,000 turned up for the replay one week later, when the sight of a wild rabbit running onto the pitch was said to have been more entertaining than anything

that had transpired seven days previously. But the game was a better one this time with Hamilton in command in the first half when the wind was behind them. The second period saw Celtic take over but, with Watson in great form in goal, it took until the 78th minute for them to score, through a long-range effort from Quinn. Two minutes from the end, McAteer produced a great solo run and finish to make it 2-0 to Celtic.

It was almost a quarter of a century before Hamilton appeared in the Final again - losing 2-1 to Rangers in 1935. They stayed in the top Division until 1947. Relegation that year saw Hamilton enter a period of decline. They have spent just four seasons in the top flight since then and even looked like going out of business altogether at the turn of the '70s. As they prepare to move to a new ground, optimism can still be found among Accies fans who live in the hope that one day their club will have some more tangible reward for their efforts than the occasional promotion and the B. & Q. Cup. If their players hadn't frozen in fright on the day, then they would already have done so - more than 80 years ago.

ON THE SAME DAY...

News: Sir Edward Elgar, on a visit to the U.S.A., has described the people of New York as living like English villagers of 200 years ago. *"Why are you not more civilised?"* he asks them.

Sport: A full programme of ten matches in the English First Division throws up a statistical oddity - not a single game ends in a draw!

Entertainment:
The Hamilton Hippodrome has Campbell & Barbour, *'The Celebrated Cycling Eccentrics'*.

HEART OF MIDLOTHIAN 3

Vs Celtic 1

April 21st 1956 Scottish Cup Final (Hampden)

Heart of Midlothian: Duff, Kirk, McKenzie, Mackay, Glidden, Cumming, Young, Conn, Bauld, Wardhaugh, Crawford.

In the early days of organised football, Heart of Midlothian were as big a club as any in Scotland. There were Scottish Cup wins in 1891, 1896, 1901 and 1906 as well as Final defeats in 1903 and 1907. And Hearts had lifted two Scottish League titles - in 1895 and 1897 - before Rangers had picked up one. With four League runners-up spots coming during the same period, it is easy to see why supporters of the Tynecastle club felt their team was on a par with any in the land.

The half-century following their last Cup win was to provide that support with poor fare by comparison. By 1956, Hearts had failed to add to their trophy tally in the two main competitions. They had finished second in the League on only three occasions since 1906. They had played in eight Scottish Cup Semi-Final ties and lost the lot. But in 1954-55 they broke their long run of failure by winning the League Cup. It was a portent of what was to follow.

Their 1956 Scottish Cup campaign was kicked gently into gear with easy home victories over Forfar Athletic and Stirling Albion. It was a sensational 4-0 Tynecastle triumph over Rangers before 49,000 fans in the Quarter-Finals that gave Hearts the confidence that, at long last, this might be their year. It took two tough Semi-Finals against Raith Rovers at Easter Road before Hearts won their way through to the Final. Their record was impressive: fifteen goals scored, none conceded. That would be tested by a Celtic team playing in their third successive Final and keen to avenge the memory of their shock loss to Clyde the previous year.

Fallon, Tully, Peacock and Evans were all looking for a third winners medal. That foursome, aided by the likes of Willie Fernie and Neil Mochan represented a potent combination. But Hearts were no slouches in the talent stakes either. The inside trio of Conn, Bauld and Wardhough was the best in the game. And the up-and-coming Alex Young and Dave Mcakay added skill and steel to the Tynecastle eleven. Their illustrious manager, Tommy Walker, reckoned he had a team which could do something he had never managed to do in his own distinguished playing career - parade the Scottish Cup down Princes Street.

A massive crowd of 132,842 saw Hearts - with the wind behind them - start on the attack. But as the wind faded, it was Celtic who started to move forward. Crawford and Bauld stood out for Hearts while Fernie and Tully did most of the Celtic prompting. With nineteen minutes played, there had been no score. Then, Celtic's Bobby Evans uncharacteristically lost the ball. Bauld swooped and started out on a run. Swerving to the right, he cut it back to Conn on the left. Conn let it run on to Crawford who cracked home an unstoppable shot from eighteen yards. Celtic struggled to recover from this setback. A Mochan header did come close but it was Hearts who were on top - Crawford and Young both missing chances to extend their lead. At half-time it was still 1-0 to Hearts.

Celtic tried to pressurise Hearts at the start of the second half but the Edinburgh team were having none of it. Bauld picked up a clearance on the touchline with Evans in hot pursuit. Bauld attempted to pass, but the ball rebounded, luckily, back off Evans, allowing him to try again. This time he crossed to the far side where Young headed down for Crawford to knock in the second. 49 minutes played and Hearts were two up. Just four minutes later, a Tully free kick was caught by Willie Duff but the 'keeper was charged by Haughney and dropped the ball. Haughney prodded home to make it 2-1. In 1956 this was a perfectly legal goal. Today, Haughney would most probably have been booked.

The goal gave Celts hope and they enjoyed their best spell of the game - even Bauld was forced to fall back into defence, belting the ball into the stand. And Hearts had been effectively reduced to ten men. Cumming - injured in a first half clash with Fernie - had blood streaming down his face, but refused to leave the field. As the game progressed, Hearts recovered their composure and resumed the offensive. With nine minutes to go, a Kirk free kick saw Bauld beat Evans to the jump and knock the ball on. It fell to Conn who made no mistake with his shot, restoring Hearts two-goal lead.

The end of the match was the signal for a flaming torch to be lit on the terracing while police rugby-tackled celebrating Hearts fans on the pitch. Trainer John Harvey (a winner with East Fife in 1938) hugged and kissed every Hearts player. As their bus reached Harthill on the way back to Edinburgh it was stopped by Rangers fans on their way back from a League game at Easter Road, in order for the Gers to congratulate the Jambos. In the capital itself, the bus was brought to a halt in Charlotte Street by the thronging mass of success-starved Hearts fans. The 50-year famine was over and their supporters wanted to celebrate.

The Cup win marked the onset of a new 'golden age' for Hearts. Although not successful again in the premier knockout tourney, the next seven seasons saw some marvellous moments down Gorgie way. Hearts played in a further four League Cup Finals, winning three times. In the League, while they blew their chances after leading in 1956-57, the following year saw them lift their first title of the 20th Century in style - thirteen points clear of the field, just one game lost all season. 62 points out of a possible 68 and 132 League goals scored - an average of nearly four a game and a new Division One record. They failed to retain their title after again leading for a long stretch but won it back in 1960.

Life has not been so good at Tynecastle since those days. There was the agony of losing the title at home on the last day of the season in 1965. Cup Final defeats in 1968 and 1976. Even the ignominy of relegation - three times - from the ten-club Premier Division. Revival came in the 1980s. But that decade also saw the 'double' lost inside seven days in 1986 when Hearts again lost the title by losing their last League game and went down to defeat in the Cup Final a week later. Another pair of runners-up slots - a long way behind the winners - was scant consolation for Hearts fans. They know that a winning side will draw crowds which can only be beaten by those at Parkhead and Ibrox. But, with more than 30 years having passed since they last had to hire an open-top bus, Hearts are well on the way to another barren half-century.

ON THE SAME DAY...

News: Workers at Sellafield Nuclear Plant are demanding a wage rise on account of the isolation and loneliness they are enduring in Cumberland.

Sport: Another huge crowd - 95,000 - turns up at Wembley at the Schoolboy International where Scotland - inspired by Jimmy Gabriel - beat England - for whom Barry Bridges had a good game - 2-1.

Entertainment: The Glasgow Metropole features Johnny Victory - *Scotland's son of Fun*.

Founded by Edinburgh's Irish Catholic community, Hibernian were only given grudging acceptance by the Scottish Football Association who originally banned the club from participation in the Scottish Cup on the grounds that it was a competition for Scotsmen only. Hibs overcame such prejudice and won the Cup in 1887 and again in 1902. In the League, they were denied entry at the foundation of the Championship and had to join the Second Division. Manifestly superior to that company, they were admitted to Division One where they performed with distinction, winning the title in 1903. They went into decline in the inter-war period, even spending a couple of seasons in Division Two. They recovered from this blow to their prestige and by 1939 had assembled a talented outfit. The War prevented them from demonstrating how good they were. But the first official post-war season - 1946-47 - ended with Hibs finishing runners-up in both League and Cup. In 1947-48 they vowed to go one better.

As in the previous year, the League race was contested by only two teams - Hibs and Rangers. Since 1904 only one team - Motherwell in 1932 - had broken the Old Firm's grip on the title. Many had come close, but all had failed at the last. Cynics expected the same to happen with Hibs, and few outside the ranks of their own supporters expected manager Hugh Shaw and his side to land the title. But as the season neared its end, Hibs led the way. On the morning of the game against Motherwell, the top of the table looked like this:

	P	W	D	L	F	A	Pts.
1 Hibernian	28	21	4	3	80	24	46
2 Rangers	26	19	3	4	58	23	41

Given Hibs overwhelming advantage in goal average, three points would secure the flag. Victory over Motherwell would take them to within a point of the title and really put pressure on Rangers to win their games in hand. It would mean Hibs having to lose their last match while Rangers won all four they had to play. On the other hand defeat would hand the initiative back to the Ibrox side. The Hibs players and the 20,000 spectators knew how much was riding on this 90 minutes.

The Easter Road side started off in tremendous form. Motherwell - keen to protect their status as the only non-Glasgow Champions for almost half a century - were clever but they weren't allowed to get within shooting distance, thanks to the half-back line of Finnigan, Howie and Buchanan who were all outstanding. Up front, Combe spurned early chances for the Hi-bees by shooting straight at the keeper. But he made amends in the twelfth minute, scoring following a Smith corner. That goal signalled a torrid time for the Motherwell defence. Just one minute later, the 'Well 'keeper made a diving save at Linwood's feet to prevent a second goal. But it wasn't delayed long. Turnbull drove through a ruck of players with a terrific shot to make it 2-0. Then a Linwood cross set up Gordon Smith for the third. It had been less than three minutes since the opening goal.

Hibs kept up their dominance but couldn't add to their score in the remainder of the half. In 53 minutes Linwood hit the post. But shortly afterwards the same player manoeuvred between two Motherwell defenders and, thanks to a fine pass from Lawrie Reilly, knocked in the fourth. A Turnbull cross allowed Linwood to claim his second goal and Hibs' fifth shortly before the end. The Hibernian supporters were ecstatic. The title was now in their grasp.

HIBERNIAN 5
Vs Motherwell 0

April 19th 1948 Scottish League Division One

Hibernian: Farm, Govan, Shaw, Finnigan, Howie, Buchanan, Smith, Combe, Linwood, Turnbull, Reilly.

But the reporting of the game in The Scotsman the next day was minimal. Perhaps the Edinburgh press didn't want to jump to conclusions too soon.

The following Saturday it was Motherwell who did Hibs a big favour. They drew 1-1 at home to Rangers leaving the Ibrox men six points behind with three to play. They also needed to knock in 26 goals without reply to match Hibs goal average. In their next game they could only beat Clyde 2-1. Even so there were those who would not acknowledge Hibs success until the last mathematical improbabilities were ruled out. On Saturday May 1st that should have happened. But while Rangers laboured to a 2-1 success away to Airdrie, Hibs lost their last game, 3-1 at Dundee. Rangers needed to beat Hearts 17-0 in their final game to keep their title. Naturally, even the Hi-bees arch-enemies weren't going to lose by that margin to anybody. In fact they went out and beat Rangers 2-1. Hibernian were the Champions by two points. It may have taken a couple of weeks to be acknowledged, but the 5-0 demolition of Motherwell was the day which convinced all except a few Ibrox fantasists that the League flag was on its way back to Edinburgh after a 45-year absence.

Hibernian went on to win the title again in 1951 and 1952 and only goal average prevented them from doing the 'hat-trick' in 1953. They also became the British pioneers in Europe, being invited to take part in the inaugural European Cup in 1955-56 when they reached the Semi-Finals. But the 40-odd years since the days of Smith, Turnbull and Reilly have rarely seen the Edinburgh team hit the high spots. There have been a couple of League Cup wins and a few runners-up places in both League and Scottish Cup. But nothing to suggest that the glory days of the late '40s and early '50s will ever come round again. Indeed, Hibs even had to endure a year in the intermediate First Division at the start of the '80s. Like their city rivals Hearts, there is a huge support lying dormant - best expressed at the time of the proposed takeover by their rivals when the 'Hands off Hibs' campaign was so spectacularly successful. With that kind of backing from the stands of their revamped Easter Road home, Hibs may get back in the trophy hunt again.

ON THE SAME DAY...

News: The Christian Democrats win the Italian general election.

Sport: After 25 years service to the county, W.R. Hammond has been invited to serve on Gloucestershire C.C.C.'s Council.

Entertainment
Those who have faced the skills of Gordon Smith and Lawrie Reilly can breathe safely. the 'Dangerous Corner' at the Edinburgh Lyceum is the play by J.B. Priestley.

Founded as far back as 1869, Kilmarnock are Scotland's oldest professional club. Joining the Second Division in 1895, they reached the First before the end of the 19th Century and stayed there for almost 50 years. They established a reputation as Cup-fighters rather than League contenders, winning the Scottish Cup in 1920 and 1929 and appearing in another three Finals. Relegation in 1947 was a disaster for the club and it took them seven years to regain their Division One status. An appearance as losing League Cup Finalists in 1952-53, while in the lower division, re-established their credentials as a Cup side. A reputation enhanced by a narrow defeat in the Scottish Cup Final of 1957. It was after this match that manager Malcolm McDonald left, to be replaced by Willie Waddell. Under Waddell, Killie were to reach heights previously only dreamed of.

In eight seasons at the club, Waddell built one of the finest teams in Britain. There was another Scottish Cup Final appearance (and defeat) in 1960. And twice more they reached the League Cup Final as well, also losing both times. But it was in the League that Killie were a team transformed. Previously never higher than 3rd in the table, Waddell's outfit finished runners-up four times in five seasons between 1959-1964. The manager announced that he was retiring from football at the end of the 1964-65 season and his players were determined to present him with a trophy - preferably the Championship - before he departed.

Despite the distraction of a debut in Europe - Killie eliminated the famous Eintracht Frankfurt from the Fairs Cup after being four goals down - the side soon established themselves as title contenders once more. A dip in form in the New Year threatened their chances and by the beginning of March they were quoted as the 25-1 outsiders of the five clubs in contention for the flag. But a splendid winning run and the fading of others such as Rangers, Hibs and Dunfermline meant that Kilmarnock approached their final game two points behind the leaders, Hearts. It just so happened that Hearts were their final opponents. The Edinburgh side had a superior goal average. If the Ayrshire team were to win the League, they had to go to Tynecastle and beat Hearts by two clear goals. Anything less and they would be runners-up again. It was a tall order and most people in Scottish football reckoned that Hearts would win. They had discounted the determination of a team out to atone for so many near-misses.

There were 36,346 including over 10,000 from Ayrshire inside the ground at the kick-off. Hearts started well - determined to grab the lead and leave Killie facing a task almost as big as against Eintracht. Norwegian winger Roald Jensen left the Killie defence trailing as he homed in on goal. Mercifully for Kilmarnock, his shot cannoned off the post. Buoyed by this early let-off Kilmarnock's rearguard began to display the qualities which had made them the best in Scotland. The half-backs, Murray, McGrory and Beattie repulsed wave after wave of Hearts pressure, allowing the Ayrshire forwards the chance to find their form.

Midway through the first half, Killie moved forward. Big inside-right Jackie McInally - a deceptively agile player for one of his build - received a pass from Brian McIlroy. McInally sent the covering defender the wrong way, darted down the line and crossed to Tommy McLean who stood just outside the box. The 18-year old winger - one of the discoveries of the season - quickly slung over a cross for the on-rushing Davie Sneddon to head downwards into goal. Less than three minutes later, Bertie Black kept possession despite a series of Hearts challenges until he could

Heart of Midlothian 0 Vs
KILMARNOCK 2

April 24th 1965 Scottish League Division One

Kilmarnock: Ferguson, King, Watson, Murray, McGrory, Beattie, McLean, McInally, Black, Sneddon, McIlroy.

see McIlroy in position. He released the ball to the winger and McIlroy calmly struck a low, hard shot past Jim Cruickshank in the Hearts goal. Killie had their two goal lead. Now they had an hour in which to protect it.

The rest of the first half was controlled by Killie but Hearts started the second period as they had the first - pouring men forward to try and break the Ayrshire defence. Even now, one goal would bring the title to Edinburgh. But the young Bobby Ferguson, playing only his eighth League game, was in tremendous form, coping easily with everything thrown at him. As the Kilmarnock fans bayed for the whistle to blow, the referee allowed four minutes of injury time. Hearts flung everything into one last desperate attack. For once the long-serving Killie skipper Frank Beattie was beaten, as Alan Gordon advanced through the middle. Gordon hit what looked like an unstoppable shot to Ferguson's right hand side. Somehow the youngster managed to throw himself at the ball and tip it round the post. Hearts' corner was frantically cleared as the final whistle sounded. Kilmarnock were Champions of Scotland by 0.04 of a goal.

Waddell raced onto the pitch to congratulate his team. And Ayrshire witnessed celebrations on a scale hitherto unknown. It was, said the **Sunday Mail**, *"a truly glorious effort."*

The newspaper was right. All the years of second prizes paled into insignificance as Killie lifted the title. For only the third time ever (and to date the last) the Scottish League Championship had been won by a team from outwith Scotland's four major cities. Waddell kept his vow and re-entered sports journalism. Later he returned to management to lead Rangers to success in Europe. Kilmarnock had reached a peak which could not be maintained. For a few more seasons they posed a threat to the best, reaching the Fairs Cup Semi-Finals in 1967, but eight years after their title success they were in Division Two.

Since the 1975 reconstruction, their fortunes have ebbed and flowed. At first they hovered between Premier and First like so many clubs of a similar size. But they had to endure the humiliation of relegation to the Second Division in 1989 before they could emerge phoenix-like as a power in the land again. Returning to the Premier in 1993, the reborn enthusiasm of their fans paid off with a dramatic alteration of Rugby Park into an all-seater, all-covered stadium in less than a year while other, 'bigger' teams struggled to build as much as a new stand. An impressive tribute to all connected with the club. But Kilmarnock supporters know that if there is to be any return to the status they held in the '60s, there must also be a return to a sensible number of teams in Scotland's top division.

ON THE SAME DAY...

News: Pakistani forces attack Indian positions in the disputed border area of Kutch.

Sport: Celtic win their first Scottish Cup for eleven years when Billy McNeill heads a late winner against Dunfermline in the Scottish Cup Final.

Entertainment:
        Stay-at-home Killie fans could enjoy *'Juke Box Jury'*, *'Dr. Who'* and *'The Dick Van Dyke Show'* on TV.

For a club little over half a century old to have had three different names is a bit odd. At the time of this fixture they were known as Meadowbank Thistle which accounts for their alphabetical location in this book. Founded in 1943 as works side Ferranti Thistle, they played under that name in the East of Scotland League. The Scottish League needed a new side to make up the numbers in 1974-75 for the agreed reconstruction taking place at the end of that season. On the strength of reaching the third round of the Scottish Cup in 1974 (and despite the fact that they had beaten only non-League opposition to progress as far, nor had they ever reached the competition proper prior to 1974), Ferranti were elected to the League, changed their name to Meadowbank and took up residence at the athletics stadium bearing the same name.

At a time when pools cash was divided up on the number of points won, cynics (or realists) contended that Meadowbank were there as easy to travel to cannon fodder, as opposed to the stronger sides from the distant Highland League who had also applied for League membership. For a few years such suspicions were justified. But, under the astute management of Terry Christie, Meadowbank surprised everyone by gaining promotion in 1983. They surprised Scotland again by retaining their First Division status and the following year embarked on an enterprising League Cup run. Premier Division side Morton were beaten at the Meadowbank stadium in the first round. Next, Thistle created more of a sensation by winning 2-1 after extra time away to Hibs. A home win over St. Johnstone (their third successive 2-1 win in the competition) took them, incredibly, to the Semi-Finals, where they were drawn against Rangers. After just ten years in the League, Meadowbank stood 180 minutes away from a Cup Final.

If the thought of Meadowbank turning out at Ibrox at this level of the competition had seemed absurd at the start of the season, it didn't any longer. At least, not so far as Rangers were concerned. The victory over Hibs had opened many eyes to Terry Christie's achievements and the Ibrox club fielded their strongest eleven for this tie. 15,000 isn't a lot inside Ibrox but it was thirty times the crowd Thistle normally played before. It was to the credit of both management and players that they didn't 'freeze' as they took the pitch.

Meadowbank were well-organised and determined to make life hard for Rangers. Stewart marshalled the defence superbly and, in the opening minutes, Thistle matched the 'Gers in attack, but lacked sufficient punch to force a way through. After fourteen minutes, Ian Redford set up Ally McCoist with a right-foot shot to open the scoring. The Ibrox fans sat back in expectation of a goal rush. They were disappointed. By half-time, that single goal was all that separated the sides.

Rangers 4 Vs
MEADOWBANK THISTLE 0

September 26th 1984
Scottish League Cup Semi-Final (1st leg)

Meadowbank Thistle: McNab, Duncan, Boyd, Godfrey, Stewart, Armstrong, Hendrie, Lawson, Lawrence, Smith, Sprott.
Subs: Robertson, Leetion.

For the first 20 minutes of the second half the game followed the same pattern. Meadowbank kept Rangers out of their penalty area, forcing them to shoot from a distance. It was one such effort, a Ferguson 30-yarder in the 65th minute, which put the 'Gers two up. In a rare Rangers foray into the Thistle goalmouth in the 73rd minute the two Edinburgh veterans Walter Boyd and Arthur Duncan both kicked off the line before McCoist headed the third goal. With six minutes to go a free kick by Rangers' Fraser took a deflection and rolled under McNab to complete the scoring. At 4-0 it was hardly the cricket score most had expected and Meadowbank left Ibrox with their heads held high.

The second leg was switched to Tynecastle and 5,100 saw Meadowbank give a good account of themselves drawing 1-1. Sadly, they were relegated at the end of the season. Two years later, they won the Second Division title, the precursor to a six-year tenure in the middle division. In their first year back (1987-88), Meadowbank actually finished second. (14th of the 38 clubs). But only one club went up that year and so the fantasy of Meadowbank playing in the Premier never came true.

Or maybe it was only postponed? Although Terry Christie has departed to work his miracles elsewhere, Meadowbank have moved on too. Frustrated by lack of support in Edinburgh, it looked like the same fate which had befallen other League clubs in the capital, like Edinburgh City, Leith Athletic and St. Bernard's - extinction - might soon threaten Thistle. Despite the opposition of their diehard fans, they are now known as Livingston and have taken up residence in the new town of the same name where they hope that greater support will be forthcoming. Whether or not that happens, one thing is certain: Meadowbank Thistle confounded all those who criticised their admission to the League by their subsequent playing record and with their thrilling League Cup run - almost to the very gates of Hampden Park.

ON THE SAME DAY...

News: Publisher Robert Maxwell, who is taking legal action against print union the NGA, is told that the Union will press for his expulsion from the Labour Party.

Sport: More joy for the minnows. Hamrun Spartans 2-1 win over Ballymena United in the Cup-Winners Cup is a remarkable result. It's only the fourth time a Maltese side has won a European tie, it's the first time a Maltese side has won both legs and it's the first victory over opposition from other than Iceland or Luxembourg.

Entertainment:
          'Jackanory' has Prince Charles, telling his own story 'The Old Man of Lochnagar'.

MONTROSE 1

Vs Rangers 5

October 8th 1975
League Cup Semi-Final (Hampden)

Montrose: Gorman, Barr, Lowe, McNicholl, D'Arcy, Markland, Guthrie, Stewart, Cameron, Johnston, Livingstone.

For most of the period up until 1975, Montrose were a makeweight in the Scottish League. They played in the old Third Division in the 1920s, returned to regional football when that division collapsed, entered Division Two in 1929, the 'C' Division in 1946 and returned to Division Two in 1955. Nor was the Scottish Cup a source of any great solace for the Links Park fans. Runs to the last eight in 1930, 1948 and 1973, the last of which brought a record 8,983 to watch Dundee win 4-1, summed up their best efforts. The same stage of the League Cup had been reached just once - in 1966-67. Promotion was a word never uttered in all that time.

Under manager Alex Stuart, Links Park began to buzz though. In the last year of the old Division Two, Montrose finished 3rd - their highest ever and good enough to win them a place in the new First Division. The start of the next term saw them perform creditably in their League Cup section. They lost only once in six matches as they finished top of the group, ahead of East Fife, Raith Rovers and St. Mirren. Their reward was a Quarter-Final tie against Hibernian. Hibs were doing well in the new Premier Division and had a side brimful with international players like Brownlie, Schaedler, Stanton, Blackley, Harper, Munro and Duncan. But Montrose too had made an impressive start to their League campaign. When they lost the first leg 1-0 at Easter Road, confidence in their ability to progress was high. By half-time in the Links Park leg, that confidence had dissipated - Hibs led 1-0 on the night, 2-0 on aggregate.

But Montrose turned in the performance of a lifetime to score twice, taking the game into extra time. And when they scored again in the extra period, their supporters in the crowd of 4,000 went wild. One of the finest sides in Scotland had been humbled at Links Park. The Semi-Final draw paired them with Rangers. Reigning Champions and on course for the treble, the Ibrox side were hot favourites to win. All the plucky Gable Endies could offer was the skill, effort and application which had brought them closer to Cup glory than at any time in their history. They were determined to give it their best shot.

The identity of one of the Finalists - Celtic - was already known when the teams took the field at Hampden. The crowd of 20,319 was small for a Rangers game but an amazing experience for the Montrose players used to playing in front of a few hundred in League games against Queen's Park at the same ground. But they didn't let the occasion overawe them. It would be true to say that in the first half there was only one team in it. But that team was Montrose. They outclassed their illustrious foes. Apart from the inspiration of skipper John Greig and the heroics of Peter McCloy in goal, the Ibrox side had nothing to offer.

Montrose attacked and attacked but the invincible McCloy held them at bay until a minute from the interval. Rangers defender Colin Jackson fell, handling the ball, in his own penalty area. The penalty was given. Les Barr stepped up to crash the ball unerringly into the net despite McCloy getting a hand to it. The half-time score read an unbelievable Montrose 1 Rangers 0.

The goal seemed to galvanise Rangers however, for they came out fighting at the start of the second half. Greig, Sandy Jardine and Ally Scott led the assault but it was a Derek Parlane shot in the 54th minute which bought the sides level. Three minutes later, Links Park hearts were broken when Derek Johnstone fired Rangers into the lead. But Montrose refused to fall apart. They continued to take the game to Rangers and were unlucky not to have equalised by the 69th minute when Rangers were awarded a spot-kick. Alex Miller made no mistake and suddenly the Gable Endies faced an uphill task. Scott's goal for Rangers in the 74th minute sealed Rangers victory and Jardine added another with five minutes to go. It may have finished 5-1 but that was a false reflection of a game Montrose had dominated for long stretches and which, for a long time, looked like they could win.

It went on to be Montrose's nearly year. They finished 3rd in the League (13th in Scotland) but were never quite in the promotion hunt. They reached the last eight of the Scottish Cup, and it took three games and 5½ hours play before Hearts overcame them. This season was the finest in all their history. They were relegated in 1979, though they have ended up back in the First on three occasions since then. However, apart from a League Cup Quarter-Final defeat in 1978-79, Montrose have never risen to such heights again. Today they are trying to recover that lost First Division place and dreaming, again, of taking on the mighty Rangers.

ON THE SAME DAY...

News: A rare sight at the Tory Party conference: ex-Leader Ted Heath and his successor Margaret Thatcher smile and shake hands.

Sport: The holders, Aston Villa, are knocked out of the League Cup in England, beaten in the third round by Manchester United.

Entertainment: TV choice for the evening is 'Softly, Softly', and, sadly for Montrose, 'It's a Knockout'.

MORTON 1
Vs Rangers 0

April 15th 1922 Scottish Cup Final (Hampden)

Morton: Edwards, McIntyre, R. Brown, Gourlay, Wright, McGregor, McNab, McKay, Buchanan, A. Brown, McMinn.

Morton, or Greenock Morton as they prefer to be known these days, were original members of the Second Division in 1893 and were elected to the First Division in 1900. During the First World War they assembled a powerful side, finishing runners-up in the League in 1917. But although regularly finishing high in the League around this time, they were never serious contenders for the title. For Morton, and many clubs like them, the best hope of silverware lay in the Scottish Cup. They had played in three Semi-Finals prior to 1922, but had always come unstuck at this hurdle.

The 1922 campaign opened gently enough with a 4-0 Cappielow win over non-League Vale of Leithen but after that it was First Division opposition all the way. A 1-1 draw at home to Clydebank was a poor result but the Greenock men pulled off a smart 3-1 away replay win. Clyde were crushed 4-1 at Cappielow before Morton notched up an impressive 2-1 victory at Motherwell to set up another Semi-Final clash. Dens Park was the venue for the tie with Aberdeen and this time Morton made sure there would be no last-four exit. They were always in control and the 3-1 triumph could have been much greater.

Their opponents in the Final - Rangers - hadn't won the Cup since 1903 and never at the present Hampden Park, yet the Ibrox men were overwhelming favourites. They had six current internationals in their side. The League record between the two clubs read: Rangers 31 wins, Morton 9, Draws 4. In the cup, Rangers had never lost a goal to Morton, let alone a game. Ten of the Greenock side had played in a losing cup-tie against Rangers the previous year. George French - Morton's top scorer who had netted twice in the Semi-Final, was injured and would miss the Final. Perhaps most damning of all, Morton themselves didn't appear to think they had a chance. Although they spent the week before the match preparing at the Wemyss Bay Hydro, they made no provision for post-match celebrations. Indeed, Morton weren't even scheduled to return to Greenock after the game. Instead, they were off to North-East England for a friendly the following Monday against Hartlepools United! It seemed they didn't even entertain the possibility of a Cup Final replay.

75,000 fans were in attendance as the match kicked off. The loss of French had been described as *"like losing Wellington before Waterloo"* by one reporter. But Morton played with determination. The early minutes were scrappy. One scribe declaiming that there was *"no spirit of fair play"* between the sides. After eleven minutes, Rangers 'keeper Robb ran out to pick up a poor pass back and in doing so, carried the ball over the 18-yard line. Jimmy Gourlay had to endure an agonizing wait, preparing to take the free kick, as Referee Tom Dougray coaxed the Rangers defence to go back ten yards. Gourlay struck his shot over the heads of the defensive wall and straight into the top corner of the net. The outsiders were ahead.

It was all Morton now. Twice, Gourlay nearly increased the lead and Jock Buchanan - the late replacement for French - harassed the 'Gers defence at every opportunity. The rugged nature of the tackles took its toll. Buchanan, McMinn and Wright of Morton took nasty knocks and Rangers' Andy Cunningham had to leave the pitch with a broken jaw. Morton held their lead comfortably until the interval, but in the second half Rangers came more into it. In the last twenty minutes they pulverised the Morton goal. Davie Edwards was in great form in goal. Another having a fine game was right-back Jock McIntyre who had been delegated to take care of the peerless Alan Morton - 'The Wee Blue Devil'. McIntyre headed off the line in 75 minutes then, with fifteen players in the Morton penalty area, and six on top of him, Edwards emerged from the scrum with the ball in his arms. Alan Morton tried a solo run. He got round Gourlay and McIntyre but Edwards somehow managed to scramble his shot away for a corner. In desperation, Rangers' Dixon barged Edwards into the net but Morton were awarded a free kick. That was Rangers last throw. Morton had won the Cup and had done so deservedly.

It was said, by a Vale of Leven official present to have been, *"the roughest Final I've seen in 40 years."* That didn't bother Morton though. They had earned their victory. Their Chairman accepted the trophy while Manager Robert Cochran hastily 'borrowed' come champagne from Queen's Park. And while Greenock celebrated into the early hours, one of the strangest welcomings ever given to a Scottish Cup-winning side took place the next day. In Hartlepool, Morton alighted from their train to be met by officials of the local club, the town band and a crowd of curious locals who accompanied the Scottish Cup winners on their march to their hotel. It was the Wednesday evening before the people of Greenock got a chance to see the trophy. Following a 1-1 draw at Hartlepool, Morton beat Hamilton in a League game at Cappielow in front of 10,000 happy fans.

It should have been the start of a glorious era for the Greenock club but just five years later they were relegated. That was the start of a see-saw existence which has plagued them to the present day. They were relegated six times between 1927-75. There have been a further three relegations from the Premier. And in 1994 they dropped briefly into the Second Division. Trophies have been scarce too. Losing appearances in the Cup Final of 1948 and the League Cup Final of 1964-65 are the best that can be boasted. Repeating the success of more than 70 years ago seems an unlikely prospect for those who still follow the fortunes of the Cappielow club.

ON THE SAME DAY...

News: *"Ireland is yours for the taking; take it,"* is the Easter message to the young of his country from Eamon De Valera.

Sport: The Football League orders a cut in players wages to a maximum of £8 per week in the season, £6 close season, fuelling fears of a players strike.

Entertainment: New at the Theatre Royal, Glasgow, having transferred from London is 'The Faithful Heart' by Monckton Hoffe.

The Cup-winners:
The players and officials
proudly display the trophy.

MOTHERWELL 4

Vs Dundee United 3

May 18th 1991 Scottish Cup Final (Hampden)

Motherwell: Maxwell, McCart, Nijholt, Paterson, Boyd, Griffin, Angus, O'Donnell, Cooper (O'Neill 117), Ferguson (Kirk 61), Arnott.

Motherwell had been one of Scottish football's great names. Original members of Division Two, they had played in the First since the early days of the century and, during the inter-war period, had almost single-handedly challenged the might of the Old Firm. Their League Championship success of 1932 was the only occasion between 1904-1948 that the title had gone to a side other than Rangers or Celtic. But they had known heartbreak too. In the same era they had finished League runners-up four times and had lost three Scottish Cup Finals. Post-war, 'Well had lost another Scottish Cup Final - in 1951. But the same season saw them lift the League Cup. And the following year they finally won the Scottish Cup beating Dundee 4-0 in the Final.

Yet just twelve months after that success they were relegated. Although immediately regaining their top flight place and reaching another League Cup Final (which they lost) in 1954-55, Motherwell faced a long lean period. There was another relegation - in 1968 - followed by a quick promotion, but they were never in the hunt for trophy success nor did they ever qualify for Europe. For the first decade of the Premier League's existence they struggled, being relegated twice and saved from a third drop only by League reconstruction.

With Tommy McLean as manager, they came to settle down in the Premier and supporters thoughts began, after a gap of almost 40 years, to turn to trophy-winning again. Since that 1952 victory they had played and lost in seven Semi-Finals. But in 1991 Motherwell were touted as potential winners after their first game. The reason for that was their stunning 1-0 away win over the holders, Aberdeen. A fine 4-2 Fir Park win over Falkirk was followed by a tricky Quarter-Final against Morton. A 0-0 draw at Fir Park meant a replay at Cappielow. After 120 minutes the sides were still deadlocked at 1-1. It was Motherwell's nerve which held better as they emerged successful 5-4 in a penalty shoot-out. A 0-0 draw with Celtic in the Semi-Final seemed to have ended their hopes. For conventional wisdom held that you only got one crack at the Old Firm in the Cup. They always win the replays. Not this time though, as Motherwell entered the Final in style, beating Celtic 4-2.

Their opponents - Dundee United - were a modern-era equivalent of Thirties Motherwell - always reaching, and losing, Cup Finals. This would be the Tannadice side's sixth Final since 1974 and they had lost all the previous five. Yet, on the basis that they had to win sometime, United were the favourites. They were managed by McLean's brother Jim but the unique flavour of a Final with sides led by two brothers was tragically marred three days before the match by the death of the McLeans' father.

Naturally, the occasion was no longer the joyous prospect it should have been for the McLean family. But the supporters were happy to turn up in numbers for what promised to be an enthralling game. Despite live TV coverage, there were 57,319 present. That is a huge number for a 1990s match lacking the presence of the Old Firm and they were rewarded with the best Scottish Cup Final in living memory.

United started like a whirlwind - determined to end their Hampden jinx. Inside 90 seconds, Hamish French had the ball in the net but the 'goal' was disallowed. Then a 20-yarder from Freddie Van der Hoorn spun off the post and rolled along the goalmouth before being cleared. But Motherwell gave as good as they got. In 32 minutes, Ian Ferguson (who had played twice for Dundee United in the Final), sent Griffin off on the right. Ferguson met the return cross and headed past United 'keeper Alan Main to give Motherwell the lead. It stayed like that until half-time.

The Second half saw a frenzy of goal-scoring as the ball lay in the back of the net four times in only twelve minutes. But before the extravaganza, there was a dangerous moment for Motherwell when, following a challenge from United's Clark, 'keeper Ally Maxwell went down clutching his ribs. He was in obvious distress but, with no substitute goalkeeper available, opted to play on. The Tayside team immediately capitalised on Maxwell's misfortune. In 55 minutes Dave Bowman seized on a clearance and shot under Maxwell to equalise. It was obvious to all that a fully-fit Maxwell would never have been beaten. Three minutes later, 'Well hit back. A free kick from Davie Cooper saw Clark, under pressure from Motherwell's Craig Paterson, make a hash of his headed clearance. 'Well's talented youngster Phil O'Donnell stepped in to send a stooping header past Main to restore the Lanarkshire side's lead. In 65 minutes, substitute Steve Kirk combined with Cooper to set up Angus with a cracking shot past Main at the left hand post. 3-1 up and 25 minutes to play. Surely the Cup was won? The answer to that was a devastating no as United's substitute Michael O'Neil met a Bowman cross with a header which gave the injured Maxwell no chance.

Even so, Motherwell were only sixty seconds from victory when a defensive lapse allowed United's Jackson to stroll through their ranks and equalise. 3-3 and extra time. Four minutes into the first extra quarter-hour, a Cooper corner was fumbled by Main and Kirk nipped in at the back post to crash home his side's fourth, and as it turned out, winning goal. The exhausted Tannadice side couldn't come back into it. Motherwell had re-established themselves among the big boys with this stunning victory. And both sides had proved that big games can be great games as well. The streets of the Lanarkshire town were filled with fans eager to acclaim their heroes. For an area devastated by closures in the steel industry, it was a welcome shot in the arm.

McLean built a fine team at Fir Park and the directors have helped ensure there is a modern ground to match it. And although McLean is no longer in charge, his side goes from strength to strength, competing at the top of the League for the first time in a generation and playing in Europe too. Motherwell supporters are confident that they won't have to wait another 39 years for trophy success. They reckon the present team is good enough to enter the winners enclosure. Tragically, one who will never see them do that is Davie Cooper. The ex-Rangers player, who orchestrated 'Well's 1991 triumph and played a large part in reviving the club's fortunes, had returned to his first club, Clydebank and was playing his last season before retirement when he died suddenly at the age of just 39. A talent taken away all too soon, but a talent which will live forever in the memories of those Motherwell fans who were at Hampden in May 1991.

ON THE SAME DAY...

News: Helen Sharman, in a Soviet Soyuz craft, becomes the first Briton in space.

Sport: Brian Clough, having reached the FA Cup Final at last, sees his Nottingham Forest team beaten 3-1 by Tottenham Hotspur who lost Paul Gascoigne early in the match after a wild tackle on Forest's Gary Charles.

Entertainment: Top new film is Stephen King's 'Misery', which sums up the feelings of Dundee United fans after their sixth Cup Final defeat.

PARTICK THISTLE 4

Vs Celtic 1

October 23rd 1971
Scottish League Cup Final (Hampden)

Partick Thistle: Rough, Hansen, Forsyth, Glavin (Gibson 74), Campbell, Strachan, McQuade, Coulston, Bone, Rae, Lawrie.

Football in Glasgow, outside the Old Firm, has always been a precarious profession - the two giants commanding the loyalty of the bulk of the citizenry. Partick Thistle know this as well as anyone. For almost the first decade of their League history, Thistle struggled to maintain a First Division place. But when they were elected to the top flight for the third time, in 1902, they stayed for nearly 70 years. But it could hardly be described as a glorious era. In the League, though seldom fearful of the drop, they never finished higher than third place. The Scottish Cup brought a victory in 1921 but even this was somewhat tarnished as the twin effects of a doubling of admission prices and a transport strike in the city produced an attendance of under 30,000 to see their win over Rangers. They reached the Final again in 1930, this time losing. After the Second World War, Thistle enjoyed their forays into the League Cup, reaching - and losing - three Finals in five years in the fifties. Worse came in 1970 when, after 68 years, the Jags were relegated.

They won the Second Division title in 1971 and prepared for their return to the big time with a gentle stroll through their League Cup section, finishing ahead of rivals Arbroath, Raith Rovers and East Fife without losing a game. They had to dispose of Alloa in a supplementary round before taking on St. Johnstone in the Quarter-Finals. Here, Thistle lost their first match in the tournament, 2-0 at Muirton, but their 5-1 home leg triumph easily ensured their qualification for the Semi-Finals. A 2-0 victory over Falkirk took them to their fourth League Cup Final.

No-one outside Maryhill thought they were going to Hampden to do anything else other than make up the numbers. For their opponents were Celtic, at the time regarded as invincible in the domestic game. At the same time as Thistle had been relegated, Celtic were playing in their second European Cup Final. And in 1970-71 they had won another 'double'. It was their sixth successive League title and their third Scottish Cup triumph in the same period. In the League Cup, this would be their eighth consecutive Final and they had won five of the last six. The only subject of any interest was how big the winning margin would be.

With the exception of captain Billy McNeill, Celtic were at full strength and even the Jags fans among the crowd of 62,740 must have felt apprehensive at the kick-off. No-one could have known that they were about to experience football history in the making. Yet, after nine minutes, it was Partick who made the first serious chance. Frank Coulston and Jimmy Bone opened up the Celtic defence and sent McQuade through. An anxious and relieved Davie Hay booted clear. Sixty seconds later, a McQuade cross to Bone was touched on to Coulston, then knocked back to Rae who lobbed over 'keeper Evan Williams from 20 yards to give the Jags a shock lead. It was also the 100th League Cup Final goal.

In fifteen minutes came more despair for Celts as Lawrie beat Hay to a loose ball and fired a low shot into the corner of the net. The favourites ran into more trouble when injured winger Jimmy Johnstone had to be replaced by full-back Jim Craig. Then Celtic tried their first shot on goal through the powerful Tommy Gemmell. But his attempt hit Hansen on the head and the Thistle defender had to wait a full three minutes for treatment. But Thistle still held the initiative. Bone and Coulston had the beating of Brogan and Connelly, and Lawrie and McQuade's fast running was a constant threat on the flanks. In 28 minutes, a Lawrie corner found Rae. But his header hit off Coulston, fortunately rebounding to McQuade who squeezed in the third.

Thistle fans, all too used to the annual jibes in the Scottish press about 'when will it be Thistle's year?" roared their heroes on, singing *"We want four."* After 35 minutes, Alan Rough saved from Callagan - the first direct shot on goal from Celtic. One

minute later, the Celtic defence were guilty of ball-watching as a Lawrie free kick found Bone who scored a fourth. The half-time score of Partick Thistle 4 Celtic 0 was met with disbelief at every other ground in the country as spectators assumed it had been given the wrong way round.

Yet such was Celtic's standing in the game at this time that no-one assumed Thistle had won yet. The second half was all Celtic. A Dalglish shot was saved by Rough. As were two from Macari. Only Gemmell and Brogan remained in defence as Celts set up a non-stop barrage for the first 25 minutes of the half, culminating in Craig and Macari setting up Dalglish for a goal in 70 minutes. But it was too little too late. Celtic's heaviest defeat for six years prompted loss Jock Stein to congratulate Thistle manager Davie McPartland and admit: *"They deserved to win and it won't do the game any harm".*

As jubilant Thistle supporters took to the streets, the players celebrated the first trophy in 50 years by drinking champagne on the clubhouse steps at Firhill. It was the most surprising upset a Cup Final in Scotland had ever seen, surpassed since by only Raith Rovers victory over Celtic in 1994-95.

But it didn't signal any change in Thistle's fortunes generally. Players were sold and the club struggled. They were relegated form the Premier in 1982 and spent ten long years in the First Division. But Partick have survived where others have failed. Third Lanark are dead. Clyde have departed the city. Queen's Park stay loftily amateur and no longer pretend to compete at the top level. Only Partick Thistle offer a home to the Glaswegian football fan unwilling to share in the sectarianism of the Old Firm. But Thistle's continued existence comes at a price - the knowledge that it may be another 50 years before champagne is drunk on the clubhouse steps again.

QUEEN OF THE SOUTH 5
Vs East Fife 0

December 26th 1953
Scottish League Division One ('A' Division)

Football clubs had existed in Dumfries for many years but the present-day Queen of the South were only formed in 1919. They were the one undoubted success story of the otherwise tragic Third Division in the 1920s, winning promotion from that sphere in 1925 and landing in the First Division eight years later. In their first year in the big time - 1933-34 - they finished fourth - their highest-ever placing. They held on to their place until relegated in 1950 - ironically the year they produced their best performance in the Scottish Cup, when they took Rangers to a replay before losing in the Semi-Finals.

Those who thought they'd seen the last of the Doonhamers in the top League were confounded by their immediate return the next season - a year which also saw a run to the Semi-Finals of the League Cup where it took Champions Hibernian to stop their progress. The Dumfries side proved their worth over the next couple of seasons and in 1953-54, for a few months, it seemed that a miracle might happen at Palmerston Park - that Queen of the South could become the Scottish League Champions.

They started the season in sensational style - with five straight wins which shot them to the top of the table. Although tailing off a bit after that, they retained the leadership and as they lined up at home to East Fife in front of 9,500 supporters, they knew that victory would take them into the New Year in the same position they had held since August - League leaders.

But it was a poor first half in which, if anything, East Fife were the better side. Cynics in the Palmerston Park crowd suggested that the strain of leading from day one was beginning to take its toll on the side. The second period was to show how wrong that idea was. After 52 minutes, McGill and McBain set up Bobby Black to open the scoring. After that, Queens were a team transformed. Walter Rothera turned in a virtuoso performance. He reduced the East Fife full-backs to a state of distress as he waded his way through the defence single-handed, leaving players trailing in his wake. In the 63rd, 83rd and 85th minutes, Rothera scored brilliant individual goals. The Fifers inside-forwards rushed back into defence to aid their stricken comrades, but could do nothing to prevent Rothera's hat-trick.

Just as they thought their agony was about to end with the final whistle, Queens' Brown knocked in a fifth to compound the misery of the Fife side and cap a magnificent second half display by the home team. Boxing Day satisfaction also brought a delayed Christmas present as Queen of the South supporters studied the League table.

Queen of the South: Henderson, Sharp, Binning, McBain, Smith, Greenock, Black, McGill, Brown, Rothera, Oakes.

Even if their rivals won their games in hand, Queens were still the leaders. Having led from August to December, could anyone now doubt that the League flag would fly in Dumfries?

	Pld.	Pts.
1 Queen of the South	17	24
2 Dundee	16	21
3 Hearts	17	20
4 Celtic	15	19

Alas, for Queen of the South, the moment of their greatest optimism was illusory. They collapsed, taking just eight points from their remaining thirteen games to end up in tenth position. Five years later they were relegated again. In 1960-61 they reached another League Cup Semi-Final but were hammered 7-0 by Rangers. They returned to the top flight in 1962 but after two seasons were relegated once more. It was to be the last time they experienced life at the top.

It's now more than 30 years since Queen of the South have played at top level and in that time they have struggled to remain even in the intermediate First Division, spending more time in the Second since the 1975 reconstruction than anywhere else. But recent seasons have seen a modest rise in support. They can now command regular four-figure gates - a far cry from their days at the top, but better than a Second or Third Division side should expect. Ambition now means a return to the present First Division. That glorious period when it looked like the Championship was on its way to Dumfries must remain what it always really was - a beautiful mirage.

ON THE SAME DAY...

News: Missing British diplomat Donald McLean is reported to be working for the U.S.S.R.

Sport: It is announced that St. Andrews will host both the British Open and Walker Cup golf contests in 1955.

Entertainment:
The Ayrshire coast, a few miles north-west of Dumfries, is the setting for the top new film, *The Master of Ballantrae*, based on the novel by Robert Louis Stevenson.

Without the pioneering spirit of Queen's Park, Scottish football as we know it may not exist today. They are the oldest club in the country, having been formed in 1867, and have stuck doughtily to their amateur principles ever since. They were both midwife and nurse in the early years of the game - helping other clubs to come into being and encouraging their development. And, by urging the formation of the Scottish Football Association, they bequeathed a legacy of development independent of England which is still in force today. Indeed, it may not be going too far to suggest that, without Queen's Park, the Scottish League may never have come into being. An ironic reflection, given that Queen's opposed both the League and professionalism. And while they resisted the lure of the latter they eventually joined the detested League.

The Scottish game was dominated by Queen's in the amateur era. They won the first three Scottish Cups between 1874-76 then completed another treble in 1880-82. Further successes were achieved in 1884 and 1886 and they were also F.A. Cup Runners-up in 1884 and 1885. By the 1889-90 season they remained a formidable force. They eliminated Celtic in the first round 2-1 before going on to conquer lesser opposition like Summerston Athletic (11-0 away), Vale of Leven Wanderers (8-0 home) and Aberdeen (not the present club, 13-1 away). The fifth round provided sterner foes and they had to be content with a 1-0 home win over St. Mirren. A similar score at home to Leith Athletic took them into a home Semi-Final against Paisley side Abercorn which Queen's won 2-0. They had reached the Final for the ninth time in seventeen seasons.

Their opponents Vale of Leven were Queen's greatest rivals. They were the first side to beat them in a Cup tie, had recorded their own treble of Cup wins in 1877-79 and this was their seventh final. The match was originally intended to be played on February 8th but fog forced a postponement until the following Saturday. Then, in a poor game, played in dreadful conditions, Vale took the lead ten minutes from half-time and held it until Sellar equalised in the 89th minute - forcing the clubs to meet again seven days later. Conditions were much improved and the 15,000 crowd saw a fast, entertaining game played in sportsmanlike manner.

QUEEN'S PARK 2
Vs Vale of Leven 1

February 22nd 1890 Scottish Cup Final Replay (Ibrox)

Queen's Park: Gillespie, Arnott, Smellie, McAra, A. Stewart, Robertson, Berry, Gulliland, J. Hamilton, Sellar, Allan.

Vale were the better side in the first 45 minutes but their goal, in eighteen minutes, was somewhat lucky - Arnott impeding Gillespie's view of the shot from Vale's Bruce. But it was enough to give them the interval lead. It was Queen's turn to take charge in the second period but their constant pressure looked like being doomed to failure until ten minutes from the end when Hamilton equalised. Five minutes from the end, Stewart scored the goal their second half control had merited and for the ninth time in nine Finals, Queen's Park had their name engraved on the Scottish Cup. It was, said a contemporary report, *"a fitting termination to a brilliant season."* The same report warned *"those who never have a good word for the game,"* that they would have been *"surprised at the respectability of the crowd."*

The players too enjoyed themselves both on and off the pitch. At the dinner on the evening, there were songs and speeches of mutual praise between the teams - the evening ending with a lusty rendition of *'Auld Lang Syne'*. But of all their victories in those early days, why single this one out? Why not their first win? Or their last? It strikes the writer that this was the end of an era - the last Final played in the old amateur spirit. Less than three weeks later a letter was written by the Secretary of Renton F.C. inviting clubs to establish a Scottish Football League.

The League was up and running the following year and professionalism was legalised in 1893. Ironically that was also the year when Queen's Park won the Scottish Cup for the tenth and, to date, last time - beating Celtic, the great proponents of paid players, in the Final. As the League expanded, creating a Second Division, Queen's found themselves with fewer and fewer opponents of a reasonable standard to play against. In 1900 they reached the Scottish Cup Final one more time, losing to Celtic. That was in April. By August they had joined the League.

For almost half a century Queen's managed to stay mainly in the First Division. Up until 1948 they had spent just one full season and a handful of games in 1939 in the lower flight. Indeed, they had one last flourish in the late 1920s, reaching the last four of the Cup and scoring 100 League goals, finishing in fifth place. But after World War Two, they found things more difficult. They had their occasional moments. Like the 27,205 who turned out for a 'B' Division game against Kilmarnock - a record crowd for a non-Premier/Division One match. Or in 1956 when they returned to Division One for two seasons. Nowadays though, it is a struggle just to survive in the Third Division, the only success in recent years came when Queen's spent two years in the new First Division in the early eighties. All clubs live on past glory to some extent. But in Queen's Park's case, it is as certain as anything is in football that the glory days died along with the amateur era over 100 years ago.

QUEEN'S PARK FOOTBALL CLUB 1889-1890

Back row l to r: J. McTavish (Sec.), J. McAra   Middle row: W. Arnott, R. Smellie, G. Gillespie, A. Stewart, W. Gulliland, D. S. Allan. Seated: W. Berry, W. Sellar, D. C. Brown (Pres.), T. Robertson and J. Hamilton.

Raith Rovers had little to show for 111 years of football prior to this game. Beaten Scottish Cup Finalists in 1913, they had joined the League in the early years of the century, reached the First Division in 1910, dropped out during the First World War and rejoined in 1919. Thereafter they oscillated betwen the First and Second Divisions, never staying in either for long. Another Cup Final was reached in 1949 - the League Cup Final. Although they lost that game to Rangers, they won promotion and stayed for fourteen years in the First Division - the nearest they have ever come to a 'golden age'.

RAITH ROVERS 2
Vs Celtic 2
(Raith won 6-5 on penalties)

November 27th 1994
Scottish League Cup Final (Ibrox)

Raith Rovers: Thomson, McAnespie, Broddle (Rowbotham 93), Narey, Dennis, Sinclair, Crawford, Dalziel (Redford 112), Graham, Cameron, Dair.

to Boyd who hit it across to Galloway. He headed on into the goal area and Celtic's Andy Walker was 'first to respond, heading past a wrong-way diving Thomson to equalise. Celtic put Raith under the cosh after this and the fact that they reached the interval with the scores still level pays tribute to the Fife side.

Celtic enjoyed a good spell of pressure in the second half. Boyd saw an attempt blocked in 51 minutes and, in the 69th minute, Donnelly evaded the offisde trap but Thomson pulled off a fine save. But Rovers weren't out of it by any means. Dalziel tried to break the deadlock but his shot was saved by Marshall.

Another brief spell in the First was terminated in 1970 and for almost a quarter of a century, Raith took a back seat in the game. The arrival of Jimmy Nicholl as player-manager proved to be a turning point in Rovers history, for they swept to the First Division title in 1993, finishing eleven points clear at the top. But their chances of surviving in the Premier took a knock before a ball was kicked when one of their five directors - in direct contravention of a Board decision - voted for three clubs to go down. Although Rovers played an open, attractive game, admired by many, they just couldn't stay the distance in this cut-throat League and eventually finished second bottom, nine points adrift of safety.

It was thought that Raith would return to semi-obscurity and Nicholl would try his hand elsewhere. But the Starks Park manager was surprisingly overlooked for the post of Northern Ireland manager and the Board refused to entertain a request for his services from Kilmarnock. So Nicholl remained at the helm as he tried to restore the club to the Premier League.

But first came the 1994-95 League Cup. Rovers opened up confidently with a 5-0 win away to League newcomers Ross County, then shocked Kilmarnock with a 3-2 Starks Park triumph. A 3-1 away victory over St. Johnstone put them into the last four of a major tournament for the first time since they'd reached the 1963 Scottish Cup Semi-Finals. Cup fever reached a pitch at McDiarmid Park in the Semi-Final against Airdrie. Rovers had 'keeper Scott Thomson dismissed and replacement Brian Potter had to withstand the drama of a penalty shoot-out. The youngster was the hero as Raith squeezed through 5-4 to book a Cup Final spot after a 45-year wait.

Their opponents Celtic - though fielding one of the poorest teams in their history - were overwhelming favourites to win the trophy and book the European place that came with it. Jimmy Nicholl spent the week before the Final scoffing at suggestions that Celtic were there for the taking and fantasising about AC Milan asking for training facilities at Burntisland. What Nicholl was really doing was piling all the pressure onto the Celtic players and their manager Tommy Burns. Celtic were under immense pressure to deliver a trophy for new owner Fergus McCann, and the wily Nicholl knew the best way to keep the heat off his own players was to turn it up on the opposition.

Nicholl's tactics worked. Raith weren't fazed by the 45,384 crowd inside the impressive Ibrox Stadium. Indeed, in the first minute Crawford was almost through before being checked by Celts' Tony Mowbray. Amazingly, the big Teessider wasn't even booked. Raith, with Colin Cameron in commanding form, matched Celtic man for man and ball for ball. After nineteen minutes they won a corner on the left. Broddle sent over the ball to Stevie Crawford and the Celtic defence stood and watched as Crawford turned and shot past 'keeper Marshall. The Celtic fans fell deafeningly silent as Rovers supporters whooped with joy. But the goal seemed to wipe out Celtic's lethargy. With 32 minutes gone, Paul McStay released Tom Boyd down the left. Boyd's shot crashed off the post but Raith failed to clear. The ball came back down the left

Then, with only six minutes left, came a sickening blow for Rovers. Walker's shot hit the post and the ball rebounded straight to Charlie Nicholas. With no hesitation, the old-stager knocked it in. All of a sudden the prospect of Fabio Cappellini or Johan Cruyff phoning up to enquire about train times on the Fife cirle line seemed terribly remote. But while the green-and-white hordes were still celebrating, Raith struck back three minutes later. A Jason Dair shot was fumbled by Marshall and Dalziel knocked the loose ball home to make it 2-2 and take the game into extra time.

The extra half-hour failed to separate the sides so it all boiled down to the drama of a penalty shoot-out. Shaun Dennis slotted home the first for Raith. Willie Falconer did likewise for Celtic. Jason Dair scored for Raith. So did John Collins for Celts. Colin Cameron netted Rovers third. Andy Walker responded for Celtic. Stevie Crawford for Raith and Paul Byrne for Celtic both tucked their spot-kicks away. 4-4. One penalty each left. Up came young defender Steve McAnespie. He coolly slotted the ball home. Next was Mike Galloway. For a split second it looked like he had missed, but the ball just trickled over the line. 5-5. It was now sudden death.

Despite the noise emanating from the Celtic suport, substitute Jason Rowbotham acted as if he had ice in his veins as he calmly despatched the sixth penalty for Raith. Next to the mark was Celtic skipper Paul McStay. His shot lacked power and Rovers 'keeper Scott Thomson leapt to his right to beat the ball clear. Raith Rovers had won the Cup. Fans and players went wild with delight. A scene imitated all over Scotland. For, outside the ranks of the Celtic faithful, there were few who weren't wishing for a Kirkcaldy triumph. Celtic were devastated by this defeat but Raith fully deserved their victory. As they prepared for a civic reception for the players on the Wednesday, the people of Kirkcaldy took to the streets on the Sunday evening. And, as had been said in error a long time ago, they truly "danced in the streets of Raith" that night. After 111 years, Rovers finally had something tangible to celebrate. In years to come this victory will become 'the good old days' as far as Raith are concerned. The icing on the League Cup cake was provided courtesy of the First Division title, and a return to the Premier Division, at the season's end.

For much of their 120-year plus existence, Rangers have dominated the domestic Scottish football scene. Championships and Cups have been won in abundance. The **worst** they have finished in the League is **sixth**. So, it was only natural that when European competition started in the 1950s, that Rangers would develop an appetite for the fresh challenges of the continent. They took some time to find their feet but reached the Semi-Finals of the European Cup in 1960, only to be outclassed by Eintracht Frankfurt. The following year they reached the Final of the inaugural Cup-Winners Cup but lost over two legs to Fiorentina. In 1967 they were back in the Final but the agony of extra-time defeat by Bayern Munich was compounded by the triumph in the European Cup of Rangers greatest domestic rivals, Celtic. The Ibrox side were determined to match their Parkhead foes.

But while Celtic ruled the roost in Scotland, Rangers had to look beyond the Champions Cup for European success. In the Fairs Cup, they reached the Semi-Finals in 1969, but lost to Newcastle United. In 1971-72 it was back to their old stamping ground of the Cup-Winners Cup, courtesy of losing the Scottish Cup Final to domestic 'double' winners Celtic. Although the competition is sometimes accused of lacking in quality, the entry this year was of a fine vintage and there were no easy ties for Rangers. Rennes, of France, were beaten in the first round, then came an away goals win in Lisbon against Sporting, after extra time. A home win and away draw was enough to see off the threat of Italians Torino. In the Semi-Finals, the same formula was good enough to despatch Bayern Munich - sweet revenge for 1967. Rangers had reached the Final for the third time - the first club to do so.

Their opponents Moscow Dynamo were playing in Europe for only the second time and if the opposition they had eliminated to reach the Final - from Greece, Turkey, Yugoslavia and East Germany - wasn't quite as high in quality as Rangers victims, it still intimated that here was a Soviet side which could compete at the highest level. At first there was some dispute as to whether the Final would be played in the designated venue - Barcelona. For the Russians were reluctant to play in still-Fascist Spain and the Franco regime didn't want to admit the Soviets. As events were to prove, it was the Scots both countries should have worried about.

Rangers had a vastly-experienced side and in Willie Waddell and Jock Wallace the shrewdest management combination in the game. They made a magnificent start in front of 45,000 fans in the Nou Camp stadium. For the opening 20 minutes they ran the show, hardly allowing the Russians a look in. But a foretaste of what lay ahead came before the kick-off, when a group of Rangers supporters invaded the pitch as the teams entered the field. An invasion which was repeated in 24 minutes when a shot from Colin Stein gave Rangers the lead. Five minutes from the break, a superb cross from Smith was met with a glorious - but rare - sight, Willie Johnston **heading** a goal. It was the signal for the third pitch intrusion of the evening.

Three minutes into the second half and Johnston struck again to make it 3-0. Surely the game was over? The fans seemed to think so. This time they were content to stay on the terraces. The Russians - bystanders up until now - refused to recognise defeat and brought on two forwards as substitutes. With Rangers content to protect their lead, chances were bound to come. And in the 60th minute, one of their replacements - Estrekov - pulled a goal

RANGERS 3
Vs Moscow Dynamo 2

May 24th 1972 European Cup-Winners Cup Final (Barcelona)

Rangers: McCloy, Jardine, Mathieson, Greig, D. Johnstone, Smith, McLean, Conn, Stein, MacDonald, W. Johnston.

back. The situation was suddenly transformed. Now it was the Scots who were pegged back in their own half, hanging on in the face of relentless Muscovite attacks. Derek Johnstone - just 18 and a forward converted to centre-half - was immense for the Ibrox side. As were Dave Smith and goalkeeper Peter McCloy. But, in 88 minutes, Makovikov scored for Dynamo. Sixty seconds later, with their idols desperately trying to hang on, came the fourth assault on the pitch as a group of Scots fans thought the game was over. It wasn't. Order restored, the 'Gers clung on for another nervous couple of minutes before the whistle blew. At last, Rangers had triumphed in Europe. Their delighted fans took to the field for the fifth time and in greater numbers than before - perhaps encouraged by the lack of police action at the previous intrusions.

This time it was different as the hitherto impassive Spanish police waded into the crowd with a baton charge. In turn the fans drove the police back across the pitch. The fighting spilled over into the streets, although - incredibly - there were no arrests. The Rangers players had seen their moment of glory marred. It took them ten minutes to escape to the dressing room and it proved impossible to present them with the trophy - the sight their fans presumably most wanted to see.

It was more peaceable the next day in Glasgow when the team paraded with the trophy in a motorcade round their Ibrox pitch as thousands of fans expressed their appreciation. The scenes of joy in the Stadium were in sharp contrast to the events of the previous evening. Although there was talk of cancelling the result, UEFA let Rangers keep the trophy, though they were not allowed to defend it; being banned from Europe for two years - later reduced to one year after appeal. It had been the greatest night in the Glasgow club's history, but it had been spoiled by the actions of some of their own supporters.

Rangers target remains the European Cup. But their attempts to win the premier club prize have thus far been unsuccessful. Two Quarter-Final appearances was their post-1972 tally until 1992-93 when they missed out on the Final itself by just one point, finishing second to Marseilles in their group. But by and large their form has been poor in Europe. Whether they can ever lift the big one is debatable. What is not is question is that it is the burning ambition of everyone at Ibrox that they do.

When Ross County decided to apply for one of the two vacancies the Scottish League created for 1994-95, there were few outside their native Dingwall who would have bet on their being successful. The Victoria Park side had a strong enough pedigree - since foundation in 1929 they had competed regularly in the Scottish Cup. And since the early 1960s they had beaten League opposition in that tourney on several occasions. Also in their favour was the fact that their 1990s side was the strongest in their history. They had won two Highland League titles to add to their previous triumph in the 1960s. And they could draw decent crowds. 5,500 for a cup tie against Queen of the South and 4,374 Vs Meadowbank were the kind of figures that some **First** Division sides would have envied.

But County had to contend with strong opposition. Opinion among the League clubs favoured granting League status to the combined Caledonian and Thistle bid from Inverness. Many doubted the wisdom of electing two Highland teams when there were Southern contenders in the shape of Gala Fairydean and Gretna. Even if they did plump for two teams from the North, County also faced a challenge from Elgin City. County manager Bobby Wilson realised that his side's best hope was to **play** their way into the League.

The Scottish Cup presented the ideal opportunity. In the first round they demolished South of Scotland League side St. Cuthbert's Wanderers 11-0, having scored **nine** by the break. The next round gave them the ideal tie in which to prove themselves. Forfar Athletic away. The Station Park side were on a roll - unbeaten in their last eight games, including an 8-3 trouncing of Queen of the South in the Cup. If Ross County could win this tie - with the vote on League admission taking place four days later - they might just swing enough support to land the big prize.

Interest in the tie was immense. 1,400 highland fans travelled south, bringing the gate to 2,439 and outnumbering the home support. The BBC TV cameras were there too, to record a potentially historic game. And within three minutes of kick-off, County received a taste of the supposed 'superior skills' of League players when Forfar's Archibald hit County's Andy McLeod *"with a forearm jab which could be heard in the stands,"* according to one reporter. The miscreant was ordered from the pitch but that is no excuse for what happened next. The Dingwall men were simply determined to show they had what it takes to join the League. In sixteen minutes, Billy Ferries broke past Forfar's McPhee on the right, centring into the middle of the box for Grant to side-foot a volley past 'keeper Arthur from eight yards. Two minutes later, Grant turned provider - sending a great pass to Barry Wilson. The manager's son made no mistake. 2-0 to County.

Forfar Athletic 0 Vs
ROSS COUNTY 4

January 8th 1994
Scottish Cup Round Two

Ross County: Hutchison, Somerville, Reid (Ross), Williamson, Bellshaw, Alex McLeod, Ferries, Grant (Robertson), Andrew McLeod, Connelly, Wilson.

The Highland side dominated the rest of the half without adding to their score. But five minutes after the re-start, Grant took advantage of a dreadful back-pass from Forfar's Hamill to nip in and score the third. The striker - who had notched five in the first round - was having a field day and in 71 minutes audaciously lobbed Arthur from 25 yards to make it 4-0. The Ross County fans delight was expressed in no uncertain terms as they took over the Station Park terracing. And when Grant retired from the fray, he took not just the supporters acclaim, but also the knowledge that his hat-trick now made his Scottish Cup tally eight goals - a figure none would better by the competition's end.

Bobby Wilson was ecstatic. But for once his mind was not on the next round, but on the following week. *"We have come here and done very well,"* said the manager about his team's 4-0 success, *"but the right result on Wednesday would mean even more for those great fans who followed us in huge numbers to Forfar today."* He was right. **Scotland On Sunday** summed it up, saying of County: *"Their final arrives on Wednesday."*

And it was a glorious Wednesday too. The League clubs couldn't ignore the Forfar result. The Inverness amalgam did indeed take first place in the ballot. But County were only just behind them - polling more than the other three contenders put together. After 65 years, League football was on its way to Dingwall and Ross County earned the distinction of becoming Britain's most northerly League club. It was an honour richly deserved. There were no more heroics though, County losing 2-0 at Alloa in the 3rd round.

But County did not disgrace themselves in their higher surroundings. Despite taking some time to settle, the Victoria Park side quickly outpaced the Inverness combine and earned the respect of their longer-established foes.

But in a desperately close finish to the season, County were just pipped for further promotion. However, Scottish football is all too aware that the rise of the men from Dingwall isn't over yet.

TACTICS TELL AS COUNTY CRUISE

Another senior soccer cup scalp for Ross County

THE fact that Ross County manager Bobby Wilson is one of the game's leading soccer tacticians was emphatically emphasised last Saturday as

dee defender explained after watching his team canter past Forfar Athletic to a 4-0 cup victory, "Early on Saturday morning I was told from Forfar that

were like. "As soon as I saw the ice-covered pitch and how hard it was I knew our rubber studs were no use and we would require multi-

preferring two out and out wingers and bringing in former Don Andy MacLeod. And at the end o 90 minutes it prov canter for County

win Man of the Match for was the second successive tie Grant who has taken up haul to eight and well be in line for the sponsor's prize for

In the end, however, Forfar, quite understandably, tired and County coasted to yet another famous victory. After an early shock when Konel almost put

and shout the County faithful did in no uncertain terms as the home fans looked on in dismay no doubt wishing they had a support like the

to his charge hell leather as County w on the attack again In 71 minutes it v well and truly all over Forfar's cup hopes as t

136

ST. JOHNSTONE 0
Vs Celtic 1

October 25th 1969
Scottish League Cup Final (Hampden)

St. Johnstone: Donaldson, Lambie, Coburn, Gordon, Rooney, McPhee, Aird, Hall, McCarry (Whitelaw 33), Connolly, Aitken.

St. Johnstone joined the Scottish League shortly before World War One. The spent the bulk of the inter-war period in Division One, although never challenging the teams at the top. Placed in Division Two by Scottish League diktat in 1946, they took fourteen years to gain promotion. A further relegation ensued before they regained their Division One place in 1963 and began their longest spell in the top flight.

Their record in the Cups was poor. Prior to 1968 they had played in just one Scottish Cup Semi-Final and two in the League Cup - losing each time. But in 1967-68 they began to emerge as a Cup-fighting side, reaching the last four in both domestic knockout tourneys. Two seasons later they demonstrated their mettle by annihilating strong opposition - Kilmarnock, Dundee and Partick Thistle - in their League Cup section. Saints won all six matches, scoring 22 goals (including an 8-1 away win at Firhill) for the loss of just 6. They turned over Falkirk in the last eight winning 5-1 at home and 6-2 away before going on to beat Motherwell 2-0 at Hampden in the Semi-Finals. It was an impressive tally: Nine games played, nine games won. Thirty-five goals scored, nine conceded. Average match result - 4-1 to Saints.

But it still didn't make them favourites to win the Cup. Their opponents, Celtic, were going for their fifth successive League Cup win and Finals were second nature to Jock Stein's side. By contrast, St. Johnstone, managed by the Willie Ormond, were playing the first major Final in their 85-year history.

Latecomers among the Hampden gate of 73,067 missed one of the most sensational openings ever in a Cup Final. Celtic kicked off but McPhee halted their charge. He sent the ball through to Connolly, who pushed it on to Henry Hall in an excellent position. Hall didn't connect strongly enough and his shot was saved by John Fallon in the Celtic goal. It had taken just fifteen seconds for Saints to demonstrate the attacking prowess which had made them the talk of Scotland. Almost immediately, Celtic showed off their own deft touches. Murdoch found Hughes who took his time to set up a cross which Chalmers headed onto the bar. The rebound fell to Bertie Auld - six feet out from goal. Auld could hardly miss. Just two minutes played and Celtic were ahead.

That was usually the signal for a Celtic goal avalanche. And for the next twenty minutes it was one-way traffic as Celts tried to kill the game off. In four minutes, Hughes blasted over an open goal. Then a fine cross from Harry Hood found no-one in the middle to take advantage. McNeill headed against the bar. Even full-back Jim Craig got into the action, heading over the top. But somehow St. Johnstone weathered the storm. And when they won possession, Connolly, Hall, Aird and Aitken all looked good on the ball. After half-an-hour, Connolly was pulled down by Celtic's Brogan when in a good position. But the free kick came to nothing. McCarry had to retire injured shortly afterwards to be replaced by Whitelaw. In 35 minutes Aird's shot beat Fallon but McNeill was on hand to clear. Celtic returned to the attack just before the interval with Callagan having two attempts saved by Donaldson. At half-time it was still just 1-0 to Celtic.

Aird almost equalised in 48 minutes but McNeill managed to put the ball out for a corner. Celtic's Chalmers had to go off with a broken ankle, being substituted by Jimmy Johnstone. The pace of the game dropped a bit. Unsurprising, in view of what had gone before. But with seven minutes to go, Hughes dispossessed Donaldson and 'scored'. But the referee had blown for a foul on the 'keeper. Then, with only two minutes remaining, Benny Rooney hit a first-time shot to the near post which Fallon finger-tipped away. Saints had come so close to glory, but that single goal from Auld settled the affair.

"St. Johnstone gave us a terrific game," said the always-magnanimous Jock Stein, while Willie Ormond asserted: *"I felt we were as good as Celtic."* Rooney could scarcely believe his late effort had failed, saying: *"When I hit that shot near the end, I was sure we had gained a replay."* It was one of the finest League Cup Finals ever and St. Johnstone were desperately unlucky not to have earned a draw at least. Few could believe that such a furiously-played attacking game could produce no goals other than the one scored after just two minutes.

Two more Semi-Finals in the Scottish Cup and one in the League Cup are all St. Johnstone have to show for the 25 plus years which have since elapsed. They have struggled to come to terms with the post-1975 set-up, even falling into the Second Division in the 1980s. The absurdity of the Scottish League was demonstrated by Saints in the early 1990s. In 1993 they amassed 40 points by winning 10, drawing 20 and losing 14 of their 44 matches. They finished in sixth place, one below European qualification. In 1994, they won, drew, and lost exactly the same number of games as previously to gain 40 points again - but with a better goal difference. This time they were relegated! Without a change in the direction of sanity, St. Johnstone remain fated to flit from First to Premier and back again.

ON THE SAME DAY...

News: *'News of the World'* owner, Rupert Murdoch, buys *'The Sun'*.

Sport: British Tennis Womens No. 1, Virginia Wade, records her second victory in a week over Wimbledon Champion Ann Jones.

Entertainment:
As St. Johnstone's great run comes to an end, the latest cinema release is, ironically, *'The Undefeated'*, starring John Wayne and Rock Hudson.

ST. MIRREN 1
Vs Dundee United 0

May 16th 1987 Scottish Cup Final (Hampden)

St. Mirren: Money, Wilson, Winnie, Cooper, D. Hamilton, B. Hamilton, Abercromby, Lambert (Fitzpatrick 88), I. Ferguson, McDowall (Cameron 74), McGarvey.

Along with Celtic, Hearts and Rangers, St. Mirren can proudly claim to have played in every Scottish League season from the very start in 1890. But unlike the above-named trio, honours have rarely found their way to Love Street. Although they spent just two seasons out of the top flight up until 1971, their best placing was 3rd, back in 1893. They did win the Scottish Cup twice during this period - in 1926 and 1959 - and lost in the Final in 1908, 1934 and 1962. There was also a losing League Cup Final in 1955-56. But Saints best footballing days came after the club reached its lowest point. Relegated in 1971, they failed to regain their place before reconstruction. It took until 1977 and a side assembled by manager Alex Ferguson, before Saints returned to the big time - now the Premier Division.

The early and mid-eighties saw Saints consistently finish high in the table - 3rd in 1980 being their best - and they played regularly in Europe. But success in the Cups eluded them. Three years in a row - 1982, 83, 84, - they fell at the Semi-Final hurdle in the Scottish Cup. And in 1981-82 they lost at the same stage in the League Cup. So it was hardly surprising that no-one outside Paisley tipped Saints - now managed by Alex Smith - to win the Scottish Cup.

An easy 3-0 stroll against Inverness Caledonian kick-started their campaign. That was followed by a tough 3-2 victory away to arch-rivals Morton. A 2-0 success at Raith Rovers took them into another Semi-Final, where they met Hearts. Saints were expected to lose to the side which had come so close to the double the year before, but they pulled off a stunning 2-1 win to take them into their first Scottish Cup Final for 25 years. Their foes were the great nearly-men of the Scottish Cup - Dundee United. But United's previous Final defeats had all come at the hands of the Old Firm. The Tayside side - already through to the UEFA Cup Final - were strongly fancied to win this time.

A respectable crowd of 51,782 turned up at Hampden to see United make the better start. It wasn't until the 17th minute that Saints got going when a low shot from an awkward angle by Frank McGarvey tested United 'keeper Thomson. But both sides suffered from poor passing, though the Tayside rearguard looked the more reliable. The game was going through a dull patch when it was enlivened by United's Bowman firing a 20-yarder just wide. The same player tried another long-range shot which was well-held by Money. The second half followed much the same pattern as the first. The Buddies best effort came in the 62nd minute. An Abercromby corner found McDowell who shot on the volley, only to find Thomson positioned perfectly to hold the ball. The regulation period passed without a goal being scored.

The first half of extra time also elapsed without much incident. But in the second extra fifteen minutes, the game exploded into life. Sixty seconds after the restart, Redford produced a dazzling run for United and crossed into the area. Money touched the ball away, but only as far as Gallacher - who missed the ball totally. United's Iain Ferguson didn't, however. He 'scored' only for the 'goal' to be disallowed by the alert linesman who had spotted Gallacher standing on the goal-line. There was a feeling that Dundee United had blown it again.

After 111 minutes play, Abercromby passed to Brian Hamilton. As the United defence hesitated, he pushed the ball to Saints Iain Ferguson. From fourteen yards out, his left-foot shot flew into goal. Having seized the initiative, Saints refused to sit back for the remaining nine minutes. They pushed forward again. With five minutes to go, Cameron fired in a terrific 20-yarder which Thomson magnificently fisted over the bar. That was the last of the action. After a 28-year absence St. Mirren had won the Scottish Cup.

Paisley was brought to a standstill the next day as the Cup was shown from the Town Hall balcony prior to the players tour of the town. The highlight came at 2p.m. with the display of the Scottish Cup at Love Street.

Unfortunately for St. Mirren, the Cup win was the end of the good years. By 1992 they had been relegated to the First Division after fifteen years in the Premier. At present they look far from returning. It is difficult to believe that they can have fallen so far so fast. Hard to comprehend that, under a decade ago, they were the proud holders of the Scottish Cup.

ON THE SAME DAY...

News: Ex-convict Jimmy Boyle is to take the British Government to the European Court of Human Rights, alleging that his mail was tampered with during his time in Saughton Jail.

Sport: After more than ten years out of top-class swimming, 1976 Olympic Gold Medallist David Wilkie breaks two records in a triumphant return at the Scottish Masters in Glasgow.

Entertainment:
After another Cup Final defeat, it is unlikely that Dundee United will take in this week's top new film: 'Little Shop of Horrors'.

SCOTTISH FOOTBALL ASSOCIATION
SCOTTISH CUP FINAL
Sponsored by the
Scottish Health Education Group

SECURITY WATERMARK

ST. MIRREN
v.
DUNDEE UNITED
HAMPDEN PARK, GLASGOW
SATURDAY 16th MAY 1987
Kick-off 3.00 p.m.
(30 minutes extra time if necessary)

VISIBLE IN THIS WINDOW

E. Walker, Secretary

PRICE	COVERED SEATING	SOUTH EAST STAND	TURNSTILE	Row	Seat
£7			B	D 113	

TO BE RETAINED — SEE BACK FOR PLAN AND CONDITIONS

Won nothing, done nothing - that could sum up a cynic's account of Stenhousemuir. An understandable attitude - but quite wrong. Every club - even the smallest - has had its moments and Stenhousemuir are no exception. Their League record may be mundane in the extreme - joined in 1921 and never promoted - but they have produced the occasional upset in the Cup. None more so than in 1902-03 when the Warriors played in the Central Combination. The draw favoured them in the early stages, other non-League outfits Inverness Caledonian and Douglas Wanderers were beaten at Ochilview to take them into the last eight for the first time. It was then things began to get tough.

STENHOUSEMUIR 3
Vs Partick Thistle 0

February 21st 1903
Scottish Cup Quarter-Final

Stenhousemuir: Skene, Duff, Mirk, Silcock, McBride, Weir, Buchanan, Law, McNair, W. Clarkson, T. Clarkson.

It was a long time before anything similar happened, but after the Second World War, 'Muir enjoyed a few Cup runs. They lost 2-0 away to Rangers in the League Cup Quarter-Finals in 1947-48 and in the following two seasons reached the last eight in the Scottish Cup, losing 1-0 at home to Clyde (who had also beaten them at the same stage in 1933), and 3-0 to East Fife - that latter match producing the ground record attendance of 12,500. Quarter-Final defeats in the League Cup were also recorded in 1960-61 and 1975-76, while there was the glory of a 2-1 win at Ibrox in the League Cup in 1972-73. But since Rangers had already won the first leg 5-0, that counted for nothing.

A home draw against First Division Partick Thistle should have seen the end of the Central Combination side's dreams. 'Muir thought differently. A crowd of 4,000 turned up to see the two sides do battle. For the first ten minutes Stenhousemuir did the pressing, but their illustrious foes looked confident in defence . Then Silcock tried a shot which was held by Thistle 'keeper Wilkie. Left-winger T. Clarkson charged the goalie - ball as well - into the net and under the prevailing laws, the goal was given. The First Division side tried furiously to equalise but a combination of poor finishing and excellent goalkeeping from Skene kept them out. 'Muir didn't just try to hold on to their advantage though. They attacked too. Buchanan tried a long-range effort which Wilkie parried away. But in the ensuing melee, McNair scored for the Warriors. 'Muir kept on top until half-time arrived with the unlikely scoreline Stenhousemuir 2 Partick Thistle 0.

In 1994, under the managership of Terry Christie, 'Muir finished 3rd in the Second Division, keeping their position in that echelon the next year. It wasn't the long-awaited promotion as such, but it did keep them out of the bottom sphere. And 1994-95 saw a return to the Cup-fighting glories of old as the Warriors knocked out St. Johnstone in the Scottish Cup before going on to record one of Scottish football's greatest ever upsets by eliminating Premier Division Aberdeen 2-0 at Ochilview. That brought a last eight game at home to Hibs but a 4-0 defeat prevented the modern-day side from equalling the achievement of their Edwardian non-League predecessors by reaching the Semi-Finals.

For the first fifteen minutes in the second half, Partick were well on top. Duff and Mirk were reduced to making wild clearances. Fortunately for 'Muir, Thistle's shooting was just as wild. Eventually, 'Muir came more into it. From a Stenhousemuir corner, Wilkie fisted away, but only to McNair. The centre-forward fluffed an easy chance to wrap the tie up. Then McBride sent the ball forward to T. Clarkson who, running onto the ball, belted home past Wilkie to make it 3-0. There was no way back for Thistle now and the final whistle brought delirious scenes as *"players and spectators indulged in a regular war dance,"* according to the **Scottish Referee**. In the end it had been a surprisingly easy victory as Stenhousemuir basked in the glory of becoming the first Stirlingshire side to reach the Semi-Finals of the Scottish Cup.

Their reward was a home tie with either Celtic or Rangers - the Ibrox side winning through. The game produced a record gate of £190 - almost 8,000 spectators - and at half-time 'Muir were holding the 'Gers 0-0. The second half saw Rangers run riot. They won 4-1 and were 4-0 up before Stenhousemuir scored. But even that goal was an achievement - it was the first conceded in the Cup by Rangers that season. Indeed the score could have been doubled to 8-2, 'Muir having one 'goal' disallowed and Rangers four. It had been a magnificent run by Stenhousemuir - the last non-League side to reach the last four of the Cup.

ON THE SAME DAY...

News: Laying the cornerstone of the new US Army War College in Washington, President Theodore Roosevelt said that circumstances had forced the USA to become a world power.

Sport: Both Cup holders, Hibernian in Scotland and The Wednesday in England, are knocked out of this year's tournaments, beaten by Dundee and Bury respectively.

Entertainment:
On tour was the popular musical comedy 'Isle of Champagne' - a fair estimate of where Stenhousemuir's players felt they were after beating Partick.

Raith Rovers 0 Vs
STIRLING ALBION 0

April 2nd 1949
Scottish League Division Two ('B' Division)

During the Second World War, King's Park F.C., a Second Division side from Stirling, had their Forthbank ground destroyed by a Luftwaffe bomb. The club folded and in their place in 1945 came Stirling Albion. Their founder, Tom Ferguson, had been Managing Director of King's Park, so the connection between the two clubs was strong. Despite this, the Scottish League, in accepting Albion's membership, decreed that they would play in the 'C' Division. In their first year (1946-47) in that footballing twilight zone, Albion won the title and promotion to the 'B' Division, as Division Two had been renamed. They consolidated in 1947-48 and made a strong push for promotion the next season. As 1948-49 drew to a close, four clubs were still in with a chance of going up. Albion's last match was against one of their promotion rivals, Raith Rovers, away from home.

Over 2,000 fans travelled from Stirling, swelling the crowd to 10,000 strong. They saw a typical promotion clash, full of hard kicking, and desperate tackling. Stirling were on the defensive for 75% of the game, including the entire second half. But inside-left Martin gave a superb performance, as did 'keeper Hoey. And centre-half Whiteford controlled Rovers dangerous forward Willie Penman. In the first half, Hoey made some fine saves, cutting out a dangerous cross from Raith's Brady, then holding a fierce shot from Stockdale, before beating out two successive corners. At the other end, Jones produced a powerful header which Rovers 'keeper Westland needed two attempts to save. At half-time it was goalless.

In the first minute of the second half, Collins of Raith fired over the top. Jones retaliated with a stinging shot which almost shaved the post. Then came wave after wave of Raith attacks. Hoey punched out a Stockdale header, then held a rocket shot from Collins, despite being off-balance. A wicked grounder from Stockdale was also saved by the intrepid 'keeper. To the relief of their travelling support, Albion held out for a 0-0 draw, following which the table looked like this:

	P	F	A	Pts.	G.Av.
1 **Stirling Albion**	30	71	47	42	1.510
2 Dunfermline Ath.	29	80	54	41	1.481
3 Airdrieonians	28	73	39	39	1.871
4 Raith Rovers	27	72	44	36	1.636

As the Stirling Observer wryly noted, it was *"Time for a good spey-wife to be called in to help us out."*

Albion's programme was complete but two of Raith's remaining fixtures were against Airdrie and Dunfermline. Two agonizing weeks later, Raith won 3-0 away to Airdrie and the Broomfield club were ruled out of contention. The

Stirling Albion: Hoey, Sherrington, Clark, Wilson, Whiteford, McLean, Dick, Aitken, Jones, Martin, Drury.

only way Dunfermline could go above Stirling was by beating Raith and if that happened, Raith could only finish on 40 points.

There was no need for the spey-wife after all - the Broomfield result heralded the popping of champagne corks at Albion's Annfield ground. Raith duly won their last two to take the title but, had three points for a win applied, Albion would have been home and dry before Raith's triumph at Airdrie. As it was, to rise from nowhere to the 'A' Division in such a short space of time was an incredible achievement. One of which Tom Ferguson and all of Stirling could be justifiably proud.

Sadly for them, Albion couldn't live at the higher level and gained the reputation of a 'yo-yo' club. They were promoted six times and relegated on an equal number of occasions between 1949-1968. And they were spared a seventh drop thanks to League reconstruction. Life has been a bit duller since. They have spent the bulk of their time in the old and new Second Divisions. The only high spots have been promotion to the new First Division in 1977 and 1991.

Albion have now departed Annfield for a new ground, named Forthbank in honour of their King's Park roots. And even if they never play at the top level again, they can take pride in that incredible climb of theirs in the 1940s. The legendary phoenix could not have risen so far so fast.

ON THE SAME DAY...

News: London's West End is lit up for the first time in nine years.

Sport: Former World Snooker Champion, Walter Donaldson, has two century breaks in the final session of his 49-22 World Championship Semi-Final win over John Pulman.

Entertainment:
One of this week's new films has a title Stirling Albion supporters can identify with. It's *'Once Upon a Dream'*, starring Googie Withers.

Founded as far back as 1870, Stranraer achieved little during their first 80 years - the Scottish Qualifying Cup in 1937 was the only trophy of any substance to take up space at Stair Park. They joined the 'C' Division's South-West section in 1949-50 and were admitted into Division Two six years later. But League membership did nothing to spur them on to greater things. They never looked like promotion candidates - even in the revamped post-1975 set-up. They never progressed further than the last sixteen of the Scottish Cup and their solitary League Cup Quarter-Final appearance in 1968-69 ended in an embarrassing 10-0 aggregate defeat at the hands of Dundee. Stranraer - or so it seemed - were there simply to make up the numbers.

But the arrival of Alex McAnespie as manager proved to be a turning point in the little Wigtownshire club's fortunes. He signed a battery of experienced players - mainly from Ayrshire clubs Kilmarnock and Ayr United - and wielded them into a formidable outfit. On the last day of the 1992-93 season, hundreds of Stranraer fans invaded Stenhousemuir's Ochilview ground, convinced that their club had won promotion for the first time in their history. Alas, they were premature. A late winner from Brechin City at Clyde meant that Stranraer had lost out on goal difference. Ochilview joy became tears on the long road home.

McAnespie was undaunted though. Despite a shaky start the following season - losing three of the first seven played - his side set off on a run which was to see them lose just another three all season. By early November Stranraer reached the top of the table - a position they never looked like losing. Despite the occasional stumbled draw, the prize so cruelly denied them in 1993 looked set to become reality in 1994. With four games to play they led closest rivals Stenhousemuir and Meadowbank by six and seven points respectively. If the results fell the right way, then their visit to East Stirling could set the seal on their campaign.

Over 600 supporters - a massive amount for a club the size of Stranraer - travelled to Firs Park, swelling the crowd to 862, easily East Stirling's biggest gate of the season. Yet the away fans were dismayed when they saw their heroes line up. Steve Ross was a last-minute replacement in goal for the injured Barney Duffy and the absence - also through injury - of Graham Miller meant that the versatile Graham Duncan would wear the No. 2 shirt - the seventh number he had worn this season.

After just ten minutes play, it seemed that all the worrying about the new-look defence was unnecessary when Lex Grant shot in a terrific 20-yarder to put Stranraer in front. They looked like protecting their lead till the interval when disaster struck in the 43rd minute. In his first game at right-back, Duncan put through his own goal. Worse was to follow in the 56th minute when Russell scored for East Stirling. Now Stranraer knew they had a real battle on their hands.

East Stirling 2 Vs
STRANRAER 3

April 23rd 1994
Scottish League Second Division

Stranraer: Ross, Duncan, Hughes, McCaffrey, Brannigan, Gallagher, Sloan, Grant (Spittal), T. Walker (Ferguson), Cody, Henderson.

But neither they, nor their army of fans, knew that the next four minutes would not only be crucial, they would transform a villain into an instant folk hero.

For it was Graham Duncan - scorer of the own goal - who rescued his team. One minute after falling behind, it was Duncan in possession who saw a space. From fully 25 yards he cracked the ball past McDougall in the 'Shire goal. 2-2.

Three minutes later, and from five yards further out, Duncan repeated the trick to restore Stranraer's lead. This time there was no stopping them. There were no further goals at Firs Park, but the news that both Stenhousemuir and Meadowbank had been beaten sparked off another pitch invasion. And this time it was no false alarm. Not only had Stranraer won promotion, they had also clinched the Second Division Championship. After 124 years, there was cause for celebration at long last, as the table shows:

	P	W	D	L	F	A	Pts.
Stranraer	36	21	10	5	58	33	52
Stenhousemuir	36	18	8	10	60	40	44
Meadowbank Thistle	36	15	13	8	58	45	43

There was only one promotion place on offer and Stranraer had won it with three games to spare. *"I thought Grant's opening goal was fit to win any trophy,"* said McAnespie, *"but what about the other two? These players have shown character and skill I didn't even know they had,"* added the Stair Park boss in a worthy tribute to his team.

Life in a higher division though, was always going to be fraught for Stranraer. More so as a result of further reconstruction. Instead of going up into a division of 14, they joined a 10-strong First Division, including three teams just relegated from the Premier. With none of their rivals having finished lower than seventh in the First Division at the time of Stranraer's promotion, they were, in effect, jumping two divisions at a single bound. Add to this the fact that Stranraer were the only part-time club in the new set-up then it is not surprising that they lasted just one season at the upper level. But the disappointment of relegation cannot erase the glorious memories of April 23rd 1994 - the day Stranraer left the also-rans of Scottish football and carved out their own very special piece of history.

- INDEX: (English) Football League Clubs -

- INDEX: Scottish Football League Clubs -

FORGOTTEN CAPS (England Football Internationals of two World Wars) *(Bryan Horsnell and Douglas Lamming)*
A much acclaimed book written by the two leading authorities on the subject. A complete Who's Who record of every England player (including non playing reserves) - over 100. A biography and photograph of **every** player (the famous and the not so famous) has been included. Full match statistics, modern interviews with the players, the programmes feature, etc. A truly complete record! 112 large pages, price £8-95 plus £1-30 P/P.

WHO'S WHO OF LINCOLN CITY F.C. 1892 - 1994 *(Donald & Ian Nannestad)*
Every Football League player is included, together with several additional sections, e.g. a brief history of the club, managers and secretaries, etc. 190 pages, price £9-95 plus £1-15 postage & packing.
　　　　　(Also 'Who's Who The Stags' - Mansfield Town. Former titles include Coventry City and Newport County)

DONNY - The Official History of Doncaster Rovers *(Tony Bluff and Barry Watson)* Written by two supporters of the Club, the full statistics (from 1879) and including line-ups (from 1901). The book is well illustrated, including many line-ups, and also contains the full written history of the Club. Hardback with full coloured dustjacket and 240 pages. Price £14-95 plus £1-80 postage & packing.

COLCHESTER UNITED - The Official History of the 'U's' *(Hal Mason)*
With football involvement from the 1920's, the Author - a former journalist and Colchester programme editor - is well qualified to relate this complete history of the Club since its formation in 1937 (including complete statistics and lineups from this season). Large Hardback, 240 pages, priced £14-95 plus £2-70 postage.

AMBER IN THE BLOOD - History of Newport County: *(Tony Ambrosen).*
The full written story of football in Newport from the pre-County days up to and including the recently formed Newport AFC club. The text is well illustrated, and a comprehensive statistical section provides all the results, attendances, goalscorers, etc. from 1912 to 1993 - the various Leagues and principal Cup competitions; additionally seasonal total players' appearances are included. Large hardback with 176 large pages is exceptional value at £13-95 plus £2-60 postage.

BREATHE ON 'EM SALOP - THE OFFICIAL HISTORY OF SHREWSBURY TOWN *(Mike Jones).*
Written by long time supporter and local radio broadcaster, and aided by the club's official statistician, this 256 large page hardback book tells the full story - including statistics from 1886. It is very well illustrated, and includes a 'one-liner' Who's Who section, and a feature on all the managers. Price £14-95 plus £3-50 P/P.

Other Club histories: 'Killie - The Official History' (Kilmarnock F.C.) by David Ross, author of 'Simply The Best' plus: Bristol City, Southend United, Rotherham United, Carlisle United, Maidstone United and Notts County

REJECTED F.C. VOLUME 1 (Reprint) *(By Dave Twydell)*
The revised edition of this popular book - now in hardback - this volume provides the comprehensive histories of: Aberdare Athletic, Ashington, Bootle, Bradford (Park Avenue), Burton (Swifts, Wanderers and United), Gateshead/South Shields, Glossop, Loughborough, Nelson, Stalybridge Celtic and Workington. The 288 well illustrated pages also contain the basic statistical details of each club. Price £12-95 plus £1-30 postage.

REJECTED F.C. VOLUMES 2 and 3 (Reprints) The revised and extended former volume 2 has now been reprinted in two volumes, and includes the rest of the 'ex-League' clubs: Accrington/Acc. Stanley, Barrow, Darwen, Merthyr Town, Thames Association plus new addition Leeds City (Volume 2), and Durham City, Gainsborough Trinity, Middlesbrough Ironopolis, New Brighton/New Brighton Tower, Northwich Vics., Southport plus new addition Wigan Borough (Volume 3). 256 pages (hardback), and each priced £12-95 plus £1-30 P/P.

(Also Rejected F.C. of Scotland: Volume 1 covers Edinburgh and The South (Edinburgh City, Leith Athletic, St.Bernards, Armadale, Broxburn United, Bathgate, Peebles Rovers, Mid-Annandale, Nithsdale Wanderers and Solway Star - 288 pages). Volume 2 covers Glasgow and District (Abercorn, Arthurlie, Beith, Cambuslang, Clydebank, Cowlairs, Johnstone, Linthouse, Northern, Third Lanark, and Thistle -240 pages). Each priced £12-95 plus £1-30 postage.

FOOTBALL LEAGUE - GROUNDS FOR A CHANGE (By Dave Twydell). A 424 page, A5 sized, Hardback book. A comprehensive study of all the Grounds on which the current English Football League clubs previously played. Every Club that has moved Grounds is included, with a 'Potted' history of each, plus 250 illustrations. Plenty of 'reading' material, as well as an interesting reference book. Price £13-95 Plus £1-70 Postage.

THE CODE WAR (Graham Williams)
A fascinating look back on football's history - from the earliest days up to the First World War. 'Football' is covered in the broadest sense, for the book delves into the splits over the period to and from Rugby Union and Rugby League, as well as Football (Soccer). Potted histories of many of the Clubs are included, as is a comprehensive index. 192 page hardback, price £10-95 plus £1-20 postage.

Non-League football is also covered, including the 'Gone But Not Forgotten' series (histories of defunct non-League clubs and grounds). Plus unusual items, e.g. 'The Little Red Book of Chinese Football', etc.

• NEW OXFORD WORKBOOKS

A Parent's Guide to Pre-School Learning

Jackie Holderness

Senior Lecturer in Education at Oxford Brookes University

and

Bill Laar

Educational Inspector and Consultant

OXFORD

UNIVERSITY PRESS

For Alexander

Oxford University Press, Great Clarendon Street, Oxford OX2 6DP

Oxford New York

Athens Auckland Bangkok Bogotá Bombay Buenos Aires Calcutta
Cape Town Dar es Salaam Delhi Florence Hong Kong Istanbul Karachi
Kuala Lumpur Madrid Melbourne Mexico City Mumbai Nairobi Paris
São Paulo Singapore Taipei Tokyo Toronto Warsaw

and associated companies in Berlin Ibadan

Oxford is a registered trade mark of Oxford University Press

© Jackie Holderness and Bill Laar 1999

British Library Cataloguing in Publication Data

Data available

ISBN 019 838251 0

Cover photograph by Bubbles Photo Library

Designed by Oxprint Design, Oxford

Printed in Hong Kong

■ CONTENTS

■ 1 *BASIC PRINCIPLES*

Parents as teachers

Most people agree that parents, other adults and other children play a vital role in helping youngsters learn. Indeed, as a parent, you are the first and most influential educator in your children's lives. This is something you already know and it is assumed that this is why you are reading this book. You are very likely a parent or care-giver who is interested in helping, as far as you can, to prepare your child to:

• learn about the world.

• start school with confidence.

• learn the four fundamentals of survival, which are:

1. Learning to be safe

There is a phase in every young child's life when you feel that you only ever say "No!". Making up a story and inventing other children who have experienced difficulty in dangerous situations can be a useful way to relieve a potential confrontation: e.g. *I knew a little boy who put something into a socket in the wall and he had to go to hospital ...*

2. Learning to be a person

Children need to be allowed to develop a sense of identity and self-esteem. It is important to accept your child as an individual, not a carbon copy of yourself or another member of the family. Through listening, you can discover what makes your child tick as an individual.

3. Learning to get along with others

Learning to share with and listen to others can take a long time. Through calm reasoning, most children come to understand the value of friendship and accept the need to give and take. Some children go through periods of shyness but, if allowed to watch from the sidelines, usually gain enough confidence to join in with a group.

4. Learning to learn

Asking questions is an important way learners learn. Encourage your child to ask you questions. If you are not sure of an answer, explain how you might find the answer: *We could go to the Library ... we could ask Mrs ... ... we could watch someone who can do it very well ... etc.*

It is always valuable, in encouraging independence of thought, to ask a child, *What do you think it could be? Or what do you think might happen?*

Encouraging learning

Parents, therefore, are a child's first teachers. Just think about all the things you do, on an almost daily basis, which lead to important kinds of learning:

• You talk about stories (real and make-believe) and steadily teach your child facts about the world.

• You listen seriously to problems your child has identified and help to solve them.

- You prepare your child for school by talking to them about letters, words, numbers, shapes and colours.
- You model and share useful skills with your child.

A special relationship

You enjoy a special and unique teaching and learning relationship with your child because:

- children spend four times more time with their parents than with anyone else – even after they have begun school.
- parents know their offspring best. They recognise their interests, their feelings and moods.
- parents and children enjoy a shared environment with shared routines and meanings.
- parents can provide pleasurable, familiar and secure experiences and routines within daily life that can help their children learn to read, write and count.

This book is intended to offer practical guidance and activities which will help you make the most of the times you have together with your child. It does not assume that you will have access to many materials other than those you are likely to have at home already. Examples from OUP's "At Home" series are used here as reinforcement activities to support activities which you and your child can enjoy at home, e.g. in the kitchen or in the open air.

This book also tries to recognise the fact that many parents work long hours and may not have unlimited amounts of time with their child. You may only see your child outside working hours but you can still encourage good language development and prepare effectively for those first days at school.

■ 2 *LEARNING AND DEVELOPMENT*

Developing as learners

When a baby is born, the parents may worry whether the baby feeds well and watch anxiously as health visitors monitor progress and make little marks on distribution curves to reassure them. The parents hope that their baby will gain steadily in weight so that it is neither lighter nor heavier than "the average". Yet, within only a few months, most parents realise that there is no point in looking for averages or norms. Each child is an individual and is unique and seems to have been programmed with its own personal timetable, which cannot be rushed or delayed. Gina may crawl before Ben but Ben may be walking first.

Parents come to trust nature and start to relax about children's physical progress. And, inevitably, as time goes by, nearly all their babies achieve the same goals, e.g. holding a spoon or climbing a play ladder.

However, where school is involved, parents seem to forget that children differ wildly, even after an apparently similar start, at birth. They seem to expect their children, because they all started school at five, will somehow stay level and pass through important stages of development at precisely the same time as their classmates, simply because they all started school at five. They expect younger brothers and sisters to start reading, writing, counting and drawing triangles at precisely the same age as their older children, even though not one physical milestone was probably reached at the same chronological age.

People would be horrified to see parents trying to force a six-month old to ride a tricycle, because it would be clear that the child was just not ready, in developmental terms, to do so. Yet many parents, keen that their children should succeed at school, may be tempted to introduce reading, writing and counting activities to their children before they have reached a stage of development where they can cope with and enjoy

them. The ages written on each of the "At Home" books are only loose guidelines, therefore. Whenever you share the activities with children, their response, body language and facial expression should be taken as your signals to continue or to stop. In other words, if your children are not having fun and are not keen to go on, put the book away and do something else. If the activities are clearly beyond the understanding and abilities of the child, swallow your disappointment, remember Albert Einstein, Gladys Aylward and Winston Churchill were late developers, and save the book for another time, some months or even years in the future. Focus instead on learning less formally through sharing your home with your child.

A learning environment

The environment will be made up of all the resources and opportunities you can provide inside and beyond the home, ranging from toys to saucepans; photos to holiday souvenirs; spiders found behind furniture to houseplants; cardboard tubes to pasta shapes. Beyond that will be the wider world: visits to the park or shopping centre; trips in cars or public transport; woodlice under stones or caterpillars inside leaves; trips to the countryside, beach or river. Finally, the environment will include all the words and numbers which you have in and around the home. Children can benefit from books in the home from their earliest days and few things promote language more powerfully than experience with stories, poems and rhymes.

Opportunities for learning

Much of children's early language development grows out of their day-to-day experiences and the environment in which they grow. The opportunities for learning and experiences that you can share with your child would inevitably include all kinds of play, games and adventures; outings and visits; planning for and making records of events, like birthday parties, Christmas, weddings etc.; learning to play with others, to take turns, to share and to be hospitable; learning to do and make things; sharing TV, songs, videos, plays, pantomimes, puppet shows and films; preparing for the experience of starting nursery and school.

■ 3 LEARNING AND COMMUNICATION

Talking about activities for learning

Building up children's confidence and self-esteem are more important
than accuracy and detail at this stage. If you work on pre-reading, pre-
writing and number activities such as those in the "At Home" series, you
can do a great deal to foster positive attitudes towards learning.

It is always helpful, whatever the task, to:

• Be enthusiastic about the activity, *e.g. Ooh, look, this page looks exciting!*

• Talk about the purpose of the activity, *e.g. Now, what does this page want
  us to do?*

• Help your child appreciate the wider application of each skill, *e.g. Once
  you can write s's, you can write about all sorts of things which begin with S,
  like snakes, and stars and ...* (let child supply other S words).

• Acknowledge a child's initial difficulties, *e.g. It is difficult to count big
  numbers isn't it? Let's try again ...*

• Be prepared to join in and help to avoid anxiety and frustration,
  *e.g. You've managed really well so far, but let's finish the page together. ... I'll
  hold your hand this time and show you how ... .*

Quality communication

What really counts is the quality of communication within the family
when you are together. You can help to develop your child's language by
encouraging them in several ways:

– by listening with real care to what they say and by responding with
  interest

– by allowing them time to express themselves

- by reflecting back to them what they have said and extending the talk, remodelling the language if necessary, e.g. CHILD: *Daddy goeded to work today.*
- PARENT: *Yes, Daddy went to work, didn't he? He works at the big factory.*
- by clarifying confusions and by helping children find the right words to say what they mean
- by modelling language, using wider vocabulary to "stretch" children's understanding, e.g. CHILD: *Look! a big lorry!* PARENT: *Yes, it's enormous. It's very tall and very long, isn't it?*

Developing as communicators

Peek-a-boo games and roly poly rhymes, like "What shall we do with a lazy Katy?" or "Humpty Dumpty" are valuable introductions to turn-taking and conversation. You will already have found yourself listening to burbles and giving them meaning, e.g. *Goo..goo mooo* may have meant *I want my toy cow* and you probably reacted with *Oh, you want your cow, do you? Here you are!*

The tantrums which are typical of many pre-schoolers provide opportunities to introduce children to reason and to ways of controlling their emotions (e.g. "time-out" to calm down) or learning to share.

Learning to talk to other children and adults is often accompanied by a phase of shyness, but most children become sociable, eventually. They learn to use talk to express their feelings, to explore their imaginations through play and to find out more by asking questions. You may have already experienced, with both exasperation and affection, the *Why?* phase, when children ask endless questions.

Children's vocabularies grow at an astonishing rate during the pre-school phase. Their command of grammar and sentence structure develops as well. Children experiment and practise with rules, e.g. *mouse/mouses ... mouse/mices ... mouse/mice ...* until the correct form becomes acceptable and almost automatic. Impressively, many children perform these experiments in two or more languages. Children who speak two languages manage, after some initial confusions of course, to separate the languages and learn to use them correctly in different settings.

Children learn by recognising the relationships between things, and by making distinctions. At this stage, they need to explore similarities and differences. They become aware of what is real or true and what is "made-up". They start to appreciate jokes and nonsense. They learn to describe things, exploring size, colour, shape and numbers: *There's one in this box and lots (more than one) in that box. This costs £50 and that cost no pennies.* They start to compare things: *Mine is betterer than yours. It's bigger.* And to use superlatives: *It's the bestest!!*

They can use these skills to start to look at words and numbers, e.g. *A one is like a road ... and a zero is like a polo-mint; S looks like a snake ...* Such discussions are valuable in preparing children to learn to count, write and read.

■ 4 SPEAKING AND LISTENING AT HOME

All families talk but how they talk to each other is very important. Children need to feel they can share the events of the day and things that are interesting, exciting or puzzling them. They need to know that the adults in their life will listen sympathetically and take them seriously. Listening to children can be tiring because what is important to them may not always be of interest to you and often the timing isn't right. You want to get them to the doctor on time but they want to show you a fly in a spider's web and tell you a story about it.

Talking together

Here are some ways to encourage discussion at home:

- Make mealtimes special and encourage everyone to sit together and talk through the day's events, whether they are still to happen (breakfast) or have happened (supper).

- Talk about shared experiences, e.g. television programmes, visits, visitors.

- Make a Memories Scrapbook, where you stick souvenirs of important and happy times, e.g. outings, holidays, great occasions etc. Discuss the events with children and let them share them with others.

- Spend time with children, sharing simple things which are fascinating to them but which we adults may take for granted, e.g. how water goes down the plughole, how ants carry biscuit crumbs which are bigger than themselves.

- Be prepared to talk about challenging or uncomfortable topics, e.g. teasing, news items, bereavements ...

- Stimulate children's thinking by asking open-ended questions, e.g. I *wonder where that could have come from? What if ... ?*

- Chant rhymes while getting dressed or walking in the park. Make up your own versions of nursery rhymes – *Oh the grand Old Duke of Scunthorpe ...* or make up new chants to suit an occasion, e.g. *What a windy day! What a windy day! Hold on tight so you won't blow away!!*

- Sing songs together, taking turns with lines or leaving the last word for your child to complete.

- Go on a sound walk, either outside or in your home, with a paper and pencil. You write down all the sounds your child can identify. When the child's interest wanes, share all the sounds you have collected.

- Encourage social activities, mixing with other children of different ages. Some pre-schoolers find it hard to share and get along with others but, with encouragement and reasoning, most children come to understand the value of friendship and accept the need to give and take.

Toys for talk

The following toys and resources will all help develop children's talk:

- Toy telephones, e.g. two paper cups, joined with string
- Puppets, made from paper bags or socks
- Children's cassette players, with microphone and blank tapes
- A selection of home-made musical instruments, e.g. shakers, drums, etc. Use these to "talk" to each other in rhythmic phrases, taking turns, as in a spoken conversation.

Talk and play

Children's language is often at its richest when they are engaged in some form of roleplay, acting out a fantasy with their friends or on their own.

You may be invited to join in: *You can be the mummy policeman ...* but once "inside" the play, you will need to act out your part with as much seriousness as the children. Within your role, you can extend the children's vocabulary by feeding in new words and ideas, e.g. *We need a stretcher, don't we? What's a stretcher? It's something injured people are carried on, like at football matches ... . It's carried by two people, one at either end ... . Let's pretend.*

Talking games

Young children enjoy games and these help to develop their language:

- I-Spy. The traditional game can be played with letter sounds, e.g. *I spy with my little eye, something beginning with buh ... Bus! Yes!*
- I-See-Something. This is based upon the colour of an object. *I see something and it sees me and it's as (yellow) as (yellow) as can be ... . Is it my shirt? Yes!*
- Rhyme-time. The parent says the first part and the children try to guess the rhyme.
  I know a word and this word is ... (dark) ... And I can hear it rhymes with ... Child: (bark!)
  (See also pages 15–29 *At Home with Sounds and Rhymes*)
- Guess-the-Animal. Player 1 thinks of an animal and says, *I'm thinking of an animal, what can it be? Ask me questions and you will see.* The other players have to ask questions, e.g. *Can it swim? Has it got four legs? Does it live in our garden? Has it got fur??* Player 1 can only answer *Yes* or *No* until the animal has been guessed correctly.
- Chinese whispers. The first player thinks of a sentence to whisper, e.g. the first line of a nursery rhyme. He/she whispers it to the next person and on around the group until the line is whispered to the last person. He/she has to say the line aloud and everyone listens to see whether the whisper has survived the journey.
- In order to help children express their feelings, you can choose any subject and take turns to say *A good thing about ... is ... . A bad thing about ... is ... .*
- Play a feelie bag game. Collect some everyday objects or toys in a cloth bag. Without looking the child has to feel an object and describe it.

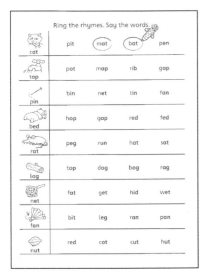

Sounds and Rhymes p.16

■ 5 AT HOME WITH COLOURS

Visual development

Children are drawn to bright colours and strong visual contrasts, which they notice even during their first few months. You may have seen or hung mobiles with bold images above your child's cot.

Most toddlers can identify the primary colours (red, yellow, blue) by their third year. They can appreciate that colours like dark green and light green are still green.

Being able to identify sameness and difference is very important in visual development. Several visual discrimination games are included on pages 8, 20, 21, 22, 24, 28, 30 of *At Home with Colours*. For example, children have to identify which image is the odd-one-out or which objects are hidden in an overlapping collection.

In the "At Home" series, the book about Colours is a good one to start with, because it focuses on only three words (red/blue/green) and three numbers (1, 2, 3). The activities are self-explanatory and they help to develop hand-eye co-ordination and enable children to practise pre-writing skill and to learn concepts like *straight*, *curved* and *zig-zag*. These are useful when teaching children to form letter shapes. The activities are also designed to develop early number recognition and formation, up to three.

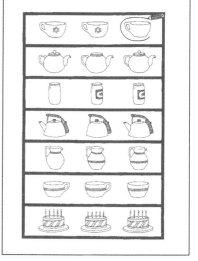

Colours p.22

Learning colour names

Colour names are best learned through conversation, while looking at things which your child is interested in.

Here are some suggestions:

- Whenever you teach your child a new word, e.g. *plum*, you can add the colour, e.g. *purple*

- Encourage your child to explain which object they want by describing the colour of it. E.g. *You want your snake, do you? Now, what colour is it? Is it black? No? Ah, it's green. So you want your green snake? Here it is!*

- Look out for cars and lorries of different colours, when travelling. Each traveller chooses a colour and can score a point whenever they see a car of their colour choice.

- Sing songs and rhymes which feature colour, e.g. "Yellow submarine" or "Little Boy Blue".

Once your child can tell you the main colours, you can move them onto more subtle descriptions, e.g. sunflower yellow, lemon yellow, pale yellow, bright yellow, dark yellow etc.

Colourful resources around the home

In order to encourage discussion about colours, it is helpful to make "Colour collections".

- Buy a scrapbook and label each page with a colour. Onto these pages, stick pictures cut from magazines: an orange car, an orange chair, an orange sun, a real orange flower, a piece of orange wool etc.

- Make up a set of containers, e.g. shoeboxes, and start collecting coloured objects. Your "collections" could include balls of wool, balloons, feathers, buttons or marbles. Naturally, some of these carry a safety risk. Young children would need to be supervised when playing with buttons or marbles, for example, because of the risk of choking.
- Use painting and decorating colour cards or fabric swatches so children can sort colours into families, e.g. cool, blue colours or hot, reddish colours or pale pastel shades.
- Make simple folded or zigzag books (My White Book, My Red Book) to show things that are nearly always a certain colour, e.g. snow is always white, tomatoes and strawberries are always red.
- Provide opportunities to experiment with coloured paper, colouring books, sets of crayons and pens.
- Give children the chance to sometimes indulge in more messy colour activities, using paints, sponge shapes, printing etc.
- Talk about colour on a daily basis in connection with your child's clothes, with getting dressed and undressed.

Learning to read colour names

Children can recognise a colour adjective, e.g. *red*, long before they can write it for themselves. Here are a few ideas:

- Make small flashcards with the colour name on a piece of paper or card of the same colour. Stick these up somewhere, and point to, "read" and discuss them together.
- Let your child paint blobs of the main colours (red, blue, green, yellow, orange, white, black, purple, brown). Cut these out and make labels for each one. Put them up somewhere in your child's bedroom.

Using colours

The kitchen table can become a studio with some scrap paper, newspaper on and below, and whichever mark-making tools you can find. Pre-schoolers often start to draw recognisable items at this stage.

They choose to paint colours for specific purposes, e.g. *This is the blue sea and this is me swimming in the sea with my friend ...* They can roughly colour in blank areas in a colouring book and draw a circle or line, face or animal.

You can help to encourage this development by:

- Responding with enthusiasm whenever your child "writes" or "draws" something.
- Praising the use of colour, line or shape within what may appear to be a confusing muddle of marks on paper.
- Mixing colours with your child and discussing the results.
- Using an element of mystery, e.g. *Guess what I'm drawing – a blue circle, a red square or a green triangle.*

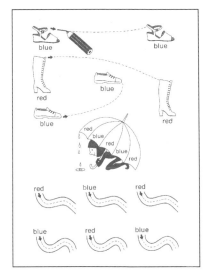

Colours p.9

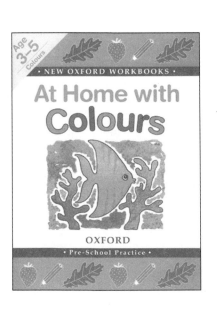

■ 6 PRACTICAL STEPS TOWARDS LEARNING AT SCHOOL

Home and school – a partnership

It is hoped that home and school will encourage similar positive attitudes to learning. The partnership between home and school need not be restricted to hearing reading or practising numbers or tables. It is a partnership about learning in general. When the powerful influences of home and school are united, children's learning is exciting and rewarding. As parents of a pre-schooler, we have tried to develop some ideas and approaches which may serve to build a helpful bridge between home and school. We hope that the practical guidance we offer may be useful to you and that you and your child enjoy learning together.

Learning about shapes and numbers

Very young children can recognise shapes and lines. There are many ways you can build up your children's awareness of shape, through games, within conversation and through children's play. The same is true for numbers. Recognition of numbers can be encouraged through counting rhymes and finger plays, through sorting and matching, sequencing and sharing activities, all embedded in everyday living. Children need to build up the concept of a number or a shape by encountering them frequently and in a meaningful situation, e.g. two cats on a wall, asking for and receiving two balls, adding one doll to another or even sharing ten cookies between five children. The concept of two can be deduced by a child on their own but you can make the understanding of an idea more fun, more memorable and more reliable by explaining it, by looking for other examples and by helping children make links for themselves. All this is achieved by talk, by listening, and by asking and answering questions.

Becoming a reader

Everyone agrees that learning to read is one of the most important steps in a child's education. Being able to read makes it easier to learn other subjects at school.

If you are a reader, you can find things out for yourself. You can explore things that interest you, from growing vegetables to paragliding. You can be a more independent learner.

The more children read, the more they learn about language. They widen their vocabulary, improve their spellings and find it easier to learn to write their own ideas. Being able to read opens up a wonderful world of books and stories that can thrill, inspire, amuse and entertain. Reading opens up an infinite range of sources of information, from encyclopædias to the internet.

Reading to children

Extensive reading of stories to children is particularly important in leading them into reading, for the following reasons:

- children are won over and enchanted by the excitement of story, by the need to know what happens next
- the pleasure is added to by being shared with a loved adult and the book provides a shared experience to talk about
- children learn what reading is about. They understand books can reveal interesting information about places, people, animals, earthquakes, heroines, aliens and distant stars
- they learn that the words and pictures remain the same even when they are read by different people, at different times and in different places
- children learn to handle books with care
- books provide children with early encounters with the language of books and teach them to develop reading behaviours
- children begin to memorise stories and can join in with words and phrases which are repeated
- children start to recognise certain words because they see them often and start to match sounds and letters as well
- children learn to use the "clues" in the story (illustrations, rhymes, storyline) to work out what is happening and to predict what is going to happen next
- books extend children's vocabulary and widen their experience

Reading and writing – a vital connection

Just as children, from an early age, take an interest in books, so they are often fascinated by aspects of writing. Children imitate adult writing behaviour, making marks and eventually making scribbled versions of letter shapes. You can help children make the very important connection between reading and writing by writing down children's words and stories, almost like "taking dictation", matching the spoken word to written language. At school, teachers will continue to emphasise the reading–writing relationship as they develop children's literacy skills.

At Home with abc

Some very early letter formation practice is offered by the activities in *At Home with abc*.

In this book, children can write the letters in various sizes in the top picture on each page. The bottom picture requires them to form the letter as closely as possible to the model letter. Where children find it difficult to write accurately, encourage them to practise the letters in the spaces between the two pictures. Try to identify the "best letter" and single it out for special praise.

my best a

abc, p.2

15

■ 7 SOUNDS AND RHYMES

Matching sounds and letters

In order to read we need to be able to match **sounds** to **letters** on the page. It is very important, therefore, that children, before they learn to read, can recognise the sounds that **spoken** language makes. They need to be able to recognise and discriminate between different sounds.

Children make a very important step towards reading when they see the connection between the sounds they hear and can make and the way in which these sounds are written down. For example:

- They recognise their own name in print.
- They connect individual letters with sounds and words. For example: "L" for "Learner" on cars; "P" for "Parking".
- They make the connection between single letters and the sounds they stand for, e.g. "S" (suh) for "STOP".
- They sound out words that relate to them, e.g. *This is Anna's room.*
- They make good guesses about words in the same "family". Once a child can read one word in the family, s/he can usually read most of the others. For example: *man, ran, can, pan, than; rake, bake, cake, sake, lake.*

How can parents teach sounds?

- Teach the alphabet names until your child knows them. Then focus on the sounds that letters begin with, e.g. *A says Ah, B says Buh, C says Kuh, Dee says Duh, Eee says Ehh,* etc.
- Talk through exceptions as you encounter them. For example, "C" has a "kuh" sound for "cat" and a "see" sound in "ceiling".
- Begin to mention the **sound** with the letter, e.g. in an alphabet frieze or alphabet book: *Let's find **B**, the first letter in your name; there it is, **B**/Buh for Bridget and also for butterfly, bus and bumble bee* until your child links the letter name with the sound.
- "Collect" families of words beginning with the same letter name and sound. Put them in funny sentences, e.g. *busy bees buzzed busily by the barn.*
- Ask her/him to listen with closed eyes to a series of three or four spoken words and to guess the letter which you're thinking of: e.g. *fish, frog, toffee, if (F).*

What can parents do to develop rhyme?

Children who have been exposed to nursery rhymes and have a good sense of rhyme are helped to learn to read by their sense of language patterns. To support your child in this area:

- Share nursery rhymes, songs and jingles with them. Stress the **rhymes** at the end.
- Play rhyming snap: you give a word and your child has to think of a rhyme for it, e.g. GORILLA – VANILLA. Take turns.
- Stress **rhythm**, e.g. *Run, run as fast as you can! You can't catch me – I'm the Gingerbread man.*

Sounds and Rhymes p.5

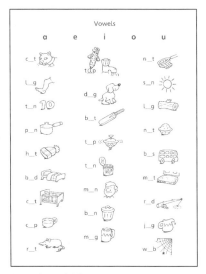

Sounds and Rhymes p.14

- Encourage your child to guess what is coming next in a rhyme when you leave out words.
- Invent nonsense words for nursery rhymes and songs and ask your child to put them right.
- Describe something in the room, giving a rhyming word (*There's a bear next to the table. Bear = chair*) and your child has to guess.
- Play I-Spy rhyming games: *I spy something round and yellow that rhymes with "fall" or "tall".*

At home with sounds and rhymes

The book *At Home with Sounds and Rhymes*, which continues from *At Home with Reading*, gives a wide range of activities that will help your child learn to read by using sounds and rhymes.

It is very important to say the sounds aloud, especially the rhyming sounds. Focus on both the similarities and the differences between words.

The early activities practise the **first** letters of words (pages 4–8). Next (pages 9–14) comes practice in sounding out the **middle vowel** of words. The following activities (pages 15–29) help children to focus on the important idea of **rhyming endings**. Once children can master this skill, together with the ability to recognise first and middle sounds, then they are well on the way to recognising whole words. The activities also move children to reading whole sentences.

Later activities (pages 30–35) take children a step forward, into **blends**. Blends are sounds that are made when two consonants come together, e.g. *fl-, cr-, sw-, st-*. These are **initial blends** because they come together at the beginnings of words. On pages 36–41, children are forming **initial consonants** with **vowels,** e.g. *do + g, du + g*. Pages 42–46 develop sound recognition skills. The aim is to help children read whole words by sounding out the first two letters. They are given picture clues to help.

The book finishes with some rhymes to read. The pictures give clues but children are likely to need some help.

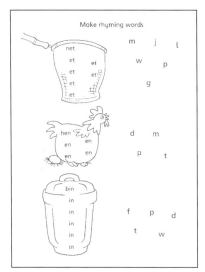

Sounds and Rhymes p.17

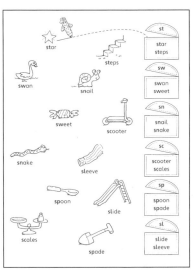

Sounds and Rhymes p.35

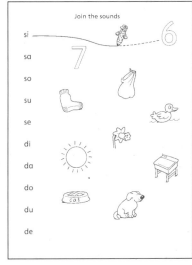

Sounds and Rhymes p.36

■ 8 *THE ALPHABET*

Children find it easier to learn to read if, when they come to school for the first time, they already:

- recognise the letters of the alphabet
- say the sounds that some of the letters make, e.g. A often says *ah*
- know the letter names, e.g. A's name is *Ay*

It is important to help your child learn all this in an enjoyable and successful way, without pressure or haste.

Recognising letters

Your child is surrounded by letters: in books, on food packets and containers, in all the post that comes through the door, on the TV, in shops, on cars and in street names and signs. Pointing out individual letters is a good place to start but it won't be long before your child is quite naturally recognising whole words and the letters that comprise them: *POLICE, EXIT, SLOW, SCHOLAR ROAD*.

To encourage children to identify letters, you can use the following:

- collections of "real" alphabets, that is letters made of plastic, wood, sponge and various other materials, including magnetised letters
- alphabet books, friezes or posters
- cardboard letters that can be pegged on a "washing line"
- a range of writing papers and pens, crayons, pencils
- a magnetic board (e.g. an old tin tray) or a flannel board to which flannel letters can be stuck
- a chalk board, with duster and chalks
- scrap books, made easily from blank scrap paper or computer print-out paper and stapled together
- a play "office", with pencils and pens, paper and post cards , stamps, envelopes, scissors, paper clips, "post its", a stapler, glue.

Learning the letter sounds and names

Once children have understood that letters can stand for sounds and make words, they are ready to start learning all 26 letters, both by their sounds and their names, e.g. *Ay can say Ah; Bee can say buh*.

Here are some ideas to help children learn the alphabet:

- Learn and sing the alphabet song to the tune of "Twinkle, Twinkle, Little Star".
- Stop singing or saying the alphabet at a certain letter so your child can say the next letter.
- Take away or cover up a letter on a written alphabet and have him/her say what the missing letter is.
- Play the alphabet I-Spy game. *I spy something that is red and shiny and lovely to eat and it begins with "Ay ... ah"*. Say both the letter name and the sound.
- Make alphabet letters using pebbles, pasta, salt or play-dough.
- Make collections of objects beginning with various letters, e.g. *Our C basket*.

Letter Forms p.2

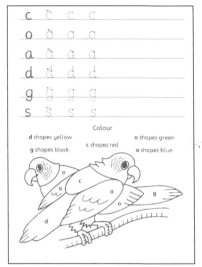

Letter Forms p.16

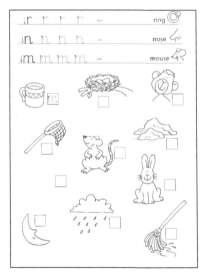

Letter Forms p.27

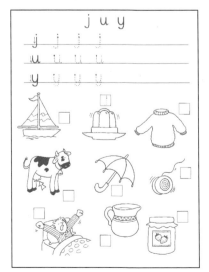

Letter Forms p.38

– Trace a letter on each other's hand or back and guess which it is.
– Have a letter of the day during which you find that letter as often as possible.
– Make alphabet scrap books. Give each letter a page and write the letter in both upper and lower case ("capital" and "small"). Cut out pictures from magazines, catalogues etc and glue them under the letter they begin with, e.g. "home" under Hh, "car" under Cc.

At home with letter forms

You can support your child's learning to write :

• by creating play situations that make the idea of "writing" attractive to them, e.g. shops, hospitals or dentists that call for bills, advertisements, admission signs, prescriptions, notices and so on.

• by showing them how to hold a pencil or other writing implement, taking into account whether they are left or right-handed (see page 2 *At Home with Letter Forms*).

• by encouraging them to make patterns based upon letter shapes. "Pattern" activities should be done before the child begins with letter shapes. This is to encourage:
  • confident and flowing left-to-right hand movements;
  • muscular control of the hand and pencil;
  • memory of individual letter shapes.

So, for example, finding the way out of a maze helps left to right movement; joining series of dots helps muscle control, hand–eye coordination and a sense of movement. These activities also help children to associate letters with sounds.

It is important to value and give time to these pre-writing activities. They are essential to prepare your child for correct letter formation.

When children learn to write letters, it is helpful if the letters are grouped in "families".

• The first group of letters *c, o, a, d, g, s* are all round letters, starting with a movement to the left (pages 10–16).

• The letter "e" is given individual attention, being the only letter that starts with an upward stroke to the right (pages 17–18).

• The group of letters *r, n, m, h, p, b* all have an initial downward stroke, followed by an upward movement from the same line (pages 23–32).

• The group of letters *l, t, j, u, y* also start with an initial downward stroke, but then lead into a curved movement, to either left or right (pages 33–38).

All the activities for letter formation show clearly the direction in which the individual letter should be formed. Help your child to follow the correct movement, practising in the air first of all. Try to prevent him/her forming the letters incorrectly, since this will show in his/her writing progress later.

As with the pattern activities it may be that at the beginning your child finds the letter activities too small to cope with easily. Where this is so, write the letters in larger script on separate sheets of paper, and encourage him/her to write as large as is comfortable for them.

■ 9 *READY FOR READING*

As soon as children realise that books are useful, interesting, sharable, transportable, permanent and attractive, they have embarked on the road to reading. The next phase of the journey, towards reading on their own, may take several years.

At school, children will be taught to read books on three levels, word, sentence and whole text. Some children will arrive at school already able to read to some extent. Others may only just be beginning to show that they are almost ready to learn to read.

Signs to look for

These are some of the signs that teachers and parents can look for which show that children are ready to begin reading independently:

- they enjoy having stories read to them and they look at favourite books on their own;
- they join in, repeating words and phrases, and finish phrases that rhyme;
- they guess words or phrases in advance because they are making sense of the story;
- they know how a book should be read, i.e. in English, starting at the top and getting to the bottom by reading along the lines from left to right; they know you have to turn over the pages, one by one;
- they know that illustrations can help readers understand the story;
- they ask questions about the characters and the plot;
- they recognise individual words and letters;
- they know the letters of the alphabet and the sounds they make at the beginning of words;
- they like to "read" back their own "writing", whether this be marks and scribbles or lists, notices, and story books they have made.

Learning to look at words more closely

Once the above behaviours appear, you can help your child:

- to recognise words that occur frequently, such as *and* or *the*;
- to recognise words that have a distinctive shape. Children often "read" longer words, like *astronaut, crocodile, power-ranger*, before they master shorter, more easily confused words, like *them, they, this*;
- to see him/herself as a reader, even when remembering or guessing the words;
- to pay more attention to text, e.g. looking for names which stand out, thanks to their capital letters, or for words in large type, such as *Oops! Wow! No. Help!* and so on;
- to look closely at words which have the same first letter, e.g. *g-, j-, m-* or which start with the same two letters *th-, cr-, fl-*, etc.;
- to look for letter families which have the same middles or ends (*-oo-, -ee-, ing*).

Supporting early reading development

Here are some other ways to help:

- Introduce your child to a wide range of fiction and non-fiction books.
- Make sure that the occasions when you share books are relaxed, and without strain.
- Encourage your child to join in and take part; to talk about characters and their behaviour; to speculate about what is likely to happen and why; to ask questions and give opinions.
- Don't overdo questioning and make sure it is not done as a test, but as something inspired by the excitement of the story: *Ooh, I don't think I'd go into that cave, would you? What do you think they are likely to find in there ... ?*
- Encourage your child to predict what will come next: *Let's look at the next page and see if we were right.*
- Treat any incorrect predictions lightly: *Oh, dear, that fooled us, didn't it?*
- Point out words your child may have encountered in other situations.

At Home with Reading

The *At Home with Reading* book aims to develop children's ability to discriminate visually between different shapes and sequences (pages 1–12). It then moves on to letter recognition (pages 13–22) and recognition of short words (pages 22–44). Finally, it focuses on environmental print, on words which children may see when out and about.

Reading p.4

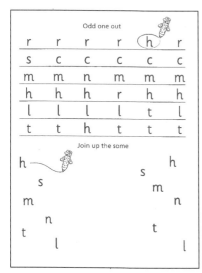

Reading p.18

Reading p.24

Reading p.46

◼ 10 LETTER FORMS AND WRITING

Children's writing develops through three main stages:

1) <u>scribbling</u> when "writing" is doodles, zigzag patterns, marks and loops. What makes these different from "drawing" is that the child thinks s/he is saying something particular: *This is a sign for my shop. It says Sweet Shop.*

2) <u>emergent writing</u> when recognisable letter shapes and words begin to appear.

3) <u>independent writing</u> when children can form all or most letters of the alphabet, can write sentences and begin to know simple rules of punctuation (full stops and capital letters).

Supporting pre-writing

Here are some other ways to support pre-writing development:

• Show great interest in what your child has "written" and talk about it together.

• Encourage her/him to tell you what the "writing" says.

• Be ready to write for your child, while s/he tells you, or dictates, what s/he wants to say. Write the letters slowly and clearly. Encourage your child to notice the letters: *That's got a long tail ...* Read the writing back together.

• Write captions and descriptions for your child's pictures, collections and models.

• Make shopping lists, scrap books and diaries together.

• Encourage your child to add messages to your letters and cards to relations and friends.

• Make small story books together which s/he can "read" with you and illustrate.

At Home with Writing

At Home with Writing suggests some pre-writing activities which give children the opportunity to practise flow and fluency, pattern-making and pencil control. For example, pages 4–23 give practice in "writing pathways" (drawing controlled lines along or between given tracks on the page).

The activities develop skills essential to successful writing, including muscle control, hand–eye co-ordination and the sense of movement essential to successful writing. They steer children towards proper letter formation and pencil control. In tracing paths around various shapes, children are, in fact, making the shapes and curves that underpin whole families or groups of letters.

Writing p.22

The mechanics of writing

At Home with Writing also gives valuable advice about teaching your child the mechanics of writing, that is, how the letters are actually formed. Talk through each writing movement you are making or helping her to make: *First I'm drawing a line down, then two arch shapes, and a little flick to finish with; that's how we write the m's in your name Emma ...*

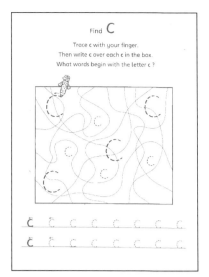

Writing p.24

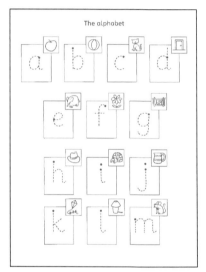

Writing p.46

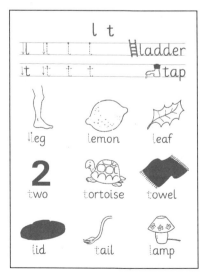

Writing p.39

Your child is likely to need help, at the beginning, in holding a pencil correctly, and in finding the best and most comfortable position to write.

Letter formation

It is not an easy accomplishment for children to write all the letters of the alphabet correctly. It takes time and patience because it is important for children to be taught how to form the letters correctly. *At Home with Writing* gives guidance on this. Pages 23–47 introduce letter forms and ways of practising them. The letter forms are introduced in "letter" families. The families are made up of similar shapes, starting with the "easy" ones, *c, o, a, d*.

Pages 24–47 deal with letter formation and give clear advice about the way and the direction in which the letters should be formed. Remember your child should be familiar with the names and appearance of letters before s/he attempts to write them formally.

The workbook suggests that with each letter you should start by tracing the shape with the child's finger. Apart from tracing over the letter shape you can encourage him/her to trace the letter in the air, and to trace it on the back of your hand. You can trace letters on your hands, necks and backs and play guessing games about the letter you are tracing. Say the sound of the letter as you trace it.

Now, on the practice pages, e.g. page 24, let your child write the letter, with you holding his/her hand. Start with the dot and join up the dots. There are several activities that lead easily into this (page 21), and the complete alphabet in dotted letter shapes for the child to complete (pages 46 and 47).

If, at the beginning, your child finds some of the letter shapes in the workbooks on the small side for them to practise on, then you can of course copy them on to larger sheets of paper and let him/her practise there first.

Talking about writing

There are features of writing and letter formation which it is helpful to discuss together:

a) Lower and upper case letters

You will notice that all the exercises here are concerned with "small" or lower case letters. It is usual to begin children's writing by focusing on lower case letters since these are the letter shapes that they will most usually encounter. However in all the activities we have encountered here, from sharing books to playing with letter shapes, to practising hand writing, you will find occasions where you can also give them practice in recognising and writing the capital letters too.

b) Letters that are ready to join

Many letters end with "exits", hooks or flicks (pages 38 and 39) to help the writer's hand movements flow fluently along the line. Even if your own handwriting does not feature these flicks, it is very important to practise this particular skill with your child. It will help when they eventually progress to joined writing. Otherwise moving from individual letter shapes to "real" joined writing becomes more difficult than it needs to be.

■ 11 *AT HOME WITH SHAPE AND SIZE*

The world around us is full of shapes, such as circles, rectangles, squares and triangles. These shapes can make deliberate or accidental patterns, from windows on a tower block to ripples in a pond. Understanding the way shapes work helps to develop your child's visual sense and is mathematically important and useful.

Shape

To start with, you can help your child to become aware of shapes and to notice the patterns they can make. Teach your child the names of the shapes and talk about their features: *Yes, it's got three corners and three sides ... (TRIANGLE)* or *It's the same both sides, isn't it? The windows are the same both sides, look ... (SYMMETRICAL HOUSE)*

Shape and Size p.28

Here are some ways to explore shapes together:

- Start to develop a vocabulary to talk about shape, size and pattern (see *Shape and Size* pages 28 and 29). Focus on the properties of the shapes *(how many corners, sides, curves and what can they do?)* and not just their names.

- Make shapes from paper and card, then let your child create "shape people" and other pictures out of circles, triangles etc. Gummed paper shapes are available from newsagents.

- Cut out enough different shapes to sort them into groups, e.g. all four-sided shapes *(QUADRILATERALS)* , all rounded shapes *(OVALS, CIRCLES)* etc.

- Choose a shape and look for it in magazines or on a "shape walk".

- Make shapes from play-dough or modelling clay.

- Make shapes using letters of the alphabet or numbers.

- Talk about and understand the difference between 2D (flat) and 3D (can be picked up) shapes. Unfold boxes and look at how a 3D shape can become 2D.

- Make shapes using your fingers, arms and legs.

- Classify shapes. Children need to realise that their features mean some shapes can be grouped together in categories, e.g. quadrilaterals, open or closed shapes etc.

Spatial awareness

Children can develop spatial awareness by drawing and painting their own shapes and by experimenting with the relationships between shapes.

Continue to develop spatial awareness, by helping your child to:

- Appreciate the concept of space and how lines can be used to contain space and join points. Talk about *points, joins and boundaries* as you draw shapes together.

- Relate shapes one to another, e.g. which can fit together or which can contain another: *Look, here's a circle inside the square,* and so on.

- Appreciate why a shape is or is not symmetrical. Spotty or squared paper can be helpful.

Shape and Size p.43

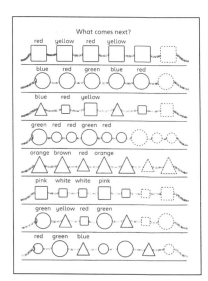

Pattern and Shape p.45

- Experiment with shapes to see what happens if they are "rolled", rotated or reversed – shapes made from stiff card or plastic are useful.

Size

In *At Home with Shape and Size* there are activities to help your child identify similar sizes (pages 30 and 31) and to compare sizes (pages 36–39 and 46–47). Your child will learn about measuring height and length (pages 40–45).

Other ways to support your child's understanding of size:

- Measure and weigh your child regularly, discussing results.
- Talk about different sizes of items, e.g. tins, packets, bottles when unpacking the shopping.
- Ask your child to line up toys, pebbles, books etc. in order of size.
- Have a ruler and tape-measure readily available so you can measure differences in length and height.

Comparing

Talk with your child about similarities and differences whenever you have the opportunity. Some things (e.g. cars) are countable while others (e.g. water) are uncountable. Nearly everything can be measured however, and comparisons made between numbers, shapes and objects:

- by size – *bigger/smaller than, the biggest/smallest;*
- by quantity – *enough, more than, the most, less than, the least;*
- by weight – *heavier/lighter than;*
- by length / width – *longer/shorter/wider/narrower or thinner than;*
- by height – *taller or higher/smaller or shorter than.*
  Comparisons about periods of time can also be made:
- by length – *longer/shorter times*
- by speed – *slower/faster or quicker than*

Workbook activities

In the "At Home" series, *At Home with Shape and Size* aims to develop children's visual and spatial skills by helping them recognise different shapes, patterns and sequences. It provides opportunities to strengthen hand–eye co-ordination and to develop language needed to describe shape and size. It also encourages children to estimate the measurements and dimensions of shapes. *At Home with Shape and Size* is followed by *At Home with Pattern and Shape*. This book provides more visual discrimination activities and more challenge, especially in terms of sequences and pattern-making.

Patterns and sequences

Ways to develop children's sequencing abilities include:

- Encourage your child to predict what comes next in a sequence in visual patterns (pages 22 and 23 *Shape and Size*) in clapped rhythms or in storybooks.
- Look for number sequences and use them to make decorative patterns.
- Use printing stamps or potato prints to print sequences of shapes.

■ 12 *AT HOME WITH NUMBERS*

Numbers

Numbers, like letters, are all around us. Your child will learn about numbers and their usefulness by seeing you use and talk about them. Children soon start to realise that numbers have names, *one, two, three*. At first, numbers are used without any real understanding, *12, 23, 50, 100's!* but it is a significant breakthrough when your pre-schooler can understand the idea of singleness, e.g. *one* and then the idea of more-than-one-ness, *lots and lots ... lots of.*

Children eventually begin to gain an appreciation of how one number relates to another, in terms of sequence or size: *24 comes after 23, doesn't it? And it's bigger than 20 but smaller than 100 ...* They also start to realise that numbers form a kind of pattern and system , e.g. *20, 30, 40, 50, 60 ...*

Number skills and language

The mathematical skills you need to encourage are identifying numbers and patterns, counting, sorting, matching and comparing. *At Home with Numbers* develops matching (e.g. pages 13 and 27) and comparing skills (page 39) and leads children into an understanding of addition (1 more) and subtraction (1 less) (pages 44–47).

It helps children to practise identifying and writing the first five numbers (pages 30–39) and to understand the idea of sets or groups of objects (pages 42–43).

Identifying and recognising numbers

Helping your child to notice and become curious about numbers is a good way to begin. To begin with, concentrate on numbers below 10.

At Home with Numbers starts with the numbers 1–5. *At Home with Counting* takes children on to 1–10. It is suggested, therefore, that you start with *Numbers* and move on to *Counting*.

Here are some ideas to help your child recognise numbers 1–10 at home and beyond:

- Look for and talk about numbers at home, on front doors, in newspapers, on food packets, TV or calendars and clocks.
- Make a number frieze, place mat or make a number line with pegs to hold numbers on card. Relate the numbers to something your child understands: That's the number five. *That's how many toes you've got on one foot.*
- Make numbers together out of play-dough.
- Write the numbers 1–5 on your child's left hand, starting with the thumb. Write 6–10 on your child's fingertips on the right hand, with 6 on the little finger and 10 on the thumb.
- Sing number rhymes and songs, e.g. *Five little ducks went swimming one day ...*
- Write each number 1–10 on sticky "post-its" or use playing cards. Arrange them in the wrong order. Help your child to arrange them correctly.

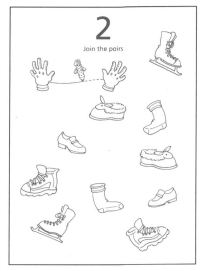

Numbers p.13

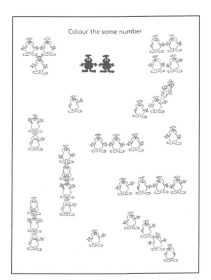

Numbers p.39

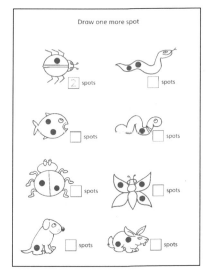

Numbers p.44

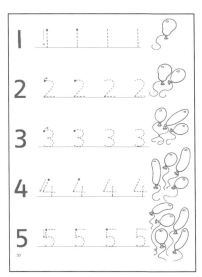

Numbers p.30

Counting p.15

- Choose a number with your child. "Collect" the number on a number walk or hunt, e.g. when you go shopping.
- Roll a dice together, count the spots and write the number down. Which number "wins" by appearing most often?
- Look for and make patterns of small numbers, e.g. using pasta shapes, buttons, beads or coins: *two small ones, then three big ones, then two small, three big*, etc.
- Gradually introduce the ordinal numbers, e.g. *She came 1st, she came 2nd, and she came 3rd*.

At Home with Counting

Try to make vocal any counting, working out or measuring you do around the home and use every chance to count items: *I think he's got about ten, but let's count and see ...* Make sure that you count stones, shells, peas etc. by touching or moving each item. This is to emphasise what is known as one-to-one correspondence. Each new item counted changes the number.

Although "At Home" does not include zero, in your conversations with your child it is helpful to talk about nothingness and introduce zero. When, for example, there are no more Smarties in a tube, explain there are none – or zero.

Using daily routines to teach 1, 2 and 3 can be fun, e.g. counting items of clothing in the morning *1 shoe, 2 shoes, 3 shoes ...*

Here are some other ideas:

- counting noises – *Listen to the shaker, one , two, three shakes. Now, let's shut our eyes and count three claps*;
- counting food – *1, 2, 3 potatoes for you*;
- counting toys – *Can you give me 2 red cars?* The following toys are particularly useful for helping children to learn to count: blocks, dominoes, dice, cards, nesting cups, beads on strings, abacus, toy animals and cars;
- counting steps, hops, bounces, swings and jumps;
- counting in the bath – *How many hands?2! How many toes?10!*

Sorting, sequencing and matching

It is important for children to be able to sort things into sets, using various attributes or features, e.g. colour, size, shape, relationships (pairs, opposites) or types (Stegosaurus or Tyrannosaurus? Fruit or Vegetable?).

- Tidy away toys or clothes into categories. Sort out the washing together.
- Categorise and sort money, e.g. into copper, silver, then into 1s, 2s, 5s, 10s.
- Collect and sort household objects, including buttons, spoons, leaves from the garden, shopping from the supermarket. *Let's sort the tins from the packets*.
- Give your child pictures, numbers and shapes to sequence in order of size. Let them count and sequence the numbers forwards and backwards.
- Play matching games, making sets that are the same colour, type or size.
- Let your child match written numbers to sets of objects, such as beans.
- Use dominoes with spots or pictures to reinforce the idea of finding an accurate match.

■ 13 PREPARING FOR SCHOOL

The transition

You will by now have done a great deal to prepare your child for the move to school. School will be different in many important ways. For a start, your child will be in a much larger and unfamiliar environment. The chances for adult–child interaction will be fewer than at home. Your child will find it is not always possible to have questions answered, to be assured something is right or to receive encouragement when it is needed.

Starting school

The first day at school is often more stressful for the parent than the child. You will need to make sure that, however you feel inside, you look and sound enthusiastic and remain positive and supportive.

Try to take your child to meet the new teacher and spend some time in the school. Local playgroups often take the pre-schoolers to the primary school for lunch, concerts or assemblies.

Helping your child adapt

Here are some ways to help your child feel more confident about starting school:

- Make sure your child is familiar with the school before s/he begins. Try to make several visits in advance. Walk by the school grounds, at break times, and watch the children playing and enjoying themselves.
- Show your child where the Secretary's Office is, in case s/he needs to phone you. Make sure your child can find his/her way around the building and name the various areas.
- Make sure your child knows where the toilets are, where to hang coats and belongings, and what the lunchtime arrangements are.
- Discuss health and safety issues together. Find out whether your child knows what to do at playtimes if there's an accident or a fall, if a ball goes into the street, or if a bigger child acts the bully. Make sure your child appreciates safety issues as far as strangers are concerned, is cautious about handling strange objects in the playground, and knows what to do in an emergency such as a fire.
- Make sure that the school knows about any physical conditions which may affect your child at school. If medication is ever required, find out about the school's procedures and make sure your child knows what to do. It will help the school if you write down dosage times and quantities.
- Try to find out and teach your child the names of as many teachers and helpers as possible.
- Try to be at the school in good time each day and avoid rushing. Make sure your child knows who will be at the school to meet them each day at home time.
- Teach your child to be independent, e.g. to be able to put on and take off shoes, boots and PE kit quickly; to use a knife and fork; to use the

toilet, then wash and dry hands; to sharpen a pencil; to cut with scissors; to know his/her home address and telephone number.

- Try to label everything your child wears or takes to school (at least with initials). Make sure your child knows what to do, whom to ask and where to look when property is lost at school.

- The school will send home letters occasionally. Establish a family routine for this, e.g. putting any paperwork in the bookbag. The bookbag is the bag or wallet in which the classteacher puts at least one reading book and a reading record card or booklet. In most schools it comes home daily, throughout the primary phase, with a request that parents listen to and read with their child.

- Provide opportunities for her/him to mix and play with new classmates.

- Remember your child is likely to find early days at school very tiring and may need more sleep, and a more relaxed programme for a while.

Providing support and encouragement

Here are some ways you can help in the early stages of school:

- Show interest in what your child has done each day, encouraging them to talk about it but without making it a kind of test.

- Find out which topics are being studied at school. Help your child, where possible, to contribute to any class activities, projects, displays and collections.

- Continue to provide your child with wide and stimulating experiences. Children are often asked to talk or write about their weekend. On Monday mornings, at breakfast, talk through what you did together over the weekend. Some children find it difficult to remember what they have done, so you might draw a picture, provide the child with a souvenir, e.g. a brochure or a ticket, or suggest some words they might use.

- Playing organised games may be new to some children. Help your child to understand about being part of a team, about picking team members, about taking part, about joining in and about being prepared to lose at times.

- Read every night with your child. Most schools send home a bookbag with a reading book. Some schools enclose two books, one for the child to attempt with help from you, and another book which is more challenging which you can read aloud. Many schools ask that the parent writes a short comment of encouragement or information in a reading journal or diary. This booklet can become a useful written conversation between the classteacher and parent, about the child's progress in reading.

Finally, one of the most important ways to support your child's education is to maintain good communication with the school. When things are not clear or when problems occur, approach your child's teacher, in a spirit of partnership, to ensure that misunderstandings don't allow small problems to grow into bigger ones.

■ 14 BASELINE ASSESSMENT AND DESIRABLE OUTCOMES

From September 1998, all children starting at primary school will be assessed within their first seven weeks, to see what they can do. Schools are required to select a government-approved baseline assessment scheme. Though these vary, they all have to assess children's learning outcomes in six aspects of Language and Literacy, Maths, and Personal and Social Development. These outcomes are summarised below, and they lead into the first stage of the National Curriculum.

Baseline assessment has two purposes:

- to provide information to help your child's teachers plan effectively for his/her learning needs
- to measure your child's attainment at age 5. The results can be used in later analysis of your child's progress. They can also be compared to National Test results at age 7 so that the "value" the school has "added" to his/her education can broadly be measured.

The pre-school learning experiences suggested in this book together with the activities in the "At Home" series will help your child to show what h/she knows and can do in the process of baseline assessment.

1. Personal and Social Development

Children should be able to:

- Show respect for self and others, including those from other cultures and beliefs
- Work independently and as part of a group
- Concentrate and persevere in their learning
- Seek help where needed
- Initiate ideas and solve practical problems
- Be independent in dressing and personal hygiene
- Be sensitive to the needs of others, taking turns and sharing fairly
- Behave in appropriate ways
- Have a sense of right and wrong and why
- Treat living things, the environment and property with care and concern
- Respond to their experiences of the world and cultural and religious events with a range of feelings such as wonder, joy or sorrow

2. Language and Literacy

Children should be able to:

- Listen to others and talk about their own experiences
- Respond to stories, poems, songs and rhymes
- Make up their own stories
- Enjoy looking at books and handle them carefully
- Know that words and pictures carry meaning
- Know how, in English, print is read from top to bottom and left to right

- Relate sounds to letters and words
- Recognise their own name and other familiar words
- Recognise letters of the alphabet, by their shape and sound
- Write their own name correctly and show awareness of the purpose for writing

3. Mathematics

Children should be able to:

- Use mathematical language to describe shape, size and quantity
- Recognise and recreate patterns
- Know number rhymes, stories, songs and games
- Compare, sort, sequence, match and count using everyday objects
- Recognise and use numbers 1–10 and recognise larger numbers
- Solve practical problems using their mathematical understanding
- Show awareness of number operations, e.g. adding and subtracting
- Understand and record numbers

4. Knowledge and Understanding of the World

These outcomes focus on children's developing understanding of other people, their environment and the natural and man-made world. They form the foundation for future learning in Science, History, Technology and Geography.

5. Physical Development

These outcomes focus on children's development of mobility, awareness of space and manipulative skills and use of tools. They include establishing a positive approach towards a healthy, safe and active way of life.

6. Creative Development

These outcomes focus on the development of children's imagination and their ability to communicate and express feelings and ideas in creative ways, e.g. through art music, drama, dance, stories and imaginative play.

■ *FURTHER READING*

Anderson J et al (1989) *Right Start for School*. Longman

Arnberg L (1987) *Raising children bilingually : the pre-school years*. Multilingual Matters

Baker C (1995) *A Parents' and Teachers' Guide to Bilingualism*. Multilingual Matters

Gee R and Meredith S (1987) *Entertaining and Educating your Preschool Child*. Usborne

Lindon J (1993) *Child development from birth to eight*. National Children's Bureau

Morrow J (1989) *Reading and Writing is Child's Play*. Longman

Pugh G et al (1994, 1997) *Confident Parents, Confident Children*. National Children's Bureau/Open University Press

Roberts R (1995) *Self-esteem and Successful Early Learning*. Hodder and Stoughton

SCAA (1996) *Nursery education – Desirable Outcomes for Children's Learning on Entering Compulsory Education*. HMSO

Watt F and Lovett P (1996) *First Skills – Starting Lettering*. Usborne

Wood L and Wragg E (1996) *Pre-school choices and Nursery Education*. Longman